Europe in the
Seventeenth Century

DAVID MALAND, M.A.

*Head Master of Cardiff High School for Boys
and formerly Senior History Master, Stamford School*

MACMILLAN
London · Melbourne · Toronto

ST MARTIN'S PRESS
New York
1966

MACMILLAN AND COMPANY LIMITED
Little Essex Street London WC 2
also Bombay Calcutta Madras Melbourne

THE MACMILLAN COMPANY OF CANADA LIMITED
70 Bond Street Toronto 2

ST MARTIN'S PRESS INC
175 Fifth Avenue New York NY 10010

Library of Congress catalog card no: 66–13437

PRINTED IN GREAT BRITAIN

Contents

EUROPE IN THE SEVENTEENTH CENTURY

IV THE RISE OF THE DUTCH REPUBLIC

V THE DECLINE OF SPAIN

VI LOUIS XIV: A STUDY IN ABSOLUTISM

VII WESTERN EUROPE, 1660–1714

VIII THE DUTCH REPUBLIC

IX THE CREATION OF THE DANUBIAN MONARCHY

X THE STRUGGLE FOR THE BALTIC

List of Plates

Acknowledgements

The publishers gratefully acknowledge the following sources
of the photographs reproduced in this book:

Mansell Collection: Plates 1a, 1b, 2, 3, 4a, 4b, 6b
Dr. Eva Frodl-Kraft, Vienna: Plate 5
Photographie Giraudon: Plate 6a
M. Jean Roubier, Paris: Plate 7a
Mr. A. F. Kersting: Plates 7b and 8

xi

List of Maps

Preface

I owe so much to so many that it is difficult to isolate particular acts of kindness and aid. Professor L. H. Butler did me a great service by putting me in touch with Messrs. Macmillan, who in turn gave me much encouragement and advice. Mr. P. D. Whitting, formerly of St. Paul's School, read the typescript twice and his comments were unfailingly helpful and pertinent.

To my own colleague Bartle Frere I owe most of all. He has read and criticised every sentence as it was written and rewritten, and this book would be much the poorer but for his sane and shrewd advice.

I am also grateful to Gladys Wyman for typing the final typescript; to Hugh Sharp for help in correcting the proofs; to Oliver and Nicholas for their work on the Index; and to my wife, who typed the early drafts and always eased the work of composition.

Stamford, 1965   D. M.

I

The Seventeenth Century

———————◆———————

ECONOMIC DEVELOPMENT

The Peasantry and Food Production

Most Europeans in the seventeenth century were peasants, though their status, their legal rights and their terms of tenure varied greatly from one region to the next. East of the Elbe where serfdom prevailed they were at their worst, subject to the jurisdiction of their landlords, burdened with heavy labour services and with little or no personal freedom.[1] In western Europe serfdom was less common — though it was not abolished on the royal estates of Portugal until 1702, and there were perhaps a million or more serfs in France, a tenth of the peasant population — but there existed many degrees of bondage short of serfdom itself, not all of them always preferable to it. The number of landless labourers for instance had grown considerably since the sixteenth century; men condemned to eke out an existence by selling their labour in an age when forced labour was too often available and when there were few industries other than farming to offer them employment. More fortunate in the greater security of their life but denied personal freedom, were most of the Danish peasantry, along with a substantial minority in other western countries where landlords, attempting to combat the price rise of the previous century, were cultivating their demesnes more intensively and thus demanding greater labour services than in the past. Since the lords were judges in their own case the peasants had little success in pleading their customary rights, and their freedom was consequently invaded.

On the other hand, there were many, perhaps the majority in France and Spain, who were free of manorial control in all but minor matters, however irksome, provided they shared their crops with the lord, paying from one-fifth to one-half of their produce.[2]

[1] See Chapter IX, page 357, on Austria, and Chapter X, pages 406 and 436, on Brandenburg and Russia respectively.

[2] In France this service was known as *métayage*, see Chapter VI, page 249.

Freer still were those who had commuted all services for a rent charge, though the landlord might also be at greater liberty to raise their rents and to secure their eviction. On the fringe of the peasantry, if not of it, were the peasant proprietors who had won possession of their own smallholdings. In France there were a million or so, grouped mostly in the north and west and especially around Paris, working their land at a profit to supply the growing population of the capital. An independent peasantry of this type was also to be found in Holland, though a few miles distant the peasants of Overyssel suffered under heavy feudal burdens. In Sweden where the peasantry enjoyed social freedom and political powers unheard of in the rest of Europe, these privileges might none the less have been reversed had it not been for the triumph of Charles XI over his nobles.[1] Indeed, apart from the rough division of European peasantry into those east and west of the Elbe, the range of serfdom was too great, the variations in gradation too subtle, too fluid and too uncertain, to be trapped within a generalisation.

Whatever changes for good or ill occurred in the status of the peasant, none took place in his methods of work, nor did he see any reason why they should. Ignorant and hidebound by tradition, he grew food principally for his own consumption, and there was little incentive to do otherwise. Throughout most of Europe stretched the great open fields, bastions of a primitive economy, which determined the time-honoured progression of the manorial calendar, preventing the adoption of new crop rotations, and compelling adherence to traditional methods of cultivation. As they had done for centuries, teams of oxen scratched the earth's surface with wooden ploughs; as always cereals were the staple crop, especially rye, oats and millet which yielded more per acre than wheat. Since cereals exhausted the soil it was necessary to leave land fallow one year in three in the north, one year in two in the south, and even two years in three in particularly infertile regions. In any given year, therefore, two-fifths of Europe's arable land was unproductive.

Variations from traditional procedures were uncommon, their causes various. One novel development took place in Ireland where the adoption of the potato was welcomed by an impoverished people who could grow sufficient potatoes to sustain them on half the land,

[1] See Chapter X, pages 400–1.

and with half the effort, required to keep them in cereals. In Holland too cereals were abandoned, but from reasons of wealth, not poverty: enriched by trade the Dutch could afford to import the cereals they required, mainly from Danzig, while they themselves developed the market-gardening of fruits and vegetables, and grew barley and hops for brewing, root crops and clover. These last crops gave nitrogen to the soil and winter feed to the cattle which, being stalled throughout the winter, not only supplied their owners with better milk and meat but with more organic fertiliser than could be found in the rest of Europe. Such intensive cultivation on a similar scale was only to be found elsewhere in the Ile-de-France and in Kent, where the demands of a rapidly expanding population in both Paris and London had to be met.

Away from the pressures created by population density there was little change, nor could any be expected until the landlords themselves desired it. The peasant was generally ignorant and poor. It was only the noble who had opportunities to inform himself on agriculture by travel and by reading; who had the power to enclose land; who had the wealth to drain it, to fertilise it and to experiment. Though it involved no revolutionary innovation in crop rotation and farming technique, none the less a most important development was taking place in Bohemia, Austria, and above all in Poland, where the tradition of self-sufficiency was being smashed by some of the nobles. The demand for corn in the west, the expanding population of Vienna, the perennial necessity to supply armies at war in Europe, were being exploited by landlords who used their monopoly of political power to secure for themselves commercial monopolies and trading privileges. They increased both their demesnes and the labour services of their serfs; they built granaries to store their surplus produce, and barges and rafts to ship it down the tributaries of the Danube and the Vistula.

Generally, however, the environment of court and camp, and the association of commercial farming with the stigma of the *bourgeois*, worked against the practice of successful estate management: it was Madame de Sévigné's cousin who explained to her that tenants neglected the land unless 'you get yourself exiled [i.e. from Versailles] and then you will be able to keep an eye on them'. Where the English were to excel was in the fact that their social system gave to the improving landlord, who had the capital with which to experiment, a prestige which stimulated imitation by lesser men.

Interest in agrarian matters was already more widespread in England than in any other country, and though there was much extolling of the Netherlands — the most famous of agricultural works was Hartlib's *Discours of Husbandrie used in Brabant and Flanders* (1652) — the English in fact were not so backward as their own writers supposed. The number of improving landlords was increasing steadily; market-gardening, land drainage, such as the immense schemes of the Duke of Bedford in the fens, and the use of root crops were expanding under the influence of a growing population and a landlord class who had the leisure, the capital and the interest to devote to their estates. It was this environment which made possible the rapid acceptance of the ideas of Tull, Bakewell and Townshend in the next century, and thus paved the way for English primacy in agriculture.

Population and Prices

The failure to achieve a general improvement in methods of food production was the most important factor determining the size of Europe's population in the seventeenth century. Political arithmetic, as demography was significantly termed, was in its infancy; it was only the more commercially minded governments who took pains to discover the statistics of their populations, and the evidence they collected was often unreliable. The sale of government annuities, for example, despite the informed advice in Holland of Christiaan Huygens on the mathematics of probability, and the compilation of the first reasonable life-table by Edmund Halley in England, was more of a Treasury gamble than an actuarial calculation.[1] For the most backward countries, such as Spain, the estimates of historians are likely to be based on nothing more reliable than a Venetian ambassador's guess.

Accepting the estimates which are available, it appears that the population increase of the sixteenth century petered out early in the seventeenth, and that numbers thereafter remained more or less static. Scandinavia, including Denmark, varied but little about the two million mark; Brandenburg-Prussia remained slightly below this, the United Provinces rather above it; Italy held steady at about 13,000,000, Poland at 16,000,000. France rose from

[1] As late as 1810 the municipality of The Hague sold life annuities at a rate which did not vary with the ages of the persons during whose survival they were payable.

16,000,000 to 19,000,000 and Austria from 5,500,000 to 7,500,000, but both examples are misleading since the increase was derived less from any change in birth or death rates than from the territorial acquisitions made by both countries throughout the century. Great Britain, alone, rising by one million to 7,500,000, provides evidence of a real increase based upon increased prosperity, just as the economic decline of the Iberian peninsula explains the estimated fall in numbers there from ten to eight millions. National statistics are deceptive in two ways; they are meaningless for many purposes without some indication of the density of the population,[1] and they fail to indicate all manner of local variations which, to the historian, might be significant. Towns for example often kept fairly accurate records of their population, and there are interesting conclusions to be drawn from the growth of London, Amsterdam, Paris and Vienna — London and Paris both exceeded 400,000 by 1700 — which relate to the increased power enjoyed in Europe by the states of which they were the capital cities. Too hasty a generalisation, however, is silenced by the reflection that Madrid also increased its population.

The general stability of the total figure of Europeans was not affected by the local fluctuations which occurred. Emigration would reduce numbers in one particular region only to create increases elsewhere, and there is evidence of considerable redistribution of the population across Europe. Religious persecution drove at least 200,000 Huguenots into the haven of Protestant states such as Holland and Brandenburg: warfare stimulated emigration from war zones, the Rhineland or the Leipzig plain, to more happily placed areas: equally there was emigration from regions of declining economic importance to more flourishing centres; more than a hundred of the richest merchants of Cologne emigrated to Frankfurt with their families between 1594 and 1637, while in France at the end of the century over 4,000 Catholic weavers left Normandy to seek better employment in England. Plague, unlike emigration, had only bad results. Sometimes it struck with devastating effect, killing for instance 130,000 in Naples in 1656: nine years later 100,000 died in the Great Plague of London: Danzig suffered severely in 1653, 1657 and 1660, as

[1] Density figures, quoted in G. N. Clark, *The Seventeenth Century*, are: Italy, 44 souls per square kilometre; Netherlands, 40; France, 34; England and Wales, 30; Germany, 28; Spain and Portugal, 17; Denmark, 15; Poland with Prussia, 14; Sweden, Norway and Finland, 13.

did Amsterdam and Frankfurt in both 1664 and 1666. Amid these major disasters the constant and universal incidence of the plague must not be ignored, since its persistent toll of the population was of greater significance than its periodically spectacular killings. Most spectacular of all in its effects, however, was warfare. Though comparatively few Europeans died in battle, the movement of armies brought famine, typhus and syphilis. Contemporaries always laid great stress on the depopulation caused by war, and if they tended to do so frequently in pleas for reduction of their taxes, no one could doubt that the Thirty Years War in Germany, the campaigns of 1650–60 in Poland, the devastation of the Palatinate in 1688 and the struggle for Spain after 1700, collectively reduced the population of Europe — though no two authorities would agree on an estimate.

Emigration, plague, warfare, causing tremendous fluctuation in particular localities, exercised a check upon the population as a whole; but since there were always some survivors, the losses wrought were made good by a sharp increase in the birth rate. The entire population was governed in fact by one simple rule: its size was directly determined by its supply of food. Far worse than an epidemic or invasion was the incapacity of European farming, apart from rare exceptions as in Poland and England,[1] to produce and to store a surplus against the inevitable years when the crop failed, not merely locally, but throughout the continent. Between 1648 and 1652, for example, the harvest failed in one country after another across Europe, adding economic distress to the political factors which brought or threatened revolution in those years:[2] there were further general failures in 1660–3, 1675–9 and, in the worst crisis of all, 1693–4.

The failure of the harvest whether local or general was a disaster for all who lived at subsistence level, and these comprised the great majority of Europeans. Such folk might survive one bad year by selling their goods and chattels — if there were any rich enough to buy them — in order to purchase food imported from other regions; but if the crops failed generally, or if they failed two years together, then famine resulted. Many died directly from starvation. Thousands more were so weakened by malnutrition that they fell prey to

[1] See above, page 4. Though the Dutch produced no surplus, their commercial facilities ensured the regular importation of food.

[2] See Chapter X, page 393, for Sweden; Chapter V, page 221, for Spain; Chapter III, page 166, for France.

the first illness to attack them. At such periods in the seventeenth century the death rate doubled or trebled and there were practically no births to offset it. The countryside was more immediately affected than the towns, since these had the means to lay in supplies and to buy further afield, but they too suffered when the famine was widespread. The famine of 1693, for example, caused food prices to rise so sharply that in Beauvais in northern France a family of five, even though they were all employed in weaving serges, could afford to buy less than half the bread it needed. Before the next harvest the father and two children had died: 'From a particularly fortunate family, because everyone worked, only a widow and an orphan remained because of the price of bread.'[1]

The harsh fact was that the population of Europe was pressing hard upon its means of subsistence, and since they were unable to produce greater supplies of food most Europeans suffered from undernourishment, poor health and a low expectation of life. One-half of all the babies born in the seventeenth century died within twelve months of birth; those who survived childhood might hope to live from 48 to 56 years if they were wealthy, and therefore comparatively well fed; if they were not, their expectation was between 30 to 40 years. For society as a whole the average expectation of life was 22 years.

Whereas famine accelerated the death rate and reduced the number of births, a series of good harvests produced an immediate parallel rise in births and a decline in deaths. The overall picture is therefore one of wild fluctuation in detail, determined primarily by the success or failure of the harvest, around a fairly constant mean. This same pattern is true also of the movement of prices, and for the same reason. In the sixteenth century the steady growth in numbers and the influx of American bullion had caused a steady rise in prices; in the seventeenth the population increase was checked, the influx of bullion fell off, and prices were again regulated by the harvest. Good harvests resulted in cheap food, and since money was thus released to purchase other goods, production was stimulated to the benefit of all classes. Conversely, a bad harvest not only caused starvation among the poor but compelled even the wealthy to economise in order to maintain their standard of housekeeping: industry and trade were consequently depressed.

[1] See P. Goubert, *Beauvais et les Beauvaisis de 1600 à 1730*, Paris, 1960.

On a European graph prices continued to rise steadily to 1625, fell to some extent by 1650, and held this level until a new rise began after 1700 — but such a general outline is wholly misleading. Europe was not an economic unit. The basic pattern was accompanied by startling variations from region to region, caused not only by the harvest, but also by the action of regional governments. The operation of tariffs, the sale of monopolies, and the debasement of the coinage[1] produced so many disconcerting fluctuations in the general pattern of European prices that merchants and manufacturers were filled with uncertainty and pessimism. This more than anything explains the fact that although the scale of economic activity continued to increase, the general rate of expansion was considerably less than in the sixteenth century with its mood of confident optimism. Because of the uncertainty of monetary values, the field of enterprise contracted; fewer new companies were founded, and established ones began to limit their activities as the investor, the merchant and the industrialist chose to take fewer risks.

Industry and Technology

If the uncertainties caused by price fluctuation checked the rate of industrial growth in Europe, there was none the less a degree of expansion stimulated by the needs of warfare, and the demand for luxuries which an increasingly wealthy middle class was able to afford. Remarkably, none of this expansion was accompanied by any significant change in methods of production, despite the fact that in the history of science the seventeenth century was a revolutionary era. Technological progress continued to depend upon the development of empirical methods by practical men, and science probably gained more from technology than she gave in return, at least before 1750.

In a few specialist fields only did the technologist benefit from scientific research: the study of pendular oscillation was applied by Christiaan Huygens to improving the measurement of time, while the study of the atmosphere contributed a great deal to pioneer work on the steam engine. This began when Galileo and his pupil Torricelli were asked by Cosimo II de Medici of Florence to

[1] See Chapter V, page 215, for the effect of this upon the Spanish economy.

account for the failure of his engineers to construct a suction pump capable of lifting water from a depth of fifty feet in the mines. In 1644 Torricelli announced his discovery of atmospheric pressure, and ten years later at Magdeburg, the immense forces exerted by it were demonstrated by von Guericke in a famous experiment with iron hemispheres.[1] In a subsequent experiment von Guericke showed that, when a partial vacuum was created below a large piston working in a cylinder, the combined force of fifty men could not prevent the atmospheric pressure driving the piston into the cylinder. Here, therefore, was a means of harnessing atmospheric pressure as a source of power, if only some simple means could be found of repeatedly creating a vacuum.

Huygens in all seriousness proposed to achieve this by means of gunpowder explosions, but fortunately his assistant, Denis Papin, achieved his object more simply and more safely by condensing steam in a cylinder: 'Since it is a property of water', he wrote in 1690, 'that a small quantity of it turned into vapour by heat has an elastic force like that of air, but upon cold supervening is again resolved into water, so that no trace of the said elastic force remains, I concluded that machines could be constructed wherein water, by the help of no very intense heat, and at little cost, could produce that perfect vacuum which could by no means be obtained by gunpowder.' The first machine to apply this principle in practice was *The Miners' Friend*, 'an engine to raise water by force', demonstrated by its inventor, Thomas Savery, at Hampton Court in 1698. A better machine, invented independently by Thomas Newcomen, appeared in 1712, capable of lifting ten gallons of water 153 feet through tiers of pumps, and so successful did it prove in the collieries and tin-mines of Great Britain that within fifteen years it was also in use in the Spanish Netherlands, France, Sweden, Germany, Austria and as far afield as Hungary.

The other inventions of any industrial significance were not adopted so speedily, nor did they owe their creation to scientific discovery. The stocking-frame, for example, developed in 1589 by an English clergyman, William Lee, was so unpopular in England that its inventor left for France — only to meet with a similarly hostile reception. The truth was that, unlike the steam pump which created opportunities for employment in mines hitherto flooded, labour-saving devices in the textile industry were suspected of

[1] On all this see below, pages 38–40.

causing unemployment: consequently it was not merely the work-men who rejected them but the local authorities too who banned their use in order to prevent riots and the spread of vagabondage. Industrialists themselves were not greatly exercised; since there was no shortage of cheap labour, labour-saving devices were not worth the trouble and expense, and the fate of the stocking-frame was shared by the ribbon loom, a device invented in Danzig by which the simple movement of one bar sufficed to produce six narrow weaves simultaneously. Introduced into London in 1616 and Leyden in 1620, it provoked such opposition that finally its use was banned not only in England and the Netherlands, but throughout Austria and the Holy Roman Empire. Even as late as the eighteenth century the city of Basle prohibited an attempt to harness it to water power.

Important though these inventions might be for the future, their impact on Europe in the seventeenth century was negligible. They represented the exception rather than the rule; technology not only made few advances on positions gained in the later Middle Ages, it was hardly considered by most business men as a potential factor in improving production and in making bigger profits. The major industries of building, shipbuilding, metallurgy and textile manu-facture, and the local crafts of the smith, the joiner and the miller, remained basically unchanged save for the empirical refinement of existing practices. In shipbuilding, for example, there were inter-esting developments but no sensational advances. While trading ships altered little in size and shape — even the great East India-men of 800 tons were not of unprecedented size — warships lowered their poops, cultivated larger, lower lines and occasionally attained to 1,500 tons: this of course was as large as the resources of the age could permit, since the *Sovereign of the Seas*, for instance, built for Charles I of England, required the destruction of two thousand oak trees, covering fifty acres of woodland. Design was largely a matter for rule of thumb: the midships section of a well-known ship was often reduced to scale and used as a model for others, but there was little attempt to modify design for novel purposes, except among the Dutch, who saw that experiment could be commercially profitable. Their herring *busses*, for example, were decked over and enlarged so that after the fish had been caught, coopers and salters could prepare the catch for market long before returning to port: the *fluitschips*, too, were a triumph of design;

transports with rigging simplified to need less crew, they were planned to carry goods swiftly and succeeded so brilliantly that their owners could fit in one extra voyage to the Baltic every year.

The endemic nature of warfare in the seventeenth century, and its greater scale, prompted a general assault on Europe's mineral resources.[1] At the siege of Magdeburg, for example, Tilly expended 12,000 to 18,000 cannon balls every day for a period of two months; yet even though the demand for cast iron increased so much the technique of smelting was still handicapped by its dependence upon charcoal, since no way was found to employ less expensive fuels without increasing the carbon impurities in the metal. Within this limitation, the pattern of production changed considerably. In 1600 England was the primary producer of iron in Europe, by 1700 she was producing 17,000 tons a year, but Sweden had overtaken her during the Thirty Years War with an annual production of 45,000 tons of which 30,000 were exported. The German states together increased their production to 30,000 tons, France reached 25,000 and Russia sprang from 5,000 to 20,000 during the single span of Tsar Peter's reign.[2] England's primacy was only to be recovered as a result of the secret experiments in coke-smelting which the Darbys of Coalbrookdale first began in 1706.

The conservatism of European industry in the seventeenth century is partly explained by three separate factors. Both in the social esteem and in the profits it offered, industry took second place to commerce and hence it rarely attracted the most acquisitive and ambitious minds. More important than this, the basic problem was the commercial one of finding new markets; a contrast to the nineteenth century, for example, when the problem was to produce goods more swiftly and more cheaply than anyone else. Consequently there was little emphasis on productivity as an end in itself: indeed, the greater part of industrial production was designed for the maker's own use. Europe was essentially an agrarian community, there was little profit from farming to devote to the purchase of commodities other than food, and as a result it was left to most men to use the local raw materials in their spare time to make their own cloth and to fashion their own tools and furniture. A few who found in this a more congenial occupation

[1] See Chapter X, page 388, for example, on the exploitation of copper-mining in Sweden.

[2] See Chapter X, page 432.

than tilling the fields set up as specialists, but their activities were severely limited by the cost and difficulty of transporting their products beyond their own locality. Very few had the skill, the capital and the enterprise to manufacture goods for markets elsewhere, and Colbert found it necessary in his plans to stimulate productivity[1] to compensate for these deficiencies by drawing upon the resources of the state itself.

The third and most important factor restraining technological and industrial experiment was that, given the capitalist, whether an industrial entrepreneur, an association of individuals, or a state-backed joint-stock company, there remained the problem of industrial control. It was difficult, often impossible, to persuade workers to adopt new techniques in order to sell their products more competitively outside their region. The industrial organisation known as the cottage or domestic system suffered greatly from this disadvantage. In theory the capitalist provided the raw materials and distributed them among the workers in their own homes, who then produced the goods according to his specifications and returned the finished product to him for sale in local or distant markets. But in practice the sanctions left to the employer were often inadequate. Because the domestic worker was usually in a position to derive an alternative livelihood from the land, since industrial activity was often a part-time occupation, he was sufficiently free to work as he pleased, even to the extent of withdrawing his labour without necessarily ruining himself. This was very important because of all those involved in the industrial process the worker was the least likely to comprehend the need for change in methods of production.[2]

A possible solution, though one generally beyond the means of the seventeenth century, was to establish factories employing full-time labour, so that the worker was not only supervised more closely, but, being thus more dependent upon his employer for his livelihood, became more amenable to discipline. This, however, was discouraged by the cost of building a factory and of supplying it with machinery; only where the nature of the product was such as to demand close supervision and the concentration of highly

---

[1] See Chapter VI, pages 267–73.
[2] See the case of the Widow Falempin, and Colbert's failure to bring French domestic workers within the aegis of a nationally regulated textile industry, in Chapter VI, page 269.

skilled workers was there any economic incentive for large work-shops. While small-scale metal production might still be carried on at home, the manufacture of cannon required the establishment of a factory: similarly the *Manufactures Royales* were initiated by Colbert to perform specialist functions, such as the great works at Abbeville set up by the Van Robais to produce luxury cloth, but they were an expensive venture scarcely typical of industry in general during the seventeenth century.

Commerce

Despite the discoveries of the fifteenth and sixteenth centuries and the spectacular efforts of individuals and companies to estab-lish trading stations across the world, most merchants were still primarily concerned with the transportation of goods from one region to another in Europe. But if the geography of European trade remained much the same, its control was passing into very different hands, and the seventeenth century witnessed the final stages in a long process by which the Italian republics and the Hanseatic cities, both based on the shores of inland seas, lost their monopolies to the states on the Atlantic seaboard. The Italians had controlled Europe's trade with the Levant, not only for the Medi-terranean produce of wines, oils and fruits to be purchased in Aleppo, Beirut or Jaffa, but also for the spices and silks shipped overland from the Indian ocean. The opening of the new route to India around the Cape had done them less harm than they had feared: their problem was to compete with English, French and Dutch interlopers in the Mediterranean itself. They were handi-capped by the growth of Turkish naval power in the previous century which had destroyed much of their trade, and their banking houses had been drained of wealth by the bankruptcies of successive Spanish governments. In the seventeenth century, therefore, though their cities retained much individual importance, their days of collective pre-eminence were over.

In conscious imitation of the Italians the member cities of the Hanseatic League, stretched around the shores of the Baltic and along the west coast of Scandinavia, had succeeded by the fifteenth century in controlling all trade between their shores and the mar-kets of Germany, England and the Netherlands. They trafficked in wares less exotic than the Italians' but no less valuable, exporting corn and naval stores, and monopolising both the cod fisheries off the Lofoten Islands and the herring grounds off Scania: salted fish was in great demand, and in a good year the catch frequently exceeded 13,000 tons. Wealth had given the Hanse political power: they had made possible the Yorkist invasion of England by Edward IV and they supplied aid to Gustavus Vasa's rebellion,[1] but they could not withstand the rise of strong national governments in Denmark, Sweden and, ultimately, Brandenburg and Russia, which destroyed the concept of commercial co-operation in the Baltic and substituted a long struggle for military supremacy. In addition there was the competition of the Dutch who broke into the Hanseatic enclave to fish for herrings, and whose competitive techniques outstripped those of their rivals. They invented a new process for salting, and their herring *busses* were equipped to process the catch at sea. Worse still, the herrings themselves had turned fickle and deserted the Baltic for the North Sea. Hanseatic towns like Stralsund and Danzig still enjoyed a measure of prosperity in the seventeenth century, though both suffered from Sweden's expansion, but the bulk of Baltic trade fell into the hands of the Dutch, the French and the English. The last Diet of the Hanseatic League met in 1669.

The first effective challenge to the supremacy of the Italian and Baltic towns had come from Antwerp. As Bruges, her local rival and a Hanseatic base, was left stranded by the silting-up of the river Zwyn, Antwerp became the Staple for the English Merchant Adventurers and replaced Venice as the European copper market; moreover, as the effect of the overseas discoveries began to take place, she became the market for the colonial produce of the Spanish and Portuguese empires. With the Dutch revolt and the blockade of the Scheldt, however, she lost her trade and influence to Amsterdam, but not so swiftly as to allay all Dutch fears of her recovery if liberated from Spanish rule in 1645.[2] Amsterdam's pre-eminence, and with it the commercial supremacy of the Dutch, coincided almost exactly with the limits of the seventeenth century. As every prince attempted to erect his own Versailles, as every court hastened to adopt French fashions in dress and deportment, so, in matters of commerce, it was the Dutch who were the exemplars of Europe. Unfortunately for them they were the first to suffer from successful imitation, and competition from England and France began to make inroads into their monopoly of the carrying

[1] See Chapter X, page 380.   [2] See Chapter IV, page 196.

trade.[1] Amsterdam, however, yet remained unrivalled as the very hub of European commerce, its principal money market and exchange.

No commercial venture could succeed without capital, and this was generally provided by the partnership of two or more individuals. Such a relationship was essentially a personal one, often restricted to the operation of a single voyage or expedition, and by its very nature could not survive indefinitely. In place of this type of regulated company, an association of traders, the English by 1600 had developed the joint-stock company, an association of capital. Its merit was that it attracted the capital of investors who knew nothing of commerce, but whose interests were safeguarded by an elected board of officials. Shareholders might sell their stock, the stock might fall in value, individual officials might resign or die, but the joint-stock company itself could remain indifferent to such events: it had achieved a type of immortality. The Dutch swiftly appropriated the idea from England, and the rest of Europe from the Dutch. The joint-stock company was of particular value in undertaking a sustained series of long range commercial ventures, such as those of the East and West India Companies, which were far beyond the pockets of any group of individual merchants. It was also a useful device for the encouragement or control of trade by the state.[2] Nevertheless there is a danger of confusing the spectacular with the normal; the joint-stock company for all its significance was still a rarity. Just as the bulk of trade was still essentially confined within the boundaries of Europe, so it was that the individual merchant, backed by his family or a few partners, remained the typical figure in seventeenth-century commerce.

POLITICAL THEORY AND PRACTICE[3]

Warfare, Absolutism and Political Philosophy

In the Middle Ages political theory and feudal practice assumed that states were not so much political organisms as interchangeable

[1] Dutch supremacy was the cardinal feature of commercial history in the seventeenth century: see Chapter IV, pages 196–206, and Chapter VIII, pages 348–52. See also Chapter VI, pages 271–2, for a study of French commercial companies.

[2] See Chapter IV, page 201, for the organisation of one such company in detail, and Chapter VI, page 272, for examples of state direction.

[3] Since this section generalises much of the material described in subsequent chapters, cross-references for all topics would be distracting, and

items of inheritance. Territories were only superficially united in the person of one prince since effective central control, except on occasion in England and Sicily, was prevented by the autonomous powers vested in local feudatories, ecclesiastical princes and corporate towns. In the sixteenth century the empire of Charles V provided a classic example of this: not only did he inherit the Habsburg lands in Austria, the combined thrones of Castile and Aragon and the Duchy of Burgundy, but within these separate states his title was further fragmented as, in the Netherlands, Duke of Brabant, Count of Flanders or Marquess of Antwerp. This personal empire was even then an anachronism: the trend in the sixteenth century was already towards the so-called 'New Monarchy' from which evolved some of the absolutist concepts of the seventeenth century.

The source of absolutism in Europe has been traced to the revival of Roman law in the twelfth century. Customary law arose from the complex gradations which had evolved in western European society; since this society was essentially hierarchic, one man's lord another man's vassal, it laid down no harsh dividing line between bond and free, between ruler and subject. Roman law, on the other hand, recognised neither the indeterminate status of the villein nor the disjunctive nature of medieval sovereignty. The villein was thus condemned to serfdom, since if he was not wholly *liber* he must be deemed wholly *servus*, and the sovereign declared absolute: 'Quod principi placuit legis habet vigorem.' Yet though the villein lost his freedom straightway, four centuries supervened before the prince became absolute; consequently some more immediate explanation of seventeenth-century monarchy must be found.

The answer probably lies in the extended scope of warfare after 1500. Operations were on a larger scale than in the past, the number of men under arms increased, campaigns were more prolonged, so that a revolution was necessary in the organisation and equipment of armies. Novel problems of recruitment and finance arose which could only be solved by strengthening the powers of the prince so that his decisions might be obeyed unquestioningly by all his subjects everywhere. Since the machinery of state was not only rudimentary but was also in the hands of the great noble families,

references will be made only where they seem necessary to assist an understanding of the text.

it was necessary to follow the suppression of regional franchises and class privileges with the creation of an efficient bureaucracy, loyal to the prince who alone gave it its authority. Moreover, since rebellion endangered security and made it impossible to mobilise the country's resources, domestic faction and religious dissent had first to be silenced before effective preparations could be made for war. Ideally,[1] therefore, the European state best qualified to wage successful war was the one in which central direction, administrative uniformity and efficiency had been established.

A philosophical justification of this political development had gained ground steadily since the Renaissance. Unlike the political philosophy of the Middle Ages the new concept was wholly secular. It paid only lip service to the notion of monarchy by divine right and it regarded the state as a self-sufficient entity, a law unto itself, with its own morality — *raison d'état*. The anarchy of the Italian wars prompted Machiavelli to demonstrate that a strong and stable community could only be secured by princely absolutism. In a similar environment, that of the French wars of religion, Bodin expounded in his *Six Livres de la République* a similar doctrine, prescribing an absolute monarchy exercising, 'supreme power unrestrained by law over citizens and subjects'. Such a philosophy justified the disregard of established rights and customs, and the destruction of rival authorities within the state, on the grounds of expediency and national strength.

So too in England during the civil war of the seventeenth century Thomas Hobbes gave classic expression to this theory in his *Leviathan*, a book which was all the more effective for its air of scientific infallibility. Hobbes indeed owed much to his scientific interests. Fired by the new enthusiasm for mathematical modes of reasoning, he tried to apply Descartes's *esprit géométrique*[2] to society at large, to construct a political philosophy as exact as a geometric proof. He agreed that if Euclid aroused as much passion as did politics, then people would argue equally as much over geometry, but he believed that by the application of a rational technique a similar science of politics was practicable. He agreed with Galileo that all explanations expressed in terms of substantial form or essential nature were tautological.[3] A pellet of wax sank or floated not

---

[1] For a summary of what tended to happen in practice see below, pages 26–27, 250–3.
[2] See below, page 60.   [3] See below, page 37.

according to its essential nature, but to its specific gravity. Similarly, man did not create the state because he was a political animal, as Aristotle maintained, but because his reason taught him that only thus could he avoid violent death. Life in Hobbes's state of nature was, 'solitary, poor, nasty, brutish and short', an atomistic view of equally competitive individuals constantly striving with each other, which clearly reflected the corpuscular theory of matter of his fellow countryman Boyle. At bottom, of course, the emotional basis of Hobbes's lay not in science but in his experience of the civil war, which he then identified with life in its natural state: 'Hereby it is manifest that during the time men live without a common power to keep them all in awe they are in that condition which is called war, and such a war as is of every man against every man.'

In these circumstances it was only to be expected that Hobbes should seek to establish security of person and property, and in doing so should be willing to pay heavily in terms of personal liberty. He thus defined his new concept of the state, combining total responsibility with total power: 'This is that great Leviathan, or rather (to speak more reverently) that Mortall God, to which we owe under the Immortal God our peace and defence.' In this state morality is no longer the basis of law, but law — the sovereign's decree — is the basis of morality. Hobbes did in fact allow for considerable modification of this totalitarian principle, since he established the origins of the sovereign power in the doctrine of popular consent, and always recognised that 'the obligation of subjects to the sovereign is understood to last as long and no longer than the power lasteth by which he is able to protect them'. Hobbes's utilitarian philosophy was too hedonist and too materialist for his contemporaries wholly to accept. Nonetheless, the divorce of political theory from theological belief was becoming increasingly clear, and the seventeenth century witnessed the gradual secularisation of political standards. Even Bossuet, with his *Politique tirée des Propres Paroles de l'Écriture Sainte*, merely used scripture to refute the Protestant apologists of rebellion, and to corroborate his own views which were clearly derived from the political circumstances of seventeenth-century France.

Also secular in outlook was Grotius, the Dutch polymath who fled from Holland after Oldenbarneveldt's execution, and whose most famous work, *De Jure Belli et Pacis*, was published in Paris in 1625. Though his plea for international law was backed by massive and detailed quotation not merely from legal authorities but from the Bible and the Fathers, it is evident that his most vital source of inspiration was the Stoic concept of natural law, a concept essentially rational and secular. Moreover he too was fascinated by the scientific advances of his day and, like Hobbes, believed that ethics and politics were potentially demonstrable sciences. To this end he sought to provide a chain of reasoning sufficiently exhaustive, sufficiently systematic, and backed by every conceivable authority in order to convince mankind of his urgent thesis, that there was a common law between nations, valid in peace and war. His experience of the Dutch revolt and the Thirty Years War gave substance to his humanitarian desire to prevent war from becoming 'nothing but a riot of fury as though authorisation had been given for every sort of crime'. Consequently he tried to apply the rules of right reason, of natural law, to the actions of sovereign states. As for the states themselves, Grotius assumed that their rulers were wholly responsible for their actions: 'That power is called supreme whose acts are not subject to another's jurisdiction in such a way that they can be rendered void by the decision of another human authority.'

The evolution of a political philosophy under the pressure of a changing environment is best seen in the work of Spinoza, a fellow countryman of Grotius, better known for his more general philosophical works.[1] Like Hobbes and Grotius he tried to make his reasoning as cogent as a mathematical proof — the *more geometrico* — but he shifted his basic premises too radically to succeed in this. He began by extolling an idealist view of democracy but, as the friend and admirer of Jan de Witt, and living in a society which promoted security, liberty, commercial expansion and a flourishing culture, he began to consider the attractions of benign oligarchy. In 1672 all this was rudely shattered by the power of absolute France: from that moment there was little to distinguish Spinoza's attitude from Hobbes's. Since nothing seemed comparable to the virtues of peace and security, the function of the state, defined in the *Tractatus Politicus* (1677), 'is purely and simply to guarantee peace and security.' Spinoza continued: 'It follows that the best state is that in which men live their lives in concord and in which their rights are inviolate', but these rights were not to be tolerated if their operation weakened the guarantor of security, the

[1] See below, page 63.

Sovereign. The clear-eyed disillusionment of the philosopher is reflected in his dictum, 'It is not wisdom but authority that makes a law.'

Absolutism

The basis of political practice in the seventeenth century was the identification of the state with the sovereign, a view expressed characteristically by Louis XIV; 'When you are working for the good of the state you are working for yourself; the good of the one constitutes the glory of the other.' To achieve this the prince had first to control the separate units of medieval society — the Estates, the great noble households, the church and the corporate towns. If the federal nature of this society presented a challenge, it also offered a means of attaining control since, so self-regarding were these separate units, the crown could play off one against the other, especially by offering to one group alone the opportunity to win rewards in the royal service which were not otherwise available. In eastern Europe, where there was no powerful middle class to set against the nobles, the rulers of Russia and Austria secured the nobles' loyalty by granting to them greater powers over their serfs, a concession which in no way weakened the crown. This was true also of Brandenburg, but here the Great Elector went further, following a practice begun in Sweden by Gustavus Adolphus, and gave the nobles an entirely new function in the state as leaders of the administration.

One feature common to the growth of absolutism in every country, except of course in England and Poland where absolutism made no headway, was the eclipse of the Estates, since the very existence of popular assemblies challenged royal supremacy. Some of them, as in Aragon, might control taxation; others, in Castile, served simply as sounding boards for public opinion, but whatever their function they naturally sought to extend it. 'The more you rely on such bodies', wrote the Great Elector to his son, 'the more you lose your authority since the Estates are always trying to weaken your sovereign power.' The Austrian Habsburgs shared his view. They took advantage of their conquest of Bohemia to annihilate the powers of the Estates, and even that most powerful and independent of assemblies, the Hungarian Diet, was brought under control by 1720: dependence upon Vienna was the price of Hungary's liberation from the Turks. In France the Bourbons solved the problem by dispensing altogether with the States-General except on one occasion, in 1614, which significantly enough was a moment of royal weakness after the assassination of Henry IV. The reduction of the provincial Estates, achieved already in the *pays d'élections*, was completed in the *pays d'état* by Richelieu and Louis XIV. Paradoxically, the Swedish *riksdag* survived, but only in order to strengthen the absolutism of Charles XI and Charles XII against the ambitions of the *rad* to establish a permanent oligarchy. The government of the United Provinces was less of an exception than might appear, since in this case it was the States-General which became the sovereign, exercising an increasing measure of control over the separate provinces of the Union of Utrecht. For all their propaganda the regents of Holland and the princes of Orange, who contested control of the States-General, worked continually to strengthen its authority at the expense of local assemblies and urban councils.

The destruction or weakening of popular assemblies was not enough: it was equally important to ensure control of the Church which, as the second estate and with claims upon men's deepest oyalties, represented a rival authority within the state. 'Rex est in regno suo imperator', ran the dictum of Roman law: henceforward, as the monopoly of Rome was replaced by royal monopolies across Europe, the monarch was also to be pope. If the prince became a Protestant, as in north Germany, Sweden and Denmark, he could then appropriate ecclesiastical revenues and secularise monastic lands: equally important, he could control appointments to benefices, supervise the policies of his clergy and make the national Church serve his needs. But Erastianism of this sort was not confined to Protestant princes. If he remained a Catholic, the prince could none the less insist upon a greater measure of control over his clergy. Orthodoxy did not entail submission to Rome, and a feature of the Counter-Reformation had been the compacts made between the papacy and such states as Bavaria and Austria, by which the prince was guaranteed greater powers in return for his suppression of heresy. Kings of France had in any case enjoyed absolute control over the appointment of their clergy since the Concordat of Bologna (1516), and, as the *régale* crisis demonstrated,[1] they were accustomed to rely on their support against the rival authority of the pope. So too in Spain, where the Inquisition

[1] See Chapter VI, pages 253-5.

was virtually a department of state and where papal bulls were promulgated only with royal permission, their Most Catholic Majesties enjoyed absolute authority over their Church.

The Churches were particularly dependent upon the state for success in their struggle with their rivals. Lutheranism was established solely by the action of princes, and the Counter-Reformation owed its successes as much to the prince as to the priest. The conflict of denominations endangered the state and thus the sovereign was as eager as his clergy to suppress heresy. Nor was his interest confined to rival Churches. The seventeeth-century ruler disliked all signs of nonconformity and diversity within the established church of his state, and the Jansenists in Catholic France suffered as severely from the secular authorities as did the Arminians of Calvinist Holland. The goal of political absolutism precluded toleration: the individual was allowed to worship freely only where the prince was not supreme, and wherever toleration had been granted there was a strong tendency for it to be revoked, as it was in Bohemia (1621), in Hungary (1678) and in France (1685), as the powers of the sovereign increased. Tolerance could only make its way unofficially when the conflict of sects had abated, as in Holland after Gomarist rigorism had become a spent force, or in England when the political circumstances of 1689 made toleration of a sort advisable: in either case it was toleration by Protestants of other Protestants. There was no truce in the rivalry of Protestant and Catholic.

The absolute power which princes sought to acquire could not be exercised through the traditional offices of state, since these were too closely wedded to the medieval system from which they had sprung. Consequently their titles were abolished, their powers emasculated or their functions transformed. This is what happened in East Prussia where the independent and powerful *Oberrathe* became, in the Great Elector's words, 'councillors and servants who derive their power only from their lord; without his will and his approval they have no power to do or to decide anything in his affairs, except in conformity with their instructions'. These great officers of state should not too readily be acclaimed as martyrs to the cause of absolutism. The liberty they championed was too often a cloak for inefficiency or for their own tyranny in local affairs. Their place was taken by men of outstanding brilliance, not merely subservient to the crown but distinguished by their comprehensive grasp of the essentials of administration. Such men, the epitome of bureaucracy, shared the same outlook whatever country they claimed their own: in the committees of the Holland Estates, in the Viennese Chancery, in the *conseil du roi*, in the *Reduktion* commissions, in the *Generalkriegskommissariat*, they strove after uniformity, good order and the rational exploitation of the states' resources. Without them the absolutist assumptions of the seventeenth-century prince would have been worthless.

Mercantilism: Political Economy

Warfare and bureaucracy imposed so great a burden on the royal exchequer that no sovereign could survive unless the economic resources of his state were exploited to the full. Since his power to tax at will was valueless if there were no wealth to be taxed, the creation of wealth became a matter for government direction. There was also a strong argument for unifying territories by economic as well as political ties by the introduction of a single currency, of standard weights and measures, of improved communications and of uniform regulations for trade and industry. Wealth, moreover, encouraged civil peace: the most significant fact about Bacon's dictum, 'money is like muck, not good except it be spread,' is that it comes not from his essay on *Riches* but from that on *Seditions and Troubles*. This clear-sighted analyst of politics knew well that poverty was a potent cause of rebellion, and thus the sovereign was required to concern himself with his people's material welfare as a necessary means of defence.

For these reasons the seventeenth-century ruler had a vested interest in promoting the economic welfare of his state. To do so he evolved a system of direction, regulation and encouragement which has been generally termed the 'mercantile system' or 'mercantilism', a term invented in the eighteenth century as a generalisation about the previous century's practices and beliefs in these matters. It has been held that these practices were simply the extension, on a national scale, of the regulations governing the economy of the medieval towns, the paternalism of the guilds being replaced by the paternalism of the state. But this was not the full story. Medieval economic thought was dominated by religious ideas of a 'just price', by a desire to protect the artisan from unfair competition, and by the notion that an adequate livelihood and a fair return for honest work were ends in themselves. The seventeenth-century state, on the other hand, was organised for the acquisition of power, and this demanded the endless exploitation of national resources. The mercantilist sought to increase the wealth of his country immoderately, and without moral limitations, so that the exchequer might replenish itself unceasingly from the accumulating wealth of the taxpayers: his purpose was not primarily to enrich the public at large but to force the economy into the service of the state.

A principal characteristic of seventeenth-century political economy was the identification of military and political power with the possession of gold. It seemed to explain, for example, the momentary ascendancy of Spain, and mercantilists therefore concentrated on measures designed to acquire greater supplies of the precious metals — hence the use of the term 'bullionist' to describe their policies. They believed that gold was a limited commodity which was a view encouraged to some extent by the ever-decreasing proportion of gold and silver to copper in the shipments from America to Spain by 1600, and that its acquisition was possible only by theft or commercial competition. Colbert, moreover, drawing close parallels between the wealth and the power of Venice in the past and of Holland in his own day, believed that commerce itself nourished national greatness, and he shared with his contemporaries the notion that commerce too was limited in its volume. Despite the fact that greater opportunities for trade were being opened up in America and in the Far East, this view was substantially sound at the time, for the bulk of European trade was within Europe itself,[1] and the steady inflation of the previous century which had stimulated economic activity had been checked. To expand their trade states would therefore have to fight.

Commerce was in any case an aggressive occupation, especially in an age of insecure craft and mutinous crews, of pirates and wreckers, and the respectable merchant slipped easily from commerce to contraband, from trade to theft. In its search for the constituents of power, the seventeenth century merely added one further hazard, national exclusiveness or commercial war. If trade had to be filched from the foreigner, governments were quick to fashion their weapons. Government agencies were established, as the *Kommerzkolleg* in Vienna and the Council of Trade in London, to direct the strategy of the operation: state companies were

[1] See above, page 13, and, for a detailed study of Colbert's application of mercantilist ideas, see Chapter VI, pages 267–73.

formed, as the Dutch West India Company and the French *Compagnie du Nord*, to drive their rivals from selected areas: tariffs were imposed and goods proscribed, as in the Navigation Act of 1651 and the Methuen Treaty of 1703, in order to deny home ports to foreign ships or to boycott an enemy's exports. When all this failed, governments turned to war. The Dutch fought the English three times for essentially commercial reasons. When the two combined against France, the French tariffs of 1667, the success of the *Compagnie du Nord* in the Baltic by 1688, the threat of a French monopoly of Spanish trade in 1702, were potent factors in the resultant wars against Louis XIV, whatever other issues were involved. Colbert was clearly justified in his report of 1669 that, 'le commerce cause un combat perpétuel en paix et en guerre entre les nations de l'Europe, à qui en emportera la meilleure partie. Les Hollandais, Anglais and Francais sont les acteurs de ce combat.'

The mercantilist thus constructed an economic system geared to the needs of warfare: in the words of the contemporary dictum, 'Trade is the source of public finance, and public finance is the vital nerve of war.' Any benefits which accrued to the individual by the regulation of industry or trade were incidental to the prime purpose of mercantilism. It was not concerned with the creation of prosperity for its own sake, nor with the raising of the standard of living as an end in itself: its purpose was political. Colbert, naturally enough, became so enthusiastically involved in his projects to revitalise industry that he clearly forgot this on occasion, but he never failed to recognise that even the interests of the economy were subordinate to those of the state in its struggle for power. Tariffs designed to stimulate the export of manufactured goods in place of raw materials could not be kept artificially low when the cost of warfare forced the Treasury to raise all taxes indiscriminately, and subsidies to newly established industries took second place to military expenditure. The periodic depreciation of the currency during the last decades of Louis XIV's reign prejudiced the success of industry, the continual recourse to higher taxation restricted consumption and expenditure, and regulations for the good of industry frequently became mere devices for taxing the worker.

It was thus the weakness of mercantilism in practice that, while it recognised that economic growth was a vital prerequisite to the pursuit of power, and that governmental direction was often necessary to promote this growth, the onset of the very wars which these policies were intended to sustain resulted in their being abandoned and, frequently, in national insolvency.

The Limits to Absolutism

The absolutism of seventeenth-century government must not be equated with totalitarianism. Arbitrary though the powers of the absolute monarch might be, and considerably more comprehensive than those wielded by his predecessors, they were yet meagre by modern standards. In the imposing façade of power there were significant flaws. In the first place there was the insurmountable difficulty of communication. The time taken for an order to be sent from Paris, Brandenburg, Madrid, Stockholm, Moscow or Vienna to royal officers in Languedoc, Cleves, Catalonia, Livonia, Siberia or Transylvania, and the difficulties involved in calling these far-flung agents to account, explain the impossibility of maintaining absolute control over the administration until the age of modern transport and communication. Local officials were only too ready to ignore despatches whose contents they disliked, and it could take many years before the central government discovered that its orders were not being implemented. The vagaries of the postal services then provided offenders with the excuse that their orders had never arrived.

Though the expansion of bureaucracy was a feature of the century, the absolute monarch still had only a few servants on whom he might implicitly rely. His councils were staffed with men whose obedience and loyalty were never in doubt, but there were very few officials to enforce his policies away from the centre of government. No matter how hardworking they were, such men could not exercise that supervision over every member of society which is the prerogative of a modern civil service, since many of the functions which today devolve upon the central government or its provincial agents were then fulfilled by the traditional local authorities. Even in France, where the work of men like Colbert did so much to bring the body of the population under the aegis of the royal councils, it was the local *parlement*, the local noble or the local corporation which still acted as the authority most directly affecting the daily life of the average individual. It was unlikely that such bodies would openly oppose the decrees of an absolute monarch, but their enforcement of them might be ludicrously ineffectual. The activities of royal intendants and inspectors were thus confined to checking the grosser abuses of local authorities and to dealing with openly recalcitrant individuals. Even the intendant, or his equivalent outside France, might tend to escape royal control by overlong residence in a particular province so that he too acquired a parochial attitude to the dictates of the central government.

Instead of ruling a society of individuals whose equality only served to expose them uniformly to the power of his government, the seventeenth-century monarch governed a society whose hierarchic structure afforded bastions of privilege to protect the separate classes from the full force of his power. He might strengthen his authority by playing off one class against another, but he could not destroy the privileges of a class if these were jealously guarded or vigorously upheld. French nobles were excluded from the administration and their ability to wage private war destroyed, but Louis XIV at his greatest did not dare to tax them as he taxed his peasants. Similarly, the *junkers* in Brandenburg, the *boyars* in Russia and the nobles of the Danubian Monarchy did not acknowledge the augmented powers of their sovereigns until they themselves had been confirmed and strengthened in their social privileges. Serfs apart, every stratum of society was hedged about and protected by time-honoured privileges, and though the prince might arbitrarily strike at individuals, and even reverse individual traditions, he could not challenge classes as a whole. Only when a class was in decline, as in the north German towns, or had been defeated in war, as in Bohemia, could its traditional privileges be overthrown. Absolutism, in short, was remarkably ineffective in a society based upon privilege, and the governments of the seventeenth century had far less direct impact upon the daily lives of their subjects than their successors in the egalitarian societies of the modern age.

By the end of the century there came a significant trend in political thought away from royal absolutism. The state had emerged as the central concept of political theory: this of course might be linked, as in the writings of Bossuet and Hobbes, with the concept of royal absolutism, but there arose an alternative notion that the prince himself might not always serve the best interests of the state. *Raison d'état* might then be invoked, not for the prince but against him, and even Hobbes had recognised that when the sovereign failed to protect his subjects they were free to rebel.

Fénelon, a man who experienced the full rigour of Louis XIV's power, appealed to a visionary past in which the aristocracy had provided a form of government which had best served the interests of the people. Though in this respect he was wholly out of touch with the realities both of the past and of the present, his denunciation of the king's personal policies as running counter to the nation's interests is most significant. In a letter to the Duc de Chevreuse in 1710, he wrote: 'Our misfortune arises from the fact that the war has hitherto been the affair of the king alone, who is ruined and discredited. It must be made the real affair of the whole body of the nation. It is necessary that there should be spread throughout our nation an intimate conviction that it is the nation itself that in its own interests bears the burden of this war.'

This deliberate separation of the sovereign and the state, in contrast to the generally held identification of the two, was repeated early in the following century by Montesquieu, who wrote of England: 'I call it free because the sovereign, whose person is controlled and limited, is unable to inflict any imaginable harm on anyone.' In England the reaction against absolutism had reached its climax in the Glorious Revolution of 1688, its permanent expression in the parliamentary settlement of 1689–1715, and its philosophical justification in the writings of John Locke. 'For all power given with trust for the attaining an end being limited by that end, whenever that end is manifestly neglected or opposed the trust must necessarily be forfeited, and the power devolve into the hands of those that gave it, who may place it anew where they shall think best for their safety and security. And thus the community perpetually retains a supreme power of saving themselves from the attempts and designs of anybody, even of their legislators, whenever they shall be so foolish or so wicked, as to lay and carry on designs against the liberties and properties of the subject.'

The emphasis was shifting from the rights of the king to the rights of his subjects: the maxim, 'quod principi placuit legis habet vigorem', was being offset by another, 'lex est quod populus romanus constituebat', which represented the obverse side to Hobbes's theory of the social contract. Its essence was to insist upon government as the action of society, delegated perhaps to one man but always revocable. The government acts as a trustee, and this fiduciary concept is also the basis of Fénelon's demand, 'Is the flock made for the shepherd or the shepherd for the flock?' There was very little thought along these lines outside France and England, perhaps because elsewhere the centralised state was only just being established, but once monarchy had become absolute in Austria, Prussia and Russia, there were strong hints of this same concept behind the behaviour of the Enlightened Despots of the eighteenth century.

THE SCIENTIFIC REVOLUTION

New Methods and New Aims in Scientific Discovery

In the Middle Ages scholars were concerned less with the exact description of natural objects than with the construction of philosophical and logical systems: 'This kind of degenerate learning', wrote Bacon, who was one of the first to attack it, 'did chiefly reign among the schoolmen; who having sharp and strong wits and abundance of leisure, and small variety of reading, but their wits being shut up in the cells of a few authors (chiefly Aristotle their dictator), as their persons were shut up in the cells of monasteries and colleges, and knowing little history, either of nature or of time, did of no great quantity of matter and infinite agitation of wit spin out unto us those laborious webs of learning which are extant in their books.'

But Bacon was less than just: the classical scientists, Aristotle, Galen and Ptolemy, had already provided explanations of the material world[1] which satisfied so fully the demands of common sense, and which were then so smoothly integrated into Christian theology by St. Thomas Aquinas in the thirteenth century, that to question them was not only to question common sense but to venture into heresy. As a result scientific study in the Middle Ages was mainly the literary transmission of classical science, experiments being conducted only to demonstrate accepted truths. Albertus Magnus of Cologne, who is credited with the close study of natural history in the twelfth century wrote of the ostrich: 'It is said of this bird that it swallows and digests iron, but I have not found this myself because several ostriches refused to eat the iron which I threw them.' There were very few who wrote like this. The majority preferred their bestiaries stuffed with biblical

---

[1] For these explanations see below, pages 36, 40, 44.

exegesis and little natural history, following St. Augustine's dictum that it mattered less whether an animal existed than what it symbolised.

Mathematicians at Oxford in the twelfth century and at Paris in the thirteenth began to query some of the principles of Aristotle's physics, the weakest element in the corpus of classical science and when Duns Scotus and William of Occam, two English Franciscans of the fourteenth century, had exposed serious flaws in the philosophy of Aquinas, the way was prepared for further inquiry. Occam was particularly important for his belief that nature does everything in the simplest manner, and his famous Razor, 'entia non sunt multiplicanda praeter necessitatem', was a plea for the rejection of unnecessary hypotheses. Under his influence Parisian scholars came close to the modern theory of impetus, and it might have been thought that a major breakthrough in science was to be expected by the time of the Renaissance. Curiously enough, though art and literature, politics and philosophy were immediately affected, the impact of the Renaissance on science was principally to reinforce the authority of the ancients, since it was they who were held up by the humanists as models of perfection. Nevertheless, the recovery of classical texts did lead to some discoveries in science: the full text of Aristotle on biology, his best subject, had never been accessible to medieval scholars, nor had the original text of Galen on medicine. Moreover, the revival of Platonic and Pythagorean concepts of the universe at variance with those of Aristotle, as well as the rediscovery of Archimedes, whose teaching did not fit into any of the accepted systems of thought, made it possible, as at the University of Padua, for Aristotle to be challenged; and it was no accident that there, in one of the few centres of relatively free thought, both Galileo and Vesalius were professors.

The great developments in Renaissance art did much to stimulate the study of anatomy, perspective and natural history, and Leonardo da Vinci, who combined the scientist's curiosity with the artist's eye has been acclaimed the symbolic figure of the scientific revolution. This he was not. He experimented widely, he brought a freshness of observation to accepted doctrines, but he had neither the experimental method — the methodical collation of material and the systematic verification of hypotheses — the mathematics, nor the means of measurement which were to be among the great achievements of the seventeenth century. Why the seventeenth century should have been so vital a period in the history of science is a complex problem. Certainly the long-term effect of both the Renaissance and the Reformation was to encourage a questioning spirit among many scholars, but a greater factor was the invention of printing, which allowed men throughout Europe to become immediately aware of the work of their contemporaries. Collaboration at a distance was now possible, and the pace of scientific advance no longer depended upon the chance concentration of scholars in one favoured place. Above all, the one development that made possible the scientific revolution was the tremendous technological advance in the manufacture of precision instruments of observation and measurement, which furnished mankind with the telescope, the microscope, the micrometer, the barometer, the thermometer, the pendulum clock, and balances, no longer accurate to 1 grain but to $\frac{1}{500}$ of a grain.

This remarkable and necessary addition to man's scientific equipment resulted from the increasing amount of accurate investigation into nature carried on by men outside the universities, in spheres where no inherent reverence for authority precluded investigation, and where the demands of practical problems compelled the formulation of new questions and answers. Artillery attacked the physics of Aristotle at its weakest point by compelling the study of ballistics. The sternpost rudder, which replaced what had virtually been an oar lashed to the stern, made ocean-going less hazardous in the sixteenth century and thus prompted a demand for better means of navigation. Mariners, therefore, became knowledgeable in the study of compasses and magnetism, of astronomy and tides. Men employed in land drainage also studied the tides, and it was Stevin, a Dutch engineer and mathematician, who produced in 1590 the first scientific tide table: others, engaged in mining and metallurgy, studied the properties of metals, the mechanics of the pump, and the problems of hydrostatics and ventilation. So it was that away from the traditional centres of learning the scientific revolution owed its greatest impetus to the practical problems, solutions and equipment evolved by countless foundryworkers, instrument-makers, mariners, miners, smiths and engineers — some well versed in Euclid, others illiterate, but all alike driven by the profit motive and curiosity to experiment in their work.

One man who profited much from the experience gained by sailors, and also from his own extensive practical knowledge of mining and metallurgy, was William Gilbert, Fellow of St. John's College, Cambridge, and physician to Queen Elizabeth I. Spending hours in the company of craftsmen, especially of Robert Norman, a retired mariner and compass-maker, he was prompted by them to examine the nature of magnetic variation, and the problem of the compass needle which tilts at various angles according to its position on the earth's surface. Gilbert made a model of the earth, a *terella*, out of lodestone, a magnetic rock, and placed upon it a series of small iron needles. These behaved exactly like compass needles. Not only did they point to the *terella*'s north pole, they also dipped at various angles in different places, horizontally at the equator, vertically at the pole. From this Gilbert demonstrated that the earth itself was a magnet with its magnetic poles near the geographic North and South Poles, and that between these poles there flowed lines of magnetic influence which governed the behaviour of the needles. In his *De Magnete* (1600), the first learned work to appear on experimental physics, Gilbert at one stroke transferred the whole subject of magnetism from the empirical to the scientific, though he did not fail in the dedication to acknowledge his initial debt to those 'who look for knowledge not in books but in things themselves'.

This attitude was shared by a more famous Englishman, Sir Francis Bacon, Lord Chancellor to James I. He himself performed no experiments, until one winter's day in 1626 he left his coach to gather snow to stuff into a dead fowl that he might observe the effect on the preservation of the flesh: the result was a chill from which he died. His true importance was as the powerful advocate of what he called experimental philosophy: 'Men have sought to make a world from their own conception and to draw from their own minds all the material which they employed, but if, instead of doing so, they had consulted experience and observation, they would have had the facts and not opinions to reason about, and might have ultimately arrived at the knowledge of the laws which govern the material world.' Bacon believed that systematic experiment was the new instrument, the *Novum Organum*, in the investigation of nature: its revolutionary value was symbolised for him by the picture on the title-page, a ship under full sail passing the Pillars of Hercules, the limits of the ancient world.

Bacon's forecast of how scientific work ought to be carried on was largely mistaken. He believed that if nature were examined sufficiently intensively and systematically, the resulting mass of data would, when correctly tabulated, automatically demonstrate the general laws of nature. This in fact never happened: the great achievements of science were made, not by such collations on a massive scale, but by intuitive guesses, by the leap in the dark, and above all by the rare ability to reconsider accepted facts in a novel way. Experiments were then conducted to satisfy the new hypothesis, or to demonstrate its adequacy. It was Bacon's enthusiasm rather than his logic which counted. As he said, 'he rang the bell which called the wits together'. It was, too, his insistence upon experiment which served a vital purpose in urging men to accept the validity of the results arrived at, whether they liked them or not — such as the experiment of Torricelli's on atmospheric pressure[1] which demonstrated the creation of a vacuum in despite of Aristotle's contention that a vacuum could not exist. Experiment was urged with equal enthusiasm by Torricelli's master, Galileo, who opposed all arguments based on *a priori* assumptions: 'I know very well that one single experiment or conclusive demonstration produced against them is enough to batter to the ground these and a thousand other probable arguments.'

Another Baconian concept of importance was the necessity of collaborating among those engaged in scientific studies. For this purpose, in his visionary Utopia, the *New Atlantis*, he proposed a House of Solomon, an institute for organised co-operative research, not only of scholars, but of technologists and craftsmen, so that intellectual activity should not be confined to the universities, which were to be distrusted as strongholds of orthodoxy. Both these desires were ultimately satisfied by the foundation of the Royal Society. From informal beginnings in the Philosophic or Invisible College which met variously after the Civil War at Gresham College and at Wadham College, Oxford, it was established in 1662 under royal patronage. Its business, in the words of Robert Hooke, was to 'improve the knowledge of natural things and all useful Arts, Manufactures, Mechanick practices, Engines and Inventions by Experiments — (not meddling with Divinity, Metaphysics, Moralls, Politics, Grammar, Rhetoric or Logick)'.

[1] See below, page 38.

On the Continent similar societies were already in existence, as in Italy, where the *Accademia Secretorum Naturae*, founded as early as the sixteenth century, was succeeded at Rome by the *Accademia dei Lincei* — the lynx-eyed. Galileo's association with this society, though intellectually stimulating, proved ultimately fatal, since the Inquisition began to investigate its members after Galileo's clash with the pope,[1] and despite the patronage of Federigo Cesi, Duke of Aquasparta, it was then closed. In 1651, however, Federigo's brother, the Grand Duke of Tuscany, founded a successor, the *Accademia del Cimento* — the experimental academy — under his own protection in Florence. The older societies had been nothing more than fraternities but the Florentine academy existed for the purpose of co-operative experiment. Several of Galileo's pupils, Torricelli among them, did much useful work there, and their results were published after 1667 in the *Saggi di Naturali Esperienze fatte nell' Accademia del Cimento*. Their work, like that of the Royal Society, was enthusiastic but undirected, their results interesting but inconclusive and lacking in coherence. Other Italian societies sprang up, the *Accademia Fisico-Matematico* at Rome (1667), the *Accademia del Scienza* at Naples (1695), and the rest of Europe was not to be outdone. In France the informal Thursday gatherings at the homes of Mersenne and Montmar of men like Gassendi, Pascal and Descartes — the *Académie Libre* — were eventually superseded in 1662 by the formation of the *Académie des Sciences*. Colbert showed much interest in its activities, particularly in its practical study of textiles and industrial techniques, but state direction was deadening, especially after the appointment of Louvois in 1683 as its protector, and men of ability were not attracted to it. In Germany the *Collegium Naturae Curiosum* specialised in medicine at Schweinfurt; Joachim Jungius, a biologist, founded the *Societas Erneutica* at Rostock in 1662, and, ten years later, students at Altdorf formed the *Collegium Curiosum sive Experimentale*. Leibniz realised a lifelong ambition when in 1700 an academy was established at Berlin; a similar ambition of Peter the Great resulted in the Academy of St. Petersburg in 1725.

Experiment, singly or in collaboration, was not however the most important feature of the scientific revolution, and chemistry, the science most responsive to experiment, made the least progress of all. The new instruments which encouraged experiment had quite

[1] See below, page 49.

another result, since without them men were geared for ever qualitative investigation of the world associated with Ar compelled to enumerate the qualities of objects, to classif accordingly and to explain phenomena in terms of their qualities: with the new instruments it became possible to establish the physical quantities of matter. Sanctorius, the inventor of a medical thermometer and of improved balances, was fascinated for hours on end by weighing himself and taking his temperature under all kinds of conditions, carefully recording his results. But if the development of tools to undertake quantitative investigation was important, equally so was the discovery of means to express the results of this type of investigation. This means was mathematics. 'Science', wrote Isaac Barrow, a professor of mathematics at Cambridge, 'is to study the sensible realm so far as it shows quantitative continuity, and mathematics is the art of measurement.'

Descartes, who denied the validity of the senses in revealing the hardness, roughness or any other quality of material objects, insisted that the nature of matter consisted in its extension in space: thus its mathematical quantities, its length, breadth, weight, mass and so on were the only ones worthy of study. Galileo went further still in stressing the function of mathematics in science by claiming that all the data produced by experiment and observation was valueless unless interpreted mathematically. 'Philosophy is written in this grand book, the universe, which stands continually open to our gaze. But the book cannot be understood unless one first learns to comprehend the language and read the letters in which it is composed. It is written in the language of mathematics, and its characters are triangles, circles and other geometric figures, without which it is humanly impossible to understand a single word of it; without these, one wanders about in a dark labyrinth.' That this is true was demonstrated by the verbal complexity of medieval scholars who wrestled with problems of impetus and motion without the aid of a mathematical language. This language — notation — was both simplified and amplified in the seventeenth century. Decimals were introduced, along with algebra, equations, logarithms and slide rules; the mathematics of probability and of centrifugal force were examined; coordinate geometry, Descartes's invention, made it possible to express the motion of a point by means of a formula, the infinitesimal calculus went a stage further by studying the point's rates of change in position. So it was that the seventeenth century was not only one of the greatest periods of progress in mathematics, but the period in which mathematical knowledge had the greatest influence on science.

The Structure of Matter

Medieval theories about the nature of matter, based on Aristotle and adapted to suit Christian theology, represented a curious amalgam of two different approaches, physical and metaphysical. The physical analysis concentrated upon the four elements revealed by the process of combustion: a twig, for example, when it burns is resolved in flame, smoke, moisture and ash — four elements which Aristotle generalised as fire, air, water and earth. These elements were believed to possess properties which accounted for their action. Earth and water had gravity, air and fire levity; and mixed up with this was the theory of the four primary qualities, heat, cold, dryness and humidity, so that fire was characterised as hot and dry, earth as cold and dry, air as hot and moist, water as cold and moist. The fusion of the elements thus produced different materials, and the mingling of the primary qualities resulted in secondary qualities like softness or acidity. The alternative approach to matter was metaphysical, a distinction being made not between the separate elements but between Form and Matter. Form was believed to be the active agent, the principle which determined not merely shape but the entire organisation of Matter: Matter was the passive agent, that which is organised by Form. Such a distinction was necessarily metaphysical since it was quite impossible to demonstrate it physically by combustion, by dissection or by any other experiment. In Christian theology there existed a hierarchy of Forms. God was Pure Form: from Him there descended the nine grades of angels down to man, and thence through the animal, vegetable and mineral grades to mere Matter, about which, since it had no Form, nothing could be said. Form determined the properties of material objects. Wood therefore floated in water because its Form dictated its activity — in other words it was its nature to float, an explanation which was both tautological and meaningless.

Whatever the method of inquiry, whether physical or metaphysical, whether things behaved according to the properties of their principal element or because of their Form, the tendency was to endow matter with attributes which explained its behaviour, as though matter was capable of self-direction. Usually these explanations were anthropomorphic, given in human terms such as horror of a vacuum. The falling stone accelerated because it was jubilant at returning home; things went where they belonged in the universe, and comets, earthquakes and other interferences with the natural order were ascribed to the power of supernatural forces. What could be demonstrated by experiment thus seemed reasonably satisfying, and what could not, and therefore required faith for its understanding, did not strain men's reason too greatly since men are essentially sympathetic to anthropomorphism.

The first to destroy the whole overburdened structure of tortuous verbosity and wishful thinking was Galileo, who performed an experiment with a ball of wax. First he placed the ball in a bowl of water, where it sank; then, by dissolving salt in the water, he caused the ball to rise. Thus were confounded all existing theories as the action of the wax ball was interpreted no longer in terms of elements, properties or Form, but of specific gravity.

True to the tradition of Renaissance learning, scientists began to search the writings of classical antiquity for alternative explanations of the nature of matter, and found what they sought in the neglected philosophy of Democritus, the first Greek atomist, who held: 'In truth there are atoms and a void.' On this the seventeenth century based its *corpuscular* philosophy, though Descartes, the first in the field, rejected the concept of the void. The universe for him was composed of infinitely indivisible matter, existing in unbroken continuity without any intervening space or vacuum. Motion was therefore something imparted by one corpuscle to the next, like the behaviour of individuals jammed in a crowd. Gassendi, his colleague in the *Académie Libre*, insisted on retaining the theory of the void, claiming that atoms were indivisible particles of the same primary material, differing from each other only in shape and size, and separated from each other by a vacuum. In England the theory was further developed by Robert Boyle, a founder of the Royal Society, who, like Gilbert, had gained much from contact with craftsmen, and who claimed that it was they who had taught him all his chemistry. In conscious rejection of all university notions based upon *a priori* reasoning he entitled his books, published in 1661, *The Sceptical Chymist*. Matter was reduced, not to the four elements but to minute particles which joined together as corpuscles: everything could then be explained by the formation of atoms into different systems with different

motions. 'Bodies exhibit colours not upon the account of the pre-
dominancy of this or that principle in them, but upon that of
their texture and especially the disposition of their superficial
parts; whereby the light rebounding thence to the eyes is
modified.'

Though their attacks on medieval theories were effective, Boyle
and his colleagues failed to propound a clear alternative in their
place, as Joseph Friend, professor of chemistry at Oxford,
shrewdly complained in 1712: 'Chemistry has made very laudable
progress in Experiments; but we may justly complain that little
Advances have been made towards the explication of 'em. . . . No
body has brought more Light into this Art than Mr. Boyle . . .
who nevertheless has not so much laid a new Foundation of Chemistry as he has thrown down the old.'

Nevertheless, one of the most important investigations of the
seventeenth century was that which led to the recognition of the
pressure of air. The fact that water rushed into the barrel of a pump
when the piston was drawn back was previously explained by
Aristotle's theory that, since nature abhors a vacuum, the water
poured in to prevent a vacuum being created. When lift-pumps
came into extensive use for mine drainage Galileo was asked to
explain why they could not raise water from a depth of more than
34 feet. So arbitrary a limit to nature's abhorrence of a vacuum
seemed curious at least, and it was Galileo's pupil, Torricelli, who
suggested the answer in 1643. A column of water 34 feet high was
clearly too clumsy an object for experiment, and so he filled a glass
tube, a yard long, with mercury and, turning it upside down, placed
the open end in a trough of mercury. The mercury level in the tube
fell to about 30 inches. As mercury is 13·6 times as dense as water,
the 30 inches of mercury in the tube corresponded to the 34 feet of
water in the lift-pump, thus demonstrating that both the water and
the mercury were being balanced by the weight of the atmosphere.
But what was also demonstrated was the fact that as the mercury
fell in the tube, a vacuum was actually created above it, since there
was no means by which air could enter the tube. 'We live sub-
merged at the bottom of an ocean of the element air', wrote Torricelli, and, noting that the height of the mercury in the tube varied
slightly from day to day, ascribed this to changes in the atmospheric pressure: 'Nature would not, as a flirtatious girl, have a
different *horror vacui* on different days.'

Mersenne, the secretary of the *Académie Libre*, passed on the news of Torricelli's experiment to his members, and to Blaise Pascal in particular. Pascal, an infant prodigy who had produced an original study of conic sections at the age of sixteen, immediately repeated the experiment on a grand scale with 50 pounds of mercury in a 4-foot tube. The mercury again stood to a height of about 30 inches, but as Pascal was unaware of Torricelli's reasoning about the vacuum created above the mercury he had to arrive at the same conclusion independently. Back in Paris he found a bitter opponent in Descartes, whose atomic theory precluded the existence of the vacuum, and who insisted that some 'subtle form of matter' made its way into the tube. To counter this, and other attacks, from traditional scholastic quarters, Pascal went on to further experiment. Believing the air to be compressed by its own weight as, in a pile of wool, 'the bottom layers would be far more compressed than the middle or top layers, because they are compressed by a greater quantity of wool', he concluded that the pressure of the atmosphere would be less great on the mountain-tops than in the lowlands. A successful demonstration of this was performed by his brother-in-law, who carried a Torricelli tube to the top of the Puy-de-Dôme, the highest point in the Auvergne, observing as he climbed the gradual fall of the mercury in the tube.

Similar lines of research into the nature of the air were followed by Boyle in England, leading to his famous law that 'the pressures and expansions' of any given quantity of air are 'in reciprocal proportion', so that when the pressure exerted on an enclosed volume of air is, for example, doubled or trebled, the air shrinks to one-half or one-third of its original volume. Otto von Guericke, remarkable for surviving the siege of Magdeburg, was to a large extent unaware of the discoveries of his contemporaries, but performed his own experiments along similar lines. Becoming interested in the problem of the vacuum, he tried to create one by pumping water out of a cask, but the air forced its way in past the wooden staves and he did not succeed until he had used a cask made of copper. He then invented an improved air pump and drew out the air from two bronze hemispheres placed together as a hollow globe. In 1651 the Emperor Ferdinand III was invited to Regensburg to witness a dramatic experiment when two teams, each of eight horses, were scarcely able to pull apart the evacuated hemisphere. Equally of value was von Guericke's action in weighing the hemispheres, and, by noticing the change in weight before and after withdrawing the air, thus determining the density of the air.

Living Matter: Medicine and Biology

In the study of the body, great stress had always been laid upon observation since from earliest times doctors had had to examine their patients and to discover connections between symptoms and diseases. But for all that, throughout the Middle Ages, men persisted in observing only what they had been taught to look for: over them all fell the shadow of Galen, physician to the Emperor Marcus Aurelius, and whose teaching had since been integrated with Christian theology. Even a practical experiment was conducted under his dead hand; the purpose of dissection was not discovery but demonstration, and if the results contradicted Galen's teaching it was assumed that the demonstrator had bungled his job.

In the study of the circulation of the blood, Galen's influence was especially pernicious because it seemed to correspond so well to the facts. Since venous blood has a blue tinge while arterial blood is bright red, he assumed that there were therefore two distinct blood systems, the venous system which nourished the tissues of the body and the arterial system which gave the tissues life. Galen also assumed that all the blood was made in the liver, part of the venous system, and thus his chief problem was to trace the blood from the liver into the arterial system. This he did by finding a connection between the liver and the right auricle and ventricle of the heart, and since he also found a special passage between the right ventricle and the lungs, he believed that once the blood had arrived in the heart it was immediately cooled by air sent up from the lungs. It then passed into the left ventricle, there to be enriched, purified and strengthened by the addition of vital spirits, *pneuma psuchikon*, essential for life. Finally it surged into the body in a kind of tidal ebb and flow, the valves of the heart to some extent restraining the violence of the flow, while the rate of absorption of the blood into the tissues was balanced by the rate at which new blood was delivered from the liver to the heart. The greatest single difficulty about the theory was that the thick fleshy wall between the right and left ventricles, called the septum, appeared impenetrable but Galen insisted that fine pores, invisible to the human eye allowed the blood to seep through: 'These indeed are seen with difficulty in the dead body, the parts being then cold, hard and rigid. Reason assures me, however, that such pores must exist.'

The discovery during the Renaissance of a Greek text of Galen's work revealed the hitherto unknown fact that all Galen's conclusions had been drawn from experiments on animals alone. Consequently, Vesalius, professor of anatomy at Padua, produced his own study of the body, *De Corporis Humani Fabrica* (1543), in which he exposed more than two hundred anatomical errors in Galen, among them the fact that the human thigh bone is straight, not curved as a dog's. The diehard Galenists immediately blamed this phenomenon on the narrow trousers of their day, and attacked Vesalius bitterly; but Vesalius himself was less of a deliberate rebel than a fervent Galenist with doubts. Above all, he was not satisfied by Galen's views on the septum, but as he could offer no alternative theory he enigmatically commented: 'We are driven to wonder at the handiwork of the Creator, by means of which blood sweats from the right into the left ventricle through passages which escape the human vision.' Four years later, in 1547, there was published a Latin translation of the theories and experiments of a thirteenth-century Arabian doctor who had not only denied the possibility of blood seeping through the septum, but postulated its movement from the right to left ventricles by way of the lungs. Another blow was struck by Leonardo da Vinci, who in his practical way tried in vain to pump air through the pipe which Galen had identified as bringing air from the lungs to the right ventricle. So great however was the authority of Galen that though his work was criticised in detail, no one presumed to challenge his general theories. Even when Fabricius of Padua discovered the existence of valves in the veins, a clear indication that the flow of the blood could only be in one direction — back to the heart — he explained them away as barriers designed to prevent the rush of blood down to the legs.

It was not until the seventeenth century that the spell of Galen was finally broken by William Harvey, a man who shared the empirical philosophy of his countrymen Bacon and Boyle: 'It were disgraceful, therefore, did we take the reports of others upon trust, and go on coining crude problems out of these, and on them hanging knotty and captious and petty disputations. Nature herself is to be addressed; the paths she shows us are to be boldly trodden; for thus . . . shall we penetrate at length into the heart of her mystery.' Harvey studied at Padua under Fabricius but found himself unable to accept his explanation of the valves in the venous system; the airpipe through which Leonardo had failed to pump air appeared to him to have all the characteristics of a major blood-vessel; he discovered that creatures without lungs have only one ventricle, which prompted him to consider that if animals with lungs have two ventricles then the second is for the flow of blood into the lungs; lastly he calculated that the amount of blood pumped out of the heart in the course of one hour exceeded the total weight of a man, and that the blood was 'continuously passing into the arteries in greater amount than can be supplied from the food ingested'. From all these things Harvey concluded that the blood must circulate through the body. 'I began to think whether there might not be a motion, as it were, in a circle. Now this I afterwards found to be true; and I finally saw that the blood, forced by the action of the left ventricle into the arteries, was distributed to the body at large and in its several parts, in the same manner as it is sent through the lungs impelled by the right ventricle into the right pulmonary artery, and that it then passed through the veins and along the *vena cava* and so round to the left ventricle in the manner already indicated, which motion we may be allowed to call circular.'

Harvey's *Exercitatio Anatomica de Motu Cordis et Sanguinis*, published in 1628, was certainly the most vital medical publication of the century, but it was not the only one. Malpighi of Bologna University took Harvey's theory a stage further by discovering the means, unknown to Harvey, by which the arteries and veins were linked. For this he made great use of the microscope and, by studying the tissue of a frog's lung, discovered the tiny capillary tubes which carry the blood through the tissue: 'Hence it was clear that the blood flowed away along tortuous vessels and was not poured into spaces, but was always contained within tubules.' Even more remarkable in some ways were the discoveries of Leeuwenhoek, a draper of Delft, who became fascinated by the new world of discovery opened to him by the microscope. A compound microscope, such as Malpighi used, could only magnify from sixty to eighty times, and the two lenses, being insufficiently ground, caused blur and distortion. Leeuwenhoek fashioned his own, consisting of a single lens, almost spherical, mounted between metal plates. This was extremely difficult to produce but by exceptional skill in setting and grinding his lens he achieved a degree of magnification up to about 300.

Leeuwenhoek studied the capillary tubes observed by Malpighi, but his greatest interest lay in the micro-organisms which he found in drops of liquid. These he termed *animalculae*, 'little animals'; in fact he was observing protozoa, the simplest form of animal life, protophyta, single-celled plants, and bacteria. He derived tremendous pleasure by alarming his acquaintances with sights of the monstrous inhabitants of a drop of fresh water. When he showed a group of ladies the 'eels' in vinegar, they immediately foreswore its use: 'But what if one should tell such people in future', he commented, 'that there are more animals living in the scum of the teeth than there are men in a whole kingdom.' In tartar he found the *animalculae*, 'moving about in a highly amusing way,' with one of the larger ones 'passing through the saliva as a fish of prey darts through the sea'. The study of tartar and spittle obsessed him, and he collected samples everywhere: one such sample however did not prove so exciting as he had hoped. 'I have also taken the spittle from an old man who makes a practice of drinking brandy every morning, and wine and tobacco every afternoon; wondering whether the animalcules, with such continued boozing, could e'en remain alive, I judged that this man, because his teeth were so uncommon foul, never washed his month. So I asked him, and got for an answer, "Never in all my life with water, but it gets a good swill with wine or brandy every day." Yet I couldn't find anything beyond the ordinary in his spittle.'

Matter in Motion: Copernicus and Kepler

Although St. Ambrose said, 'To discuss the nature and position of the earth does not help us in the life to come', natural curiosity could not be suppressed. From the earliest times the stars had aroused both interest and emotion in mankind, and their study had had practical results in the making of calendars and in navigation — and even in astrology which, if something of a bastard offspring, at least kept its parent in business: 'God', said Kepler, 'provides for every animal his means of subsistence. For astronomers he has provided astrology.' As the Greeks had inherited the vast amount of data of the Babylonians and Egyptians and then rationalised it, so the medieval Church had adopted Greek astronomy and adapted it to its theology. By 1500, therefore, the study of astronomy rested upon three apparently incontrovertible authorities — scholastic theology, Aristotelian physics, and the observations recorded in

Ptolemy's *Almagest*. More important still, perhaps, the *Almagest* tallied with common-sense observation. The earth, solid, spherical and immovable, lay at the centre of the universe. Around it the moon, the sun and the five planets were carried upon seven revolving concentric spheres, made of some translucent, crystalline substance. The eighth sphere held the fixed stars; the ninth, the *primum mobile*, imparted motion to the rest; and the tenth was believed to be heaven. The supralunary universe was deemed to be in a state of perfection; that state which the medieval mind wistfully regarded as one in which change and decay were impossible, owing to the addition of a divine quintessence to the existing four elements. Between the moon and the earth, however, there was no such preservative: the moon itself was obviously tainted by dark blotches, comets exploded across the sky in great exhalations of fire, and on earth the four elements existed in restless confusion.

Within this perfectly ordered universe the behaviour of the planets gave cause for concern since each was observed to follow an erratic course. It was for this very reason that Plato had christened them 'planets' — vagabonds — and many attempts were made to reconcile their apparent course with the theory of their uniform circular motion around the earth. Ptolemy suggested that they revolved in epicycles, the centres of which described a uniform circular path; this could be made to fit the observed facts provided that the construction of eighty such epicycles was accepted. Alphonso the Wise of Castile, a medieval patron of astronomy, complained: 'If the Almighty had consulted me before the Creation I should have recommended something simpler.' Such complexity was none the less effective since it accounted for every known irregularity of the planets, and tables composed on this system proved wholly reliable.

Less easy to solve was the problem of motion in the universe. The *primum mobile* was presumed to import motion in some way to the other spheres, and Christian thought romanticised this by assigning the nine grades of angels to superintend the motion of the nine spheres. Celestial motion was circular because circular motion was deemed 'natural' to celestial bodies, a question-begging answer which went unquestioned in an age which endowed material objects with human aspirations. Terrestial motion was more difficult to explain. Motion up or down was simple enough, since matter was endowed with the attributes of levity and gravity, but

any other type of motion had to be assigned its due caus
proved to be the weakest point of Aristotelian physics
taught that since a state of rest was natural to all objects, noth...
would move unless compelled to by some agent or force. This
failed to satisfy the perplexity of those who pointed to the arrow
which continued to fly through the air long after losing contact with
its mover, the bowstring. Aristotle's own explanation of this was
obscure and inaccurate, and the target of learned criticism from
the twelfth century onwards, with the result that by 1500 a concept of impetus was evolved as being something like heat which
gradually lost its potency.

The publication in 1543 of Copernicus's *De Revolutionibus
Orbium Celestium* was an event of unusual importance. As befitted a
canon of Cracow Cathedral, from whose tower he was permitted to
observe the heavens, Copernicus was in most respects a medievalist:
Matter was endowed with aspirations; all bodies sought to assume
the shape of the sphere since this was the perfect shape, and circular motion was perfect motion. But for many years Copernicus
had also studied in Italy under de Novara, professor of mathematics and astronomy at Bologna, a fervent neo-Platonist whose
mathematics was loaded with Pythagorean symbolism. Copernicus
was inspired by him with a love for mathematical simplicity. He
thus attacked the Ptolemaic universe as too cumbersome and
claimed, purely as an hypothesis, that the whole problem might be
simplified by assuming the sun to be at the centre. What pleased
him was not merely that the number of epicycles could be cut to
thirty-four, nor even that, in Pythagorean terms, the light of the
universe would now be in its most suitable place, but the elegant
simplicity of his proposal: 'It is so bound together both the order
and magnitude of all the planets and all the spheres and the heaven
itself that in no single part could one thing be altered without
confusion among the other parts and in all the Universe.' His
theory caused new problems. If the earth were to move around the
sun, then its position in relation to the fixed stars would alter every
month. Since no such parallactic shift was discernible, Copernicus
had to save this theory by putting the fixed stars at so great a distance from the earth that no shift could be expected, but this,
though correct, involved concepts of distance so immense that most
men found them more difficult to accept than heliocentrism itself.
Moreover, when Copernicus settled down to revise the *Almagest* in

detail he found it impossible to put the sun exactly at the centre of the planets' orbits,[1] which compelled him to construct another twelve epicycles. Nor were his tables uniformly superior to those of Ptolemy and it was possible for men of the most open mind to choose equally between the two systems.

The most damning weakness of the Copernican system was that it could not be reconciled with Aristotelian physics, for to the mind brought up on this no force in the universe was capable of moving the sluggish earth. Hence the immediate importance of the publication, also in 1543, of a Latin edition of Archimedes, the greatest geometer of classical times, who had imagined how the earth might be moved with a lever. Archimedes had been known by name in the Middle Ages, but the texts were too inadequate and too corrupt to convey the originality of his thought. One of his greatest qualities was an ability to perform mental experiments in order to abstract essential from irrelevant factors, and to present them in mathematical terms. In dealing with fluids, for example, he ignored their taste, their colour and the attributes by which other scientists explained their activity, and considered only their motion. Similarly, having measured objects in air and in water he tried to imagine them unencumbered by either. If Aristotelian physics prevented the serious acceptance of the Copernican theory of heliocentrism then the revival of Archimedean teaching was a significant step towards its re-examination.

One other feature of the sixteenth century, vital to the subsequent revolution, was the work of Tycho Brahe, a Danish noble who studied at the royal observatory in Denmark until, after violent quarrels with his own countrymen, he went to Prague in 1596 at the invitation of Emperor Rudolf II. His observations were unique alike in their accuracy and their comprehension. Equipped with quadrants and direction finders, but without a telescope, he plotted the position of the planets and stars with unrivalled care. Though he accepted that the planets revolved around the sun he was not a Copernican, since he could discern no parallactic shift in the position of the fixed stars and believed that planets and sun together circled the earth. The first man to make a detailed study of the planets at every stage of their orbit, he was perplexed to find that the orbits were never circular. More disconcertingly, in 1572,

[1] Naturally enough, as Kepler discovered, since the orbits are elliptical not circular; see below, page 47.

he observed in the constellation of Cassiopeia a supernova— previously faint, blowing up and gradually burning out — 1577 a comet which, far from moving in the sublunary sphere of change and imperfection, followed a track far beyond the moon, as trigonometrical observation confirmed. These observations ended the belief in uniform circular motion, in the immutability of the heavens, and in the crystalline spheres through which the comet must have crashed its way.

In 1600 Brahe appointed an assistant, Johannes Kepler, a poor but brilliant astronomer whose reputation had been made by his *Mysterium Cosmographicum*. A fervent Copernican, inspired by neo-Platonist and Pythagorean theories on the harmony of numbers and shapes, Kepler had been looking for one law to explain the distances between the planets. To his great delight he discovered a rough relationship between their orbits and the five regular solids: if the orbit of Mercury were imagined as a solid shell it would fit inside an octahedron whose points would touch the inner surface of the shell of Venus: Venus in turn lay within an icosahedron whose points touched the inner surface of the earth's shell, the earth lay within a dodecahedron, Mars within a tetrahedron, Jupiter within a cube. Around the cube fitted the orbit of Saturn. To Brahe this was mere romancing but he was struck by the observations Kepler had made, and he put him to observe the orbit of Mars. Within a year Brahe had died, leaving his collection of data to Kepler, who thus possessed more information on the behaviour of the planets than anyone had held before. He at once set out to postulate a theory to explain the motion of Mars in keeping with the recorded observations. This was soon done but, on comparing the positions computed from his system with the corresponding positions observed by Brahe, Kepler discovered a discrepancy of eight minutes of arc. This was negligible: even Ptolemy and Copernicus had been accurate only to ten minutes of arc, but so great was his respect for Brahe's records that Kepler refused to make the facts fit into the theory. 'And thus the edifice which we erected on the foundations of Tycho's observations we have now again destroyed. . . . For if I had believed we could ignore these eight minutes I would have patched up my hypothesis accordingly.'

Kepler's scrupulous regard for eight minutes of arc caused him eight more years of intense labour, but at last he found the answer: the planets move in an elliptical path with the sun at one focus: as they near the sun they accelerate, as they veer away they slow down so that a line drawn from the planet to the sun sweeps out equal areas in equal times. Having published these laws in his *Astronomia Nova* in 1609, Kepler returned to his mystic preoccupation with the harmony of the spheres, preparing for publication his *Harmonica Mundi*. There among discussion as to whether Mars is a tenor and Mercury a falsetto, was included almost fortuitously the third of Kepler's laws, that the time taken by a planet to complete its orbit increases the further it is from the sun: indeed, the squares of the time of the planets' revolutions bear a constant ratio to the cubes of their mean distances from the sun. As for his explanation of the dynamics of the universe, he derived this from Gilbert's work on magnetism,[1] and assumed that the sun maintained the planets in rotation by exerting an *effluvium magneticum*.

Matter in Motion: Galileo and Newton

The man who paved the way for a more satisfactory explanation of planetary motion was Galileo, professor of mathematics at Padua, and a man of many interests who examined practically every scientific subject under discussion in his day. In the study of the universe his first great contribution was to convince most people that the Copernican system, operating by Kepler's laws, was fundamentally sound. This he did with the help of the telescope, the chance invention of a Dutch spectacle-maker between 1590 and 1600, which he copied and improved to a degree of magnification of thirty. Through this he studied the heavens more closely than ever before, and published the results in his *Siderius Nuncius* of 1610. Among many other novelties he recorded his observations of blemishes on the face of the sun; of 80 stars in the constellation of Orion and of 40 in the Pleiades where even Brahe had seen only nine and six respectively; of the four satellites of Jupiter, a Copernican system in miniature; of the Milky Way which he described as 'nothing else but a mass of innumerable stars planted together in clusters', not, as believed, planted at a uniform distance from the earth in the sphere of the fixed stars. These observations compelled men to reconsider long-held beliefs, but the Church having successfully integrated Ptolemy into its theology, was reluctant to approve of change, and Galileo deliberately provoked a conflict.

[1] See above, page 32.

He left Padua in the free territory of Venice for Florence, and then for Rome, the centre of the controversy, having published in 1613 his *Letters on the Solar Spots* and in 1615 a *Letter Concerning The Use of Biblical Quotations in Matters of Science*. The opposition to him however was more powerful than he had suspected. Indeed those who claimed that the moons of Jupiter existed only in the telescope had unknowingly some justification: the danger that so novel an invention might distort the truth was not illusory since spherical aberration, the failure of the lens to give a rectilinear image, was not identified and corrected until 1637, and the cause of chromatic aberration, the light from different colours coming to a different focus, was not analysed before Newton studied the problem in 1671. In 1616 the Church exacted from Galileo a promise to cease his public advocacy of the Copernican system but in 1632, after the accession of a pope whom he believed to be sympathetic, he published his major assault on the Ptolemaic universe, the *Dialogue concerning the Two Chief World Systems*. Though Galileo pretended to state both cases fairly, he portrayed the defendant of the old system as a thick-witted gull, aptly named Simplicio, who obligingly fell into each of his antagonists' logical traps. For this work Galileo was disgraced, the pope mistakenly believing that Simplicio was based upon himself, but in 1633, on an apparently different topic, the *Discourse on the Two New Sciences*, he fulfilled his second major achievement, the destruction of the Aristotelian laws of motion, and with them the last remnants of the medieval world picture.

Galileo realised that if his enemies denied the evidence of the telescope because it conflicted with their concepts of motion, then motion itself would have to be studied afresh. He began by observing the movement of the pendulum, discovering that a long swing took the same time to complete as a short one, and putting his discovery to practical use in the invention of a pendulum clock. Equally practical was his interest in gunnery. It had been proposed by another Italian, Tartaglia, that projection was most efficient at an elevation of 45 degrees and that the trajectory was curved. Galileo identified the curve as a parabola and wondered if the speed acquired by the falling canon ball was in any way proportional to the time it took to fall. This led to his experiments with metal balls in which he rolled them down grooves lined with polished leather to reduce friction, and found that their final speed varied with the height at which they were released, not with the angle at which the plane was inclined. He also discovered the relationship he sought between the distance and the time, expressing it as $d = \frac{1}{2}at^2$ where a represents the constant acceleration caused by gravity. The formulation of the hypothesis was not new since medieval mathematicians at Oxford had arrived at the same truth in verbal terms: where Galileo broke new ground was first by conducting his experiments and then by expressing his findings in a mathematical equation.

Equally important was Galileo's attack on the problem of inertia. First he rolled a ball down one plane and observed it run up a second until halted by the force of gravity. Modelling himself on Archimedes from whose work he derived his greatest inspiration, he then tried to imagine what the ball might do if gravity and friction were dispensed with. He concluded that it would rise to the same vertical height from which it had started. Finally he realised that if the ball, instead of climbing the second plane, followed a horizontal course, it would continue to roll for ever, seeking to regain its original height. The problem of inertia was thus put in an entirely novel setting. For the first time in history attention was thus directed not to the causes of motion, but to the forces which cause a body in motion to stop or alter course.

It was Descartes who pointed out that, since Galileo's horizontal plane was one parallel to the curved surface of the earth, the motion of the ball along it was in fact circular. To Descartes, however, natural motion, that is, motion in an ideal Euclidean sense, frictionless and free from interference, had to be in a straight line. Consequently the problem was to discover why the ball in motion along the horizontal plane did not fly off at a tangent to the earth. If Descartes's formulation of the problem marked a significant advance towards the discovery of the truth, his answer unfortunately obscured the issue. Like Aristotle, his metaphysical assumptions underlay his physics: like Aristotle, he drew his illustrations from the immediately recognisable world of common-sense experience. The Cartesian world was dualistic, consisting of Mind and Matter.[1] Matter he defined as *res extensa*, that which is extended in space. By this he meant that colour and taste, for example, were of secondary importance in identifying an object, and that the essence of matter consisted in its geometric characteristics. The uni-

[1] See below, page 62.

verse represented an infinite extension of continuous matter in which there was no room for a vacuum to exist. Motion was imparted by one particle to another, just as the jostling of one individual in a crowd causes the movement of those around him. Moreover, as eddies form in the course of a river, trapping and carrying round a passing leaf, so, in the universe matter forms vortices whose circular motion carries the planets in their orbits. Suction towards the centre of the vortex was thus the cause of deviation from a straight-line path.

To Descartes this represented a satisfying demonstration of his belief in a mechanical universe, and many of his contemporaries found it wholly intelligible. Unfortunately it flouted Kepler's law that the motion of the planets was not circular but elliptical. Borelli in 1665 suggested that it was centripetal force which prevented Galileo's metal ball from flying off at a tangent to the earth, and which kept the earth and the planets for ever circling in orbit around the sun, but until Huygens had published his *Horologium Oscillatorium* in 1673 there was no public explanation of how this force could be calculated. Huygens said that the force required to make a point describe a circle uniformly was equal to $4\pi^2 r/t^2$ for each unit of mass, where t is the time taken to describe the circle. With the aid of Kepler's third law, $r^3/t^2 = C$, he then expressed the force more simply as $4\pi^2 C/r^2$. In other words, the force required to keep a planet in circular orbit was inversely proportional to the square of its distance from the centre. Huygens, however, was not satisfied that his formula held true of elliptical motion, and until this could be demonstrated his work could no more relate to the universe of Kepler's laws than did the vortices of Descartes.

Both the formula and the proof of its application to ellipses had already been discovered independently by Isaac Newton in 1665-6 when, during the plague year in Cambridge he took refuge at Woolsthorpe in Lincolnshire, and worked out the principle of his laws of motion. These, however, were not released to the world until the publication of his *Principia Mathematica* in 1681. His ideas taken singly had mostly been anticipated though he himself had arrived at his conclusions independently, and he was especially ahead of his contemporaries in taking Galileo's concept of inertia as a quality or property of matter in motion, and developing it into a quantitative concept of mass — even though he was later proved wrong in his calculation of mass in terms of weight and density. Of

C

greater importance than the novelty of individual concepts was
Newton's ability, his genius, to select from all the varied notions of
the age the ones most capable of fitting together; to isolate Kepler's
three laws, for example, from twenty volumes of mystical nonsense
which enshrined them, and to create an imaginative synthesis sustained by proofs so detailed that no more rigorous a publication
than the *Principia* appeared in the whole century.

Newton agreed with Descartes that the important problem was
to seek the causes of divergence from a straight line, but he rejected
the theory of vortices, preferring to study the operation of a centripetal force than to identify its nature. 'That by means of centripetal
forces the planets may be retained in certain orbits, we may easily
understand, if we consider the motions of projectiles; for a stone
that is projected is by the pressure of its own weight forced out of
the rectilinear path, which by the initial projection alone it should
have pursued, and made to describe a curved line in the air; and
through that crooked way is at last brought down to the ground;
and the greater the velocity is with which it is projected, the farther
it goes before it falls to the Earth.' He argued that if the velocity
were increased sufficiently the stone would then 'reach at last quite
beyond the circumference of the Earth', and go into orbit. The
moon, he argued, was such a satellite, its motion controlled by the
same centripetal force which caused stones to fall upon the earth's
surface — a force proportional to the inverse square of the distance.
'And this same year', he wrote in 1666, 'I began to think of gravity
extending to the orb of the Moon, and having found out how to
estimate the force with which a globe revolving within a sphere
presses the surface of the sphere, from Kepler's Rule. . . . I deduced that the forces which keep the planets in their Orbs must be
reciprocally as the squares of their distances from the centers about
which they revolve; and thereby compared the force requisite to
keep the Moon in her Orb with the force of gravity at the surface of
the Earth and found them answer pretty nearly.'

This comparison of forces, stated so simply, was in fact a task of
great complexity. First he had to compute the rate at which the
path of the moon as it circles the earth diverges from a straight line,
and then to compare this with the rate at which objects fall at the
earth's surface. Finally, he had to demonstrate that these rates were
in the appropriate ratio according to Huygens's formula. The
solution he arrived at in 1666, which satisfied him 'pretty nearly',

was not sufficiently accurate for publication in the *Principia*, partly because current estimates of the moon's distance from the earth were unreliable. This was remedied soon after 1680 when a Frenchman, Picard, produced new calculations based on extremely accurate observations, which estimated that the distance between the earth and the moon was sixty times the radius of the earth — this last being calculated at 4,000 miles. Another factor which delayed Newton was the difficulty of calculating the force that the earth exerted upon the moon, since he faced the impossible task of calculating the attraction of every point on the earth's surface for every point on the moon's unless he could prove that the earth attracts bodies to it as though all its mass were concentrated at its centre. Once satisfied on this point, he began the formal demonstration of his theory, though even then the work might never have been undertaken had it not been for Newton's colleagues in the Royal Society, whose urgent insistence compelled him to return to problems which had been solved for his own immediate satisfaction at Woolsthorpe fifteen years earlier.

In the *Principia* Newton demonstrated that the moon, on account of the earth's attraction, diverges from a straight-line path at the rate of 0·0044 feet in the first second. If Huygens's formula were correct, and if the attraction varied inversely to the square of the distance, then since the distance between the moon and the earth was believed to be sixty times the earth's radius, the attraction must be 60^2 times as intense at the surface of the earth. In other words, a stone should fall at 16 feet in the first second — which is in fact the case. The behaviour of an object falling upon the earth and of the moon encircling it were thus attributed to one and the same cause. But Newton was not concerned solely with the forces of attraction between the earth and the moon. He demonstrated that the universe as a whole represented a complex set of mathematical relationships, with each planet exerting influence upon the others, the whole being dominated by the attraction of the sun. To understand this universe he formulated three laws. Any body will remain either at rest or in a state of uniform motion in a straight line unless it is compelled to change its state by an external force: the rate of change of motion will be directly proportional to the external force acting on the body and will take place in the direction in which the force is acting: when a force of attraction exists between two bodies this force acts equally on both — but the motion which it produces in the more massive body is less than that produced in the other.

For all that he revealed the universe in an entirely novel and revolutionary way, Newton's achievement was deceptively simple. He made three reasonable assumptions about the movement of matter under the action of forces, and made a fourth assumption about the one particular force, gravitation, by which motion within the solar system was explained. It was in this simplicity that his genius lay, and also in his ability to give the whole theory a logical, mathematical expression: if as Galileo had said, 'the book of Nature is written in mathematical symbols', it was Newton who deciphered much of the code. The universe was thus demonstrated to be something of a machine whose behaviour could be accounted for by considering the attraction that its various parts exerted upon each other. Unlike a machine, however, the parts acted upon each other across empty space, and this was a notion which horrified Descartes and Leibniz, who could only think of forces being impacted upon bodies, such as by bats upon balls. Newton himself believed that attraction at a distance was only apparent, and that someone might subsequently discover the true nature of the mechanism. For the time being he was content to know that his system worked. 'I have not yet been able to deduce the reason of these properties of gravity from phenomena and I do not frame hypotheses. For whatsoever is not deduced from phenomena is to be called hypothesis; and hypotheses whether metaphysical or physical or of occult qualities or mechanical, have no place in experimental philosophy. In this philosophy propositions are deduced from phenomena, and are rendered general by induction. So impenetrability, mobility, the impetus of bodies and the laws of motions and gravity have become known. And it is enough that gravity really exists and acts according to the law explained by me and suffices for all the motions of the heavenly bodies and of our sea.'

THE INTELLECTUAL REVOLUTION

Philosophy and the Scientific Revolution

So great an accession of scientific data, so revolutionary a transformation in interpreting it, was bound to have a fundamental impact on philosophy. In a later age a generation might well have passed before the men of one discipline succeeded in re-educating those of another, but in the seventeenth century, since there was no formal division between natural science and philosophy — the term 'Natural Philosophy' embraced them both — changes in physics were immediately reflected in metaphysics. With men like Descartes and Leibniz prominent in both spheres, ideas moved swiftly and with dramatic effect.

In the Middle Ages 'natural philosophers' had been pre-occupied with the analysis of function and properties: their basic approach was qualitative, their prime achievement classification. Hence the syllogism, the basic tool of medieval logic, made classification appear to be the standard expression of knowledge:

> All Xs are Ys;
> This is an X;
> Therefore this is a Y.

With the syllogism as the model of rational inference, medieval philosophy was thus restricted to terms of definition — of essence, substance and attribute; of essential properties and accidental properties. From this attitude to the world as a museum of things and creatures, eternally divided, distinguished and determined by their Forms,[1] there sprang the notion of hierarchy, since classification was naturally followed by comparison and grading. Important analogues were made between, for example, the hierarchy of the heavenly spheres and that of earthly society, so that good order on earth came to be considered a reflection of the orderly progress of the planets — 'The heavens themselves, the planets and this centre, observe degree, priority and place.'[2] In consequence, all violent disturbances in society were regarded either as the cause of disturbances in the natural world, or, alternatively, as the result of these.

When Harvey revolutionised physiology by thinking of the heart and the body in mechanical terms as a pump and a system of pipes, and Newton revealed the entire universe as one vast mechanism, the whole structure of scholastic philosophy was discredited. Things could no longer be described in terms of their final causes, their purpose or their attributes, but in terms of their interaction as part of a machine. Physical change was thus explained as the effect of the motion and impact of matter in space; matter itself was

[1] See above, page 36.   [2] *Troilus and Cressida*, i. iii. 85.

regarded as the action of atoms in motion; the difference between one object and another could only be assessed quantitatively in terms of their extension.

Alarmed bewilderment was the immediate reaction to this intellectual upheaval. The world had lost its order: 'The new philosophy puts all in doubt', wrote John Donne in 1611:

> 'The sun is lost and th'earth and no man's wit
> Can well direct him where to look for it.'

It was not surprising that fear of change prompted some to discredit the new science in order to salvage the old philosophy, especially since the Church, by uniting its theology with Aristotelian physics had thus bound itself to theories of matter and motion which were being proved false. The comet of 1572 was shrugged off as a miracle, despite the retort that *miraculum est ignorantiae asylum*; Copernicus's books were put on the Index, and in 1616 the Holy Office, in a vain attempt to save the situation, pronounced: 'The view that the sun stands motionless at the centre of the Universe is foolish, philosophically false and utterly heretical, because contrary to Holy Scripture.' This was not altogether the work of bigotry. Churchmen had good reason to be worried about the possible impact of the discoveries. If Donne, an educated man, a poet and an Anglican priest, confessed himself baffled then the effect on the ignorant might be disastrous. Once the medieval cosmology was uprooted, the popular imagery and conceptions of the world that everyone had taken for granted would be undermined. As it happened this fear was exaggerated; popular imagery remained geared to medieval cosmology for at least two centuries, and is still reflected in statements about the sun rising or in the concept of descending into hell.

Despite the perplexity and fear, there was in fact no question of a serious clash between science and religion. If the case of Galileo had aroused as much interest as his theories, it was the only one of its kind; nor was his treatment at all harsh in comparison to the martyrdom and imprisonment meted out to heretics. Galileo himself deliberately provoked a conflict in order to attack those churchmen who involved the Church in matters on which it was not theologically required to pronounce, and whose wilful adherence to outworn concepts only made it more difficult for the Church to shed its Aristotelian shackles. 'Take note, theologians', he wrote in a note added to his copy of his *Dialogue*, 'that in your drive to make matters of faith out of propositions relating to the fixity of sun and earth you run the risk of eventually having to condemn as heretics those who would declare the earth to stand still and the sun to move — at such a time as it might be physically or logically proved that the earth moves and the sun stands still.'

Those who came to regard the universe, and the human body, as mechanisms were not destroying spiritual values. Machinery was still something rare enough to be wondered at — like the famous Strassburg clock, so complex that even the simplified and miniature model in the British Museum not only tells the time, the day and the phase of the moon, but stages five simultaneous mechanical pantomimes. In this context to consider the universe as a clock was not to denigrate it; on the contrary, by revealing it to be an orderly, intelligible mechanism of the highest degree of complexity and skill they were thereby exalting its Creator. Hobbes alone adopted a wholly materialist view, interpreting the discoveries to mean that 'the universe is material, all that is real is material, and what is not material is not real'. Mind was merely the product of matter: 'There is no conception in a man's mind which hath not at first totally or by parts been begotten upon the organs of sense.' Hobbes's atheism was shared by none. Robert Boyle, who challenged the traditional theories of matter, believed that though the immediate causes of motion in the world might be explained in terms of a mechanism, the ultimate causes were non-mechanical: man's body might be corpuscular, but within it there existed a rational soul, the image of God in man, 'a nobler and more valuable being than the whole corporeal world'. The other scientist-philosophers shared Boyle's assumption, though sometimes in ways that could scarcely have satisfied an orthodox theologian, however willing he was to embrace the new science. Descartes, for example, made the existence of God one of the self-evident propositions upon which his philosophy depended,[1] but his vision of God was scarcely that revealed by Christ. Abstract and impersonal, the divine geometer rather than the loving Father, the Cartesian God was no longer active in the world; and Pascal[2] complained that Descartes brought God into his philosophy in order to start the world and could then find no further use for Him. Descartes none the less insisted that his attachment to the Catholic Church was sincere, and, though the

[1] See below, page 61.   [2] See below, page 76.

Church condemned his writings, he himself made no attack on the Church.

Newton, more than any other man, removed the magic from the universe by replacing the supernatural spirits and mysterious intelligences by his laws of motion: 'The gloriously romantic universe of Dante and Milton that set no bounds to the imagination of man as it played over space and time has now been swept away . . . The really important world outside was a world, hard, cold, colourless, silent and dead; a world of quantity, a world of mathematically computable motions in mechanical regularity.'[1] But Newton did not see his universe in such terms. The world of mathematically computable motions was far more romantic and imaginative for him than that of medieval thought — nor was it silent and dead.

> 'What though in solemn silence, all
> Move round the dark terrestial ball;
> What though no real voice nor sound
> Amid their radiant orbs be found:
> In reason's ear they all rejoice
> And utter forth a glorious voice,
> For ever singing as they shine:
> The hand that made us is divine.'

Joseph Addison's hymn gave fervent expression to Newton's own faith. The removal of outdated mysteries and physically impossible laws did not remove the need for God, 'who being in all places', wrote Newton, 'is more ably by his Will to move the Bodies within this boundless uniform Sensorium and thereby to form and reform the Parts of the Universe, than we are by our Will to move the Parts of our own Bodies.' Unlike Descartes, Newton believed that God was fully active in the universe, partly because this was the teaching of the Church, partly because he discovered certain problems in the daily running of the universe which only God could solve by perennial intervention. It worried him that motion was always being dissipated within the universe; 'by reason of the tenacity of fluids and attrition of their parts, and the weakness of elasticity in solids, motion is much more apt to be lost than got and is always upon the decay.' In addition, the gravitational interaction of the planets caused minor 'perturbations' in the orbit of each, and Newton was not sure if this indicated a stable system

[1] Professor E. A. Burtt, *The Metaphysical Foundations of Modern Science*.

in which the variations could all cancel each other out, or if the 'perturbations' were cumulative. The constant intervention of God was thus required to keep the planets in their courses, and to restore motion.

The Cartesian Revolution: Descartes

René Descartes was born into a typically *bourgeois* family of doctors and *officiers*, who sent him to the Jesuit college of La Flèche in Anjou, and subsequently to the University of Poitiers where he graduated in law. He then took everyone by surprise by becoming a soldier, leaving France in 1618 to serve at Breda as a gentleman volunteer in the army of Maurice of Nassau. His pursuits were more scientific than military since the Dutch were then at peace with the Spaniards, and the current vogue among the officers was the creation and solution of problems in military engineering and mathematics, at which Descartes excelled. He left in 1619, travelling in a desultory fashion across Europe for the next ten years as a soldier in the Thirty Years War, though he took part in no major engagements. It was the opportunity to travel and to study human nature which attracted him to the life, and he also enjoyed the long winters between campaigns which allowed him leisure for reflection.[1] In 1629 he settled in Holland, where he wrote three short discourses on physical and mathematical subjects, prefaced by the celebrated *Discours de la Méthode* (1637), the *Meditationes de Prima Philosophia* (1641), and the *Principia Philosophiae* (1644), which he dedicated to Elizabeth, the wife of the Elector Palatine. Another patron was Christina of Sweden, who persuaded him to visit Stockholm in 1649. The climate, however, proved too severe, and his patron too demanding in her insistence upon philosophical instruction at five in the morning. Within a few weeks Descartes caught pneumonia, and died in 1650.

Such a man was scarcely a cloistered scholastic, and his contempt for traditional philosophy was boundless: 'I had become aware, even so early as during my college days that no opinion, however absurd or incredible, can be imagined which has not been maintained by some one of the philosophers.' Since he believed the

[1] See for examples Part II of the *Discours*. 'The setting in of winter arrested me in a locality where, as I found no society to interest me, and was besides fortunately undisturbed by any cares or passions, I remained the whole day in seclusion, with full opportunity to occupy my attention with my own thoughts.'

mathematical and physical principles of the schoolsmen to be inaccurate, he also lost all confidence in their philosophy, deliberately
trying to clear his mind of all *a priori* assumptions and to subject
all traditional authorities to his own independent criticism. In
words which almost echoed those of Francis Bacon[1] he wrote: 'We
shall not, for instance, become mathematicians even if we know by
heart all the proofs that others have elaborated unless we have an
intellectual talent that fits us to solve difficulties of that kind.
Neither, though we have mastered all the arguments of Plato and
Aristotle, shall we become philosophers if we have not the capacity
for forming a solid judgement on these matters.'

The new approach was to be established on mathematical lines.
Descartes shared none of Kepler's Pythagorean mysticism, and
indulged in no rhapsodies about the theory of number, for 'there
is nothing more futile than to busy oneself with bare numbers and
imaginary figures in such a way as to appear to rest content with
such trifles'. It was the method of mathematics which fascinated
him, and he believed it capable of application to other disciplines.
'These long chains of reasoning all simple and easy, which geo-
meters use to arrive at their most difficult demonstrations, suggested
to me that all things which came within human knowledge must
follow each other in a similar chain; and provided that we abstain
from admitting anything as true which is not so, and that we always
preserve in them the order necessary to deduce one from the other,
there can be none so remote to which we cannot finally attain, nor
so obscure but that we may discover them.'

Armed with *l'esprit géométrique* Descartes set out to establish the
first principles of philosophy: 'I thought that I ought to reject as
absolutely false all opinions in regard to which I could suppose the
least ground for doubt, in order to ascertain whether after that
there remained aught in my belief that was wholly indubitable.'
A programme of systematic scepticism might thus establish a surer
basis for belief than one based on adherence to traditional doctrine.
Rigorously he doubted the reality of the world and the validity of
the senses, calling into question all experiences and wondering
whether or not 'the objects that had ever entered into my mind
when awake, had in them no more truth than the illusions of my
dreams. But immediately upon this I observed that, whilst I thus
wished to think that all was false, it was absolutely necessary that I,

[1] See above, page 29.

who thus thought, should be somewhat; and as I observed that this truth, *I think, hence I am*, was so certain and of such evidence, that no ground of doubt, however extravagant, could be alleged by the sceptics capable of shaking it, I concluded that I might, without scruple, accept it as the first principle of the philosophy of which I was in search.'

Cogito ergo sum was in no way the conclusion of a syllogism —

> All thinking things must exist;
> I think;
> Therefore I exist —

but a purely intuitive maxim whose very clarity and distinctness made it indubitable: 'by intuition I understand, not the fluctuating testimony of the senses, nor the misleading judgement that proceeds from the blundering constructions of imagination, but the conception which an unclouded and attentive mind gives us so readily and distinctly that we are wholly freed from doubt about that which we understand.' Descartes said, in effect, 'I know I exist because I am conscious that I exist.' Thus consciousness is made the starting-point in the discovery of truth, so that philosophy undertakes the interrogation of the consciousness in order to discover those concepts which are more certain and distinct than anything else. One such concept, for Descartes, was the knowledge of God. 'In the next place, from reflecting on the circumstance that I doubted, and that consequently my being was not wholly perfect (for I clearly saw that it was a greater perfection to know than to doubt), I was led to inquire whence I had learned to think of something more perfect than myself . . . accordingly, it but remained that the idea had been placed in me by a nature which was in reality more perfect than mine, and which even possessed within itself all the perfections of which I could form any idea; that is to say, in a single word, which was God.'

Since the existence of God guaranteed that the evidence of the senses was not illusory, Descartes believed he was justified in studying the material world. This, he claimed, was composed of one extended substance, *res extensa*, which might vary in density but was never discontinuous — thus denying the existence of a vacuum — which could only be comprehended by its mathematical quantities of length, breadth and height; which had no life of its own but operated mechanically according to the laws of physics.

But human bodies, composed of this lifeless matter have the capacity for thought. Descartes avoided Hobbes's materialist conclusions by making an absolute distinction between mind and body, between *res cogitans* and *res extensa*. This dualism was vital to Descartes's attempt to reconcile the Catholic Church to the advances in scientific knowledge, since it withdrew soul and spirit from the material world, whose investigation was giving rise to controversy, and left them securely in the hands of the Church.

The Church none the less was disturbed by Descartes's philosophy and condemned his works. His equation of matter with extension raised serious difficulties concerning the doctrine of the Creation and of Transubstantiation. His dualism raised equally serious problems about the soul's intimate connection with the mechanism of the body. It could not be part of the body, nor could it be the principle of life within it: 'It is not that the body dies because the soul leaves it but that the soul leaves because the body had died.' Yet it was true that mind and body produced effects within each other; pains in the stomach were related to the mind's clear and distinct desire for food, fears in the mind were reflected in the trembling of limbs. Just before leaving for Stockholm in 1649 Descartes published a less famous work, *Les Passions de l'Âme*, in which he suggested that the soul inhabited the pineal gland at the base of the brain, where it might affect and be affected by the operation of the body. The theory particularly appealed to him since he could find no pineal gland in animals — brute, mechanical creatures without souls.

The Cartesian Revolution: Spinoza and Leibniz

It was Nicholas Malebranche who attempted to make his master's teaching more acceptable to the Church by stressing Descartes's arguments for the necessary existence of God. His *Recherche de la Vérité* (1674) went further by claiming that, since the evidence of the senses is suspect, all knowledge results from the divine illumination of the intellect. Malebranche, moreover, adopted the theory of occasionalism, first published in Antwerp by Arnold Geulincx (1665), in order to solve the problem of body and soul by explaining the apparent interaction between them as the result of divine intervention. *On the occasion* of a man's desire to move his hand, God miraculously causes a corresponding effect to take place in the body in conformity with the desire: he similarly produces experiences in the mind on the occasion of changes in the body. 'Here then was a queer outcome of the new search for truth: miraculous interventions had been banished from the physical universe only to reappear within the narrow compass of the individual human being. God had made the world in such a way that it could run "of itself", but he had made man so fearfully and wonderfully that he could not act or perceive without God's continuous intervention.'[1]

If orthodox minds were only partially reassured by the efforts of Malebranche to make Cartesian philosophy respectable, their worst suspicions were to be confirmed by the development of this philosophy by Baruch Spinoza. Born in 1632 into a family of Portuguese Jews who had sought refuge in Amsterdam, he caused alarm by his boldly critical exposition of the Old Testament in which he subjected inspiration to the judgement of reason. In consequence he was excommunicated from the synagogue in 1656, since his views not only scandalised the members but made them afraid lest they cause offence to their Dutch neighbours and hosts, orthodox Calvinists whose views on Holy Scripture were as fundamentalist as their own. Spinoza made a living by grinding lenses, but his fame resulted from his quick understanding of the new ideas in science and philosophy, and from the shrewd analysis of his *Principles of Descartes' Philosophy*. By 1663 when he finally settled at Voorburg near The Hague he was a prominent figure, the friend of many scientists, including Oldenburg, the first secretary of the Royal Society in London, Huygens and Leibniz, and also of men like Jan de Witt and the Elector Palatine — who offered him the chair of philosophy at Heidelberg, which Spinoza refused lest the responsibility of such a post should constrain his freedom of thought. He remained at Voorburg until his death at the age of 45, writing the *Tractatus-Theologico-Politicus* (1670), the *Tractatus-Politico* and the *Ethica*, the last two appearing in print immediately after his death.

Spinoza's thought was greatly influenced by that of Descartes. He adopted *l'esprit géométrique* so literally that the *Ethica* consisted of a system of definitions, axioms, theorems and corollaries, and he accepted the notion of intuitive knowledge, agreeing that, 'he who has a true idea knows at the same time that he has a true idea'. The rigid distinction which Descartes drew between mind

[1] Professor Basil Willey, *The Seventeenth Century Background*, p. 82.

and matter did not, however, appeal to him, since he believed that the world as a whole constituted a single substance, none of whose parts was logically capable of any separate existence. The foundation of his system was the idea of God as a substance which exists independently, *causa sui*; God is in fact identified with *natura naturans*, nature which creates, as opposed to *natura naturata*, nature which is created. God's attributes are infinite, but two of them, Thought and Extension, are known to men. Thus the dualism of mind and matter was resolved in the greater unity of God, while the problem of how soul and body interact no longer arose since mind and body were inseparably correlated attributes of one and the same divine substance.

But, since thought and extension were attributes of God — not created by Him but essentially of Him — then there could be no distinction between God and His creation. Such a view, Spinoza claimed, could trouble only those whose anthropomorphic imagination identified God as a person simply because they judged everything in terms of their own experience. Of them he wrote: 'They necessarily estimate other natures by their own . . . they consider all natural things alike to be made for their use; and as they know that they found these things as they were and did not make them themselves, they have cause for believing that some one else prepared these things for their use. Now having considered things as means, they cannot believe them to be self-created; but they must conclude . . . that there is some governor or governors of nature, endowed with human freedom, who take care of all things for them and make all things for their use.' According to Spinoza they thus had to explain how God could be the author of evil and of suffering in the world, a dilemma which he himself tried to resolve by saying that evil and suffering were merely subjective terms. 'As soon as men had persuaded themselves that all things which were made, were made for their sakes, they were bound to consider as the best quality in everything that which was the most useful to them, and to esteem that above all things which brought them the most good. Hence they must have formed those notions by which they explain the things of nature, to wit, good, evil, order, confusion, hot, cold, beauty, and ugliness, etc.; and as they deemed themselves free agents, the notions of praise and blame, sin and merit, arose.'

Spinoza, however, did not deem men to be free agents. If everything sprang from God's nature, nothing could be independent of it. 'All things are in God and so depend upon Him that without Him they could neither exist nor be conceived; and all things were predetermined by God, not through his free or good will but through his absolute nature or infinite power.' The Cartesian Revolution thus took one more turn. Where Descartes had raised the vitally important questions, 'How do we know things? Is there a fundamental distinction between mind and matter?' Spinoza asked, 'Is God distinct from His creation? Does free will exist?' Determinist and apparently pantheist, Spinoza horrified many contemporaries; but, if there was clearly no place for him in Christianity and Judaism, he was a deeply religious man, and the metaphysical views which aroused controversy were designed principally as the background for his ethical teaching, the release of the mind from mundane things for the eternal love of God.

One of the most brilliant, certainly the most versatile, men of the seventeenth century was Gottfried Wilhelm Leibniz. After training in law he entered the service of the Elector-Archbishop of Mainz as both jurist and diplomat, revising the statutes of the city and proposing schemes for German unity as a defence against the power of Louis XIV. He then became historian-librarian to the House of Brunswick-Wolfenbüttel at Hanover, though his fame spread further afield and both the Elector of Brandenburg and Peter the Great conferred upon him the title of Privy Councillor of Justice, a title he also received in Hanover in 1704. As a theologian he was welcomed equally at Protestant and Catholic courts, even at Rome, and he worked in vain to promote reconciliation between the churches. As a scientist he discovered the infinitesimal calculus independently of Newton and contributed the concept of kinetic energy to mechanics: he was also largely responsible for the foundation of scientific academies at Berlin and St. Petersburg. As a philosopher he met and corresponded with Malebranche and Spinoza and, like them, owed everything initially to the inspiration of Descartes.

Like Spinoza, Leibniz sought to unite the separate realities of extension and thought, but he was repelled by Spinoza's notion of them being attributes of one divine substance. His own theory sprang from his great interest on the mathematics of infinitesimals. Extension, he claimed, could not be a reality after all, since whatever was extended was infinitely divisible, and what was made up of parts could not be regarded as an ultimate reality. Since the essential factor in all substances was force, or energy, Leibniz envisaged a universe consisting of centres of force which he termed 'monads'. The monad was 'a simple substance without parts': it was not to be confused with physical atoms since it was metaphysical and without extension of any kind. It was indestructible, unchanging, and completely independent of other monads, 'having no windows by which anything could get out or come in'. Leibniz thus avoided Spinoza's pantheism only to raise a new problem of explaining how things in fact work together in the world. This he solved in a manner reflecting the influence of occasionalism by assuming that the monads operated according to a plan of divine harmony, preordained by God, acting together without actually influencing one another like a set of clocks timed to a master clock.

Monads which lacked consciousness were those of which bodies were composed. Souls were monads of a higher degree of activity since, through the power of the mind, they were capable of knowing the system of the universe. This made them capable of entering into communion with God. Moreover they enjoyed free will, in the sense that their free and spontaneous activity was allowed force in the pre-established harmony of all monads and their states. The world was therefore something more than extension and thought; it was an ensemble of spiritual forces which, in preordained harmony, conformed to the will of God who created the best of all possible worlds.

Monads, as centres of force, could not be static but were capable of development, and by attempting to solve the problem of the mind's development Leibniz became involved in controversy with John Locke[1] over the latter's *Essay on Human Understanding*. The monad, as Leibniz conceived it, was created with innate ideas, the germs of development, while Locke denied the whole concept of innate ideas. 'Our differences', wrote Leibniz, 'are important. The question between us is whether the soul in itself is entirely empty like tablets upon which nothing has been written, according to Aristotle and the author of the *Essay*; and whether all that is there traced comes wholly from the senses and experience; or whether the soul originally contains the principles of several notions and doctrines which the external objects only awaken on occasions as I

[1] See below, page 68.

believe with Plato.' This was vitally important to the followers of the Cartesian method since all certainty was established by appealing to the consciousness. If, however, true and universal ideas were not innate but were acquired through the experience of the senses, then there were no grounds for certainty since Descartes had begun by denying the solidity of everything revealed through the senses. Leibniz agreed that though the senses were necessary for the acquisition of knowledge, yet they could not reveal the full picture. At the best they provided a set of particular, individual truths, but 'All the examples which confirm a general truth, however numerous, do not suffice to establish the universal necessity of that truth, for it does not follow that that which has once occurred will always occur in the same way.'

The Transition to the Eighteenth Century and the Idea of Progress

No one better illustrates the transition from the seventeenth to the eighteenth century than Fontenelle, who was born in the middle of one (1657) and lived through a hundred years to the middle of the next. For much of this time he was secretary to the *Académie des Sciences* and played an important part in the process by which the discoveries of the scientists were made intelligible and were transmitted to the layman. In France, of course, there were many wealthy and leisured families of the *officier* class, who were eager to gain prestige by associating with men of letters, and who were especially welcomed by the scientists as a court of public appeal since they had no vested interest in adhering to the older views. Descartes had deliberately written his *Discours* in French, in order to appeal, as he said, to a reading public which had not been biased by a scholastic education: Fontenelle's *Projet d'une Science Universelle* was also in French, 'which is my native language, because I hope that those who employ only their natural reason will judge better of my opinion than those who only trust to ancient books'.

His most famous work, *Entretiens sur La pluralité des Mondes*, was a discussion between an astronomer and a lady, in which the revelations of the telescope and the new physical expanations of the universe were simplified for popular consumption. In this respect the book was no different from the series of public lectures on geometry, chemistry and astronomy which were becoming fashionable in Paris, but what is so remarkable about its author was the attitude of rational scepticism which presaged the *philosophes* of the eighteenth century far more than it reflected the natural philosophy of the seventeenth. The *philosophes* — men like Montesquieu, Voltaire and Diderot — were prompted by the great advances in knowledge made in the seventeenth century to claim that man's mind had been emancipated from authority, from innate ideas and from revelation. Endowed with the supreme faculty of reason, man was not only autonomous but capable of perfectability. The *philosophes* believed they were emancipating the human spirit by rational enlightenment: the mood, however, was largely secular and ultimately arid since it reduced God to a disinterested first cause, and subjected all authority to a critical scrutiny which destroyed more than it could replace.

Pierre Bayle was another influential writer who provided scientific literature for popular consumption. The appearance of a comet in 1680 had focused attention once again on the popularly held theories of planetary influence on human life, and in particular on the notion that comets had some especial and probably malignant power. Bayle determined to reveal the ignorance and irrationality underlying such beliefs and his *Pensées* were published in 1682. Two years later he began a monthly series of writings on scientific subjects for the general reader, *Nouvelles de la République de Lettres*, and in 1695 he embarked on a task which in its scope foreshadowed the efforts of the *philosophes*. Like them he hoped to assist in the spreading of knowledge by the compilation of a *Dictionnaire historique et critique*: like them, too, his work was largely critical of the Church, discounting revelation and fostering a sceptical spirit which made his book a source of inspiration to the Deists and other opponents of Christianity in the eighteenth century.

Altogether different in character but equally revolutionary in effect was the *Essay concerning Human Understanding* by John Locke,[1] whose rationalist assumptions brought him nearer in spirit to the eighteenth century than Leibniz and others whom in point of time he preceded. The belief that ideas were innate was common to Descartes, Spinoza and Leibniz and went back, as Leibniz said, to Plato, but an age which established an empirical science produced its most modern philosopher in Locke, who denied the innateness of ideas. In doing so, Locke also abandoned the philosophy underlying such a belief, namely the philosophy which postulated the

[1] Locke's political philosophy is described above, page 28.

existence of universals. Such a philosophy had already been challenged in part by the nominalists of the later Middle Ages who asserted that universals, for example truth, beauty, or man, are only names which had been invented for linguistic convenience. Locke, however, was even more thorough-going, for he stated that the finite is prior to the infinite, the particular precedes the generalisation, and that knowledge must reject all those beliefs which can only be justified by an appeal to universal concepts. Just as Galileo or Bacon had ignored the general theory until they had built up a system of particular facts and observations, Locke in his *Essay* denied that universal ideas could be evolved except by the acquisition of particular experiences. The mind he compared variously to an empty cupboard or a *tabula rasa*, a clean blackboard, being entirely dependent upon experience for its ideas, and he sought proof of this by showing that children or savages reveal no trace of possessing any universal concepts innately. Complex ideas were merely the sum total of the simple ideas derived from experience.

The interesting point is that Locke, while he attacked the Cartesian or Platonic theory, deliberately avoided any confusion of his own ideas with those of the materialist Hobbes. Hence he refused to derive all knowledge from sensation, taking care to distinguish between sensation and 'another fountain from which experience furnisheth the understanding with ideas', and this source he termed 'reflection'. 'Though it be not sense, as having nothing to do with external objects, yet it is very like it, and might properly enough be called internal sense.' The mind by reflection, therefore, comes to consider the ideas of sensation and builds upon them, and naturally, the sum of the whole can be greater than the sum of the parts. 'When the understanding is once stored with these simple ideas, it has the power to repeat, compare and unite them, even to an almost infinite variety, and can make at pleasure new complex ideas. But it is not in the power of the most exalted wit or enlarged understanding, by any quickness or variety of thought, to invent or frame one new simple idea in the mind not taken in by the ways aforementioned.' As Locke accepted the idea of God he assumed that it must therefore be one of the clearest and most certain of the complex ideas. He was, in fact, a deeply religious man but even in his Christianity he retained his staunch empiricism. He disliked intolerance and distrusted enthusiasm. The enthusiast, he argued, was only too ready to abandon common sense and substitute revelation. Hence 'revelation must be judged of by reason'.

As the seventeenth century broke so decisively with the past, the Golden Age, for the first time in European history, was transposed to the future. The battle between Ancients and Moderns was mostly a literary affair, but ammunition was drawn from most aspects of contemporary culture, not least from science. Corneille, in a preface to *Clitandre*, argued that the Ancients did not know everything, and in view of the discoveries of Galileo, Harvey and Newton it was difficult to refute him. Fontenelle, not unnaturally, made his own contribution to the controversy with two works, *Dialogues des Morts* and *Digression sur les Anciens et les Modernes*, which emphasised the advantages of his own age: 'A man of culture is, as it were, compounded from the distillation of all the cultures of preceding ages. Such a man will have no old age; for men do not degenerate, and there will be a steady accumulation of sanity and wisdom as one age succeeds the other.' Here is a novel concept, not simply of superiority over the Ancients with their misguided notions of motion and matter, but of progress yet to come.

No doctrine of progress could be fully evolved until the zoologists and botanists had arrived at some theory of evolution, which was not to happen until the nineteenth century. Even so, the excitement and enthusiasm created by the new philosophy induced in many a mood of optimism to rival the perplexed pessimism of men like Donne.[1] The most excited, and if not the most characteristic, certainly the most prophetic, voice of all was perhaps that of Joseph Glanvill, who wrote the *Vanity of Dogmatising*. Its title might be prosaic but in the course of the book Glanvill became rhapsodic about the unlimited possibilities of the future. He cited the work of Galileo, Harvey and Descartes — though not of Newton, since he wrote in 1661, as examples of the revolutionary achievements of the age, and continued: 'Should these Heroes go on as they have happily begun, they'll fill the world with wonders. And I doubt not but posterity will find many things that are now but Rumors, verified into practical Realities. It may be some Ages hence, a voyage to Southern unknown tracts, yea possibly to the Moon, will not be more strange than one to America. To them that come after us it may be as ordinary to buy a pair of wings, to fly into remotest Regions; as now a pair of Boots to ride a journey. And to

[1] See above, page 56.

conferr at the distance of the Indies by Sympathetic conveyances, may be as usual to future times, as to us in a litterary correspondence. The restauration of gray hairs to Juvenility, and renewing the exhausted marrow, may at length be affected without a miracle: and the turning of the now comparatively desert world into a Paradise may not improbably be expected from late Agriculture.'

The Church in the Seventeenth Century

The Reformation, springing from Martin Luther's repudiation of papal authority in 1521, and the Counter-Reformation this evoked in the Roman Catholic Church, established the sixteenth century as an era of violent religious conflict. Justification by faith alone, the priesthood of all believers, the sole authority of the scriptures and the sanctity of the individual conscience in interpreting them, were to remain the characteristic tenets of Protestantism generally, but the Lutheran Church in particular, by its emphasis on the individual conscience, became fissiparous. A new leader had only to arise to challenge the teaching of his day for a new sect immediately to form around him, its life rarely being prolonged beyond his own. Of the many sects which broke away, Calvinism alone was to prove vigorous and effective. Unlike Luther, who arrived at his doctrines over a period of many years and whose teaching was not only liable to inconsistency but was never efficiently collated in his lifetime, Calvin formulated in the *Institutio* a comprehensive, logically cohesive theology which served as an invaluable frame of reference for his followers.

Calvin's doctrine of predestination, that only God's elect were to be saved, gave tremendous confidence to his followers in the face of persecution since each confidently assumed his own inclusion among the elect. Moreover, the international structure of the Church, centred upon Geneva as a source of inspiration and instruction, gave them a strength and a cohesion denied to the members of Lutheran State Churches, each reflecting the personality of local princes and ministers. Calvin's social teaching, too, was as positive and as comprehensive as his theology. In sharp contrast to Luther, whose revulsion from the mechanical performance of duties, which he associated with the belief in justification by works, prevented him from laying down precise rules for his followers, Calvin demanded of his fellow-elect that they showed by their behaviour in this world their fitness for salvation in the next. Hence the severe and comprehensive regulations he laid down, which, in an authoritarian age, attracted many Lutherans who preferred to be told what to do, especially as Calvin was less conservative than Luther in his frank recognition of the necessity of commercial life and his approval of thrift, hard work and sobriety. Less happy for the future was the possible implication that successful business men were, by the evidence of God's favour, among the elect while the poor were damned.

Calvin was more radical than Luther in his repudiation of Catholicism, rejecting entirely the concept of the Real Presence, which Luther had tried to preserve by a complicated doctrine of consubstantiation, and creating an entirely novel administration in which the consistory of laymen and ministers replaced the traditional hierarchy of clergy. The Lutheran in consequence tended to be left in a midway position, exposed to the cross-fire of both Calvinist and Catholic, especially when the Catholic Church at the Council of Trent responded to the challenge of the Reformation by reforming its abuses and restating its doctrine. Where the Protestant believed in salvation by faith alone, and the priesthood of all believers, the Catholic Church uncompromisingly asserted the value of good works and the necessity of its own mediation by means of the confessional and the sacraments. Thus the dividing-line between orthodoxy and heresy, unwittingly crossed by many Catholics in the early days of the Reformation, was distinctly drawn, and the Society of Jesus was formed specifically to recover ground lost to the Catholic Church. The Jesuit was required to have attained a respectable standard of education before admission to the Society; he then devoted two years of his novitiate entirely to a routine designed to develop his character in holiness and obedience, after which he resumed his studies for the priesthood. The *Exercitia Spiritualia*, drawn up by Ignatius Loyola, the Society's founder, trained him not only in meditation, self-knowledge and humility, but also prepared him for martyrdom. Though they were not the only champions of the Counter-Reformation, the Jesuits were remarkable in their achievements. As skilful debaters, thoroughly grounded in theology, they recovered many to their Church: as confessors they gained the ears of rulers, urging them to renew their efforts to fight heresy: as educators they formed the minds of many of the new generation.[1]

The impetus given to the conflict by the Calvinists on the one hand and by the Jesuits on the other, ensured that the controversy was no less bitter, no less intense in 1600 than it had been in Luther's day; and in the Thirty Years War the passions roused by theology burned fiercely. But to the devout and the dogmatic on both sides they did not burn fiercely enough: for them the war proved sadly inconclusive. The denominational frontiers of 1648 differed only slightly from those of 1618 — remaining virtually fixed for the rest of the century — and though religious faith continued to be a vital force in seventeeth-century life it lost its importance as a prime cause of warfare. Consequently, the rival Churches had to come to terms with a state of compulsory coexistence. For this reason the papal bull *Zelo Domus Dei* condemned the peace as 'null and void, accursed and without any influence or result for the past, the present or the future', but it could not alter the realities of seventeenth-century politics. Coexistence did not necessarily imply toleration of a rival faith in one's own country. Most states opposed the existence of religious dissent on grounds of security; a few allowed it to some extent as good for trade. In both cases *raison d'état* decided the outcome, though, generally speaking, the clergy themselves held no brief for toleration.

Reunion, however, was a cause which won a surprising amount of lip-service, and if few took it seriously it was given much publicity by men like Grotius and Leibniz.[2] Exiled from Holland both for his tolerant sympathy with the Arminians and for his friendship with the Catholic Oldenbarneveldt, Grotius had advocated reunion in two books, *Via ad Pacem Ecclesiasticum* and *Votum pro Pace Ecclesiastica*, published in 1642, but to little effect. Leibniz, after his appointment to Hanover, found himself in an unusually tolerant court, his patron, the duke, becoming a Catholic, but his successor marrying the daughter of the Calvinist Elector Palatine. It was easier for him than for Grotius, therefore, to believe that all confessions could find agreement in the fundamental rules of faith provided they gave themselves to honest discussion. By way of a preliminary to this he began a correspon-

[1] Maximilian of Bavaria and Ferdinand of Styria were both pupils of the Jesuits.
[2] For Grotius see above, pages 18-19, for Leibniz see pages 65-67.

dence with Bossuet, the distinguished French theologian; but Bossuet was handicapped in this, as were all Catholics, by the dogmas of the Council of Trent, and it was over the question of the Council's authority that the correspondence ended. This same point was taken up by another Catholic bishop, Cristobal de Roja y Spinola, who, sent by the pope on a mission to rally all German opinion against the Ottoman peril in 1673, became convinced of the possibility of reunion. He wanted to pave the way for the summoning of a new General Council, but realised that in order for it to succeed the decisions of Trent would first have to be suspended. This was not a proposal which won support, and it died with him in 1695.

Paradoxically, while reunion, an officially respectable guest, failed to secure admission, toleration, universally reviled, began to creep in at the back door. It had few advocates. Not only did Catholics and Protestants abhor each other, but within each Church intolerance and exclusiveness prevailed whenever a serious division of opinion arose. Paul Gerhardt, famous for many Lutheran hymns, left Brandenburg after many conflicts with the Calvinist clergy, exiling himself to Saxony with the bitter words, 'I cannot regard the Calvinists as Christians'. Saxony, because of its traditional link with Luther's University of Wittenberg, remained the fount of purest Lutheranism — or so it believed. Others were more critical: 'If things are to go on according to the intentions of the Elector of Saxony . . . we shall have a new papacy and a new religion', wrote George Calixtus, but he was a liberal Lutheran of the University of Helmstedt, who advocated syncretism, the belief that it was more profitable to establish points of agreement between the Protestant Churches than to emphasise the disputed ones. He was attacked from all sides, and elsewhere the supporters of toleration awoke little response. Nevertheless, though in most countries the limits of religious freedom were contracting, the practice of unofficial toleration began to grow haltingly, especially in those areas where men became less fearful, or more indifferent.

The Churches, however, had serious problems to face other than their own rivalry or intolerance, for as man's horizons widened the centre of his interest changed. Trade expanded, standards of living for the wealthy began to improve, and the quest for material comfort was redoubled. Men absorbed in the present had less time for the eternal. This was not the consequence of commerce

alone but of something more general. While it is true that the sense
of God's presence in every act of daily life remained an integral
feature of life in general, there were none the less aspects of life
which, formerly spiritual, were becoming increasingly secular. The
service of the state was an all-absorbing occupation with its own
morality; science and philosophy began to move away from theology; international relations eluded the control of the Churches.
This last was due in part to the greater control exercised by the
State over the Church. The long conflict of the faiths had left the
secular State to rise as arbiter between them, while the idea of
sovereignty as an attribute of the prince alone left little room for
the concept of the Church as an equal partner in the State.

As men travelled throughout the world in search of trade they
discovered not only new merchandise but old religions. The *Koran*
was already known to Europe, but from further afield such works
as the *Analects* of Confucius awoke a surprised response in European minds. Pagans though they might be, Chinese and Indians
were seen to have concepts of virtue and morality, of God and of
eternity, without ever having heard of Christ. In consequence, the
discovery of such unsuspected wisdom in these alien religions
induced a relativism which in turn gave rise to scepticism, as La
Bruyère commented: 'Some complete their demoralization by extensive travel, and lose whatever shreds of religion remained to
them. Every day they see a new religion, new customs, new rites.'
It also promoted a tendency to call in question the unique character of the Christian Church, to think of a 'natural religion' to
which all religions approximated; this especially since the collapse
of scholasticism and the schism of the Reformation seemed to
point the moral that no religion had a monopoly of wisdom or of
inspiration. 'Who can doubt', wrote the sceptic Bayle, 'that the
Church is sometimes more, sometimes less enlightened and that
in this diversity of illumination and knowledge, it may quite
legitimately have different opinions on the same things.'

Nothing, however, was quite so devastating in its ultimate effect
upon the Church than the impact of the scientific and intellectual
revolutions. Descartes was implicitly a religious man, convinced of
the truth of the Christian revelation, but Cartesianism opened up
paths which Descartes himself never thought to tread; nor did his
disciple and apologist, Malebranche, fully realise that the Cartesian
God was not altogether congruous with the God of the New Testa-

ment. Locke never challenged the necessity nor the value of revelation but the relative position he assigned it implied that it merely confirmed what could be acquired in other ways. His successors accordingly deified reason, deposed revelation, and subjected the Scriptures to intensive, and often unsympathetic, scrutiny. Most of this of course took place in the eighteenth century, but long before the damage was done the Church might well have taken effective counter-action. Unfortunately, as an institution wedded to medieval principles of science and philosophy, it seemed more concerned to oppose the revolution than to play a part in it. Scholastic thought continued to dominate Catholic theology as though no revolution had taken place. Protestant response varied greatly. Luther had condemned Copernicus, but his successors were free to reject the ancient cosmology since it was not specifically taught in the Scriptures, for them the sole source of authority. For the Calvinist, in particular, the Cartesian concept of God setting the universe to work according to unalterable laws coincided reasonably well with the doctrine of predestination, and Descartes's ideas were accordingly permitted to be taught in the United Provinces and at Puritan Cambridge.

Nonetheless, no one but Blaise Pascal realised that the challenge of the new ideas had to be met if the victory were not ultimately to go by default to the freethinkers. A gifted mathematician with tremendous powers of imagination and analysis,[1] he abandoned his scientific pursuits after a mystical religious experience in 1654 which entirely altered his life. From then he devoted his time to the preparation of material for a defence of Christianity. His death supervened in 1662 before he could complete it, but his *Pensées* indicated the pattern of his work. His concern being to expose the inevitable weakness of human reason and the necessity of faith, he used the scientists' own regard for factual truth to challenge those who gave reason pride of place over revelation, by demonstrating that human life was in fact entangled in irrational confusion. The endemic misery of mankind indicated man's fallen state from which nothing but the operation of divine grace could raise him. Pascal thus offered an attitude to the rational science of his day which, if the Church had adopted it, might have given it greater strength with which to face the free-thinking assault of the succeeding century. Religion, he argued, was not detachable from the rest

[1] See above, page 39.

of life. 'It illuminates our nature and experience. It draws into a unity the scattered elements in our life. It guides our minds and controls our science, because it alone can unfold the full mystery of nature. It answers the questions which reason can only raise, and it brings us to that fulfilment of life towards which science in its more limited way is struggling. It cannot be set in opposition to reason or science, because it includes yet transcends both.'[1]

The Varieties of Christian Experience

Whatever the difficulties and inadequacies of the Christian Church in the seventeenth century, its spiritual life was both intense and varied. In France during the first half of the century the *dévots*, as they were termed, led a spiritual revival, a natural outcome of the Counter-Reformation though altogether different from the more emotional, almost sensational, movements in Spain and Italy. Its keynote was active Christianity, its inspiration the Cardinal Bérulle, who founded the French Oratory as a means to train clergy; this was, perhaps, the most necessary reform the Gallican Church required since there were few seminaries and the average *curé* was often invincibly ignorant. Bérulle's followers maintained his characteristic blend of devotion and practical action. St. Francis of Sales, titular bishop of Geneva, wrote two classic works of devotion, the *Treatise on the Love of God* and an *Introduction to a Devout Life*, persevered successfully against enormous odds to recover the inhabitants of the Chablais from Calvinism, and founded the Order of Visitation, the Visitandines or Salesian Sisters, who were to leave their convents to care for the sick and to teach, an innovation eventually suppressed by the Archbishop of Lyon. The Sisters of Charity, however, founded by St. Vincent de Paul, secured permission to work in the world, particularly to alleviate the poverty of the country districts caused by the warfare of the Fronde: The spiritual poverty of these areas especially concerned St. Vincent and he established the Lazarist Fathers to assist and to educate the country *curés*.

A movement which aroused St. Vincent's bitter opposition, and indeed the pope's too, sprang from the teaching of Cornelius Jansen, bishop of Ypres in the Spanish Netherlands. Jansen condemned the ceremonial of the Church which, to him, merely disguised the fact that man could only be saved by God's grace, which, once

[1] G. R. Cragg, *The Church in the Age of Reason (1648–1789)*, p. 43.

granted, resulted in man's love for God and, through love, faith. His *Augustinus*, a study of the saint most drawn upon by Protestants in the sixteenth century, not unnaturally resulted in a system which had much in common with Calvinism, not least in its belief in predestination and in its puritan spirit. Two things in particular — that man cannot fulfil God's commands without the assistance of a special Grace, and that God's grace is irresistible so that there is no withstanding it — proved objectionably pessimistic and determinist to many other Catholics, and not least to the Jesuits. Indeed it was their conflict with them, rather than their own theology, which won the Jansenists their fame. In France the movement was led by Antoine Arnauld, a doctor of the Sorbonne, and by his sister Angélique, Abbess of Port-Royal in Paris. Arnauld's publication of *De la Fréquent Communion* (1643) brought the conflict into the open by criticising the laxity of the Jesuits in the confessional. Their doctrine of probabilism urged the confessor to be lenient if there were good grounds for granting absolution, in order that the morally frail be not for ever barred from the Mass, but it was true that probabilism had often degenerated into a lax casuistry. The Jansenists were not alone in criticising this, but Arnauld's demands were typically rigorous in that the penitent was to be denied absolution until his confessor was absolutely satisfied of his contrition.

Later the Jansenists won the support of Pascal, whose *Lettres Provenciales* eternally branded the Jesuit with the stigma of casuistry, and gave the controversy immortality by the brilliant sarcasm of his style. The Jesuits mobilised their reserves, the movement fell foul of Louis XIV[1] and was proscribed by the popes. Independently of its persecution, the movement degenerated as it lost the impetus of its founders. It tended to become associated with the type of reformed sinner who demands a regimen of unattainable rigour in order to compensate for his past life by making his present one unbearable. Its puritanism, originally a valuable and necessary warning against the dangers of ceremonial developed into a harsh and narrow doctrine, reinforced by an unduly pessimistic view of mankind and by the spiritual pride which often accompanies belief in the predestination of the elect to salvation. This attitude was to be found in the writing of Pierre Nicole (1625–95): 'All these blind sinners, abandoned to their passions, are proofs of the rigour and

[1] See Chapter VI, page 261.

justice of God which delivers them to the devils who torment them and, after inflicting infinite miseries upon them in this life, plunges them into the abyss of eternal torture.' Toleration, denied them by Louis XIV, was not something the Jansenists were likely to grant to anyone else. In this respect they resembled the rigorist Calvinists of Holland who condemned Arminianism.

Arminius, a student of Calvinist theology at Leyden, had subsequently studied both at Geneva and at Rome, an education which had confirmed him in his naturally charitable and humanist outlook. On his return to Leyden he questioned Calvin's doctrine of predestination since it seemed to him incomprehensible that God should deny men free will and that He should preordain most men to damnation. It was an ancient problem: Arminius could not deny God's prescience lest he limit God's omniscience, but his humane instincts compelled him to modify the harsher implications of predestination. 'God has of all eternity established this distinction among fallen humanity, that those who renounce their sins and place their trust in Christ are granted forgiveness of their sins and life eternal; those, however, who remain impenitent are to be punished. Moreover, it is agreeable to God that all men should be converted. . . . But He compels no one.' The divinity school at Leyden became an arena in which Arminius was challenged at every point by his rigorist colleague, Gomarus: 'An eternal and divine decree', he thundered, 'has established which men were to be saved, and which were to be damned.' The conflict then turned to the sources of Calvinist theology as the contestants argued over the interpretation of sentences, but neither side could allow its emotional philosophy to be decided by logical discussion. In the event the appeal was made to force, and the Gomarists were victorious.[1]

Despite the evils associated with rigid and intolerant dogmatism, the formulation of theology was a necessary process and it had been one of the weaknesses of the Lutheran Church that it had lacked a coherent body of dogma. Under pressure of attacks from Geneva and Rome, the second and third generations of Lutherans undertook to remedy this. Unfortunately their approach was tediously scholastic, and resulted in arid controversy. Preaching, once the greatest strength of the Lutheran Church, became notoriously argumentative about minor points of doctrine. Consequently the

[1] See Chapter IV, page 191.

Church lost touch with the ordinary people, who looked for a more personal faith, immediately relevant to their own lives. To satisfy this need, a religious revival began which drew its inspiration not only from Luther but from an older tradition of mysticism, established in the fourteenth century. Pietism, as it was termed, owed its foundation to Philipp Jakob Spener, a Lutheran minister, whose *Pia Desideria* presented a programme of reform in which personal piety and the fear of God were to be the central features, and the sermon to be restored to its devotional character. In addition, he established centres of fellowship, *collegia pietatis*, so that his followers might find by shared experience that faith was less a matter of doctrine than a way of life. If Pietism was characterised by faults of emotionalism and contempt of learning, this was only to be expected in the circumstances, reflecting as it did a passionate discontent with the arid formalism of the official Lutheran Church. In Saxony the authorities made known their disapproval, but Spener at last won the support of the Elector Frederick of Brandenburg, later to become king of Prussia, and in 1694 established the University of Halle, which became a centre from which Pietism expanded in the eighteenth century, not only throughout Germany, but even reaching through its organised missions, the shores of India and America.

Another reaction from formal theology was to be found in the Catholic Church as a result of the mystic doctrines of Miguel de Molinos, a Spanish priest who became famous among fashionable society in Rome. By abandoning all effort, by resigning itself to complete passivity, the soul, he claimed, would lose itself in God and thus attain perfection. But the concept of passivity, of becoming a vessel filled with God, could easily be corrupted into the notion that such a soul was therefore incapable of sin; from this it was but a short step to suppose that the body containing it could go through the actions of sin without being contaminated. The Catholic Church, moreover, while accepting the fact of mysticism, has always been suspicious of those who insisted on their direct access to God since, strong in their immediate knowledge and experience of God, they become intolerant of authority and frequently dispense with dogmas, rites and the entire priesthood. This, in fact, happened among the nuns whom Molinos directed in Rome when they discarded their rosaries and refused to go to confession or to recite their office. Condemned to lifelong imprisonment by the Inquisition for various propositions in his works and for irregularities in his private life, Molinos yet continued to exert great influence through his most popular work, the *Guida Spirituale* (1675).

The mystic concepts of Molinism appeared in France, under the name of Quietism, through Madame Guyon, a remarkable widow, obsessed with the need for spirituality in religion. Whereas the Church accepted as valid the experience of the great mystics of the past, she affirmed that such communion with God was possible for lesser people who were not acclaimed as saints: by an act of total passivity, the love of God could be directly experienced by a large number of virtuous, but ordinary, Christians. Moreover, in her *Moyen court et très facile de faire oraison* (1685) she claimed that there was no need to ponder the great truths of the Gospel since these were not the proper objects of pure contemplation. The one thing needful was to yield, 'to the torrent of the forces of God'. Her confessor was arrested by Harlay, Archbishop of Paris, and she herself was threatened with removal to a convent as a lunatic until, through the mediation of a cousin among the ladies of Madame de Maintenon, she was released and brought to Versailles. There she won the friendship of Fénelon, whose *Explication des maximes des saints*, published in 1697, distinguished true from false mysticism in a sincere attempt not only to protect Madame Guyon, but also to moderate her own extravagant opinions. Bossuet, however, who could see none of the qualities of Quietism which attracted Fénelon, but only its threat to orthodoxy and authority, appealed both to Rome and to Louis XIV. Though Fénelon was high in the king's favour, and tutor to his grandson, he could not overcome the pathological dislike of nonconformity which inspired Louis's religious policy in general.[1] Madame Guyon was arrested, and finally exiled, while Fénelon was compelled to submit to a papal condemnation of his ideas.

THE AGE OF THE BAROQUE

The Principles of Roman Baroque Architecture

Baroque architecture was born of very diverse parents. As a child of the Renaissance it inherited the classical standards of Vitruvius[2]

[1] See Chapter VI, pages 256-62.

[2] Marcus Vitruvius Pollio, a Roman architect whose *De Architectura*, written shortly before the birth of Christ, was recovered during the fifteenth century.

which had inspired and guided the work of Brunelleschi, Alberti, Bramante and Michelangelo. Since they were men of universal genius not one of them had applied the rules of composition slavishly: their styles had expanded and developed within a common form, and because of their work Renaissance architecture was never allowed to stagnate into mere formalism. Michelangelo had become absorbed by the tremendous struggle between the engineering skill of the architect and the overpowering masses of masonry, and his response marked the transition from the Renaissance proper, as formally codified by art historians, to the Baroque. But the next step was long delayed. If the discovery of Vitruvius had supplied the basic grammar for the language of Renaissance architecture, its later effect was to enable mechanical academicians to preach grammar when they had nothing new to say. After Michelangelo's death in 1564 there ensued such a phase, termed 'Mannerism', in which accepted motifs and rules were handled either too rigidly or too self-consciously. Intellect triumphed over inspiration, and the result was as arid as the sermons of the Lutheran pastors.[1] Just as some Lutheran congregations had therefore embraced Pietism, so Italian architects evolved the Baroque as their protest against the exclusion of the emotions from building.

But Baroque owed even more to its other parent, the Counter-Reformation. It was a style with an avowed missionary purpose. The champions of the Counter-Reformation, after an initial period of ascetism — in reaction to the pagan hedonism they identified in the Renaissance — recruited the fine arts in a new campaign to recover the heretic to the faith. For the Roman Catholic the miracle of transubstantiation made the Real Presence a sacred reality. A church, therefore, was not simply a preaching box or a place for private meditation, but the House of God, which in pomp and majesty could not rank second to a temporal palace. The humanist detachment of Bramante's Tempietto in Rome or of Brunelleschi's church of S. Lorenzo in Florence afforded the Church no support in its war with heresy. To sustain the fighting spirit of the Counter-Reformation it was necessary to appeal directly to the eyes and to the emotions of the people by a splendid display of magnificence and drama. Hence, the Counter-Reformation, through the medium of the Baroque, 'overwhelmed heresy by splendour; it did not argue but proclaimed; it brought

[1] See above, page 80.

1a. Chiesa del Gesù, Rome

1b. Bernini: The Vision of S. Teresa
(S. Maria della Vittoria, Rome)

2. *The Worship of the Holy Name of Jesus*
(*Ceiling of Il Gesù, Rome, by Gaulli*)

3. *Sant' Agnese, on the Piazza Navona, Rome*

4a.
*San Carlino
alle Quattro
Fontane,
Rome*

4b.
*Sant' Andrea
al Quirinale,
Rome*

5. The Karlskirche, Vienna

6a. *The Church of Les Invalides, Paris*

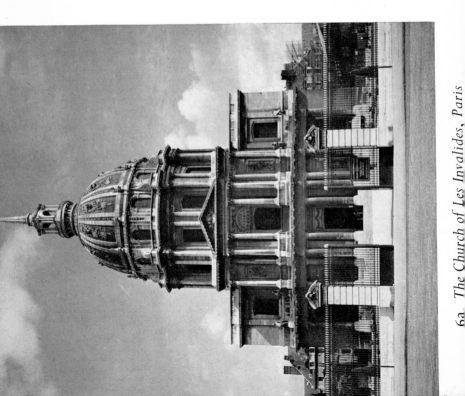

6b. *The Church of the Sorbonne, Paris*

7a. *The Orléans Wing, Blois*

7b. *The Louvre, East Front, Paris*

8. *Versailles: the Garden Front*

conviction to the doubter by the very scale of its grandeurs; it guaranteed truth by magniloquence.'[1]

The propaganda values of painting and architecture were first exploited by the Jesuits, and the Gesù, their church in Rome begun in 1568, gave some indication of what was to follow. The interior by Giacomo Vignola is not as he left it, since a great deal was added by way of decoration in the last quarter of the seventeenth century, but the basic structure still reveals his purpose. By means of massive columns, by a heavy cornice running along the nave to carry the eye eastwards, by dramatic lighting and by the bright blue pigment of lapis in the ornate side chapels, he set out to design a church of palatial splendour to reassure the faithful and to silence the sceptic. Materialist in its profuse ornamentation, it is wholly spiritual in inspiration, and within these polarities much of the Baroque was to be defined. The façade by Della Porta was as novel as the interior and equally as important in setting a trend for the future. The features were indeed those of classical architecture, but his treatment of them was revolutionary: pilasters were doubled up to achieve variety and grandeur, while the bold use of volutes, two massive scrolls, to link the first and second stories gave a dramatic unity to the whole. The Renaissance architect had defined and differentiated each part of his composition, articulating the stories by the use of the appropriate orders, to establish a mood of serene mastery and control, of balance and logic. The Baroque architect merged all the parts together in an organic unity so that one form appeared to grow out of another, instead of being placed beside it for some logical principle. Boldness, strength and power became the characteristics of the architecture of the militant Counter-Reformation.

From Michelangelo and the Renaissance, from the Gesù and the Counter-Reformation, sprang the drama and the opulent florescence of Roman Baroque in the seventeenth century. It has horrified the purists, who seem to believe that the conventions of the Tuscan tradition, of Brunelleschi and Alberti, should be frozen for all time, and who have coined the word 'baroque' from the Portuguese for a deformed pearl. It has aroused the suspicion of the northerner, perennially contemptuous yet fearful of the operatic qualities, both sensuous and sensational, of the Latin races. It has frightened the puritan out of his wits. Discomfited by the blatant

---

[1] W. Sypher, *Four Stages of Renaissance Style*.

appeal to his senses, he has sniffed behind the most devout Catholic art to discern latent traces of paganism and idolatry. In fact Baroque architecture is nothing more than an attempt to excite, to uplift and to impress; by the dramatic use of mass, light and colour it seeks to create a sense of grandeur and movement which will overwhelm the spectator.

Since propaganda is the art of public proclamation, the exterior design and decoration of the churches acquired an interest and an importance for the Baroque architect which his predecessors of the Renaissance had not always shared, and though the difference between the two styles is, in this respect, one of degree and emphasis only, it is still a valid one. The classic Renaissance interior of the church of S. Lorenzo in Florence is married to external walls and an incomplete façade which have as much dignity and charm as a warehouse: this example, if an extreme one and the result of chance, none the less reflects the Renaissance architects' preoccupation with the interiors of their churches. The Baroque architect from the very beginning conceived of his church as an integral part of its neighbourhood and could not leave its outer appearance to chance. Hence, when circumstances allowed, he delighted in the siting of fountains and statuary, the planning of squares, colonnades, and flights of steps with ornate balustrades, so that at the dramatic centre of the scene his church might rise. The dome, among the most dramatic of all architectural features, had an especial appeal and was constantly exploited since it gave majesty to the skyline of the church and, almost literally, crowned it in its regal setting.

Of great importance was the façade, the flat surface at the centre of the vista which had to be related to the whole by means of its decoration. To achieve this the accepted rules of the sixteenth century were abandoned. Curves replaced straight lines, and forms swelled and writhed instead of merely standing. The impressive façade of S. Agnese in Piazza Navona at Rome, designed by Borromini and Rainaldi, curves outward to bring it in line with the bases of its flanking towers. The towers themselves are novel in that the first storey is square, the second round, and as such a juxtaposition was inconceivable in classic rules the method of reconciling them by a curiously broken entablature had to be unique also. But so successful is the dramatic effect that it is only upon examination that the novelty of the individual features is noticed.

It is the impact of the whole which counts. For this same reason, the stories of the façade were rarely articulated by the appropriately decorated capitals and pillars of the Renaissance; in their place the use of giant columns or pilasters, stretching from top to bottom gave a dramatic unity to the façade. Frequently, to enhance this effect and to catch the eye, the columns might be grouped in pairs, or their stonework carved into spiral patterns soaring to the crowning pediment.

The handling of masses, the swelling domes, the spiral columns, the curved façades with their exciting patterns of concave–convex surfaces all indicate the sculptural quality of Baroque architecture, and, like a piece of sculpture, a Baroque church is an organic whole. The exterior was planned as the focal point of the neighbourhood; within, the unity of the decorative plan was equally imperative. If the architect were to succeed in his object of exciting, uplifting and impressing the spirits of the spectators, then he had to stage manage his effects with care. The sculptured figures are not merely placed upon pedestals or in niches along the walls but seem to have grown there, living parts of the organism, blending not only with their setting but also with the painted figures from which at a distance they can scarcely be distinguished. By tricks of perspective, and by exploiting the theatrical nature of the setting, Gaulli could paint the ceiling of the Gesù so that the formal lozenges and volutes of the patterned roof are broken in the centre as though the roof had opened to admit a heavenly host, enraptured in the worship of the holy name of Jesus. Not only is the line of the ceiling broken, it is broken irregularly so that while some of the figures appear against the sky, others seem to be borne upon cloud within the very canopy of the roof. For those who are not too busy protesting at the *trompe-l'œil*, the effect is tremendous.

Where the Baroque succeeds it represents a union of the arts of the architect, the painter and the sculptor, acting in concert to attack the emotions of the spectator. Total effect is more important than obedience to formal rules, and in this respect the Baroque is essentially theatrical, not least in its concealment of structural features behind statuary of stucco work and in its skilful understanding of the dramatic qualities of light. Statues and altar figures were often lit by concealed windows, and the windows themselves were coloured so that the exact hue might be predetermined, as for example, in Bernini's S. Andrea al Quirinale where the panes of the lantern are stained yellow so that even on dull days the light filtering through appears to be sunlight. Like most other features of the Baroque, lighting was first exploited in the Gesù. The nave is lit by windows over the side chapels, but the last one before the crossing was deliberately made smaller in order to admit less light than the others: this serves to heighten the dramatic effect of the flood of light which pours from the windows of the lantern, to illuminate the crossing and to draw the eye towards the altar.

After the Council of Trent had deliberately reasserted the dogma of transubstantiation the need to stress the importance of the altar, and its primacy over all other features, made it impossible to continue the use of the central plan which had been a prominent feature of the Renaissance, since this gave no particular emphasis to the east end. In its place the Baroque exploited the oval, which lent itself to exciting variations in treatment, especially so in the relationship of concave–convex lines. Moreover, and this was the specific function of the oval, its two axes of different lengths gave a more formal definition to the structure, thus creating an awareness of length and breadth which helped to focus the eye more directly upon the high altar.

The Architects of Rome, Vienna and Paris

The chief characteristics of the Baroque — its sculptural quality, its rejection of the restraints imposed by the Mannerists, its fervent championing of the Counter-Reformation — were reflected in the personality of its foremost exponent, Gian Lorenzo Bernini, who was not only a sculptor but devoutly practised the *Spiritual Exercises* of the Jesuits. His father, a sculptor also, brought him to Rome from Naples while still a child and trained him in the Mannerist tradition of the day. This tradition Bernini soon abandoned. Dissatisfied by the taste for multiple silhouettes, an effect which often creates an impression of uncertainty and strain, at once disturbing and disturbed, he preferred to achieve a more dynamic, more dramatic and yet much calmer effect by emphasising a single frontal viewpoint. Between 1621 and 1624, by a series of commissions for Cardinal Borghese, which included the *Rape of Proserpina, David, Apollo and Daphne*, he established a reputation as the finest artist since Michelangelo, whose brooding temperament and latent violence he shared but whose concept of sculpture he rejected. Instead of letting the figure adhere closely to the block, as Michelangelo insisted, he tried to liberate it from its material limitations so that it might break through into the world of the spectator. This in essence was the nature of Baroque; an attempt to shatter the formal distinction between virtual space, created by the artist, and real space, inhabited by the spectator. The audience and the action were thus made one.

Bernini brought to the task a consummate skill, especially with marble; he also exploited the effects created by using coloured lights and mixed materials, as can be seen in his chapel dedicated to Saint Teresa in the church of S. Maria della Vittoria in Rome. The walls are richly faced with marbles of amber, gold and pink, but the spectator's attention is riveted by the heavy coupled columns and the broken pediment which frame the altar: these are projected at an angle to the wall to catch his eye and to lead it within the frame, not to the traditional altar painting but to a sculptural group of astonishing vigour. Saint Teresa, apparently rising through the air, swoons in an agony of pain and blissful ecstasy as the angel raises the golden arrow with which, in the legend of her vision, he pierced her heart. The effect is heightened by the diagonal tilt of the group, by the golden light admitted from a hidden window, and by the golden beams, gilt metal shafts, which conceal the blank wall of the altar niche. In order to grant whole-hearted admiration to Bernini's work it is clearly important to be sympathetic to the legend which inspired it, and much of the controversy which has raged around the altarpiece has reflected religious rather than artistic prejudices. One objective comment, however, seems justified: in contrast to his penetrating studies of Louis XIV or Cardinal Borghese, Bernini's treatment of religious themes in general was perhaps too emotional and too contrived. His David appears too self-consciously righteous, his Teresa too ecstatic, to be wholly convincing.

In the altarpiece of Saint Teresa Bernini established an intimate relationship between sculpture and architecture, as he had already tried to do in his *baldaquino*, the majestic bronze canopy he constructed in St. Peter's in order to give the greatest possible dignity and emphasis to the most important high altar of the Catholic Church. Its four spiralling columns soar one hundred feet to a canopy which, for all its weight, deceives the eye by the lightness of its sculptured drapery. But the total effect is marred by the setting. The unrestrained grandeur and extravagant detail, breath-taking in themselves, contrast uneasily with the austerity of Michelangelo's walls. Bernini, therefore, seized avidly upon the opportunity to supply the architectural background for his own decoration when he was invited to build S. Andrea al Quirinale in Rome.

The result was a perfectly integrated Baroque church. Bernini made no deliberate pursuit of novelty: in 1625 he had designed the façade of S. Bibiana in a manner conventional enough to be wholly uninspiring, and his subsequent exterior work rarely broke the accepted conventions. If a curve would do the work of a straight line then he would use it, as he did in St. Peter's Square, where he transformed a correctly devised classical loggia of free-standing colonnades by laying them out in an elliptical curve; but if his treatment of classical forms endowed them with a new significance, he never abandoned them in the revolutionary manner of his contemporary, Borromini.[1] Hence his façade to S. Andrea al Quirinale is correct enough, save perhaps for the convex portico and for the quadrants formed by two retaining walls on its flanks. Inside, however, his blend of painting, sculpture and architecture is more revolutionary. The ground plan is an oval, set against the façade so that entry is at the most obtuse point of the ellipse, from where the eye can take in the entire church. The three most dominant features are the sanctuary, heavily framed by coupled columns and flooded with light; the figure of Saint Andrew, who soars above it to the gilded dome; the dome itself, ornately decorated with hexagonal patterns in white and gold which diminish in size towards the lantern. The windows of the drum are dramatically alive with the marble figures of god-like young men whose lively nonchalance makes the spectator feel an intruder, while above them angels in stucco hover around the frame of the lantern.

In the history of Roman Baroque architecture Bernini's name is permanently linked with that of Francesco Borromini, though in every important respect the two men were remarkably dissimilar. Borromini, the son of an architect, was first trained in Milan as a mason. From there he went to Rome in 1615 at the age of sixteen to work under his cousin, Carlo Maderno, who had built the nave and façade of St. Peter's. It was an auspicious start and he learned much from his cousin, but he was still only a mason in 1629 when Maderno died and was succeeded as papal architect by Bernini. It was not easy for Borromini to serve a man of passionate moods who was only one year older than himself, and, though he avoided any

[1] See next paragraph.

open breach, he resigned his post as chief mason in 1633. Six more years elapsed before he won his first independent commission as an architect. This slow burgeoning of his genius resulted in part from inborn modesty and caution so that he appeared to be diffident and unambitious, but there was a deeper cause. Where Bernini was subject to frequent fits of tempestuous passion, Borromini was the slave to sombre moods of melancholy. Labouring only to glorify God through the perfection of his art, he was perpetually aware of his deficiencies, and, lacking his rival's self-confident *bravura*, the illusion of his own inadequacy preyed upon his mind. In the end, despite nearly thirty years of acclamation as an architect, he destroyed all his drawings in a paroxysm of despair and took his own life.

Despite the hesitancy, despite the inner turmoil which ultimately paralysed his creative spirit, Borromini was in comparison with Bernini by far the more fearless innovator. From his intense admiration for Michelangelo's sculpture he came to believe that proportion was God's special gift to mankind, having its origin in His creation of the human form.[1] Consequently he maintained that none could succeed as architects but painters and sculptors who were familiar with the human body, since they alone would have the ability to fashion buildings into true living forms. In this organic view of architecture he propounded a basic principle of the Baroque, but one which revealed a profound difference from Bernini. There was little in the plans and elevations of Bernini's work at which Vitruvius might have cavilled. His basic structure was classical; it was in his sculptural treatment of it and in his decoration that he was novel and, by classical standards, extravagant. Borromini's extravagance lay in his original and dramatic handling of the basic structure itself; the greater his audacity here, the more restrained became his surface decoration.

His greatest single-handed achievement was the church of S. Carlino alle Quattro Fontane, and one which spanned his working life as an architect from 1638 to 1667. The façade he completed just before his death, and the numerous designs he made in an attempt to integrate the separate parts may have indicated the

---

[1] Vitruvius had said, in his rules for sacred edifices, that these buildings should have the proportions of a man. This however was simply to establish a geometrical relationship between a man, a square and a circle. Borromini's view of proportion was more organic.

growing lack of confidence which precipitated his suicide. Whatever the cause, the decoration of the façade — a complicated series
of bays, oval windows, Roman sacrificial altars, with columns,
statutary and a massive oval portrait to boot — has rarely been
considered entirely successful, even by devotees of the Baroque;
but few can deny the lively sense of movement it imparts. This is
suggested by the pattern of the bays of the lower storey, which are
successively concave, convex, concave, creating an undulation
which is emphasised and repeated by the unusually solid entablature
between the storeys. The bays above are all concave, but the
introduction of a small oval pavilion in the lower half of the central
bay gives the effect of balancing, and yet contrasting with, the
lower storey. But it is the interior which is one of Borromini's
greatest triumphs, and one which almost defies description, it is so
personal and so overwhelming. This effect is brought about neither
by sumptuous decoration nor by dramatic lighting, but by brilliant
mastery of the structure. The plan is an oval, with an oval dome,
and with the side and entrance chapels all representing fragments
of ovals, so that the complex interrelation, though not immediately
apparent, is gradually apprehended by the spectator. As Professor
Pevsner writes, 'five compound spatial shapes merge into each
other. We can stand nowhere without taking part in the swaying
rhythm of several of them. . . . Space now seems hollowed out by
the hand of a sculptor, walls are moulded as if made of wax or clay.'[1]
Such is the sensation of motion that one is scarcely aware of the
astonishing smallness of the church, the longest axes of which are
barely 50 and 70 feet and the whole plan would fit comfortably
inside any of the four piers which support the dome of St. Peter's;
but it is the very smallness which helps to create the illusion of
movement, since one has only to move a single pace to find all the
features of the interior change their relative position.

The greatest days of Roman Baroque were those of Bernini and
Borromini, from 1630 to 1670. Thereafter its influence spread
across Europe though the nature of its reception varied greatly
from one country to the next. The Spaniards, for example, adapt-
ing it to their own techniques and to their own temperaments,
arrived at a style which placed more emphasis on colour and
ornamentation than can be found anywhere else in Europe. It was
an unfair comment, perhaps, on the work of José Churriguera that

[1] N. Pevsner, *An Outline of European Architecture*.

his name should have been given to extravagances of style which he himself would have rejected. At Salamanca he designed the town hall, decorated the cathedral and laid out a magnificent square surrounded by ninety arcades, thus combining the Baroque's love of colour and decoration with its flair for town planning. The style of his contemporaries and successors, *churrigueresque*, however, became a wild and wayward version of *il stilo borrominesco*, in which the principle of decoration was over-elaborated to such a point that fantasy and intricacy became ends in themselves. It thus degenerated into mere eccentricity.

In north Italy the Baroque was adopted in a more orthodox fashion by Guarino Guarini, an architect who was also a mathematician, a philosopher and a devout Oratarian. Neither Bernini nor Borromini had confined themselves solely to churches, but it was Guarini who demonstrated the peculiar adaptability of Baroque for secular purposes. The style of the church militant was easily assimilated to the glorification of princes, and the dramatic undulations of the Roman façades were repeated on the palaces of Turin. Guarini to some extent succeeded in analysing the principles of his style in his *Architettura Civile* and though it was not published before 1737, engravings from it were circulating after 1668, and played an important part in stimulating the exciting growth of German architecture. Asam and Neumann, its greatest masters, worked mainly between 1720 and 1760, but before the seventeenth century was out the Baroque was already established in Vienna. The relaxation of tension produced by the relief of the city in 1683, the pride engendered among its citizens by the creation of the Danubian empire, and the sense of triumph achieved by the destruction of heresy within the Habsburg domains, combined to create a mood of celebration and self-glorification, of extravagance, expansion and exhibitionism.

To satisfy this mood, the Viennese imported Italian architects but these were soon eclipsed by a native rival, Johann Bernhard Fischer von Erlach, who returned to Austria imbued with *il stilo borrominesco* after barely three years in Italy. His ideas, stimulated by his experiences in Rome and Naples, were original and exciting; and, although they were not published until 1721, the basic principles he then enunciated in his *Entwurf einer Historischen Architektur* were those which inspired his work from his appointment in 1687 as architect-engineer to the Emperor Leopold. One especially important innovation was his admiration for the exotic; not the flamboyant excesses of Baroque extravagance, but the styles, hitherto regarded as mere curiosities, of China and the East. Pagodas and Islamic mosques were analysed and acclaimed in his book on the grounds that a barbaric monument deserved as much study and respect as a classical temple: 'Artists will see here,' he wrote, 'that nations dissent no less in their taste for architecture, than in food and raiment, and by comparing one with the other they themselves may make a judicious choice.'

The way was thus opened to eclecticism, as for example in the Karlskirche, commissioned by the Emperor Charles VI in 1716. So great is the number of motifs, so varied their provenance, that the church defies purely verbal description. A pedimented portico, supported by six pillars, evokes the mood of ancient Rome, and within the curved recesses of the facade as it sweeps back to join the side towers stand two gigantic columns, modelled on Trajan's. Unlike Trajan's, however, they are surmounted by platforms and cupolas so that they give the impression of minarets. On their flanks stand the side towers, a product of Baroque imagination run riot. Each tower begins as a triumphal archway decked out with coupled pilasters; above the arch, is a square window under an oval pediment bearing a circular motif; above that is a window, shaped in the form of an heraldic blazon; thereafter the line is lost in the bizarre eccentricity of a pagoda roof. It is almost with relief that the eye returns to the centre where, above the façade, stands a Baroque dome on a massive drum: in such an exotic context it seems reassuringly conventional. But an inventory of the features is misleading, since, in the true tradition of the Baroque, it is the total effect which counts, and few can deny the exotic and exciting impressions conveyed by the Karlskirche.

Before his death in 1723 von Erlach had transformed Vienna. The medieval centre he left untouched, since it was scarcely feasible to destroy fortifications which had so recently been tested by the Turks, but by building the Karlskirche to face across it to the Imperial Palace, and by siting his other palaces in a semicircle around them, he gave a focal point for the sprawling suburbs of the city. The Imperial Palace, as befitted its importance in Vienna, represented one of the most distinctive features of von Erlach's style, the secularisation of the Baroque to extol not the divinity of the Godhead but the divine right of the Habsburg monarchy. His

original intention was to place the palace on a hill overlooking the
valley in which it was eventually built, and, as is shown in the
illustrations preserved in the *Entwurf*, to lay it out on a scale to
dwarf Versailles, with colonnades, pavilions, fountains and lakes,
culminating in an Imperial entrance flanked by two Trajan's
columns. The enterprise was too costly and too ambitious, but its
more modest successor echoed the classical theme, being clearly
modelled on Nero's Golden House which was also featured in the
Entwurf.

The art of the Counter-Reformation, though it was so eminently
suited to the adulation of monarchy in general, could not take root
in Protestant soil. It transformed Bavaria during the eighteenth
century but made no impact on Brandenburg, and the divisions between the Catholic and Protestant states of Europe were reflected
in their architecture. The one important exception to this rule
was France: Catholic beyond question, monarchist to excess, the
French were never swept away by the tide of Baroque exuberance.
Italian models were respected, Bernini was invited to Paris, but the
Roman style never became dominant. The classical tradition in
France was of more recent date and was therefore the less readily
abandoned. Moreover, the austere phase of the Council of Trent,
so short-lived in Italy, was ideally suited to the spiritual climate of
Louis XIII's reign, to the France of Bérulle and St. Vincent.
French Catholicism differed from the Italian in two important
respects. The Cistercians and the Jansenists re-emphasised the
importance of prayer and meditation, and opposed the theatrical
quality of Baroque decoration as an unwelcome distraction from
spiritual communion. The French, too, had an unusually high
regard for the intellect: they respected the rational, which they
identified with the classical, and disliked the blatant appeal of
Baroque to the emotions. 'Clarity, logic, balance, a happy medium,
such were to be the characteristics of the art of this period. It
respected antiquity but not too much, taking practical necessities
more and more into account, and combining good sense with
reason.'[1]

None the less, the sky-line of Paris owes much to the intrusion of
Baroque motifs. In Jacques Lemercier's chapel of the Sorbonne
the ribs of the drum are heavily emphasised, rising across the line
of the dome to the lantern where, instead of being rounded off by a

[1] P. Lavedan, *French Architecture*.

gentle cupola, they are drawn vigorously upward by a short spire to point restlessly at the heavens. The effect of this, and of the façade, is both impressive and exuberant, and Richelieu ordered the Place de la Sorbonne to be cleared in order that a better view might be obtained of it — a Baroque device if ever there was one. In 1645 Anne of Austria commissioned François Mansart, the first of a famous dynasty of French architects, to design the convent and chapel of the Val-de-Grâce. Within a year he had run into so many difficulties with his patron and his work that he was replaced by Lemercier, though his plans were largely carried out, in particular those for a dramatic dome whose lofty line was achieved by constructing a false timber dome above the masonry of the inner shell. This same device was adopted by Hardouin-Mansart, François's great-nephew, for the splendid church of Les Invalides which combines classical proportion and elegance with Baroque magnificence. The two storeys of the façade are correctly articulated with Doric and Ionic orders, but not only is the line of the façade advanced in four stages, culminating with the four columns of the portico, but the columns themselves stand freely away from the walls. Above the façade soars the great dome which, for all its air of ordered serenity, is, upon analysis, wholly unconventional. With its double drum, itself a novel feature, it accounts for more than half the total height of the church so that the facade appears to be reduced to the level of a podium; while above the classic line of the dome, for all its Gothic associations, stands a simple spire. But none of this is apparent: the contrasts, the novelty, the medley of features are combined so skilfully that the total effect is one of grace and ordered majesty.

In domestic architecture, the Palais du Luxembourg represented the most typical French palace. Built for Marie de Medici, its main buildings are flanked by two projecting wings to form a *cour d'honneur*, which is closed on the fourth side by a screen. At first this was also to have been the plan for the Louvre, but its history was chequered by many delays and alterations: between 1610 and 1664 the Louvre was extended from two small buildings forming a right angle to an entirely square block around a courtyard. The problem was then to design a façade which would be majestic enough for so important a palace, and Bernini was called in in 1665 to solve it. His plans did not reflect the style of his Roman churches. Relying on the effect of unadorned mass, he proposed to leave the basement and ground floor to run the full length of the palace without decoration, to link the second and third storeys by a series of giant columns detached from the walls, and to crown the façade with a terraced roof ornamented with balustrades and statuary. In front of it all he planned to create a colossal square. By 1667, however, after Bernini's return to Rome, his plans had been replaced by those of Charles Perrault. The flat unbroken line of the façade and the balustraded roof were preserved, but Perrault reduced the other features to a more restrained design. The ground floor, with regular tall windows, became a podium for a single great storey with a free-standing colonnade of pillars grouped in pairs. Baroque principles were thus reconciled to the classical, rational mood of French architecture, and cool formality took the place of impetuous grandeur.

Traditionally, the rejection of the Baroque in French domestic architecture is identified with the decision to adopt Perrault's design in place of Bernini's, but in this field Baroque influence had never been pronounced. François Mansart had introduced a subdued hint of it when he designed the Orléans wing at Blois with a curved pediment on the third storey, and with two short colonnades to round off the right angles of the courtyard. At Vaux-le-Vicomte, begun in 1657 by Louis Le Vau, the influence was more pronounced, since the ground plan was clearly suggested by that of the Palazzo Barberini designed by Carlo Maderna in Rome. Instead of the solid blocks presented to the public by earlier palaces, with an entrance to the *cour d'honneur* within, Maderna had projected the wings from the façade to create a courtyard exposed to public view, and if the wings at Vaux-le-Vicomte are only slightly projected beyond the line of the façade, the principle of the *cour d'honneur* concealed from the world is none the less rejected. Also typical of the Baroque was the landscaping of the gardens by Le Nôtre so that the flower-beds and pools, framed by two massed groups of trees, lead the eye onward to the culminating point of a grotto. The experience gained at Vaux-le-Vicomte by both La Vau, Le Nôtre, and by the painter Le Brun, was then applied at Versailles with tremendous effect, until Louis XIV expressed his preference for the classical style.[1] Only in its immensity and its landscaped gardens did Versailles remain in any sense a Baroque creation. The sense of movement was destroyed and, under Hardouin-Mansart's direction, the exciting variations of Le Vau's design were replaced

[1] Versailles is dealt with in some detail in Chapter VI, pages 240-6.

by a façade of immense but uninspiring uniformity; a criticism which reflects the fate of the fine arts generally under the absolutism of Louis XIV.

Painting in the Seventeenth Century

In the fifteenth century the Italian painter learnt to master the parts of the human body. In the sixteenth he learnt to compose a perfect figure from these parts and to find a satisfactory means of linking one figure with another in a group study. In the seventeenth he began to relate figures more successfully to their environment, to visualise the picture as a whole and not merely as the sum of its parts. Rembrandt, for example, 'was no longer conscious of painting a set of definable and therefore separable objects. His eye could pass from a figure to the floor under its feet and the wall behind it and the cloud seen through the window in the wall without being conscious of passing from one thing to another. The whole texture of his picture is one.'[1] Similarly the architects abandoned the rigid articulation of each storey in order to find ways of stressing the unity of the whole building, and also where possible to emphasise its relation to its environment. But the analogy between architecture and painting can be misleading. Though the term 'Baroque' admirably reflects the mood of certain seventeenth-century paintings, it cannot be applied so universally to Catholic art as it is to Catholic architecture. Art which is wholly Baroque is always part of a whole, a detail which loses its meaning when detached from its context in a greater architectural whole. Moreover, the differences between the styles of Rubens, Velazquez and Poussin are too complex to be resolved within a single definition.

The death of Raphael (1520) and of Michelangelo (1564) provoked a crisis in Italian art. Their very excellence inspired emulation, but so great was their genius that their work could not be surpassed. Those who followed their style fell into exaggeration, and even caricature, and what had been a sincere mode of expression degenerated into a set of artificial mannerisms. By the end of the sixteenth century, however, a new way forward was suggested by Annibale Carracci and his brothers. Having fallen under the spell of Raphael's work they too set out to recapture something of its simplicity and beauty, but they brought to the task a skill in

[1] E. Newton, *European Painting and Sculpture*. Rembrandt and the Dutch school are treated separately in Chapter VIII, pages 331-8.

using colour acquired from a study of the Venetian painters. Where Raphael had concentrated upon line they gave the emphasis to surface, and this distinction between the two styles saved the Carracci from producing mere *pastiches*: it also led to their style being termed eclectic, having as its aim the imitation of all that was best in the Tuscan and Venetian schools.

More to the point, the Carracci were especially concerned to cultivate the ideal of classical beauty. From Giotto's day it had been generally agreed that the art of painting consisted in reproducing the appearance of nature; but as nature was not always attractive the artist began to modify what he saw in the interests of beauty. Raphael, for example, had said that he had no model for his *Galatea* but, 'a certain idea', an abstraction derived from models he had considered beautiful. From this it was but a short step to the making of formulae for the creation of beauty in art as though this were an end in itself, as is shown in Carracci's altarpiece of *The Virgin Mourning Christ*. Clearly derived from Raphael is the triangular structure of the scene, and from the Venetians the technique of illumining Christ's body in a flood of light; the total effect is an idealised version of heroic beauty with not a hint of the agony or the horror of the Crucifixion. Painted as it was to be adored in the light of altar candles, it is unfair to expose it to the daylight but, lacking sincerity by its failure to recognise the truth of death, it is merely sentimental. The most prolific and the most talented of the Carracci school was Guido Reni (1575–1642). For many years he was extolled for his ability to recapture the mood of Raphael but his art, inspired by art itself rather than by life, was too self-conscious: what flowed freely in Raphael was contrived in him.

The pursuit of beauty by falsifying the truth, the sentimental evasion of ugliness and pain, angered Caravaggio (1569–1609) beyond measure, and led him to evolve a new style of painting. In place of emulating the successes of Raphael or Titian he determined to explore new country and to attempt new summits. Using the same technical skills evolved by his predecessors he deliberately chose to present the world as it was, neither bereft of beauty nor artificially redolent with it. This did not mean that he literally painted what he saw: Caravaggio's realism was expressed in a dark and vivid way, his pictures brilliantly composed, the gestures rehearsed and emphatic, and the models carefully selected. His characters, set against a background of shadows, were illumined by a

MAP I

Years War

harsh light which makes every gesture peculiarly significant, and in a manner which invites comparison with the Baroque; but, more revolutionary than the technique, was the choice of the characters themselves. Caravaggio shared the Jesuits' desire to give new life to the Bible stories and to impress the world with their immediacy. In his portraits of biblical scenes, therefore, he refused to idealise or ennoble the characters. The disciples were modelled as peasants, their features lined and their feet dirty, while Christ Himself in the *Christ at Emmaus* is a far cry from the idealised figure of the Carracci school. So accustomed, indeed, had people become to the latter tradition, that the portrayal of saints as earthly, earthy men aroused initial cries of horror and charges of blasphemy.

In France it was the classical tradition which triumphed, partly because of the French temperament which prefers form to feeling, and also because Richelieu, Colbert and Louis XIV regarded this tradition as the one most suited to a well-ordered monarchy.[1] There were significant exceptions. The Le Nain brothers pursued an independent course, wholly unaffected by the Italian schools, painting the French peasantry in a simple, sincere way which, by its frank confrontation of the spectator with the reality of peasant life, can be compared with the techniques of photography. A similar degree of social realism was also to be found in the work of Georges de La Tour (1593–1652), who learnt much from the school of Caravaggio, though his personality was too strong for his art to be wholly derivative. In *The Prisoner*, for example, the *chiaroscura*, the light from a candle illumining the two figures against the shadows, is wholly in the manner of Caravaggio, but the forms are uniquely his own since he has stylised and progressively simplified them, almost reducing them to abstract geometric shapes. The loss of individuality resulting from this elimination of superfluous detail lends a degree of ambiguity to his later work — *The Prisoner* has been variously entitled *St. Peter delivered from Prison* and *Job taunted by his Wife* — but it creates a mood of static calm far more akin to the French classical tradition than to the realist school. Against the work of these artists that of the official leaders of the classical tradition at court seems too consciously derivative to have any value of its own. Simon Vouet (1590–1649) and his pupil Eustache Le Sueur merely demonstrated that if uncontrolled

[1] For this point see above, page 93, and also page 242 for the French reception of Baroque architecture.

romanticism degenerates into sentimentality, academic adherence to classical principles too easily results in lifeless pedantry. In such an arid environment it is not surprising that two great French artists in the classical tradition, Nicholas Poussin (1594–1665) and Claude (1600–82), should have chosen to spend their lives in Italy.

In Italy Poussin tried to absorb something of the Baroque manner, but found that he could not reconcile it with his need for formal coherence, a need only satisfied by the discipline of the classical tradition. Like the Carracci he tried to purge the visual world of its imperfections and oddities, and as this involved the adoption of a criterion Poussin deliberately chose that of classical antiquity, believing that the Greeks alone had arrived at a definition of ideal beauty. His method was formally adopted in France: 'When a painter has made a drawing from the living model', said one of the academicians in a discussion of Poussin's style, 'he should make another study of the same figure on a separate sheet and should try to give it the character of an ancient statue.' In 1640 Poussin visited Paris for eighteen months; he found the French Court uncongenial and his rivals incompetent, but he secured a list of patrons for whom he worked after his return to Italy, and whose intellectual temperament and Jansenist mentality accorded well with his own. For the rest of his life he produced work in which the moral content of the story is matched by the intellectual context of the composition. Since the formal essentials of drawing and design assumed prior place in his painting, he deliberately had to tone down his use of colour lest, by its sensuous appeal to the eye it might distract the intellect. His control of his own style was supreme: 'Je n'ai rien négligé', was his boast, and as a composer he had few equals. The logical discipline to which he freely subjected himself did not however result in frigidity or sterility. Though his followers in France violently criticised the *Rubénistes*, Poussin gave to his *Bacchanals* a sense of rhythm and movement which, for all the inherent classicism of his work, is closely akin to Rubens's *Rape of Proserpine*; and there is a moving sense of poignancy in his *Death of Narcissus* and his *Mourning over the Dead Christ*.

Poussin had been attracted by the portrayal of landscape, but with Claude it became an obsession. His purpose was not so much to capture nature's moods as to show that the landscape could in itself furnish material for a satisfying picture in the classical manner, and nature itself was generalised and idealised much as Raphael had treated humanity. This process of generalisation began with a series of sketches drawn from nature with no thought of the picture but simply to learn the secrets of the landscape. Back in the studio the scene was then arranged, often with one feature overlapping another, so that an illusion of infinite depth was achieved, the eye being led back into the heart of the landscape. It was from carefully proportioned scenes such as these, the classical portrayal of a romantic ideal, that men in the eighteenth century derived their view of natural beauty, and were led to re-create it for themselves in landscaping their estates: the beauty of English parkland thus owed much to the inspiration of Claude's works.

When Claude gave narrative titles of some complexity to his pictures, such as, *The Story of how Ascanius shot the Stag of Sylvia, Daughter of Tyrrhus, Virgil, Book 7,* he was to some extent seeking to protect himself against those who thought that landscapes alone were unworthy of consideration; and the rather inadequate figures in the foreground of his landscapes seem to have been hastily added for the same reason. But there was a deeper motive for both these things. The title set the mood of the picture, by invoking an ancient legend at a point of impending crisis, and in peopling the ancient landscape of the Campagna with these ghosts from the past he deliberately refrained from making them so robust as to recall the viewer to the present. For all his classicism, Claude revealed a romantic nostalgia, heightened by the powerful use of a gentle light to touch each part of the broad landscape with an air of mystery, creating a dreamlike vision of the past. These landscapes, it has been suggested, 'are pictures of something which one would have thought it impossible to put into visual form, of what Virgil calls *lacrimae rerum,* which nobody has succeeded in translating but which means something like that mood of poetic sadness which scenes of natural beauty evoke by suggesting the passage of many centuries of human history.'[1]

Whatever the multiple and complex traditions of classicism, realism and romanticism, of portraiture and landscape, of pagan illustration and of Christian illumination, they were all absorbed and exploited by the universal zest and genius of Peter Paul Rubens. Born at Antwerp in 1577 he worked in the studios of several

[1] Ellis Waterhouse, from a B.B.C. talk, published in *The Listener,* 18th February 1960.

Flemish painters, acquiring the local tradition of Brueghel and Van Eyck with its intense love of detailed representation, until in 1600 he went to Italy. There he learnt the new techniques of colour and *chiaroscuro* and also the intellectual concepts which underlay contemporary controversy in art. After a term as court painter at Mantua, he returned home in 1608. Apart from occasional employment in diplomatic missions to Holland (1629), Spain (1628) and England (1629), which he used to become acquainted with other artists, notably Hals and Velazquez, his life was based upon Antwerp. Not only was he court painter to the Spanish Governor in the Netherlands but he established what can only be termed an 'artistic practice' which made him one of the wealthiest painters in history.

His studio closely resembled a factory, for not only did his assistants work at specialised tasks in each painting but a team of engravers made copies available for reproduction; yet without some formal division of labour Rubens could never have satisfied the demand for his work nor have successfully maintained his standards over the years. He himself would make sketches, freely painted or drawn in flowing lines, touching in the type of colour he required. These instructions given in a kind of painter's shorthand, were carried out by a staff of supremely talented assistants, some of whom, like Van Dyck, won fame in their own right. Their skill in execution, and that of Rubens's in planning, are exemplified in the *Return from Egypt*. The original drawing, recently identified in Moscow, was a rapidly executed pen and ink sketch, but so clear and implicit were its instructions that the design, the proportions and the movement are realised almost exactly in the finished work. The completed picture was always touched up by Rubens, supremely confident as he was that his own magic brushwork would bring the canvas swiftly to life and restore to it something of the unity of his first sketch. Indeed it was this technical brilliance, animated by the joyful exuberance and impassioned zest of his own nature, which gave him the power to transcend the mechanism of production. By imparting his own sincerity and vitality to the work, he ensured that it not only lived but lived as he had wished.

His style was never consciously eclectic, but so voracious were his interests and activities, so determined was he to turn his hand to everything, that he found no impediment to absorbing the dramatic sincerity of Caravaggio with the classically ordered composition of Carracci, or in blending Venetian colour with Flemish realism. What he absorbed he transmuted. In addition to buoyant energy and a sense of joy he possessed astonishing powers of invention and organisation in the grand manner: 'I confess', he wrote, 'that my natural inclination is to execute large works rather than little curiosities.' It was this which appealed to him in the commission to provide 39 ceiling paintings and 3 altarpieces for the Jesuit church of St. Ignatius Loyola in Antwerp, since, in a manner essentially Baroque, he was to be intimately involved with the architect and also with the sculptor who made the external figures. This Baroque quality is to be found for example in his *Betrothal of St. Catherine* in the sculptural, indeed architectural, treatment of space, in the light flooding in behind the Virgin, and in the throng of attendant saints and martyrs whose confused spiral pattern answers the stately counterpoint of the ascending staircase. Such a work also illustrates his capacity to introduce endless subsidiary elements without compromising or interfering with his main theme.

Rubens was gifted beyond all else with powers of observation and the ability to render what he saw in paint, an ability not confined to one genre alone. At first he paid little heed to landscapes; they scarcely lent themselves to allegory, and a painting without people offered nothing to interest him. In 1618 he referred to a painting from his studio as, 'by my hand, except for a most beautiful landscape done by the hand of a master skilful in that genre'. Nevertheless, increasingly his eye was engaged by the possibilities of landscape work. The result may be seen in the *Landscape near Moulins* in which he achieved a vivid image of an otherwise unspectacular stretch of countryside. This gift of observation explained his brilliance in portraying the nude, though his skill in the genre was not acquired without a long period of study. He began by drawing from antique models and by copying the work of other artists, of Michelangelo in particular, until from this intellectual discipline certain ideal forms emerged in his mind. With his mind thus informed he could then paint directly from nature itself, instinctively moulding nature to the patterns established in his imagination, without consciously checking the freedom of his brush. Thus 'he gave to his learned reminiscences so much of his own peculiar style and his own responsiveness to nature that we are seldom conscious of his sources'.[1] This 'peculiar style' was characterised as in all his work by a strong sense of movement, in-

[1] K. Clark, *The Nude*.

tensified in this case by rich modelling of the contours to convey a sense of solidity and weight, and thus of being truly alive. Above all else, he possessed a superb technique of rendering both the colour and the texture of flesh in which, save perhaps for Renoir, he surpassed all painters.

The ancient antithesis between flesh and spirit has led many critics to assume too readily that no artist could succeed equally with both; and Rubens's undoubted mastery of the flesh has prejudiced opinion against his spiritual subjects. Indeed his comfortable life, free from outstanding crises and sorrows, his lucrative studio techniques, and his exuberant acceptance of the world have appeared as faults to those who expect artists to sacrifice the world for their art, and who therefore hold that Rubens could never rise to the challenge of a religious theme. His *Visitation* has been described as a merely terrestial encounter, his Madonnas 'strike appropriately noble gestures but they are none the less Flemish wenches who cannot fill those gestures with meaning',[1] and Sir Joshua Reynolds commented that, 'instead of something above humanity, the spectator finds little more than mere mortals such as he meets every day.' Nevertheless, to judge Rubens as a religious painter one must stand, not before the *Visitation* or the *Assumption of the Virgin* where too many of the strictures seem to apply, but before the *Three Crosses* in the Van Beuningen Collection or the *Descent from the Cross* in Antwerp Cathedral. Different though these works are from the spirituality of, for example, a Rembrandt, and though they belong to an iconography wholly different from that of Protestantism, they yet have a pathos and a sincerity of sentiment which mark them as classics of religious art.

By way of contrast, no painter has been more wholly spiritual than El Greco (1541–1614). He eschewed the material world altogether and, after his retirement to Toledo in 1584, invoked a mood of increasingly mystic excitement, symbolised in the flame-like patterns, the elongated limbs and the shrill greens, blues and pinks, of his later works. He belonged, if indeed so individual an artist can be assigned to any category, to the Mannerist tradition of sixteenth-century Venice where he was trained, and to the tradition of Byzantine painting still preserved in his birthplace, Crete. Neither reflecting nor founding a national tradition in Spain, he remained wholly eccentric and inimitable.

[1] E. Newton, op. cit.

Born half a century later than El Greco, it was Velazquez (1599–1660) who was to dominate Spanish art in the seventeenth century. In 1613 he became a student under a minor artist Pacheco, whose daughter he married, who taught him something of the techniques of Caravaggio. His early paintings showed this interest in the naturalistic representation of things seen in a strong light, and one of these, *The Water Carrier*, won him the attention of Olivares and appointment as court painter in 1623. His work was deliberate and sober, but at court he developed a greater degree of simplicity in handling detail, and began to infuse a touch of transparency into the dark shadows which silhouetted his figures. A visit to Spain in 1628 by Rubens gave him his first opportunity to talk with an artist of greater gifts than himself, and it aroused in him a desire to broaden his experience more fully by travel to Italy. Such a visit was essential to his development since at home he was unrivalled; Ribera, Zurbaran and Murillo, his only contemporaries worthy of mention, were not only unable to match his skills but were wholly derivative in their styles. Velazquez returned home in 1631 without having modified his basic realism but with a much enlarged range of colour: 'Raphael', he wrote, 'does not please me at all. In Venice are found the good and the beautiful; to their brush I give the first place; it is Titian that bears the banner'. For the next seventeen years he was occupied with commissions at court, but a royal embassy to Italy in 1648 gave him a second opportunity to visit Naples, Rome and Venice. On this occasion he painted a vividly impressive portrait of Innocent X and was so far influenced by the new environment as to share in its enthusiasm for the female nude — an art form discouraged in the Escurial — which resulted in the *Rokeby Venus*.

In many respects Velazquez resembled the genre painters of Holland in that his work was deliberate and sober, his view of life unimpassioned. Like the Dutch too he found interest in the familiar round of ordinary events, and it was by a series of *bodegones*, scenes of everyday life, that he first made his name. Of these the *Water Carrier* was perhaps his greatest success. The action is suspended, as in a Vermeer, while attention is focused on a boy and two men, one barely visible in the shadow, the other the water carrier with his pots. The use of light is remarkable, falling on the crumpled collar of the boy and the carrier's sleeve, catching a drop of water, giving form to a glass, and revealing the texture of cloth, wood and earthenware. So satisfying is the total effect of light and texture, of balance and harmony, that the problem is less to analyse the work of art than to know exactly why it is so satisfying. Velazquez, in fact, seemed to have followed Pacheco's advice — 'I hold to the principle that Nature ought to be the chief master' — that to observe and to record is in itself art. This of course was not so. Though his pictures came to him through the eye rather than through the imagination, he did not simply copy nature. Velazquez, by instinct rather than by formal training, had a firm intellectual grasp of his work, and the *Water Carrier* is far from being a mere glimpse of everyday life. Its design is complex, the balance and counterpoint of masses contrived, and all insignificant detail has been simplified away to reveal only essentials.

This combination of the steady imperturbable eye with the unerring hand induced an element of impersonality in all but his final works, so that the subjects of his paintings are treated less as individuals to be loved or hated than as objects to be represented on his canvas. This does not make them less interesting since it was the problem of representing them which so clearly excited Velazquez, and which he solved by means of brilliant brush-work. The realism of his work is found upon analysis to be conveyed by a series of impressions so that the spectator is required to grasp his intention and to supplement it from his own imagination, a technique which was not to be fully exploited until the nineteenth century. As for the impersonality, Velazquez acquired from his second visit to Italy a much deeper interest in the problem of studying his sitters for what they were rather, than for what they seemed to be. His subsequent studies of the ageing king Philip IV, of the ladies-in-waiting, *Las Meninas*, and of the tapestry-weavers, *Las Hilanderas*, thus revealed a new dimension to his work, a greater sense of atmosphere and more sensitive appreciation of character.

II

The Thirty Years War

THE BACKGROUND TO THE CONFLICT

The Peace of Augsburg

The Peace of Augsburg, which followed upon Charles V's abdication in 1555, revealed two facts of great importance: the
Lutheran Church was firmly established in Germany, and the
princes, Catholic and Lutheran alike, were too strong to be overawed by imperial authority. The principle of *cuius regio, eius
religio*, adopted at Augsburg, meant that throughout the Holy
Roman Empire the inhabitants were to accept the religious views,
not of the emperor but of their local ruler. This, of course, was
virtually what had happened already. For many of the princes,
who had fought each other for a generation or more, the Peace
represented a practical compromise. It was in no way an Edict of
Toleration since it did nothing more than sanction an existing
state of affairs. This was its main weakness. Once the situations of
1555 were to be altered in any way the settlement would
collapse.

The Peace was not designed, for example, to withstand the
vigorous and disruptive forces which were being unleashed by the
Counter-Reformation on the one hand, and the Calvinist Church
of Geneva on the other.[1] The Council of Trent, meeting at various
intervals between 1545 and 1563, did much to reaffirm those basic
tenets of Catholic theology which had been challenged by Luther,
and ensured that every member of the Church should know the
dividing line between true doctrine and heresy. By rejecting any
compromise with Lutheranism, the Council strengthened both the
will to resist it and the missionary impulse to overcome it. This
new spirit was to have a disturbing influence on the Catholic
princes. Many of them, who might well have sat on the fence with
their Lutheran neighbours, were urged by their confessors to
become more active and aggressive in the Catholic cause. As for the

[1] See Chapter I, pages 71–73, for a general account of religious controver-
sies in this period,

Lutherans, it was not long before they lost the initiative to the Calvinists, whose revolutionary Protestantism perplexed and alarmed them almost as much as the new assault from Rome. The Calvinist, strengthened by the coherence of his doctrine and secure in the assurance of predestined salvation, was better fitted than the Lutheran to oppose the militancy of the Counter-Reformation. In defeat he withstood persecution; in victory he offered no toleration. Under the pressure of these new forces, the Augsburg settlement could offer no sure ground for future peace.

One of the great attractions of Lutheranism for many German princes was the opportunity it provided to seize the estates of the Catholic Church. The Diet of Augsburg had been silent on the matter, but Charles V, of his own authority, had laid down a ruling in the so-called 'Ecclesiastical Reservation' confirming the secular-isation of all property seized before 1552, but prohibiting it for the future. Futhermore, if any abbot or bishop were to join the Lutheran Church, he was to forfeit his estates immediately to a Catholic successor. In 1555 this compromise was reasonable: by 1600 its application had become intolerable. The Lutheran would not permit the rich enclaves of a rival religion to exist within his own territory, and he sought by one device or another to establish control over them.[1] The Catholic could not stand by unmoved when, year by year, more and more church land fell into the hands of heretics. It was a process which threatened the very survival of Catholicism in Germany.

In 1577, for example, the Archbishop-Elector of Cologne an-nounced not only his conversion to Lutheranism but also his determination to retain the Electoral title, marry a nun, secularise his diocese and make it an hereditary possession. If he were allowed to succeed in this, the Archbishop-Electors of Trier and Mainz might eventually follow suit, and conclude the affair by voting for a Protestant emperor. It was an alarming prospect for the Catholic princes. In the event, they managed to forestall the archbishop's plan, but they could do nothing to prevent the less dramatic trans-fer of such wealthy bishoprics as Magdeburg, Bremen and Halber-stadt to Lutheran control. By 1600 a strong Lutheran *bloc* had

---

[1] One device adopted by Lutheran princes was to introduce younger sons and reliable agents into a cathedral chapter until there were enough to secure the election of a Protestant bishop. Such a bishop could not be canonically invested, but he would be able to administer the revenues of the diocese on behalf of his prince.

been created in north Germany, and it was not surprising that many Catholics welcomed the possibility of renewed warfare. Only in this way might the territories, and the subjects, of a Lutheran prince be restored to the Catholic Church.

Finally, the Peace of Augsburg so clearly reflected the impotence of the emperor that any subsequent revival of his authority would immediately threaten the settlement and prejudice its chance of survival. Such a contingency seemed unlikely since the Catholic princes were as eager as the Lutherans to prevent any extension of imperial control; so much so that a triumph for their church was unwelcome to the Catholics if it also augmented the emperor's power. At the same time, the authority which the Habsburgs exercised in Germany was not based entirely upon their imperial status: their vast possessions, including Austria, Bohemia and Hungary, made them the greatest single power in Central Europe. They had many serious problems to contend with,[1] but if ever their possessions could be organised into an effective single unit, the Habsburgs might intervene in German affairs with commanding force.

The Formation of Leagues and the Jülich–Cleves Problem

The personal hostility and rivalry between the German princes was given a more definite and organised form as the result of an incident at Donauwörth in 1606. A Catholic minority within the city organised a religious procession in defiance of a ban imposed by the Lutheran Council. Naturally enough, a riot broke out in the streets. The Emperor Rudolf II seized upon this as a pretext to assert his authority and ordered an inquiry to be made. His next move was unexpected, and quite contrary to the terms of the Augsburg settlement. The Lutherans were blamed for the riot, the privileges of the city were therefore revoked, and a Catholic majority created in the council. As Donauwörth lay within the Swabian Circle[2] of the Empire, whose director was also a Lutheran, the emperor decided to make his action more effective by transferring the city to the Bavarian Circle. That is to say, he left it at the mercy of Maximilian of Bavaria, one of the most zealous champions of the Counter-Reformation.

[1] See below, page 113, and also Chapter IX, pages 355-8.
[2] In the sixteenth century the Empire had been divided into ten administrative areas known as 'Circles'. The Swabian Circle included Württemberg, Baden, the bishopric of Augsburg, and many imperial cities.

Such a violation of the Peace of Augsburg had an immediate effect on the Protestants. Many Lutheran and Calvinist princes, despite the doctrinal differences which separated them, combined to form the Evangelical Union in 1608, with Frederick Elector Palatine, as their leader. In many ways Frederick was an unfortunate choice. As a Calvinist he was eager to organise resistance against the emperor, and his Electoral title singled him out as a prince of great importance. Unfortunately he was timorous of heart, and far too dependent upon others for counsel. His Chancellor, Christian of Anhalt, was a man of supreme self-confidence and charm, whose ambition for himself and his master knew no bounds. It was he who had engineered the Union and secured its leadership for the Elector. There were many who would have preferred to see the Lutheran Electors of Brandenburg and Saxony at their head, but for the time being both these princes stood aloof from the conflict. Lulled, perhaps, into a false sense of security by the importance of their own position, they refused to believe that the situation was as critical as the other Protestants maintained. John George of Saxony, indeed, had no sympathy at all for the Calvinists and was not prepared to jeopardise the Peace of Augsburg on their behalf. Conservative and afraid of change, he remained obstinately loyal to a settlement which was no longer viable. More wisely, he foresaw that the formation of the Union would provoke the Catholics to greater hostility, and he mistrusted the motives of Henry IV of France, who had promised to act as the Union's patron.[1]

Within twelve months the Catholics had organised their own league with Maximilian of Bavaria at its head, thus carefully excluding the emperor. Maximilian was as hostile to the extension of imperial authority as any Lutheran or Calvinist, and he intended that the League should not only safeguard the Catholic cause but also provide a counterweight to Habsburg power in Germany. Rudolf watched his activity with some suspicion, but his cousin, Philip III of Spain, was more enthusiastic. His ambassador had played a secret part in the original negotiations, and Philip promised to give the Catholic League financial support provided its policies were approved by the emperor.

As the Elector of Saxony had foreseen, the formation of leagues only served to heighten the tension within the Empire, and in 1609 there came a crisis. The Catholic Duke of Jülich and Cleves died

[1] See Chapter III, page 173.

without direct heirs, his duchies being claimed by two Lutherans, Philip Ludwig of Neuburg and the Elector of Brandenburg. The Catholics realised from the start that, whoever triumphed in the dispute, the fertile regions of the lower Rhine and the Ruhr would pass into Protestant hands. Nor was this the full extent of the problem. The fortresses of Jülich controlled the Rhine crossing, and thus threatened the last link in the tenuous line of communications which the Spanish Habsburgs had created between Milan and Brussels. The emperor occupied the duchies with his own troops, pending arbitration, but the Protestants interpreted this as a device to exclude the Lutheran candidates and establish a Catholic succession. Immediately they confirmed their alliance with Henry IV, while Spain renewed its promise of support to the Catholic League.

The assassination of Henry IV in May 1610 completely altered the situation. The Evangelical Union did not dare to stand alone against the Catholic League, the emperor and Spain; nor was there any hope that France would continue Henry IV's policy since his widow, Marie de Medici, sought an immediate *rapprochement* with Spain.[1] As the tension eased, another unexpected event paved the way for a compromise: Philip Ludwig's son chose to marry the daughter of Maximilian of Bavaria and announced his conversion to Catholicism. The Catholic powers could now support him in his claims, while the Evangelical Union stood by the Elector of Brandenburg. Eventually, by the Treaty of Xanten (1614) both sides agreed to a partition of the duchies, Cleves being assigned to Brandenburg and Jülich to Philip Ludwig's son.

A major war was, for the moment, averted, but the crisis had revealed that any conflict between the Evangelical Union and the Catholic League could not be confined to the empire alone. The situation in Germany was closely linked with the dynastic rivalry between Bourbon and Habsburg. From Flanders, Franche-Comté, Italy and the Pyrenees, the French were constantly threatened by Spanish armies. There were occasional gaps in the encircling ring of Habsburg possessions, but the general effect was to induce a sensation of claustrophobia which had moved Henry IV to welcome any opportunity to break through to the Rhine. Such had been his intention in 1610. His sudden death, however, led to an easing of this greater conflict until the emergence of Richelieu, fourteen years later.

[1] See Chapter III, page 173.

The Treaty of Xanten was followed by a lull in German affairs. The League, the Union and the emperor remained perpetually suspicious of each other's intentions, but nothing arose to disturb the peace until the Bohemian revolt broke out in 1618.

The Bohemian Revolt

In 1617 the agents of the Elector Palatine reported that the Habsburg monarchy in Austria was about to collapse. There was some justification for their opinion. The vast dominion which the Habsburgs had extended over Austria, Carinthia, Carniola, the Tyrol, Styria, Bohemia and Hungary seemed to be hopelessly divided on linguistic, racial and religious grounds. There was no central body to control the empire as a whole, nor had the Habsburgs established their authority effectively within each separate territory.[1] In Hungary, for example, the Ottoman Turks occupied most of the kingdom while the Magyar nobility remained virtually independent in what was left of it, but it was Bohemia which presented the most immediate and the most serious problem of all.

Rudolf II (1576–1612) had not proved an effective ruler of the Habsburg lands. In his younger days he did much to suppress Lutheranism in his Austrian provinces, but after 1600 his faculties began to fail. Alarmed by his inept handling of a Hungarian revolt in 1605, the family decided that his brother Matthias should take over most of the government and Rudolf was left with only the kingdom of Bohemia. His position as emperor was in no way affected: it was simply a family device to keep the old man out of harm's way. But Bohemia, with its attendant provinces of Moravia, Silesia and Lusatia was not an easy kingdom to rule. There were four separate capitals and four separate Diets which kept alive a strong tradition of local autonomy. Germans and Catholics were to be found in Prague and a few other cities, but the population was predominantly Slav and generally Protestant.[2] As in Hungary, the monarchy was elective and the Habsburgs had to pay some deference to local customs and privileges in order to ensure the suc-

[1] For a fuller treatment of the Habsburg monarchy see Chapter IX.

[2] The religious situation was remarkably complex. Five major sects existed: the Lutherans; the Calvinists; the Hussites, who observed the doctrine of the fifteenth-century Bohemian reformer John Hus; the Bohemian Brethren, evangelical and apocalyptic, living by the social teaching of the Gospels; the Utraquists, who were, to all intents and purposes, Catholic in doctrine, except for their custom of admitting the laity to both the bread and the wine in communion.

cession of their family. The threat of rebellion was very real. It was this, in fact, which forced Rudolf to appease his subjects even further by granting to them the Letter of Majesty (1609), which allowed much greater independence to the separate Diets and also provided a measure of religious toleration. Separatism, nationalism and heresy went hand in hand.

Ideally, the Habsburgs longed to establish a centralised regime, staffed by German officials, to implement the decrees of the government in Vienna and to further the progress of the Counter-Reformation. To prevent this, the Bohemians took shelter behind the traditional liberties and franchises of each province, each Diet, each class and each city. The Letter of Majesty strengthened their defences.

The Letter was not destined, however, to survive for long; its only guarantee being the inability of the crown to get its own way. Once the Habsburgs intensified their hold over the country, the terms of 1609 would be whittled down. Matthias hoped that he could be the man to do this when he succeeded Rudolf in 1612, but he was already old and preoccupied with the problem of choosing his own successor. He selected the Archduke Ferdinand as the most able man to follow him and then took steps to secure his election to the thrones not only of Bohemia but also of Hungary and the Holy Roman Empire. In each case it was traditional to elect a Habsburg but the succession was never automatic. As a result, Matthias dared not act too vigorously in Bohemia to undo his brother's work lest the Estates should retaliate by rejecting his choice of Ferdinand. The little he did do, by introducing more Germans into the central government at Prague, and by attempting to exert greater authority over the separate provinces, was almost too much. The Bohemians awaited the election with alarm and resentment.

Ferdinand of Styria was, in private, a cheerful man with freckles and sandy hair, who beamed reassurance on all his courtiers; in public, 'one of the boldest and most single-minded politicians that the Habsburg dynasty ever produced,'[1] a remorseless enemy of heresy. He had already shown his abilities as the ruler of Styria, where the Lutherans had been suppressed and the voice of the Estates silenced. There was no doubt that in his hands the Habsburg territories would be transformed into a more effective and

[1] C. V. Wedgwood, *The Thirty Years War*, p. 58.

MAP 2   Bohemia and its Neighbours

coherent empire. Why, then, did the Bohemian nobles accept this ominous candidate as the heir-designate in 1617? In part they feared the consequences of electing anyone else, and there were many who, out of inertia, accepted the traditional right of a Habsburg to rule Bohemia. Above all, they were disunited and could not agree on an alternative candidate. When Ferdinand promised to observe the Letter of Majesty, even though few believed him, there was no further obstacle to his election.

Once the election was over, Matthias felt free at last to act without too much regard for local opinion. Thurn, a prominent Calvinist, was deprived of all his posts, and when Matthias left Bohemia to supervise the election in Hungary, the Catholics were given a majority in the council of regents. They were led by Martinitz and Slavata, men of particular ability, eager to extend the authority of the central government and to suppress heresy. Their first act was to order the surrender of all religious foundations to the purpose originally intended by their founders. At one stroke, the churches which the Protestants had taken over, along with their endowments, were restored to the Catholics. If the Protestants had been disorganised and at a loss during Ferdinand's election, this all too intelligible and specific attack on their religion provoked them to rebellion. In Thurn they found a leader, in the Letter of Majesty a cause. A series of public meetings demonstrated the unpopularity of the regents, and on May 22nd, 1618, a strongly supported deputation marched on the Hradcany Palace in Prague. Invigorated by the thrill of rebellion, and well aware of their most dangerous enemies, Thurn and his colleagues hurled both Martinitz and Slavata from the palace window. Their twenty-foot fall was broken by a pile of rubbish and dirt, and, astonishingly, neither was seriously hurt.

The significance of this celebrated defenestration was immediately apparent. By assaulting the regents, the rebels had challenged the emperor's authority and there was no chance to retreat. The Bohemian Estates, therefore, set up a directory of thirty deputies to administer the kingdom, appointed Thurn commander-in-chief, and called upon the provinces of Silesia, Lusatia and Moravia to join the revolt. In July, 1619, the Act of Confederation created a new constitution. Each province was to be independent, and Protestants were to occupy all the important offices of government. Ferdinand could never be expected to agree to such terms, and it was clear that the rebels only awaited the opportunity to renounce him altogether. The Habsburg monarchy was damned twice over in Bohemian eyes: it threatened them with religious persecution, and with subordination to the dictates of German officials from Vienna. The revolt was a last, desperate gamble to preserve for Bohemia an independent existence.

The Prelude to War

Matthias died in March 1619. To the end he had laid a restraining hand on Ferdinand, vainly trying to conciliate the rebels without actually conceding anything, and with his death the revolt reached its climax. When Ferdinand refused to give his consent to the Act of Confederation, the Estates renounced their allegiance to him. The throne of Bohemia was declared vacant.

This was a matter of particular importance to Ferdinand since the King of Bohemia was one of the seven Electors who were about to choose a successor to Matthias as Holy Roman Emperor. Ferdinand was the strongest candidate, certain of support from the three archbishop-electors, but there were also the three Protestants of Saxony, Brandenburg and the Palatinate who had the right to vote. If they had exploited the occasion of the Bohemian revolt to put forward another candidate, the long succession of Habsburg Emperors might have been broken. Instead, they were unable to agree among themselves and eventually cast their votes for Ferdinand, who was thus elected unanimously on August 28th, 1619. It was characteristic of him that he ignored the presumption of the rebels by insisting on his right, as King of Bohemia, to vote for himself.

Meanwhile, the Bohemian Estates cast about them for a new king and an offer was made to Frederick, the Elector Palatine. He consulted his council, the princes of the Evangelical Union, and his father-in-law, James I of England. In turn, they all advised him to reject the proposal; but there were voices nearer home which carried greater weight. His wife Elizabeth, like her father in England, was greatly attached to the divinity with which kings were encompassed, and she urged him to take the crown. Christian of Anhalt, as ambitious and self-confident as ever, added his opinion to hers. Finally, for all his timidity, the anguished searching of his own conscience led Frederick to accept the trust reposed in him by the Bohemians, and to risk all for the Protestant cause: 'It is a divine calling which I must not disobey . . . my only end is to serve God and His Church.' Religious fervour and political ambition were so closely interrelated in the minds, not only of Frederick, but of Ferdinand, of Maximilian and of nearly all the great leaders in the conflict which followed, that it would be rash to accuse the Elector of self-deception. In the Thirty Years War, the cause of religon was something more than a mere rallying cry to the masses. Princes were often self-seeking but the defence of their faith was as much a matter of self-interest as the acquisition of territory, influence and power. There were few who could remain coolly dispassionate in the clash of confessions.

With the election of Ferdinand as emperor, and the acceptance of the Bohemian crown by Frederick, the Thirty Years War began. The Bohemian revolt drew into it all the hostile elements which had been preparing for battle in Germany for the last twenty years. It was the occasion rather than the cause of the conflict. Nor may the war be considered within a framework of Germany alone. All the major European powers were sucked into the vortex, whereas many German states, Saxony for example, were directly involved for only a few years. Spain, with its vested interest in the Habsburg family and the Catholic Church; France, ready to resume under

Richelieu's direction the aggressive, expansionist policies of Henry IV; Sweden, ambitious to establish control of the Baltic; Denmark, determined to gain territory in north Germany; the United Provinces, eager to safeguard their new-found independence. All these states found good reason to intervene in the war, and it was their action which prolonged it. Theirs, in fact, was a greater conflict which took little account of the interests of the German princes. Against this wider background may be seen, not a Thirty Years War, but a struggle for power which was not resolved until long after the Peace of Westphalia had ended the warfare in Germany.

THE IMPERIAL VICTORIES, 1619-29

The Conquest of Bohemia and the Palatinate, 1619-23

In October 1619 Frederick arrived in Prague, and the Bohemians, after an initial display of enthusiasm, began to examine him more critically. Timid and even fatalistic, he had none of the qualities required in a leader of rebels and he failed to inspire much affection. The Slav population became suspicious of the Germans who filled his court, the Lutherans were affronted by his extreme Calvinist views, and worst of all, he arrived without effective support. The governments of Sweden, Denmark, Venice and the United Provinces had only recognised his title to spite the emperor; of his colleagues in the Evangelical Union, many were alarmed at the rashness of his action, and the remainder suspected that he had not the ability to stay the course. His one ally was Bethlen Gabor, the strange Calvinist ruler of Transylvania, who suddenly erupted from the far side of Hungary to strike a blow against the Habsburgs and claim the Hungarian crown. With Thurn and the Bohemian army he had advanced up the Danube during the summer of 1619, but after threatening the frontiers of Austria the troops returned to Prague for the winter.

Ferdinand, for all his galaxy of titles, was unable to recover Bohemia on his own, but soon found a way to attract allies to his cause. By his sedition, Frederick could be said to have forfeited his titles and his lands, and Ferdinand was free enough with them during the next six months. He promised the Upper Palatinate, together with Frederick's Electoral title, to Maximilian of Bavaria; the Lower Palatinate, west of the Rhine, was offered to Spain, and Lusatia to John George of Saxony. Thus the armies of the Catholic

League, of Spinola in the Netherlands, and of Saxony were at Ferdinand's disposal. John George's action might seem to have been unexpected, even unscrupulous, but he had no reason to endanger the Lutheran cause and his own solid gains on behalf of a Calvinist prince whose actions he condemned as rash and inexcusable. His view was even shared by the Evangelical Union, for when the Catholic League offered to respect the neutrality of the Protestant states, the princes of the Union agreed to remain inactive.

The campaigns began in the autumn of 1620 and Frederick was swiftly overwhelmed. Spinola invaded the Lower Palatinate, John George seized Lusatia, and on November 8th the Bohemians were defeated by the army of the Catholic League at the Battle of White Mountain, near Prague. It was the first great battle of the Thirty Years War, and the most decisive. Bethlen Gabor renounced his claim to Hungary and withdrew to the remote strongholds of Transylvania; Frederick, deserted even by the citizens of Prague, fled to Germany, and the rebels had no choice but to submit. The desperate attempt to preserve their traditions and liberties had failed, and Ferdinand was free to exploit his victory to the full.

The subjection of Bohemia and its transformation into an obedient province of the Austrian empire were achieved in the years which followed the Battle of White Mountain. No mercy was shown to the rebel leaders, most of whom were executed. As for the Protestants, their clergy were outlawed, their chapels destroyed and their schools and universities taken over by the Jesuits. The progressive debasement of the coinage destroyed the wealth of the cities, and over half the land was confiscated and sold. In this it was the speculator rather than the emperor who reaped the immediate profit, but in the long run Ferdinand's own ends were also served. With the nobility deprived of its estates, the townsmen ruined by the currency changes, and the peasants burdened with the troops of the victorious army, the kingdom might be worth little as a source of revenue, but its inhabitants were in no condition to oppose their sovereign, especially as the new landowning class was predominantly Catholic and German in its outlook. In 1627, when a new constitution was drawn up, Ferdinand's triumph was complete: the Letter of Majesty was annulled, the succession to the throne vested in Ferdinand's heirs, the power of the Estates curtailed, and the combination of Germanic custom and Roman law as practised in Austria was applied to Bohemia. As a final blow to local patriotism, the Chancellor was to travel with the King; in other words, Vienna was to be the effective centre of Bohemia's administration. It remained so for nearly three centuries.

Meanwhile, Frederick's hold of the Palatinate was weakened with every month. Spinola had already occupied the provinces of the Rhine, and in 1620 Tilly, with the Catholic League army, invaded the Upper Palatinate. Once again Frederick fled from the combat, taking refuge in the United Provinces which were then at war with Spain.[1] The reversal of his fortunes had been so swift, the triumph of his enemies so alarming, that at last he found allies. Maurice of Nassau, Stadtholder of the United Provinces, and one of the finest soldiers in Europe, came to his aid with a Dutch army; and Christian of Brunswick, who made much of his romantic, if innocent, attachment to Frederick's wife, rushed to her defence in a flurry of chivalrous enthusiasm, his banners bearing the device, 'For God and For Her'. Maurice, however, dared not leave his country undefended for long, and Christian was no match for Tilly. There was also the professional mercenary captain, Ernst Mansfeld, but his services to Frederick were of little value. He had proved singularly ineffective in Bohemia, and his activities in the Rhineland were more harmful to the inhabitants than to the enemy. By the winter of 1623 the Palatinate had been overrun.

It was clear that Ferdinand's success had enhanced his authority, both as ruler of the Habsburg kingdoms and as Holy Roman Emperor, and a reaction of some sort was to be expected. For the moment it was only a mild one. The Imperial Diet, meeting at Regensburg in 1623, opposed his action in transferring the Electoral title from Frederick to Maximilian. The Protestants, of course, objected to the clear majority created for the Catholics in the Electoral College, but the Catholic princes also had reason to protest. Any extension of Ferdinand's power was a threat to their own, and such a dramatic use of imperial authority was alarming. A compromise was arrived at by which Maximilian was to retain the title for his own lifetime, but when he died the Diet, not the emperor, should determine the succession.

The Conflict Extended, 1624–9

With the suppression of the Bohemian revolt and the expulsion of Frederick from the Palatinate, the war might well have ended.

[1] See Chapter IV, page 192.

MAP 3   The Val Telline

Unfortunately for Germany the tension was heightened, the area of conflict broadened, by the intervention of France and Denmark.

Henry IV had realised that France could never be secure until the long line of Spanish bases which encircled her frontiers had been destroyed. For this reason he had planned to intervene in the dispute over Jülich–Cleves. His widow, however, preferred to seek security in friendship with Spain, and it was not until the control of affairs passed into the hands of Cardinal Richelieu, in 1624, that Henry's policy was revived. France was in no way strong enough to challenge Spain outright, for her own resources had been wasted in the prolonged series of internal conflicts which had characterised Marie de Medici's regency;[1] but Richelieu believed that much might be gained from cautious interference with the Spanish lines of communication between Italy and the Netherlands. It was a wise policy for it threatened Spain at her weakest point, at a time when her war with the Dutch had been resumed. Two routes led north from Milan; one through Savoy to Franche Comté, the other along the valley of the Adda, through the Val Telline into the Tyrol. The first could not be relied upon as Charles Emmanuel of Savoy was

[1] See Chapter III, page 151.

an unstable ally and the route was open to French attack from
Lyons. It was all the more necessary, therefore, to keep the Val
Telline open and it was there that Richelieu chose to intervene.
The villagers of the Val Telline were Catholic, but control of the
pass was often contested by the Protestants of the Grisons, a
Swiss canton near to its upper reaches. As recently as 1622 they had
been defeated by the Governor of Milan, but, encouraged by
Richelieu, they renewed their attack. In December 1624 they
seized Tirano and blocked the Val Telline. Savoy and Venice joined
France in promising aid to the Grisons, and Spain was faced with
disaster. She could not supply her troops in the Netherlands, her
communication with the Austrian Habsburgs was cut, and her own
control of Milan was threatened by an invasion from Savoy. The
excellence of Richelieu's policy was evident; it was all the more
bitter for him that he should now fail on account of dissension
within France. His tenure of office at this stage was still insecure,
court intrigues threatened his life, and a Huguenot rising compelled him to recall his troops from north Italy.[1] Savoy and Venice
had to be abandoned, the Grisons renounced, and a treaty concluded at Monzon in 1626, which left the Spaniards free to recover
the Val Telline without interference.

Richelieu's failure to seize control of the Val Telline was to have
important results for the future, but more immediate and dramatic
in its impact on Germany was the Danish invasion of 1626.
Christian IV was an able and energetic Lutheran with a position of
some importance in north Germany. Apart from his kingdom of
Denmark, he possessed the duchy of Holstein, within the lower
Saxon Circle of the empire, and the princes of this Circle had
elected him as director. His declared intent was the restoration of
the Elector Palatine but in fact he wanted to create a Danish enclave
to the south of Holstein by the seizure of land formerly held by the
Catholic Church. His son had been elected to the vacant see of
Verden, Halberstadt had been purchased from Christian of Brunswick, and he cast an avid eye on Minden and Osnabrück. It was
true that the successes of the Catholic powers threatened the very
existence of these territories, secularised against the terms of the
Ecclesiastical Reservation, but the Protestant princes of north
Germany had no desire to assist the expansion of Denmark. They
too wanted bishoprics for their sons, and Christian, with his sharp

[1] See Chapter III, page 155.

appetite for Catholic plunder, could not expect to be received with any enthusiasm. The only German to welcome him was Mansfeld, urgently in need of a new paymaster.

Unfortunately for Christian, the Catholic powers were now stronger than ever. Ferdinand's successes had been entirely due to the army of the Catholic League, and he had realised that so long as he remained dependent upon the troops of any German prince his power would be illusory. Some new weapon, therefore, was needed and in 1625 he found the man to forge it: Albrecht von Waldstein, more generally known as Wallenstein, offered to raise 50,000 men for the imperial service. Wallenstein was one of the most intriguing characters of the war. A Bohemian and a Protestant by birth, he had been educated by the Jesuits when his parents died, and had entered Ferdinand's service when the latter was Archduke of Styria. Superstitious and subservient to the potency of the horoscope, he nevertheless ignored all religious matters, considering them a distraction from the main issue of profiting from the conflicts they aroused. The suppression of Bohemia made his fortune. He became the military governor of Prague and speculated in the sale of confiscated estates until he finally controlled nearly a quarter of the kingdom. His estates were run systematically to provide corn for the Catholic League's army, and the profits from this went to embellish the grandiose palace he constructed in Prague. Bohemia, however, could not contain his soaring ambitions and he now prepared to invest his great wealth in the imperial cause.

What distinguished Wallenstein from the ordinary run of mercenary captains was his business acumen and the scope of his ambitions. As the north German princes were to discover, he planned to maintain his army by the systematic extortion of enforced contributions from Catholic and Protestant states alike, instead of the usual indiscriminate looting by troops; in times of adversity he could always fall back upon the imperial treasury and his own Bohemian granaries to provide it with pay and food. But it was not so much the manner of running his army which so alarmed his contemporaries, as his plans for its use. These have always been the subject of debate but, broadly speaking, he planned to establish the emperor as the all-powerful and central authority in Germany. Catholic and Protestant alike were to be forced into obedience, and the imperial writ made effective from the Danube to the Baltic, from Bohemia to the Rhine. For himself, Wallenstein

E2

intended to reap financial profit, more territory and a title of distinction among the German princes. So comprehensive and audacious was the plan that Ferdinand himself hesitated to approve it. At first he limited Wallenstein's commission to Bohemia alone and agreed to an army of only 20,000. The Danish invasion, however, compelled him to allow his agent a greater freedom of action.

In 1626 Christian engaged the army of the Catholic League in Westphalia, hoping to leave Mansfeld free to cross Germany and strike at Vienna. But Mansfeld found the way barred by Wallenstein. He was first defeated as he crossed the Elbe at Dessau, and although he slipped eastwards through the territory of Brandenburg, Wallenstein anticipated his action and overtook him in Silesia. The threat to Vienna was removed; and when Mansfeld died suddenly of phthisis, Wallenstein was able to send 8,000 men to assist Tilly and the Catholic League's army. In August Tilly defeated Christian at Lutter.

Wallenstein was now convinced that the time had come to establish both the emperor's authority along the Baltic coastline and his own reputation as a soldier. He could not expect the Catholic League to approve his plans; the League was fighting to recover the north German dioceses, not to extend imperial power — an issue reflected in the personal rivalry between himself and Tilly — but luck was with him. When the Catholic armies combined to invade Denmark in 1627, Tilly was wounded, leaving Wallenstein free to act on his own. No time was wasted. He overran the Danish mainland and then turned eastwards to Pomerania, seizing for himself the duchy of Mecklenburg. All this time he recruited more troops until by 1628 he commanded at least 125,000 men. With such a force, maintained by contributions ruthlessly levied on all the north German states, save Mecklenburg of course, there seemed no power to equal him. Wismar and Rostock were captured and only Stralsund remained outside his control. In July 1628 this too was attacked. It was a critical moment in Wallenstein's career, and he failed.

Stralsund, defended on three sides by the sea, was not an easy place to besiege, but its survival was mainly due to the sudden intervention of Gustavus II Adolphus, King of Sweden. Like Christian, he too was a Lutheran, but the dynastic rivalry of Sweden and Denmark prevented them from undertaking any joint enterprise against the Catholic powers. In any case, Gustavus was committed to warfare in Poland.[1] The attack on Stralsund, however, along with the threat of imperial and Catholic control of Pomerania, could not be overlooked: aid was sent to the city and Wallenstein was compelled to abandon the siege.

Denmark was the first to benefit from this reverse. Christian's defeat had left him little to bargain with, but the resistance of Stralsund and the possibility of further Swedish activity made his neutrality of some value. Wallenstein advised the emperor to make peace, and at Lübeck, in 1629, a treaty was signed. Christian forfeited his claims to the north German bishoprics and resigned his position as director of the Lower Saxon Circle. In return, however, he was restored to all his Danish possessions and released from the payment of any indemnity.

The Edict of Restitution: the Climax of Imperial Power, 1629

Wallenstein's deliberate and methodical exactions from the north German princes had caused widespread protest, and the Catholic princes were as alarmed by his successes as were the Protestants. In October 1627 Maximilian had summoned a special meeting of the Electors at Mülhausen to protest against Wallenstein's conduct of the war. The Electors realised only too well that these same troops might one day be directed against themselves. Ferdinand himself began to wonder how far he could control his own agent; in the face of so much opposition it might be politic to disown him, particularly after the failure at Stralsund. On the other hand, he was heavily in debt to Wallenstein and he needed an army so long as his plans remained incomplete. It was not only a question of the Baltic coastline. While the Peace of Lübeck was being negotiated, Ferdinand, fired by Wallenstein's achievements, contemplated the greatest gamble of his life.

Ferdinand's plan was nothing less than the wholesale enforcement of the Augsburg settlement: revolutionary in its implications, this involved the outlawry of Calvinism and the surrender of all land seized from the Church since 1555. At one stroke the boundaries of Germany were to be redrawn. The princes whose power depended on the secularised territories would be condemned to insignificance, their subjects to Catholicism. But this was not all, for otherwise the Catholic League would have applauded the emperor's zeal. When Ferdinand issued the Edict of Restitution

[1] See Chapter X, page 384.

in March 1629 he did so without reference to the Diet, and in terms which exalted the theory of imperial absolutism. The archbishoprics of Magdeburg and Bremen, twelve other dioceses and over a hundred monastic estates were to be surrendered to the imperial commissioners on no greater authority than the emperor's own writ. It was neither the writ nor the commissioners, however, which perturbed the princes: behind both they saw the sword in the hands of Wallenstein. In private he opposed the emperor's policy, believing it to be an unnecessary distraction from the Baltic campaign and one that might provoke the Protestant princes to rebellion, but, cynical and critical though he might be of his master's policy, Wallenstein nevertheless enforced it with characteristic efficiency and alarming speed. Magdeburg, Halberstadt and Bremen were occupied; the Duke of Wolfenbüttel was deprived of a third of his territory, and the proud city of Augsburg submitted to Catholic governance.

If the edict threatened the Protestants with disaster, the manner of its enforcement was equally alarming to the Catholics: the long-awaited triumph of their Church was not to be celebrated when it represented an even greater triumph of the imperial prerogative. The time-honoured bonds which condemned an emperor to impotence had been burst open by Ferdinand, at the very moment when his army threatened to control the Baltic coastline. The relation between these two events was even more apparent when the archdiocese of Magdeburg, the strategic key to north Germany, was assigned by the emperor to Leopold William, his younger son. But whatever his immediate gains, the emperor's action must not be misinterpreted. In the eyes of contemporaries, the Edict of Restitution might well have appeared as an unprincipled device to destroy the liberties of the German princes; for Ferdinand, it was nothing less than an offering to the greater glory of his God.

By 1629 the emperor was at the peak of his power. The Bohemian rebels, the Elector Palatine and the King of Denmark had all been defeated in battle, the success of the Jesuits in Prague and the issue of the Edict of Restitution had advanced the Catholic cause further in ten years than the policies of his predecessors had done in sixty. But the price of success was the hostility of all the German princes. To the Protestants the events of 1629 represented a declaration of war, and in this conflict Ferdinand could no longer rely on the support of the Catholic princes. It was ironical perhaps that it was Maximilian of Bavaria who, despite the manner of his appointment to the electoral title, began to invoke the liberties of the Empire against the emperor: 'Today,' he wrote to his son, 'it is not only the prosperity and liberty of the whole Empire which is at stake but also the dignity and the prerogatives of the Electors.' The struggle for power in Germany transcended the conflict between Protestant and Catholic, and in this struggle Ferdinand's long series of successes had left him in a dangerously isolated position.

THE EUROPEAN CONFLICT, 1630–48

The Diet of Regensburg, 1630

The Diet of Regensburg marked a turning point in the war. For all its variety, the conflict so far had had one principal location, the Empire, and one principal victor, the emperor. After 1630, the interests of Germany were to be subordinate to the ambitions of Spain, France and Sweden; and all the imperial triumphs, save in Bohemia, were annulled. These two developments were not co-incidental: they were the price paid by Ferdinand for his success in Germany and for his cousinship with Philip IV of Spain. Ferdinand's attachment to Spain is not easy to understand. He never visited the country nor had he met his relative, but the interests of the Habsburg dynasty as a whole weighed more heavily with him than his own immediate ambitions in Germany. When Spain found herself in serious difficulties, both in north Italy and in the Netherlands, Ferdinand could not content himself with pious ejaculations of sympathy: a sense of moral obligation impelled him to go to the aid of Philip IV. Such action, as Wallenstein foresaw but could not prevent, endangered Ferdinand's position in Germany and exposed him to the open hostility of France.

In north Italy the Duke of Mantua had died. Mantua itself was of no consequence but its dukes controlled the fortresses of Montferrat and Casale, on the borders of Milan and Savoy. When the duchy passed to the Duke of Nevers, a French prince, the danger to Spain's transalpine routes was evident. Immediately the Habsburgs put forward a rival claimant, Spanish troops began the siege of Casale, and Ferdinand came to his cousin's assistance by sequestrating the duchy. This renewal of Habsburg activity in Italy provoked the enmity of Pope Urban VIII and thus alienated the

MAP 4   The Mantuan Succession and North Italy, 1630

Papacy from the stoutest champion of the Counter-Reformation. It also gave Richelieu the chance to embarrass his enemies.[1] He went to the aid of Casale, and sent agents to Germany to rouse the princes against the emperor. Father Joseph was a brilliant emissary, but his skill was barely put to the test. Ferdinand's successes had so alarmed the princes that they were only too ready to accept a little prompting from France, and the Diet of Regensburg was to prove a disaster for the emperor.

At Regensburg, Ferdinand appeared before his subjects in the role of suitor rather than of emperor, for he had to win their assent to three separate proposals. In the first place he wanted his son recognised as King of the Romans, and thus as heir to the imperial throne. This he had planned to achieve by the sacrifice of Wallenstein, who had in any case angered him by a cynical view of the Edict of Restitution and a flat refusal to assist the Spanish in Italy. But this was not all. In his desire to assist Philip IV, Ferdinand had to win the Diet's support over the Mantuan succession, and, worse still, to persuade the princes to join Spain against the Dutch who had burst across the frontier into Brabant.[2] The task was impossible, and Richelieu's agents, making great play of all the

[1] See Chapter III, page 175.   [2] See Chapter IV, page 193.

imperial successes in the past years, ensured that the princes remained jealous and unco-operative.

By allowing the interests of the Habsburg dynasty to determine his policy, Ferdinand paved the way for his own downfall. Wallenstein was abandoned, but the Diet proved obdurate on all points. It disclaimed any interest in the Mantuan problem, refused to consider action against the Dutch, and postponed the election of a King of the Romans. Only a revision of the Edict of Restitution might have strengthened Ferdinand's position, but on this he could not give way. The true significance of the Diet, however, was not so much Ferdinand's rebuff as the fact that its discussions were dominated by questions which did not immediately concern the Germans. The issues over which Ferdinand, Maximilian, Frederick and Christian had fought were no longer important; in their place were substituted the rivalry of Bourbon and Habsburg, and the imperialist designs of Sweden.

The Swedish Invasion, 1630–2

If the emperor had met defeat at Regensburg, the spoils of the conflict had not all gone to his principal enemy, Richelieu. French agents had certainly made a good use of the princes' hostility to Ferdinand to prevent him from sending assistance to Spain; but Richelieu's own design of an effective alliance with Bavaria in order to destroy the power of the Habsburgs in Germany had been forestalled by Wallenstein's dismissal. Maximilian remained friendly to France, but with Tilly in Wallenstein's place he no longer had cause to fear the emperor. Some new agent of destruction was needed, and Richelieu proposed to commission the King of Sweden.

It would, of course, be idle to maintain that Gustavus II Adolphus intervened in the war solely at the bidding of France. He had already sent aid to Stralsund, and the interests of his country and his faith encouraged him to plan the conquest of north Germany.[1] Nevertheless, the timing of the attack was largely due to Richelieu. Until 1629 Sweden was at war with Poland and it was only by French mediation that a truce was arranged, leaving Gustavus free to occupy Pomerania in the following year. Moreover, by the Treaty of Bärwalde (1631) it was Richelieu who

[1] For a discussion of this and subsequent points relating to Sweden, see Chapter X, pages 385–6.

defined the objects of the invasion. Gustavus was to lead 30,000 men against the emperor, for which purpose France would contribute 20,000 imperial *talers* every six months. Wherever the Catholic religion was upheld its churches were to be left alone, and Bavaria's neutrality was to be respected. Richelieu still hoped to derive some advantage from Maximilian's jealousy of the emperor, and did not wish to see him driven into the enemy camp by Swedish arms. In retrospect, it is clear that Richelieu was too optimistic. Gustavus was too vigorous a warhorse to harness to the Bourbon chariot. He was a man of independent spirit, and independent means. The copper from the Stora Kopperburg and the revenues from the Baltic ports were alone sufficient to finance his army, and the threat of withholding 40,000 *talers* a year was no effective sanction against his taking matters into his own hands. But, in 1631, Richelieu rode the crest of the wave. Maximilian, a friend if not an ally, was unlikely to go to Ferdinand's assistance, and without Wallenstein the emperor would find it hard to survive the Swedish attack.

In an effort to make the outcome doubly sure, Richelieu proposed an alliance between the Lutheran princes and Sweden. Soon after Gustavus's arrival in Pomerania a conference was called at Leipzig to achieve this, but the princes refused to co-operate. It was no doubt tactful of Gustavus to speak of the defence of their liberties and religion, but the fact remained that he was a foreigner intent on acquiring territory in north Germany. In any case, John George of Saxony regarded himself as the leader of the Lutherans. He refused to submit to Gustavus and resented the invasion which, in his view, would only serve to prolong the war and prevent a settlement. His own plan was to bargain with the emperor, offering Lutheran support in return for the withdrawal of the Edict of Restitution. It was a tragedy for Germany that he failed. If the emperor had once offered to compromise, John George, who had already raised as many men as he could to strengthen his bargaining power, could then have joined with the other north German princes to deny Gustavus access to the recruiting grounds of north Germany. The Swedish invasion would thus have been prevented.

But the emperor would not compromise, and the Lutheran camp was left in a state of fearful neutrality: the princes could not support their persecutor, they dared not join their self-appointed

saviour. Their dilemma was resolved, suddenly and quite fortuitously, by the sack of Magdeburg in May 1631. One of the most
appalling incidents of a war rich in atrocities, the sack resulted
indirectly from Wallenstein's dismissal. His army had passed into
Tilly's hands, but not the granaries and storehouses which supplied
it. These remained safe in Wallenstein's own keeping and, with
every justification, he refused to provision Tilly without advance
payment. Tilly was in despair. The emperor had no money to
send him, the men deserted daily to enlist in Saxony's new army,
and the only remedy seemed to be the seizure of Magdeburg.
Apart from its strategic position on the Elbe, the city was believed
to be well stocked with provisions. The marauding army began the
siege in April, and four weeks later Magdeburg fell. Fire, famine
and disease destroyed those who survived the sack, leaving a mere
five thousand of the thirty thousand inhabitants. Unfortunately for
Tilly, the all-essential provisions had also been destroyed.

The news of the sack passed like a shock wave through the
Protestant states, doubling and redoubling its effect with every
repetition. In the midst of all the uncertainty and dismay, one
thing was clear: Tilly's army was in full cry after provisions, and
Sweden was the only defence. Even John George's reluctance was
overcome when Tilly took Leipzig, so that by the end of the
summer Gustavus was assured of the alliance of all the north
German princes. The way was clear for his advance. At Breitenfeld, in the broad Saxon plain outside Leipzig, he fought his first
great battle in Germany. His allies were driven from the field,
exposing his flank, but his own men stood firm in solid squares,
supported by light artillery and small groups of fast moving
cavalry. By this combination of strength with manœuverability he
won the day. If Gustavus had been nothing more than a French
mercenary he might then have invaded Austria, but the sequel to
Breitenfeld was to prove as alarming to Richelieu as the victory
itself had been to Ferdinand.

Gustavus knew only too well why Saxony had joined him. Now
that Tilly's men were defeated, John George might renounce his
alliance. To prevent this, and to commit him more deeply against
the emperor, Gustavus sent him to invade Bohemia while he himself turned westwards, to the rich ecclesiastical estates of Franconia
and the Rhineland, the celebrated 'Priests' alley'. As the champion
of Protestantism it was a joy to him to scatter the forces of Catholi-

cism in the area where they had been most affluent and most
secure; as the paymaster of an army he welcomed the tribute of the
wealthy Rhineland cities, and, as creator of the Swedish empire,
he was better placed to control the north German waterways from
Frankfurt and Mainz than from far distant Vienna and Prague.
At Frankfurt, too, captured in November 1631 he was at the
constitutional centre of the Holy Roman Empire, and it was here
that he outlined his plan for a new Confederation in which all the
German Protestants were to dissolve their connection with the
emperor and unite with Sweden. The proposal was coldly received.
The Protestants owed much to Gustavus as an ally, but they had no
wish to become his vassals. For the moment, however, there was
nothing they could do but await the outcome of the next
campaign.

Throughout 1632 the Swedish army continued its advance
through the Palatinate, and then turned south to Bavaria and the
Danube valley. Its astonishing series of victories, explained by the
fact that the troops were not only well organised but also well paid,
caused as much consternation in Paris as in Vienna. When Munich
fell, the last remnants of the French alliance with Sweden was
destroyed. The warhorse had broken the traces, and Richelieu was
powerless to control it. Nor could he retain his influence with
Maximilian. The rulers of Bavaria and Austria were once again
united against a common enemy, and when Tilly died from his
wounds in April, the command of the Catholic armies was entrusted to Wallenstein. He had accepted disgrace in 1630 with
characteristic fatalism, taking comfort from his horoscope, but now
the stars were in favourable conjunction. The terms on which he
accepted command were never known, but there is no doubt that
the emperor's plight compelled him to allow Wallenstein complete
and independent control over the conduct of the war. His first
action was to drive John George from Bohemia, and then to
threaten him with destruction in Saxony. As a result, the Swedish
army in south Germany was in danger of losing its bases in Pomerania. In an effort to rejoin the Saxon army near Leipzig, Gustavus
immediately moved north from Bavaria, and in November
was met by Wallenstein at Lützen. The Swedish army held
firm, forcing the Imperialists to withdraw from the field, but it
suffered a blow more disastrous than any defeat. Gustavus was
killed.

Habsburg and Bourbon, 1633–48

Gustavus's sudden irruption from the Baltic to the Danube had in one respect simplified the issue: the Protestants had combined to follow him, the Catholics to destroy him. By his death, however, both camps were thrown into confusion. The issue was no longer so clear cut, and alliances began to dissolve in an atmosphere of jealousy, fear and uncertainty. Richelieu was the first to take advantage of the situation. He realised that the Protestant princes were afraid of their Swedish ally but dared not stand alone against the Catholic powers, and so, with great skill, he brought them together at Heilbronn, in 1633, to form a new League. Sweden was also to be a member, but she would receive French subsidies as the agent of the League, and not as an independent ally. In this way, French leadership in north Germany was established, and Sweden was reduced to the status of a mercenary. Although Oxenstierna, who controlled the council of regents in Sweden,[1] bitterly opposed the new arrangements, he had no option but to accept them. Gustavus was no longer alive to impose his own dominant will over the other princes, and if Sweden were to consummate his great ambitions, she could not do it without support.

Meanwhile, in the Catholic camp, the old quarrel between Maximilian and Wallenstein had broken out afresh. This time, however, Ferdinand was not prepared to defend his servant, especially since the servant threatened to become the master. While Gustavus lived, Wallenstein could dictate his own terms to the emperor, but from the moment of Gustavus's death he was no longer indispensable. Maximilian's enmity and Ferdinand's obvious mistrust drove him to take desperate measures to safeguard his own position. In short, he planned to capitalise his one asset, the army, and sell out to the Heilbronn League, his price being the kingdom of Bohemia. In January 1634 Ferdinand ordered him to resign his command, but no one knew whether the dismissal would carry any weight with the army. Wallenstein himself never doubted the loyalty of his own officers, and he failed to perceive that some of them were genuinely attached to the emperor and to Catholicism; others were simply ambitious, seeking the promotion which might result from effective service in the emperor's cause. Despite the need for haste, the mutiny was well planned and in February Wallenstein was murdered.

[1] See Chapter X, page 388.

Wallenstein's death gave new life to the emperor. During the past three years he had lost his resilience, prayer and fasting being his only response to the disasters which befell his cause. Now, with Gustavus and Wallenstein dead, he regained his spirits and renewed his efforts to forward the cause of his family and his religion. His son Ferdinand, King of Hungary, was appointed commander in Wallenstein's place, and soon justified himself as a soldier by defending both Bohemia and Bavaria from attacks by the Heilbronn League. Better still, help from Spain was on its way. Through the Val Telline, the vital artery of the Habsburg Empire, marched 20,000 men under their royal leader, the Cardinal-Infante Ferdinand. Joining forces with the Imperialist army at Nördlingen in September 1634 they defeated the Heilbronn League in one of the most decisive battles of the war. Fifteen desperate charges were made against the impregnable lines of Spanish infantry, but the armies of the League were outnumbered and, in the event, outmanœuvred. When finally they began to withdraw from the field, the Catholic armies seized the opportunity and launched their own attack. The exhausted Protestants could make no effective resistance, and their retreat became a rout.

The immediate results of the battle of Nördlingen were startling. The Habsburgs broke the power of the Heilbronn League, recovered control of the Rhineland and strengthened their position in the Netherlands. The emperor, knowing too well that dramatic victories could be reversed even more dramatically, was now prepared to lower his demands in order to recover the allegiance of the Protestant princes. John George of Saxony was the first to make peace: he had never been happy to take up arms against the emperor, and when Ferdinand, urgently prompted by his own son, agreed to compromise over the Edict of Restitution, the Treaty of Prague was signed in May 1635. The Elector was allowed to retain all lands secularised by his family before 1626, and, in addition, was confirmed in his title to Lusatia. The reasonable nature of these terms encouraged the other princes to follow suit. Bernard of Saxe-Weimar, the unfortunate commander of the Protestants at Nördlingen, was the only one to remain defiant.

The German princes might patch up their own differences, but they were powerless to dispose of their own fate. The three great powers which had intervened in the war had reasons of their own for continuing it, and the interests of the empire were brushed aside as irrelevant in the greater clash of European dynasties. Oxenstierna, remembering the triumphs of Gustavus, was determined to achieve some more worthy gain than the barren coastline of Pomerania; Spain, unable to rest while the United Provinces remained independent, feared that a general settlement in Germany would release Protestant troops for the relief of the Dutch; and Richelieu, alarmed beyond all measure by the Habsburg victory, sounded a new call to arms in which France herself would now play an open part. 'Saxony has made his peace', he wrote, 'but that will have no effect on us save to make us renew our efforts to keep all in train.' He declared war on Spain, calling upon the governments of Holland, Sweden and north Italy to assist him in the destruction of Habsburg supremacy in Europe.

From 1635 to 1648 Germany was the victim of this European conflict. Foreign armies crossed her soil, but the causes for which they fought were not those of any German prince; and the history of three years can best be described in the relevant chapters on Spain, France and Sweden.[1] Only when the powers outside the Empire had finally reached stalemate could a general peace be made.

The Peace of Westphalia, 1648

The negotiations which finally bore fruit in the Peace of Westphalia occupied more than ten years. It was fortunate, perhaps, that as Spain and France had no intention of making peace between themselves, the negotiations could be confined to the problem of Germany, although that was a complex enough problem. Neither Sweden nor France, for example, would accord precedence to each other's representatives, and so the discussions had to take place in two separate cities, the emperor treating with France at Münster and with Sweden at Osnabrück. No general sessions were held at all until 1643, and then the long delays over procedure and points of detail were used as subterfuges by one side or another to win time while their armies struggled to gain yet one more victory. The emperor, it was noticed, raised or lowered his terms as the Swedish troops alternately evacuated or invaded his territories, while it was only the outbreak of the Fronde in Paris[2] which compelled the French to make a serious effort to end the war.

[1] In particular see Chapter III, pages 176–8, and Chapter X, page 389.
[2] See Chapter III, pages 166–70.

In January 1648 Spain unexpectedly made peace with the United Provinces, granting them full independence. This was done, partly because the Dutch could not be defeated, and also to spite the French who were thus deprived of an active ally. The possibility of further bilateral agreements so alarmed the other governments that their agents in Westphalia were hastily ordered to bring the peace settlement to a conclusion.

The details of the Peace of Westphalia can best be summarised as follows:

  (i) Within the Empire, the 343 separate states and free cities were all recognised as sovereign members of the Diet, free to control their own affairs independently of each other and of the emperor.

  (ii) The principle of *cuius regio, eius religio* was reaffirmed; Calvinism was recognised as an official alternative to Lutheranism, and the retention of all land secularised before 1624 was allowed.

  (iii) Ferdinand III, who had succeeded his father in 1637, retained the kingdom of Bohemia as an hereditary possession of his family.

  (iv) Maximilian of Bavaria was allowed to keep the Electoral title granted to him in 1623, and also the Upper Palatinate.

  (v) Charles Louis, son of the former Elector Palatine, was restored to the Lower Palatinate, and a new Electoral title was created for his benefit.

  (vi) John George of Saxony was again confirmed in his possession of Lusatia.

  (vii) Frederick William of Brandenburg, son of the feeble Elector who had played so indecisive a part in the war, was not only confirmed in the possession of Cleves, acquired in 1614, but also gained eastern Pomerania, Magdeburg, Halberstadt, Minden and Cammin. This remarkable accession of territory was due to his own skill in making alliances with France and the United Provinces just before the war ended,[1] and also to the French desire to establish stronger Protestant powers in north Germany as a safeguard against further expansion by the emperor.

[1] For a full account of Frederick William's diplomacy see Chapter X, pages 403–5.

(viii) The Duke of Nevers was recognised as the ruler of Mantua, Montferrat and Casale.

(ix) Oxenstierna failed in his bid to secure for Sweden a seat in the Electoral College. Sweden, however, acquired virtual control of the north German coastline, and the mouths of the Oder, Elbe and Weser, by the possession of western Pomerania, Stettin, Wismar, Bremen and Verden.

(x) France was confirmed in her title to Metz, Toul and Verdun (held since 1559) and to Pinerolo, Moyenvic, Breisach and Philippsburg. In addition, the district of Alsace, without Strassburg, was assigned to her, although the Alsatian towns retained their so-called *immediacy* to the Empire. No one was clear as to the nature of this clause, but all parties were satisfied that they could interpret it to serve their own purposes at a later date.

Earlier historians have tended to exaggerate the significance of the Thirty Years War. The war and the peace treaty, they claimed, marked the end of an epoch, paved the way for the greatness of France, discredited the emperor's authority in Germany, replaced religious standards in public life by those of secular self-interest, ruined the economy of the German states, and brutalised the German peoples so totally that they could never again become a civilised race. All these claims, save the last which is nonsense, did contain some element of truth, but it would be wrong to suppose that these developments were necessary consequences of the war. Some of them would have occurred in any case; others had already taken place before 1618. France did not owe her ascendancy in Europe solely to the disintegration of the empire, nor was Ferdinand III's power any more negligible than that of Ferdinand I, Rudolf or Matthias. It was only in contrast with the temporary, and unexpected, triumph enjoyed by his father in 1629 that his own authority appeared to have been discredited.

It is true that religious zeal, as a dominant factor in political behaviour, became less evident in Europe after 1648, and, with some hesitation, this process may be described as the secularisation of public life, or the triumph of *raison d'état*. Men were as devout or as pagan as they had always been, but their public utterances, their justification of their actions to the world, were being phrased in different terms. Warfare after 1648 was more frequently waged for reasons of national security, commercial ambition or dynastic pride. It would, however, be wrong to assume this to be a consequence of the Thirty Years War. The sons of Frederick and Ferdinand II were certainly less prepared than their fathers had been to hazard fortune and territory for the sake of their religion, and the alliance of Catholic France, for instance, with Lutheran Sweden, had openly subordinated the conflict of faiths to the interest of dynasties: but this was not novel.

Henry II of France had allied with the German Protestants in 1552 in order to defeat the Emperor Charles V, and the French wars of religion had already produced a new type of statesman, the *Politique,* who refused to sacrifice the security of his country to the interests of a church. Moreover by 1600, the ever-increasing preoccupation of governments with the problem of finance had led to the adoption of theories, later to be termed mercantilist,[1] which paid little heed to a country's religion but a great deal to its sources of wealth. Finally, the new methods of science,[2] the Natural Philosophy which studied things as they were and not as some idealist believed they might be, was to have a far greater effect on the future than did the events of the war. Reason, by which the seventeenth-century philosophers meant the common-sense interpretation of evidence produced by direct observation, encouraged the educated classes to adopt a fundamentally practical and secular view of life.

The misery endured by the Germans throughout the hideous progression of campaigns and sieges, with the slaughter, plague and famine which followed in their train, cannot be denied; though perhaps it was not so widespread as was formerly believed. Certainly warfare was destructive, but it was not universal. Many towns never saw enemy troops more than once perhaps throughout the whole war. The main fighting was limited to Bohemia and Austria, the Saxon plain, the Rhineland and the Black Forest, and the most intensive period of warfare for the German states was from 1632 to the Treaty of Prague in 1635.

On the other hand, it is now clear that a period of economic stagnation and decay had begun well before 1618. The German towns as centres of commercial prosperity had had their day, and the peasant cultivator was already being driven from the land by new attempts at large-scale farming. The war certainly made

---

[1] See Chapter I, page 23.   [2] See Chapter I, pages 529–54.

economic recovery difficult, but it did not cause the original decline, and its ill effects were deliberately exaggerated by Pufendorf, the propagandist of the Elector of Brandenburg, who sought to accentuate his master's achievements by painting the background as black as possible.[1]

After thirty years of conflict, who had won? The remarkable thing was that within the Empire so little had been changed. Alsace and Western Pomerania, of course, were now in foreign hands; Saxony, Brandenburg and Bavaria had increased their territory, the Elector Palatine had lost much of his, and the Bohemians had been brought entirely under the control of Austria. Apart from this, the situation established in 1648 was fundamentally that of 1618. The Catholic powers had hoped to recover the land secularised since 1559, the emperor to revive imperial authority, and Sweden to control the destinies of the German Protestants; but none of these ambitions had been achieved. The Empire remained, as it had been since 1559, an untidy collection of autonomous states, some Catholic, some Protestant. If the war had ended in 1623, in 1629 or even in 1635, there might have been many changes to record, but its wearisome prolongation had finally brought Germany full circle, to perpetuate for another hundred years the political fragmentation of the past hundred. As for the powers outside the Empire, it was not yet time to apportion the laurels of victory. Sweden was well on the way towards her goal of Baltic supremacy, Spain had suffered serious losses in north Italy and the Netherlands, and France had extended her hold over the Rhineland; but it was not until 1660, when the treaties of the Pyrenees and Oliva had been signed, that we can think in terms of one period ending and another beginning. The Thirty Years War, in fact, continued without any appreciable break for another twelve years.

[1] See S. H. Steinberg, 'The Thirty Years War: A New Interpretation', in *History*, Vol. XXXII, no. 116.

III

The Revival of France, 1598–1660

Introduction to 1598

The struggle for power between the crown and its overmighty
subjects had been the central theme of French history in the sixteenth century, and one to be repeated with variations for another
hundred years. The great kings of France had attempted to create
a more centralised and efficient administration capable of enforcing
the royal will at the expense of the traditional rights and jurisdictions of the nobility, but their successes were prejudiced by the
periods of regency and inept government which unfortunately
followed upon their deaths. As Henry II had been succeeded by
Catherine de Medici and her feeble sons, so Henry IV was followed
by Marie de Medici, and Louis XIII by Anne of Austria. What
gave interest and excitement to the theme was its quickening
rhythm, for as each period of reaction was shorter, if no less
violent, than its predecessors, the dominance of the crown became
more and more assured. The final movement represented the
stately triumph of Louis XIV at Versailles.

The French wars of religion which took place before the reign of
Henry IV had not been the cause of the crown's weakness but its
symptom, and the factious rivalry of the great families had demonstrated that France would continue a prey to civil war until the
crown was able to assert once more its authority. When Henry III
died in 1589, Henry of Navarre was little more than the leader of
one among many armies, a Huguenot in a country where Catholicism was predominant, and opposed by the city of Paris, the
formidable league of the Catholic nobles and the armies of Spain.[1]
His assets were an impeccable claim to the throne and an ability to
handle men. For four years he waited, strengthening his position
when opportunity occurred by skilful military action, and by

---

[1] By the Treaty of Joinville, 1585, Philip II had allied with the Catholic
League to safeguard the Catholic cause in France.

winning support among the *Politiques*[1] and the professional middle classes. His enemies, meanwhile, fell out among themselves and forfeited their popularity by appearing to be the puppets of Spain. Then, in 1593, Henry declared his conversion to Rome; it was a brilliantly timed stroke which removed the principal bar to his accession and opened to him the gates of Paris. From there he was able to make a fervent appeal to the patriotic sentiment of his subjects, urging them to drive the Spanish troops from the country.

Within four years this was done. Philip II of Spain had no other candidate to put forward for the French throne apart from himself, and a war of conquest was out of the question. His best general, Parma, had died of wounds, and Philip himself was an old man, his finances utterly ruined. Once Henry had succeeded in driving the Spanish from Amiens, Philip recognised that he could not pursue the war any further. The Treaty of Vervins was signed in 1598, both sides agreeing to respect the frontiers decided upon at the last peace settlement in 1559.[2] Despite the long years of civil warfare, France had not lost any territory to her enemy.

Meanwhile, the nobles of the Catholic League were handled with care. Like Philip, they were unable to find any alternative ruler to Henry, whose conversion to Catholicism had undermined the whole basis of their opposition. Henry exploited their predicament by meeting them singly to promise them indemnity, pensions and titles. This skilful, if undramatic, policy served the best interests of the king and of France by bringing an end to the civil war, and the last of Henry's opponents, the Duc de Mercœur, came to terms in 1598 for the sum of 4,000,000 *livres*.

In winning over his enemies, however, Henry forfeited the affection, and very nearly the loyalty, of his original supporters, the Huguenots. His conversion outraged those who had genuinely fought for religious principles, and the remainder were jealous of the generous pensions awarded to the Catholic nobles. Unless substantial concessions were made to them, the Huguenots were prepared to renew the civil war. The measure of their strength may be judged from the terms they secured by the Edict of Nantes in 1598, the main points of which are summarised here:

[1] A name given to those leaders, both Huguenots and Catholics, who were beginning to believe that the security of the state was more important than the triumph of one particular dogma.

[2] See below, page 170, for a more detailed account.

(i) The Huguenots were allowed full liberty of worship in all places outside Paris where their faith was already established.

(ii) The Huguenots were accorded the same civil rights enjoyed by Catholics, and provision was made for the establishment and protection of their schools and colleges.

(iii) Over one hundred fortified towns, many of them of great strategic importance[1] were leased to the Huguenots for eight years, to be garrisoned by them at the royal expense.

(iv) The provincial synods of Huguenot clergy and laymen were to meet freely, and even a national assembly could be summoned with royal permission.

(v) Special courts were established, *Chambres mi-parties*, in every *parlement* of France, made up of equal numbers of Catholics and Huguenots, to which all breaches of the Edict were to be referred for adjudication.

Not one of these concessions was made as an act of grace to former colleagues and comrades; still less was Henry giving currency to any theory of toleration. Each article represented a serious limitation of royal authority, and the Edict as a whole established the Huguenots as over-mighty subjects, whose political and military privileges gave them the power to defy the crown if they chose. Spain had gained nothing from the wars, the Catholic nobles had to rest content with royal favours and pensions, but the Huguenots had driven one of the hardest bargains that a king of France had ever been forced to accept. For the moment it was worth it. By the end of 1598 the wars were ended and Henry was recognised by all parties as the rightful king. This was the all-important issue, for, as Henry remarked, 'La France et moi, nous avons besoin de haleine.'[2]

The Restoration of Royal Authority

It was not enough for Henry IV to secure the title of king if his authority could not be exercised throughout the kingdom. The years of civil war had destroyed the centralised administration created by the earlier Valois kings, and effective power in each province was in the hands of the dominant noble family. Henry of Guise had, with some justification, claimed to be king of Paris in

[1] e.g. Saumur, La Rochelle, Montauban and Montpellier. This lease was subsequently renewed in 1603.

[2] i.e. 'France and I both need a breather.'

1590, and there were many other nobles who enjoyed similar powers in the provincial capitals: the Catholic Mercœur, the Huguenot Condé and the *Politique* Damville, for example, were able to assert an almost independent authority within their respective provinces of Brittany, Berry and Languedoc. France was in danger of becoming nothing more than a federal union of virtually autonomous states, and Henry IV's task after 1598 was to destroy this legacy of the civil wars by ensuring that his writ was obeyed in every corner of the kingdom.

His greatest advantage was his ability to win loyalty and affection from his subjects. The role of a swaggering Gascon soldier, deliberately assumed during the wars, had made him a popular figure, and his bravery and enjoyment of war added to his reputation. The long face with its incredible nose, curling moustache and aggressive beard, attracted attention and respect, and his lively tongue and quick wit could charm or rebuke without offence. He was also known to be concerned for the welfare of the peasants, the greatest victims of the wars, and there was genuine feeling as well as astute propaganda behind the legend of the king who wanted all his subjects to be able to afford 'a chicken in the pot' — *le roi de la poule au pot*. Here indeed was a man to capture the imagination of his subjects, in sharp contrast to the sickly youths, neurotic invalids and effeminate playboys who had ruled since 1559. Henry's virtues commanded respect; his vices, too, were regarded with affectionate indulgence, and his tempestuous love affairs won him popular approval. He was, as Madame de Staël once commented, 'the most French king that France ever had'.

If Henry relied to a great extent on public support in securing his throne, he was none the less determined that public institutions should not limit his freedom of action once the wars were over. By his personal skill in combining *ordres et caresses*, he could make the members of the Paris *Parlement*[1] believe that nothing would be done without their co-operation and consent, and at the same time insist that all his edicts be registered by them without question. Nor did he ever summon the States-General to meet lest it prove a

---

[1] One of the four sovereign courts claiming descent from the medieval *curia regis*. By the seventeenth century it had become at once a court of justice, an agency for royal administration and an association of professional civil servants. For a fuller account of its position and power see below, page 157.

source of faction and opposition.[1] Behind the conciliatory speeches, the disarming gestures, was a king who believed in his responsibility to God alone, and he drew strength from the fact that many Frenchmen were prepared to acquiesce in his views on absolute monarchy. The middle classes had suffered from the recession in commerce and industry, and those employed in the royal administration had found their authority flouted, and their salaries unpaid. The rigid class divisions in French society prevented the existence of any common interests between the nobility and the *bourgeoisie*, and the latter could only look to the king for protection. The notion of constitutional restraints on the power of the crown, which was being evolved by the middle class in England, found little response in France. The choice before the *bourgeoisie* was not between an absolute monarch and a constitutional king, but between an effective and an ineffective ruler.

The middle classes, and indeed the peasantry, would remain content if only the new king would guarantee them a period of peace and security, breathe new life into the administration, and restore the authority of its officials. For this to be done, Henry had to impose some restraint on the actions of the nobility, whose unruliness was inveterate. Feudal sentiment still persisted in French society. Every great lord had his clientèle of followers, bound to him by ties of close allegiance and prepared to champion his cause in any way, while he in return afforded them protection and helped them on in the world. It was an extremely personal relationship, and the reciprocal duties of lord and vassal took precedence over all others, even, if need be, over obedience to the king. No immediate solution could be found to this problem, and Henry's success in exerting some measure of control was largely due to his personal qualities. Many nobles were disarmed by his open display of friendship, others accepted pensions and titles as the price of their good behaviour, and those who challenged his authority were shown no leniency. One of Henry's own comrades in the wars, the Huguenot Biron, could not accept the strange quiet which befell the country after 1598, and, from force of habit more than anything else, intrigued with the Duc de Bouillon to promote the succession of one of Henry's illegitimate sons. Biron was executed, Bouillon exiled, and no other conspiracy came to light while Henry lived.

[1] See Chapter I, page 20, for a general discussion of the decline of representative institutions in the seventeenth century.

It was one thing to restrain the nobles from rebellion and private warfare; to secure their active co-operation in the administration of royal policy was an entirely different matter, since any extension of royal control in the provinces could only be at their own expense. On the whole, Henry left the nobles to the enjoyment of their titles and local prestige, while entrusting the reality of power to men of his own choice. The provincial governors, for example, were virtually restricted to dealing with the maintenance of order, recruitment and defence; the administrative functions of their office were transferred to the *élus*. The *élus*, or elected ones, were strangely misnamed since there was no elective principle in their appointment. Owing their positions solely to the king, their primary function was to collect the *taille*, but they also informed the council on local affairs and made sure that royal edicts were respected and enforced. By himself the *élu* could scarcely hope to exercise anything more than a general supervision of his province's administration, but he was not entirely on his own as he could rely upon the assistance of a rudimentary form of civil service which the French kings had built up since the fifteenth century. It was staffed by men from the middle classes, jealous of the privileges enjoyed by the nobility and trained in the principles of Roman Law.[1] Through these *officiers* the crown could extend its jurisdiction at the expense of the seigneurial, or feudal, courts, and secure greater obedience to its edicts.

Unfortunately for the French monarchy, its foresight in creating this nascent bureaucracy had been undermined by its financial indebtedness, which had forced it to raise money by selling the offices in the administration to their holders. As a result, the *officier*, no matter how incompetent or obstructionist, could not be dismissed unless the purchase price of his office was repaid. The evils of this system, by no means uncommon in other European states, were made worse in 1604 when the *officier*, for an annual payment,[2] could not only insure against dismissal but also secure the right to pass on his office to his heir or sell it to the highest bidder. In this way, the poverty of the crown created a situation in

[1] Roman Law tended to exalt the status of the monarch, see Chapter I, page 16.

[2] The *droit annuel*. A payment of one-sixtieth of the estimated value of the office. A newcomer to the office paid an initial fee of one-third its value. The tax was known as the *paulette* after Charles Paulet, to whom it was first farmed out.

which the administration tended to pass out of royal control into the hands of those who had purchased their offices. While Henry lived, however, this tendency was not immediately obvious. The *officiers* were eager to assist the crown by encroaching upon the powers and jurisdictions of the nobility since the value of an office was in direct proportion to the extent of its authority, and the greater the extent of the royal administration, the greater the profit for the office holders. It was not until later in the century that the interests of the *officiers* as a class began to diverge from those of the crown.

There were other serious limitations on Henry's freedom of action. The Huguenots had established something like a state within the state, and the privileges afforded to them by the Edict of Nantes could not be abolished without a renewal of civil war. The provinces had a long standing tradition of separatism, if not of autonomy, and the noble families, the *parlements* and the municipal corporations resented the growing importance of the royal council in Paris. In Henry's reign there was no open opposition to his government, but the danger of something more than passive resistance was ever present. Against this picture of very limited success, however, must be set the true nature of Henry's achievements. For the first time in fifty years France was governed as a unit, and the directing force behind this government was the king himself. Henry IV was universally recognised as the head of the state, and France remained obedient and peaceful throughout his reign.

Sully

Whatever Henry's personal achievements in securing the throne and extending his authority throughout the kingdom, the effort would have been fruitless if the perennial bankruptcy of the crown during the years of civil warfare were to be prolonged. In 1598, for example, the administration was spending nearly twice as much as it received and debts of over 300,000,000 *livres* had been incurred. The first step in remedying this dangerous situation was taken by Henry himself in putting an end to warfare, for not only was the crown able to cut its military expenditure, but the provision of internal peace and security encouraged a revival of trade and agriculture, which in its turn created a greater amount of wealth in the country to be tapped by the tax collector. The remaining steps were the responsibility of Sully, the *surintendant des finances*.

Maximilien de Béthune, Duc de Sully, had served the king as paymaster of the army in the difficult years before 1598, and it was his reward to be given charge, not only of the royal finances, but also of the French economy as a whole. A devout Huguenot, cautious, thrifty, tactless and conceited, he lacked the engaging virtues and vices by which Henry captured the imagination of the French people. No one with a sense of humour could have spent his evenings, as Sully did, solemnly dancing to the lute in front of sycophantic admirers, and the great opinion which he held of himself is one of the few reliable facts to be drawn from his *Mémoires*. Two qualities, however, he did possess which made his services invaluable to Henry IV. He was utterly devoted to his work and, by the standards of his time, singularly honest. It can be said of him that he looked after the king's finances with the same attention to detail which he lavished on his own. In no sense was he a financial expert any more than he was an innovator; and in the circumstances this too was of value. The outdated and hopelessly entangled system of French taxation could not be reformed nor put on a more rational footing without destroying the privileges of the nobility, the clergy and the middle classes; and this would have provoked rebellion.[1] Instead, Sully exerted his administrative talents in securing the best possible results from a system which remained essentially incurable.

The principal direct tax, the *taille*, was levied in some provinces on land, in others on income, but in each case the chief contributor was the peasant, for it was one of the anomalies of the fiscal system that all the classes best able to support the state, the nobility, the clergy and the *officiers*, were exempt from direct taxation. All that Sully could do was to keep the closest possible control over his tax-collectors so that the little which was collected did not disappear into their pockets, and to examine more closely the cases where exemption was claimed. Henry III, for example, had sold over a thousand patents of nobility in Normandy alone, in a desperate bid to raise money: these and all similar patents dating back to 1578, were annulled by Sully.

The other taxes were even more difficult to control since they were farmed out to speculators, *fermiers*, who then undertook the

---

[1] It should be noted that even when Louis XIV had made the monarchy far more powerful than in Henry's reign, his financial advisers dared not introduce any radical reforms for the very same reason: see Chapter VI, pages 263–6.

business of collection and usually made a handsome profit. Once again, Sully accepted a situation which he could not hope to reform, but made certain that all future bargains with the *fermiers* were more advantageous to the crown. By combining certain taxes together, thus making their collection more economical, he could sell them at a higher price; all the feudal aids, for example, were treated in this way and were auctioned for a period of five years at a time. the *gabelle*, the compulsory purchase of salt at a price determined by the government, was increased until it produced nearly one-fifth of the total revenue; some of the crown lands which had been sold or abandoned during the civil wars were recovered, and the clergy were prevailed upon to revive the payment of an annual *don gratuit* to the king. Henry himself was subjected to Sully's control. His generous impulses to donate monopolies and tax-farms to his favourites were quickly stifled by the *surintendant*, whose Huguenot austerity made him view the expenses of the gay court with a particularly disapproving eye.

The sole innovation of importance was the *paulette*,[1] and this, in effect, did nothing more than exploit the well-established practice of selling offices in the royal administration. With this slight exception, Sully broke no new ground and the only novel aspect of his administration was its success. His concern was to husband the existing sources of revenue, not to devise new ones, and the total effect was one of piecemeal gains within a highly traditional and conservative system. If Sully could not reform the fiscal system, at least he became one of the few men who ever understood its workings; and by this constant supervision and efficient book-keeping he restored the crown to solvency. By 1610 he had not only reduced the royal debt and covered all current expenses, but had secured the astonishing surplus of 12,000,000 *livres*.

Sully's work was not confined to the treasury alone, since he was also in charge of the economic recovery of France as a whole, a task no less valuable to Henry than the increased yield from taxation. State direction of the country's resources and a paternal interest in the welfare of the people were characteristic features of the type of absolute monarchy represented by Henry IV,[2] but the encouragement given to Sully's work of reconstruction was prompted by other, more personal, reasons. Henry welcomed the name of *le roi de la poule au pot*, and was genuinely eager to improve the condition

[1] See footnote on page 145.   [2] See Chapter I, page 23.

of his subjects. The devastation of the fields, the destruction or seizure of the peasants' possessions, the decline of industry, the dislocation of trade, were the results of the civil wars, and the greatest single benefit which Henry afforded his people was the establishment of peace. Free from the threat of a marauding soldiery, the peasant could once again till his fields in the expectation of reaping the harvest, and the merchant was safe to travel the country with his goods.

Many schemes were proposed by enthusiasts like de Serres and Laffemas, who won great favour with the king by their plans to establish new industries and to encourage new developments in agriculture. Laffemas persuaded Henry to create a *Chambre de Commerce*, and to require all workers to register in their appropriate guilds in order to make the direction of labour more efficient. In company with de Serres, he also planned to cultivate mulberry bushes on a vast scale, and thus to lay the foundations of a silk industry. In practice, however, the formidable regulations composed by Laffemas inhibited rather than encouraged industry, the registration of workers was of benefit only to the Treasury which received the registration fees, and the mulberry trees proved to be so expensive that the peasants who had hoped to benefit by the scheme were compelled to finance it by an increase in the *taille*.

Sully has often been blamed for these failures. It is true that he showed little interest in industry, and he even opposed the manufacture of luxury goods on moral grounds, but the real cause of failure lay in the nature of French society. No new industry could develop without capital investment, but the middle classes, in strange contrast to those of England and the Netherlands, had no interest in commerce for its own sake: for them it was merely a means to acquire sufficient wealth to invest in a government post or to purchase a title. Once this was achieved, they severed their connection with business and attempted to conceal the lowly origin of their wealth by aping noble pursuits. Capital which might otherwise have been directed to the expansion of industry was thus diverted to the pursuit of social status. Nor could any great advances be expected of agriculture while the peasant continued to bear the whole burden of taxation and the nobles showed no interest in the management of their estates. They preferred to direct their efforts to hunting, warfare, politics and intrigue, an attitude epitomised by Biron: when his son had expressed some hope that the civil war might end, he had retorted in amazement, 'Do you want to pack us off to Biron to grow cabbages?' De Serres's classic textbook on farming methods, *Théâtre d'agriculture et Mesnage de Champs*, read at mealtimes to an enthusiastic king, was given scant attention by his nobles, and it is significant that Sully failed in his attempt to forbid the practice of hunting over the crops.

Sully was no innovator, and his work was designed therefore to ease the process of recovery rather than to stimulate new ventures. To this end he gave priority to the problem of communications. Local authorities were constantly reminded of their duty to repair roads and bridges, the postal services were improved, and a start was made on a great scheme of canal construction. The Briare canal was built to connect the Seine and Loire valleys, but its extension to the Saône, which would thus have created an inland waterway from the Channel to the Mediterranean, was not completed in Henry's reign. For the rest, Sully preferred to leave the development of the economy to the individual efforts of those who were prepared to exploit the advantages of a period of internal peace.

THE REIGN OF LOUIS XIII, 1610-43

The Regency Crisis and Richelieu's Rise to Power, 1610-24

Although Henry IV had succeeded in providing France with a period of freedom from internal disorder, this did not prevent a return to civil war and anarchy after his death.[1] His achievements were the result of day-to-day improvisation, and in essence were similar to those of Francis I and Henry II in the early sixteenth century. In each case, everything depended upon the strength of the ruler's personality. Without a powerful king to restrain them, the over-mighty subjects were free to revive old feuds and, above all, to exact reprisals from the crown for the loss of power they had suffered. Sully, at least, realised this and when Henry died he remarked shrewdly, 'France will fall into strange hands.'

Henry's widow, Marie de Medici, became regent on behalf of Louis XIII, who was only nine years old. A skilful intriguer, at her best in opposition to authority, the Queen Mother was too feckless

---

[1] He was assassinated in 1610, at the moment of going to war in Germany. For this, and for Henry's foreign policy, see below, page 173.

to bear the sustained burden of governing France, and her accession was a signal for the great nobles to flock to court, demanding
pensions, titles and positions of authority. Marie could do nothing
but purchase assent to her own title at a price which made its
possession worthless: the name of *la grosse banquière* aptly combined a description of her enforced liberality with a scornful
reference to her descent from the Florentine bankers. The little
power she retained was squandered on the promotion of her
Italian foster sister, whose husband, Concini, became the principal
figure at court. The crown forfeited all respect, the revenues were
no longer husbanded with care, and the administration of France
fell into the hands of those strong enough to seize it. The Duc de
Bouillon, exiled after Biron's conspiracy, returned to flaunt his
immunity at court; the Huguenots secured exemption from the
taille for their clergy, and the great nobles made themselves masters
of their provinces. Condé, the greatest of them all, compelled
Marie to summon the States-General in 1614, in an attempt to
strengthen his own position and that of his class. The nobles,
however, had no need to seek constitutional restraints upon the
crown; it was they, not the Queen Mother, who had inherited the
throne of Henry IV. The meeting of the States-General revealed
both Henry's wisdom in dispensing with it, and its own inadequacy
as a representative institution. It existed solely as a platform for the
causes of class interest and provincial separation, all of which
cancelled each other out, leaving a political vacuum which only a
strong king might fill. It did not meet again until 1789.

It was at the States-General, however, that Armand de Richelieu made his first important appearance. As the third son of a
minor noble family he had intended to serve in the army, when his
plans were suddenly altered by his elder brother Alphonse leaving
the secular clergy to become a monk. The family had long controlled appointments to the bishopric of Luçon, and as Alphonse
was no longer eligible, Armand had to be hastily ordained and
installed in his place. Richelieu accepted his new career with good
grace, and for six years he proved to be an efficient bishop. It was a
period when the Catholic Church in France showed signs of a new
fervour. Among the leaders of this spiritual revival were Father
Joseph and Pierre de Bérulle,[1] who became friendly with Richelieu
and looked upon him as their protégé in the cause of the Counter-

[1] See Chapter I, page 77.

Reformation. Although Richelieu was active in attacking the Huguenots within his diocese, he was not prepared to live his life entirely as a minor champion of the church; and when he was chosen to compose the address to the crown on behalf of the clergy in the States-General, he made use of the occasion to promote his more secular ambitions. Catching the Queen Mother's ear by simple flattery, he emphasised the peculiar fitness of the clergy for positions of trust in the state. Marie took him at his word and gave him a minor post in the royal council.

Marie's patronage, however, nearly proved fatal to his public career. While she and Concini were able to satisfy the great nobles by sharing their power with them, they could not prevent the young Louis XIII from growing up and becoming resentful of the misgovernment which disgraced his name. Concini tried to distract the king by handing him over to the care of Luynes, a swaggering Provençal with no apparent interests beyond hunting; but the device failed. In 1617 Louis and Luynes organised a palace revolution in which Concini was murdered, and Marie was forced into retirement. Fortunately for Richelieu his comparative unimportance ensured a safe retirement to Luçon. A series of resolute campaigns by Luynes restored royal authority in the kingdom: A Huguenot rising was defeated and the nobles in general were compelled into obedience. The important thing was to drive this advantage home, but Luynes died in 1622 while beseiging the Huguenot fortress of Montauban and Louis found it difficult to replace him.

Meanwhile Richelieu was preparing for the next stage of his career. In 1619 he had acted as an unofficial mediator between the king and his mother, securing Marie's return to the court. It was an important service, for the rivalry between the two had only served to stimulate intrigue and faction, and Richelieu was rewarded with a cardinal's hat. When Luynes's successors proved ineffectual Louis was persuaded by Marie and Father Joseph to appoint Richelieu to the council in 1624. This was his opportunity and within a few months he had made himself the king's chief minister.

Richelieu's Struggle for Survival, 1624-30

Marie de Medici had expected that Richelieu would act as her agent, but from the moment of his appointment an alliance was created between the cardinal and his king which endured for the rest of their lives. Louis, as was natural for a son of Henry IV, had a strong will of his own and the intelligence to know what France needed, but for all his intelligence and determination he could not bring himself to govern alone. It was not simply a matter of his inordinate love of hunting: his lonely and neglected childhood had made him particularly dependent upon the affection and support of others, and in maturity he remained to some extent neurotic, unable to endure the violent clash of temperaments and personalities which court life produced. He disapproved of his mother's policies, but so great was her emotional hold over him that he needed the support of stronger men before he could oppose her openly. At least he knew his own weaknesses, and in appointing Richelieu he sought a man of steel who would protect him from the scenes which harassed his nerves, a man of industry who would superintend the tedious chores of administration.

Curiously enough, Richelieu was physically his inferior. He was frequently ill, especially subject to nervous disorders and migraines, but the strength of his resolution and the overriding power of his intellect defeated the weaknesses of his body. A thin, slight figure, he could silence with his glance the noisy bluster of men who towered above him, and he proved to be an ideal servant for the king. He loved the direction of affairs and was utterly loyal. For Richelieu, service to the state became an end in itself; something which superseded all other claims, even those of his Church, and in strengthening the power of France and of her monarch, he satisfied his own ambitions. There were many who believed that Louis himself was reduced to impotence, that the servant had become the master, but they misjudged both the king and his minister. Richelieu sought power, but it was power for the king and in its exercise he never forgot its true source: 'The four square yards of the king's cabinet', he said, 'are more difficult for me to conquer than all the battlefields of Europe.' Throughout the reign he remained entirely dependent upon Louis's favour and approval. At court, however, he was threatened by every other member of the royal family; by Gaston d'Orléans, Louis's effeminate and treacherous brother, whose whole life was shamelessly devoted to intrigue; by Anne of Austria, Louis's wife, who resented Richelieu's influence at court; and by Marie de Medici, outraged beyond measure by the Cardinal's defection from her and his devotion to her son. Of all these, Gaston was the most dangerous, not in ability but by his position.

Louis's hold on life was uncertain, and should he die without children of his own, Gaston would inherit the throne. The threat of this remained like a shadow at Richelieu's back for fourteen years, to be dispelled at last by the birth of a dauphin in 1638.

The very first plot to challenge Richelieu's position arose from Gaston's refusal to marry Mademoiselle de Montpensier, the wealthiest heiress in France. The match was strongly urged by Louis, but Gaston disliked the lady and hoped to free himself by conspiring to destroy Richelieu. He was abetted by the Duchesse de Chevreuse, the queen's *confidante*, and by one of her lovers, the young Comte de Chalais. Chalais, perhaps, was never fully implicated but he talked too freely of the intrigues afoot, and Gaston immediately saved himself by confessing everything to the king. His only punishment was to proceed with the marriage, at which the cardinal grimly officiated; Chevreuse, however, was exiled and her foolish accomplice was put to death. This harsh treatment of the least powerful of the conspirators was intended to point a moral: if the king's brother could not be touched, those who dared to intrigue with him did so at their peril.

Richelieu's first action against the nobility as a class was to order the destruction of their private fortresses; his second, to revive the edicts against duelling. Duelling was one of the nobles' most cherished privileges, since it distinguished them so dramatically from their social inferiors, but it made nonsense of the laws against murder and encouraged them to consider themselves above the law in general. Richelieu's prohibition was not novel, although the sequel was unexpected. Montmorency-Bouteville, a young braggart with twenty-two duels to his name, had already been exiled for duelling, but in 1627 he returned to France to fight yet again, choosing his ground under Richelieu's window in the Palais-Royal. This open affront was immediately punished by his execution, which impressed the nobility with the resolution of Louis's government even though duelling itself was never fully suppressed.

It was the Huguenot leaders who were the greatest danger to the crown. As nobles they were eager to limit royal authority, as Huguenots they were licensed to do so by the Edict of Nantes: 'So long as they have a foothold in France', wrote Richelieu, 'the king will not be master in his own house, and will be unable to under-take any great enterprise abroad.' At the height of the Val Telline crisis in 1625,[1] Rohan led the Huguenots of Languedoc in revolt, while Soubise raised a naval squadron which destroyed what remained of the royal fleet, off the Normandy coast. For the moment, Richelieu was too preoccupied with his Italian campaign and the Chalais conspiracy to take effective action, and it was not until 1627 that he was given an opportunity to deal with these over-mighty subjects. Once again the Huguenots revolted, encouraged on this occasion by the promise of English support. In general they wanted to convince Richelieu of their strength and secure his confirmation of their privileges, since the revival of Catholic fervour in France was producing greater friction between the two Churches, and the appointment of a cardinal as Louis's minister seemed particularly ominous. Rohan held Languedoc, but the main centre of Huguenot resistance was the powerful port of La Rochelle, which awaited the arrival of Buckingham's fleet from England. When Buckingham's expedition proved a failure, Richelieu was free to begin the siege of the city. It was not an easy task, since there was no royal navy to blockade the port and prevent the entry of another English fleet, but the cardinal was not to be beaten. With a bold sweep of the finger he isolated La Rochelle from the sea, his engineers constructing a mole which enclosed the harbour, leaving a small gap for the movement of the tides. It was an imaginative stroke, brilliantly executed despite all difficulties; and when two successive attempts by the English had failed to break through the artificial barrier, La Rochelle was compelled to surrender in 1628.[2]

Richelieu was prepared to offer reasonable terms to the Huguenots, being eager to intervene again in north Italy, but Rohan remained defiant in the south and had been promised aid from Philip IV of Spain. This threat of Spanish intervention on the soil of France was too sharp a reminder of the old wars of religion, and Richelieu acted swiftly. The royal army swept down the Rhône valley, seizing one Huguenot stronghold after another. Rohan could not halt its advance, and the surrender of his last fortress, Montauban, in 1629 compelled him to sign one of the more momentous of the many treaties ending civil war in France. The Grace of Alais, as it was termed, allowed the Huguenots complete

---

[1] See below, page 174.
[2] The sea wall was destroyed by a storm one week after the city had surrendered.

freedom of worship in those areas where they were already established, and protected them from discrimination in their careers.
Their political and military privileges, however, were destroyed by
the abolition of all their separate law courts, assemblies and fortresses. In this Richelieu acted as a statesman rather than as
champion of the Counter-Reformation, since he made no move to
compel the conversion of the Huguenots. It was not their un-
orthodoxy but their fortresses which had caused him alarm, and
the Grace of Alais provided the solution to one of his major
problems. Never again did the Huguenots challenge the authority
of the state.

While Richelieu persisted in his stubborn efforts to enforce royal
authority, his own position was suddenly threatened in 1630. Louis
XIII fell ill, and the court was immediately filled with envious rivals,
slighted place-hunters and discontented nobles, eagerly anticipating
Louis's death and Richelieu's destruction. Louis in fact recovered,
but his illness had left him weak and irresolute; above all it left him
in the care of Marie de Medici, who used each moment and
exploited every maternal art to persuade her son to dismiss his
minister. The struggle centred round the appointment of a new
commander for the army in north Italy. After a violent and
emotional scene, such as the king always dreaded, in which the
cardinal and the Queen Mother confronted each other in his
presence, it seemed that Richelieu had fallen. Louis appointed
Marillac, one of Marie's clientele, and retired to his hunting lodge
at Versailles, leaving the Queen Mother and her delighted followers
to celebrate their triumph. But they deceived themselves. Louis
had left Paris in a desperate bid to escape his mother's hysterical
outbursts, and that night he ordered Marillac's arrest. The *Day of
Dupes*, as it was called, not only emancipated the king from
Marie's emotional tyranny but confirmed, once and for all, his
intention to employ Richelieu as his chief minister. Richelieu himself was so overcome by the unexpected outcome of the day's
events that he could not restrain the fervour of his gratitude to the
king: 'I shall have no greater happiness in this world than in making
known to Your Majesty by ever-increasing proofs that I am the
most devoted subject and the most zealous servant that ever king or
master had in this world. I shall live and die in this condition,
being a hundred times more Your Majesty's than I am my
own.'

The Consolidation and Extension of Royal Authority, 1630–43

The royal conspirators never recovered from the humiliation they suffered on the *Day of Dupes*: within a few months, Gaston had fled to Lorraine, and Marie had taken refuge with the Spanish viceroy at Brussels. In exile they continued their irresponsible treason, no longer content to intrigue with Richelieu's personal enemies, but with the governments of all countries hostile to France itself. Richelieu, however, found them less dangerous abroad than at court, and his only precaution was to dismiss their supporters from positions of influence in the administration. Marillac was executed on a trumped-up charge; his more powerful brother, the Chancellor, was sentenced to imprisonment, and an edict declared that all who offered support to Gaston were guilty of treason.

These actions precipitated a conflict with the Paris *Parlement*, which had begun to claim that its right to register all edicts allowed it to reject those it disliked. This was to transform a judicial privilege, accorded to it as a sovereign court, into a political weapon, although the members' concern was not to propound a new constitutional theory but simply to safeguard their own interests as a class. As the administrators and officers of the law they had benefited greatly from their alliance with the crown against the nobility, but their jurisdiction was in turn threatened by Richelieu's creation of special courts and tribunals to enforce his policies: the Marillac brothers, for example, had been tried in the *Chambre de l'Arsenal*, an offshoot of the royal council, and the *parlement* was determined to remind Richelieu of its own importance and power.

By refusing to ratify the edict against Gaston's supporters, however, it chose to fight on dangerous ground, since Gaston's guilt was self-evident. Moreover, the *parlement* had no allies, and no means of enforcing sanctions against the crown. It was not a representative assembly but one of the king's own courts; and it was enough for the king to appear before it in person, in a ceremony known as a *lit de justice*, for all opposition to be silenced. When Louis XIII secured the registration of his edict against Gaston in this manner, he was prompted by Richelieu to remind the members of their limited jurisdiction: 'You exist only for judging disputes between Master Peter and Master Paul, and if you try to exceed your commission I will cut your nails to the quick.' Richelieu was not entirely satisfied by the sullen acquiescence enforced by the *lit de justice*, and he looked for other means to weaken the *parlement's* authority. Its members could not be dismissed from the positions they had purchased, but the offices of the greatest importance and profit could be effectively disparaged by increasing their number and auctioning them off. The few individuals who dared to make public protest were arrested and exiled. Finally, in 1641, the chastened *parlement* registered an edict which forbade it to discuss affairs of state without the king's permission.

It was essential to Richelieu's purpose that the orders of the council should be enforced without let or hindrance in the provinces, and his methods of achieving this were similar to those of Henry IV. Of the provincial governors in 1614, sixteen could be ranked as over-mighty subjects, ruling their provinces in their own interests; by imprisonment, exile or execution, their number had been reduced to four when Richelieu died. Their place was taken by men whose careers were made in the royal service, such men as Henri de Sourdis, Archbishop of Bordeaux, who successfully challenged the feudal pretensions of the nobility in Guienne and Provence, and whose loyalty to the crown was assured. Within the *pays d'élections*, the central provinces of France, the task of enforcing administrative uniformity was not difficult. These provinces had long been under royal control and the machinery for applying royal policy was already in existence. Once the rival authority of the nobles had been curtailed by Richelieu's stern measures, the agents of the crown, the *élus* and *officiers*, were able to do their work effectively.

Where Richelieu went further than Henry IV was in his attack on the privileges of the *pays d'état* — the outlying provinces which had been acquired more recently than the *pays d'élections*, and where the spirit of independence was still strong. In Normandy, Brittany, Burgundy, Dauphiné, Provence and Languedoc, the Estates met regularly and retained considerable powers of self-government, not least the right to vote their own taxes. It was no accident that the *pays d'état*, representing one third of the kingdom, contributed only one tenth of the revenue, and it was this which prompted Richelieu's action in 1631 when he appointed *élus* in the provinces of Dauphiné, Provence and Languedoc. Since the *élus* were primarily concerned with the collection of taxes, this was an intrusion of the utmost importance, but so great had the power of the crown become that Languedoc alone resisted. It was here that the Huguenots had repeatedly challenged the crown in the past, and the independent spirit of the Estates was so marked that Richelieu had once commented that, 'the king's authority is hardly recognised in their country.'

Like the Paris *Parlement*, Languedoc weakened its cause by associating with Gaston d'Orléans, with whom its governor, Henri de Montmorenci, was in correspondence. The appointment of the *élus* was swiftly followed by Gaston's arrival from Lorraine, and in 1632 rebellion broke out. The powerful pressure groups within the province, however, were at odds with each other. The Huguenots were afraid to risk the forfeiture of their remaining privileges, and chose to remain inactive; the middle classes, who championed the cause of the Estates, demanded the removal of the *élus*; the nobility, enrolled beneath the feudal banner of the Montmorencis, fought for Gaston and a return to the 'good old days'. Against this array of divided interests the royal army stood firm. At the first setback, Gaston forsook the rebels and rushed to make his peace with the king. His followers lost heart, the revolt was broken and Montmorenci was executed. Richelieu wisely negotiated a moderate settlement in order to prevent further outbursts and the *élus* were dismissed.

In an entirely different field, Richelieu broke new ground by creating a French navy. A fleet of galleys existed for service in the Mediterranean, but the Atlantic fleet, a mere handful of ships in 1624, was destroyed by Soubise's Huguenot squadron off the Normandy coast. The siege of La Rochelle brought home to Richelieu the dangers attendant upon a major power which could not defend itself at sea, and so in 1629 he prepared a memorandum for the king, stressing the need for a navy, 'since the sea is an open door to every state in the world'. First of all he appointed himself to the newly created office of *Surintendant général de la navigation et commerce*, and abolished the post of admiral lest its occupant should attempt to contest his authority. He quickly found, however, that the admiral's jurisdiction had extended only to the Channel; that the governors of Brittany, Provence and Guienne claimed control of the coastal waters of their provinces; and that the crown had alienated its fishing rights along the coast. Virtually nothing of the coastline was therefore under the king's direct control. Once again Richelieu found it necessary to struggle against local privilege in order to establish a centralised and efficient department of state. The *Ordonnance de la Marine*, restoring to the crown all its rights along the coast, aroused less opposition than usual to such an act of royal authority, since those who had a vested interest in the matter were informed that, unless the crown assumed control, the whole cost of constructing defence works would fall upon them. Brouage, Le Havre and Harfleur were selected as bases for the royal navy, and Richelieu launched a naval programme designed to create fifty ships of the line and the necessary ancillary craft. Every port in the kingdom with its own shipyard was invited to construct one ship, resistance to central direction being thus overcome by a calculated appeal to local pride and rivalry. New foundries and arsenals were also established, as at Brest and La Rochelle, though it still remained necessary to purchase naval supplies from the Dutch.

The central organisation controlling this vast undertaking was small but efficient. Richelieu appointed the members of the *Conseil de la Marine*, and a staff of about forty *commissaires* supervised their orders. By 1636, the Atlantic fleet boasted thirty-eight new ships. Twelve of these were over 500 tons; and *La Couronne*, displacing 2,000 tons, had seventy-two guns and required a crew of 600 men. Recruitment, however, was one of Richelieu's greatest problems, since France did not possess any great tradition of naval service, and there were more French sailors in the ships of England and of the United Provinces than in those of the French navy. Reliable officers, especially captains, were very difficult to find, and often there were only merchants and former pirates to choose from Once the navy was established, however, Richelieu revived the office of admiral and appointed Henri de Sourdis, Archbishop of Bordeaux: a strange choice, perhaps, but as a provincial governor he had proved both his loyalty to the crown and his ability to administer large organisations. He sailed out to attack the Spaniards off Fuentarrabia in 1638,[1] destroying fourteen capital ships and three frigates, a triumph which sealed Richelieu's efforts to establish France as a naval power.

Richelieu was less successful in reviving the mercantile marine. Along the well-established routes to West Africa, the Levant and the East Indies, French merchants were able to hold their ground, but the attempts to open up new routes and markets all failed. English and Dutch merchants were ready to finance their own undertakings in overseas trade, but in France the burden of invest-

[1] See below, page 176.

ment was left to the government,[1] whose financial resources were
limited. Moreover, the government officials who thus directed the
new companies, were unable to understand that mercantile expansion depended upon the initiative of opportunists; instead of
encouraging trade, their well-intentioned efforts only served to
stifle it. Under-subscribed and over-regulated, none of Richelieu's
ventures had any chance of success. The *Compagnie du Morbihan*
was founded to trade in Canada, the West Indies, Russia and the
North. It lasted twelve months, to be followed by the *Compagnie
des Cents Associés*, which limited its aims to Canada alone. This
again failed, as did its successor, the *Compagnie des Îles d'Amerique*,
and not even its imposing title could save the *Compagnie de la
Nacelle de St. Pierre Fleurdelysée*, which in an outburst of enthusiasm claimed the whole world as its market.

Richelieu improved the currency by restricting the local mints
to issuing coins of small denominations and by the general issue in
1640 of a standard coin, the *louis d'or*. He did not succeed in his
ambitious projects to abolish the *paulette* and to introduce a general
tax of a *sou pour livre* to be paid by all classes. In both these proposals he had the wit to discern the two basic weaknesses of the
ancien régime, its lack of control over its *officiers*, a result of selling
them their jobs, and its failure to tax the wealthy sections of society,
but he had neither the power nor the opportunity to reform them.
The immediate demands of war made it necessary to raise cash
immediately by all available means, the sale of offices being one,
while the dangers of war made it inadvisable to provoke rebellion
by an attempt to tax the nobles. Moreover, it was impossible for
Richelieu to imitate Sully by devoting all his time to economic
affairs since problems of administration and foreign policy constantly demanded his attention. Consequently he had no alternative but to order supplementary impositions of the *taille* and to
ignore the widespread disturbances which this caused among the
peasantry. Such riots could always be quelled by the army, and as
for the victims 'all politicians are agreed that when the people are
too comfortable it is impossible to keep them within the bounds of
duty'. But successive increases in the *taille* could only provide a
temporary solution to his problems, and an income of 43,454,166
livres in 1640 was of little value in meeting an expenditure of
116,208,911. None the less, though bankruptcy threatened before

---

[1] See above, page 149.

his death, Richelieu generally raised the money he needed for his foreign ventures, and government income in France, for all its inadequacies, was probably the largest of any European state.

Towards the end of his life, Richelieu recorded in his *Mémoires* an idealised version of the aims he had proposed to achieve in 1624. 'I promised the king to use all the industry and all the authority which it pleased him to grant me, to ruin the Huguenot faction, humble the pride of the great nobles, reduce all his subjects to their proper duty and to raise his name amongst foreign nations to the pinnacle where it ought to be.' None of these achievements, however, save perhaps the first, solved the long-term evils and weaknesses inherent in the French political system. Richelieu suppressed each rebellion and each conspiracy against the crown; he could not destroy the habit of irresponsible intrigue and factious opposition which remained endemic in France.

Gaston had made his peace with Louis after the Languedoc rising, and although he remained a centre of intrigue and disaffection his position was weakened by the unexpected birth of an heir to the throne in 1638. A more serious threat resulted from the rise to favour of a lively young noble, Cinq Mars, whom Richelieu had encouraged as his presence served to enliven the king in his old age. Unfortunately his head was turned by Louis's affection, and by the attention it brought him from the rest of the court. The cardinal's enemies assiduously encouraged Cinq Mars to believe that he might supplant Richelieu in the king's favour, and the nobles in exile at Brussels looked hopefully for a speedy return to France. Thus, in the last year of his life, Richelieu discovered a plot as dangerous as any that had occurred in the past.

Cinq Mars was executed, but his conspiracy demonstrated that the problem of the unruly nobility had not been solved. When Louis died, a few weeks after his minister, he left a five-year-old boy to succeed him; and the nobles, the provincial Estates and the *parlements*, seized with delight the opportunities afforded them by yet another regency administration.

THE MINORITY OF LOUIS XIV, 1643–60

The Regency Government

In the Middle Ages, after the reign of Philippe le Bel, the barons whom he kept under close control cried out for a return to 'the customs of St. Louis'. On the death of Richelieu and Louis XIII there arose a similar demand for the restoration of 'l'ancien gouvernement'. This appeal to some mythical constitution, to the legendary good old days, was a useful formula designed to conceal a variety of causes, reform and the redress of public wrongs, sedition and the settlement of private grievances; all were evident in the troubled years of Louis XIV's minority.

Louis XIII knew only too well the dangers that attended a royal minority, and he wanted to save France from the anarchy of his own childhood. Unhappily there was no member of the royal family whom he could trust to act as regent. His wife Anne and his brother Gaston had been perennially involved in intrigues against his government, and the young prince of Condé was already proving himself as irresponsible in politics as he was brilliant at war: he therefore appointed a council of regency in which they were to be outnumbered by Cardinal Mazarin and three other officials, all trained by Richelieu. On Louis's death, however, Anne, Gaston and Condé immediately tried to remove the official members from the council, with the support of the nobles, who dreaded a continuation of Richelieu's stern policies. At the same time they intrigued bitterly amongst themselves since none would accord precedence to the others. In the end it was Anne who triumphed. She deftly succeeded in setting Condé and Gaston against each other, while she herself appealed to the Paris *Parlement* to accord her full powers as regent. The members were so gratified by her invitation to discuss an affair of state, and so mindful of her position as the king's mother, that they rescinded Louis's will without demur. With full authority to do as she wished, Anne then took Mazarin to be her minister in public, and her husband in private,[1] to the fury and amazement of all those who had been intriguing for power and a share in the spoils.

In this strange and unexpected manner, Anne's love for Mazarin ensured the fulfilment of Louis XIII's intentions, since the great difference in character between the two cardinals obscured the fact that their aims were identical. Mazarin, an Italian in papal service, had made a dramatic début before the French and Spanish armies

[1] Their relationship has been much discussed. Their affection for each other, the extraordinary influence which Mazarin maintained over Anne in the years which followed, and the queen's own reputation for chastity, are established facts best reconciled by the explanation of a secret marriage.

outside Casale in 1632. As the battle began he had galloped between the opposing forces, waving his crucifix wildly in the air,
proclaiming a papal truce. Later he was sent to Paris where he won
Richelieu's confidence and entered his service. Richelieu respected
his abilities, but to the nobles he appeared effete and contemptible.
He surrounded himself with elegant tapestries, works of art and
carefully perfumed pets; he paraded in company with his astonishingly beautiful nieces whose arrival took the court by storm; and,
after 1643, his liaison with the regent smacked of petticoat government and backstairs intrigue. He loved ostentation, and his rapacity
in amassing a private fortune contrasted strangely with the ascetic
figure of his predecessor. Richelieu had cultivated an icy austerity
which made him aloof and unapproachable, while his commanding
features instilled fear among his enemies: Mazarin, cheerful and
pleasure-loving, could even be obsequious. 'On the steps of that
throne from which the fierce and terrible Richelieu had crushed
rather than governed mankind we saw a gentle and kindly successor . . . who was exceedingly sorry that his dignity as cardinal
prevented himself from humiliating himself before you as much as
he could have liked.' (de Retz.) For all its irony, the contrast was
well drawn, but de Retz failed to notice that Mazarin could be as
resolute as Richelieu when need arose.

His abilities were immediately put to the test. The nobles who
had already imagined themselves in positions of power resented the
destruction of their ambitions, and were furious at the way Anne
had tricked them. Among the conspirators were Vendôme, Henry
IV's illegitimate son; Vendôme's son Beaufort, idolised by the
Paris fishwives for his braggart manliness; and the irrepressible
Duchesse de Chevreuse, only just returned from sixteen years of
exile.[1] The *Importants*, as they were called, were no match for
Mazarin, however, who arrested and exiled them before their plans
were complete.

If a discontented and factious nobility had been the only source
of trouble, then the Regency might well have been a model of
efficient government; but there were other, more serious, problems
to be faced. The war with Spain was still in progress, and owing to
Richelieu's lack of financial ability, the crown was bankrupt: by
1643 the revenues were pledged in advance for the next three years

[1] See above, page 154, for her part in the Chalais conspiracy.

in order to pay the speculators who had financed Richelieu's last campaigns. Finding it impossible to solve the government's financial problems as easily as he solved his own, Mazarin had to resort to extraordinary measures to raise money. In Paris, for example, he revived a wartime edict of Henry II's reign, forbidding the construction of buildings beyond the city walls — not so much to safeguard the city's defences as to impose fines on all those who had contravened the regulation. Another expedient was the manipulation of the *rentes*, investments in the city government of Paris which represented a rudimentary kind of national debt. By deliberately defaulting on the payment of interest, Mazarin encouraged the speculators to sell their *rentes*. The market price fell and the government bought up as many as possible. It was then a simple matter to announce a payment of interest, stimulate speculation and then sell out as the price rose. More valuable than either of these measures was the time-honoured sale of offices. The prestige, the power, and the opportunity for profit which these offices afforded, along with the security of tenure assured by the payment of the *paulette*, made them attractive to the middle class. Mazarin's creation of many new offices, and the reduplication of others, was therefore of great benefit to the Treasury, but not to the stability of the administration as a whole.

These expedients met with great opposition from the *officiers*, who already had many substantial grievances. Their salaries had not been paid for several years, and the sale of new offices disparaged the value of their own. Moreover, as the crown had lost the power to dismiss, and thus to discipline, its own civil servants, Richelieu and Mazarin had employed a new type of official, the intendant and *commissaire*, who was entirely dependent upon the royal council. The *officiers*, as a result, had been deprived of some of their jurisdiction with a corresponding loss in income and prestige. Finally, as many of this class were also investors in the *rentes*, they objected to Mazarin's other expedients. It was natural for them to voice their complaints through the institutions in which their own class was particularly dominant, the *parlements*, and above all through the Paris *Parlement*.

This coincidence of noble intrigue, royal bankruptcy and middle-class opposition resulted in the outbreak of the Fronde.

The Fronde, 1648-9

In 1648 the Paris *Parlement* was compelled, in a *lit de justice*, to register seven new edicts by which Mazarin intended to raise further sums of money. It was not only the edicts which aroused opposition, but the *lit de justice* itself. The members condemned it as a novel device unfairly exploited by the crown, and they challenged its legality under a Regency. Compelled by Anne to give way on this point they attacked on a different front, demanding the right to consult with the other sovereign courts, the *Chambre des Comptes*, the *Cour des Aides* and the *Grand Conseil*. In violation of all precedents, and in defiance of all royal commands, representatives of the four courts met in the Chambre de St. Louis in the Palais de Justice to discuss their grievances; this was a significant occasion since it represented the united action of the four courts which claimed descent from the royal council of the medieval kings.

1648 was indeed a year of revolution in Europe. In Portugal, England, Naples and Catalonia there was rebellion against the crown, but it is misleading to make an analogy between these events and the resistance of the Paris *Parlement*. With the States-General in abeyance, it is true that it had become the sole outlet for public opinion and therefore enjoyed a more than local prominence. Nevertheless, it remained essentially representative of its own class, a privileged body concerned with the individual privileges of its members, and the articles drawn up in the Palais de Justice reflected this limited outlook. Some proposals indeed, like the reduction of the *taille* and the prosecution of dishonest *fermiers* who speculated in the field of taxes, represented popular discontent with the government and won general approval. More significantly, however, other proposals demanded the removal of intendants and *commissaires*, the exemption of *officiers* from arbitrary arrest by *lettres de cachet*, and the abolition of the *lit de justice*. In this way they attempted to strengthen the jurisdiction and authority of their class, and to make the government powerless to coerce them either individually or collectively.

Mazarin pretended to consider the demands of the *officiers* while he waited anxiously for news of the armies in the field against Spain. A timely French victory at Lens revived the government's prestige at home, and he ordered the arrest of three members of the *parlement*. The arrests were bungled. One man escaped. Broussel, who had attracted some attention by an outspoken attack on taxes in general, was seized in full view of the mob, and a riot broke out immediately, from which the Fronde derived its name.[1] At first it was nothing more than a spontaneous and violent demonstration, but soon the hand of an organiser became apparent, that of Paul de Gondi, better known by his later title, de Retz. Gondi's ambitions were well defined: he wanted the archbishopric of Paris, a cardinal's hat, and control of the administration; his strategy was to exploit the crown's weakness and difficulties until these ends were achieved. His close liaison with the disaffected nobility, and with the mob, made him a figure of particular importance, for it was he who transformed the riot into an act of rebellion, inspired the creation of barricades in the streets, and organised a march on the Palais Royal to demand Broussel's release.

Powerless for the moment, Mazarin released Broussel and accepted all the demands of the sovereign courts. His one hope lay in the speedy conclusion of the peace settlement at Westphalia, and the return of the army. Until then, he advised Anne to take her son away from Paris to Rueil, where the family endured a miserable winter without even the means to purchase furniture and firewood. The arrival of Charles I's widow from England in January 1649 was an ominous indication of their own predicament.

The Peace of Westphalia left Spain as the only power still at war with France, and the recall of part of the army in 1649 was therefore possible, although the noble leaders of the army were so hostile to Mazarin that they refused to march against Paris. Condé alone remained loyal, being more contemptuous of the mob than of the minister, but his brother, Conti, and most of the other princes, the *Importants* and their hangers-on, joined the Frondeurs and appealed to Spain for assistance. Treason on this scale was to be expected from the nobility; for the *officiers* it was an entirely different matter, and the *parlement* anxiously declared that, 'while we order the levying of troops, we must also indicate that it is against the minister that we fight and not the King, for we must not fall into rebellion'. The distinction was of vital importance for the men who administered royal justice, but, by the end of March 1649, they found it was no longer valid. Embarrassed by their

---

[1] A *fronde* was a sling. It was de Retz, in his *Mémoires*, who contemptuously likened his supporters to 'schoolboys who sling mud [qui frondent] in the gutters of Paris'.

noble allies, and terrified of the mob, the *officiers* made a separate peace with the court at Rueil, by which the demands of the sovereign courts were again confirmed.

The Fronde of the Nobles, 1649-53

The Treaty of Rueil did not settle anything, since the nobles who had joined in the Fronde did not want to be pacified and refused to accept its terms. For the next three years they treated France as a private battleground, settling all disputes and jealousies by a resort to arms. Condé, abandoning the regent after the submission of the *officiers*, fought to assuage the slightest affront to his vanity, which had become intolerably sensitive by reason of his spectacular victories in the Thirty Years War. In his overweening conceit he aimed at nothing less than control of the kingdom, an ambition shared by Gaston, that veteran of a hundred intrigues. The remainder took arms to avenge an insult, fulfil an ambition or because they had nothing better to do. The Comte d'Alais marched against the *Parlement* of Provence because it had denied his claim in a land suit, Gaston's daughter raised her own army in order to bargain for the young King's hand in marriage, and Madame de Longueville, a restless beauty married to a dullard, relieved the tedium of her life by inciting her lovers to deeds of martial valour. For the nobles and their ladies, the Fronde became an exciting game in which foreigners of their own class were welcome to join, exiled cavaliers from England, and princes of the Empire bored by a return of peace to their territories. Whereas the *parlement* had at least been consistent in its opposition, the behaviour of the nobles was utterly irresponsible. Treacherous to their country and to each other, their intrigues resulted in a confused series of alliances that formed and re-formed with bewildering rapidity. Gaston, of all men, confessed himself baffled: 'I remember every intrigue of the League, every faction of the Huguenots, but I have never found anything so difficult to comprehend as the present situation.'

After the Treaty of Rueil the court had returned to Paris, where Mazarin drew together Gaston, Gondi and all those who resented Condé's insufferable arrogance. Emboldened by their support, he arrested Condé, Conti and their brother-in-law, Longueville, in January 1650, but this recourse to force only served to inflame the supporters of the princes. Madame de Longueville summoned her lover, Turenne, to invade Picardy with a Spanish army; Condé's mother seized Bordeaux; and the south-west rose in revolt. By 1651 the situation had altered beyond recognition: Gondi and Gaston deserted the court, the princes were released, and Mazarin, unable to crush his enemies by force, disarmed them by leaving France, with the intention to return as soon as they fell out among themselves. When the Paris mob learned of his flight it invaded the palace to make certain that the young king had not left with him; throughout the night Louis XIV feigned sleep to reassure the noisome throng which passed his bedside. Anne, too, was in danger since the Frondeurs planned to remove her to a convent. With great courage, however, she remained in close touch with Mazarin and played a skilful part in encouraging signs of dissension among her enemies. Once Mazarin had left, in fact, the coalition against him began to collapse under the strain of irreconcilable interests.

By the end of 1651 it was safe for Mazarin to return to France, bringing with him an army of German mercenaries. Condé had still not learned to conceal his disdain for his allies, and when they showed signs of unrest he left Paris to join the Spaniards. Although the mob continued to cheer his name, the Paris *Parlement* declared him a traitor; Turenne, his greatest rival for military honours, was persuaded by Mazarin to command the royal army against him, and Gondi's allegiance was recovered by his elevation to the rank of Cardinal de Retz. Throughout 1652 the Fronde continued its bewildering course. Condé led a Spanish army against Paris, the court retired to Poitiers, and Mazarin once again left the country in order that the growing resentment at Condé's excesses should not be distracted by the hostility which still existed against himself. A dramatic struggle ensued between Condé and Turenne for the mastery of Paris, in which Gaston's daughter at once won fame, and forfeited all chance of marrying the young king, by training the Bastille's guns on the royal army. Though Condé again ruled in Paris, his tenure of power was short-lived. As in 1598, the peasantry and the middle classes began to long for the restoration of royal authority and a return to peace and security. Even the nobles tired of a conflict which had become so confused as to be unprofitable, and Condé in disgust left France to enter Spanish service. Louis XIV, though still in his teens, proclaimed his majority in October 1652, and the court was welcomed back to Paris.

The Fronde had failed because none of the Frondeurs had been able to provide the sustained direction and leadership so necessary in an enterprise against the crown. The *parlement* had evolved a policy of sorts, but lacked the capacity to enforce its demands. The nobility, with its excess of military talent, was barren of any policy save that of individual self-interest.

The end of the regency signalised the end of the Fronde. In February 1653 Mazarin returned to the court, where he remained at the centre of the administration until his death in 1661. As the Frondeurs made their submission, he began again the work of restoring royal authority. The Paris *Parlement* was deprived of all the privileges gained since 1648, and the Treaty of Rueil was ignored. Condé remained defiant in exile until 1659, but most of the nobles followed Gaston's example and retired to their estates. A few, such as Conti and Madame de Longueville, made a surprising renunciation of worldly vanities by associating with the Jansenist community at Port-Royal.[1] De Retz did not enjoy his new title for long. Imprisoned by Mazarin, he eventually escaped to spend the rest of his life in exile, committing to his *Mémoires* a mordant and satiric account of the events in which he had played so prominent a part.

The achievements of Richelieu were thus salvaged by his successor, and the way was paved for the absolutism of Louis XIV. All that survived of these troubled years was Louis's bitter memory of the discomfort, danger and indignity he had endured: a memory which led him to stifle the *parlement*, to turn the nobles into court dandies, and to make his home, not in Paris, where the mob had clamoured around his bedside, but in the remote and spacious dignity of Versailles.

THE CONTINUITY OF FRENCH FOREIGN POLICY, 1589–1660

Henry IV

The Treaty of Cateau-Cambrésis in 1559 represented the climax of fifty years of Spanish supremacy in Europe. It recognised Spain as the ruler of Naples and Milan, Franche Comté, Luxemburg and the Netherlands; France on the other hand, isolated and encircled by her enemy, fell prey to the evils of prolonged civil war.

[1] See Chapter VI, page 261.

The Treaty of the Pyrenees in 1659 inaugurated fifty years of French supremacy and recorded the collapse of Spain.

This dramatic reversal of roles was explained in part by the decline of Spain,[1] but it was a decline accelerated and exploited by the three great figures of Henry IV, Richelieu and Mazarin. For sixty years their policies were identical: their aim, as Richelieu once expressed it, was 'to check the progress of Spain. Wherever that nation aims at increasing its power and extending its territory, our one object must be to fortify and dig ourselves in, whilst making open doors into neighbouring states so that we can safeguard them against Spanish oppression whenever occasion may arise.' To this end they directed their principal efforts; to this end they subordinated their internal policies, which were essentially designed to put France on a more effective footing for the successful prosecution of their foreign policy.

Sully's *Mémoires* contain many references to Le Grand Dessein, a supposed declaration of Henry's policies which outlined the formation of a European confederation to destroy Habsburg supremacy and to drive the Turks and the Russians out of Europe, and finally to safeguard universal peace. This grandiose scheme existed, however, only in Sully's imagination. Henry himself was more practical and more limited in his aims. In 1598 he had made peace with Spain by the Treaty of Vervins, which virtually repeated the terms of Cateau-Cambrésis. He knew that France was not strong enough to wage open war against her enemy, and he planned to encroach upon the Spanish empire piecemeal, by cautious attacks at its weakest point, its lines of communication. From Milan to Brussels there existed a tenuous line of provinces which served a dual purpose: through them the Spanish armies could march at will, from them the French frontier could be invaded at any point.

Henry's first enterprise was directed against Savoy. This duchy, an important link between Spanish Milan and Franche Comté, had been for some time an ally of Spain, and its dukes had tried to expand their territory into France during the anarchy of the wars of religion. In 1600 Charles Emmanuel of Savoy had agreed to restore to Henry the marquisate of Saluzzo, across the frontier from Dauphiné, but he hoped that the conspiracies of Biron and Bouillon would make it unnecessary for him to keep his promise. Henry did not wait upon events. Seizing Chambéry, the capital of

[1] See Chapter V.

MAP 5   The Frontiers of France, 1598–1643

Savoy, he compelled the duke to offer him, not Saluzzo, but the
more valuable provinces of Bresse, Bugey and Gex, which lay along
the east bank of the Rhône between Lyon and Franche Comté.
This acquisition considerably strengthened the French frontier at
a dangerous point, and limited communication between Savoy and
Franche Comté to a narrow corridor which could be easily occupied
in time of war.

Henry wisely sought the alliance of other states who feared the
extent of Spanish power. He made treaties with Venice, Switzerland, Tuscany and Mantua in order to isolate the Spanish base in
Milan, and began negotiations with the Protestants of the Grisons,
whose canton converged on the Val Telline through which the
Spaniards communicated with the Tyrol and Austria. Even the

Duke of Savoy was eventually seduced from the Habsburg camp; but none of these alliances was put to the test of war, for Henry was merely reconnoitring the ground and strengthening his position.

Further north his action was more positive and more dangerous. He allied with the Dutch in their revolt against Spain, and did much to bring about the Truce of 1609 which recognised their independence for the time being. He also became patron of the Evangelical Union in Germany,[1] believing it to be a useful weapon with which to embarrass the Habsburgs. Because of these alliances he prepared to fight in 1610 over the disputed territories of Jülich–Cleves. The fortresses of Jülich controlled the Rhine crossing below Cologne, and the duchies provided a vital link between Henry and both his allies. The Dutch were eager to occupy Cleves, adjacent to their frontier, the Evangelical Union was ready for war, and Henry mobilised an army of 50,000 men. Nevertheless it was a dangerous venture, since he faced the formidable might of Spain, the emperor and the Catholic League. The gamble was never made. As Henry left Paris in 1610 to join the army, he was stabbed to death by Ravaillac, a Catholic fanatic who believed himself divinely appointed to destroy the apostate and friend of heretics. In one sense Henry's reputation was saved by his assassination, since it invested him with the halo of martyrdom, and prevented the outbreak of a war which might well have proved disastrous for France. As Richelieu was to realise, Spain could not yet be challenged in open war: the attack had to be by sap and mine, and 'must be done with great caution, tact and secrecy'.

Richelieu

Henry IV's death was followed by the complete reversal of his policy. France withdrew from the Evangelical Union and Louis XIII was married to Anne of Austria, daughter of Philip III of Spain; a strange *rapprochement* explained by Marie de Medici's fears of Spain, and encouraged by her feckless counsellors who were either in Spanish pay or were simply eager to spend Sully's treasure on themselves rather than on warfare. It also owed much to the new fervour which was evident in the French Church at that

[1] For a discussion of this, and of the Jülich–Cleves crisis, see Chapter II, page 112.

time.[1] Cardinal Bérulle and Father Joseph, for example, urged the need for closer co-operation between the Catholic powers to further the work of the Counter-Reformation and to drive the Turks from Europe; and it was not until their efforts to win Spanish support for a crusade had been rebuffed by Philip III, that the enthusiasm of the *dévots* for the Catholic alliance was checked. Father Joseph, henceforth, became a bitter opponent of the Habsburgs and the wheel turned full circle with Richelieu's appointment to the royal council in 1624.

'Physicians', wrote Richelieu in 1624, 'hold it for an aphorism that an internal weakness, however small in itself, is more to be feared than an external injury, be it ever so large and painful. From this we learn that we must abandon what is to be done abroad until we have done what must be done at home.' For this reason his first concern was to restore the authority of the crown in France, rather than to challenge the power of Spain in Europe. Nevertheless, he did not ignore the opportunities presented by the Thirty Years War. Like Henry IV, he realised the importance of the Val Telline to Spain, and in 1624 his troops, with those of the Grisons, occupied the pass.[2] Although Venice and Savoy promised assistance to France, the Huguenot rebellion of 1625 compelled Richelieu to recall his army and acknowledge defeat. Moreover, his hopes of an alliance with England, based on the marriage of Charles I and Henrietta Maria in 1624, proved abortive. Charles refused to send naval support against the Huguenots, and his open discourtesies to his Catholic wife, along with disputes over trade, led to war.

By 1629 Richelieu was in a stronger position. The English had failed to relieve La Rochelle, the Huguenots had surrendered at Alais, and he was therefore free to intervene decisively in the Mantuan dispute. Mantua itself was of minor importance, but its dukes also controlled Casale and Montferrat, two powerful frontier towns between Milan and Savoy. When the duchy was claimed by the Duke of Nevers, a French prince, the Emperor Ferdinand II seized it on behalf of his Spanish cousin, while Spanish troops besieged Casale. Once Richelieu was certain that Ferdinand would

---

[1] See Chapter I, page 77.
[2] For this, and for the other events of the Thirty Years War which follow in the next paragraphs, see Chapter II, pages 122–37 for a more detailed account.

fail to win German support for his action, he marched through Savoy, relieved Casale and occupied Pinerolo, another valuable frontier base. Finally, the Treaty of Cherasco in 1631 secured Mantua for the French candidate, and Savoy agreed to sell Pinerolo to France.

The emperor's intervention in the Mantuan dispute drew Richelieu's attention to the close bond existing between the Habsburg dynasties in Spain and Austria. In his enmity to the one he had to take account of the other, and Father Joseph was therefore sent to the Diet of Regensburg to encourage the German princes in opposition to the emperor's policies. This move not only bore fruit in the Mantuan crisis, but secured the friendship of Maximilian of Bavaria. Meanwhile, Richelieu had also won the alliance of Sweden, whose king was about to invade Germany. This new situation which developed in Germany to the detriment of the emperor would have occurred without French intervention, but Richelieu's actions served to exploit the general run of events to the advantage of France. In associating with both Maximilian and Gustavus II Adolphus, he was perhaps too optimistic: neither was prepared to accept his direction and Gustavus in particular proved to be too independent, too powerful and too Protestant. His campaigns in the Rhineland and in Bavaria destroyed Richelieu's plan to unite the German princes against the emperor, and gave point to Father Joseph's remark that Sweden was like a poison — useful up to a point as an antidote to Habsburg supremacy, but fatal when taken to excess. Only one good result emerged. When the Archbishop of Trier was threatened by Gustavus's army, he turned to France for protection and granted her the right to garrison Philippsburg and Ehrenbreitstein. Significantly enough, these fortresses lay along the Spanish route from Franche Comté to the Netherlands.

When Gustavus was killed at Lützen in 1632, Richelieu recovered some measure of influence over the German Protestants by organising a new combination, the Heilbronn League, in which Sweden acted specifically as a French mercenary. Unfortunately, the Heilbronn League could not withstand the combined armies of Spain and the emperor. At Nördlingen, in 1634, its forces were destroyed and the balance of power in Europe was upset: Sweden was eclipsed for the moment as a military power, the Protestant princes submitted to the emperor, and the Spaniards seized control of all French bases in the Rhineland. One course only lay open to

Richelieu if his policies were to be achieved, a declaration of war against Spain. The danger was great, since the French frontier was vulnerable at every point, and the French army had not yet been tested in any major battle. Nevertheless, the assault on Spain by sap and mine had failed: it was time to advance in the open.

Within four months Richelieu had marshalled his forces; Sweden promised to harry the imperialists in Germany; Bernard of Saxe-Weimar, a mercenary captain, was commissioned to invade the Rhineland and establish bases in Alsace; the United Provinces agreed to join forces with France in the Netherlands; while Savoy, Mantua, Modena and Parma were enrolled against Spain in north Italy. The Habsburgs, in short, were to be attacked at three vital points, Milan, the Rhineland and the Netherlands. The scheme was brilliantly conceived, but the allies lacked the strength to carry it out. All their attacks failed, and the Habsburgs counter-attacked with disastrous effect in 1636.

Richelieu tried to conceal the danger in which France stood by celebrating every minor triumph with a *Te Deum* in Notre-Dame and banner headlines in the *Gazette*, but his own nerve broke when the Spaniards from the Netherlands and the imperialists from Lorraine joined forces to overrun Picardy. They passed Amiens, seized Corbie, and their outriders approached the suburbs of Paris. While the Cardinal lay sick from nervous exhaustion, it was Louis XIII who saved France and showed himself a true son of Henry IV. He calmed the frightened citizens, rallied the dispirited troops, and rode out to Senlis, midway between the capital and Corbie, to await the final assault. His stand was decisive, for Bernard of Saxe-Weimar had recovered sufficiently to move up on the imperialist flank, and the enemy refused to risk a major engagement in these circumstances. As winter approached, the invaders left France.

The 'year of Corbie' was the most critical of Louis XIII's reign, and if Richelieu's self-confidence was soon restored, the recovery of France was necessarily slow. An invasion of Spain, and the seige of Fuentarrabia in 1638, were the first indications of a turn in the tide. The navy won its first victory by defeating a Spanish fleet which had sailed to relieve the city, and Spain had barely recovered from this before she was again defeated, by the Dutch, in the Battle of the Downs.[1] Nevertheless, Fuentarrabia was not taken by the French, and Richelieu's disgust at the incompetence of his army

[1] See pages 194–5.

commanders was only allayed by news of the fall of Breisach. Bernard of Saxe-Weimar had at last proved victorious, and his death in 1639 gave Richelieu the chance not only to enrol his men in the French army, but to use Breisach as a base for further operations in the Rhineland.[1]

The initiative at last lay with France. Harcourt defeated a Spanish army in north Italy, and occupied Turin in 1640. In the following year, he was sent to Spain to assist the Catalans in their rebellion against Philip IV.[2] Portugal too was in revolt, the Spanish Netherlands were threatened by Dutch and French armies, and the emperor was unable to prevent Swedish raids into Austria. The Habsburgs were no longer a match for the resurgent power of France and her allies. As Richelieu lay dying, in 1642, he learned that French troops had recovered the provinces of Perpignan and Roussillon in the Pyrenees, lost to Spain in 1494. Despite the disasters of the 'year of Corbie', despite the chronic shortage of money and the lack of an efficient army, he had laid the foundations of French power in Europe.

Mazarin

At last France had men of military genius, in Harcourt, Condé and Turenne, and at Rocroi in 1643 Condé destroyed not only a Spanish army but the legend of Spanish invincibility. Along the Rhineland French armies took Philippsburg, Mainz and Worms; further victories were won in 1646 at Courtrai and at Lens in 1648, whilst Turenne ventured into Bavaria in alliance with a Swedish force. Mazarin, distracted though he was by the growing unrest at home, was resourceful enough to ensure that these victories were not forfeited by his diplomats in Westphalia.

The bridgeheads, the forward bases athwart the Spanish lines of encirclement and communication, which Richelieu had striven so resolutely to establish, were finally assured in the Peace of Westphalia.

---

[1] Bernard's death was perhaps opportune, since despite his alliance with France he had refused to admit French troops into Breisach. Richelieu had protested in vain: 'It is extraordinary that His Majesty allows him 2,400,000 livres a year as well as extraordinary subsidies; yet he is not able . . . to dispose of that army to the advantage of the common cause.'

[2] See Chapter V, pages 219–23, for an account of revolts within the Spanish peninsula.

(i) Metz, Toul and Verdun, the bishoprics of Lorraine which had first been granted to Henry II in 1559, were officially confirmed as French possessions;

(ii) Moyenvic, Baccarat and Rambervillers, also in Lorraine, were ceded to France, along with Breisach and the right to garrison Philippsburg;

(iii) The Treaty of Cherasco (1631) and the sale of Pinerolo to France were confirmed;

(iv) In Alsace, save for the city of Strassburg, France obtained virtual control, although there was some doubt over the legal status of the Alsatian towns. Either they were ceded in full sovereignty or else they retained their status as imperial fiefs, with membership of the Diet. Mazarin was so eager to conclude the negotiations, on account of the Fronde, that he accepted a final draft riddled with ambiguity. This in no way perturbed him; rather, as a skilled diplomat, he even hoped to derive some advantage from this in the future.

The settlement negotiated at Westphalia did not end the war between Spain and France since neither side was prepared as yet to concede victory to the other. Philip IV was handicapped by revolts in Portugal, Catalonia and Naples, but Mazarin was equally at a disadvantage because of the Fronde. Although Condé deserted to the Spanish army in 1652, Turenne remained loyal, and the two rivals manœuvred endlessly against each other in the Netherlands, with great caution and to little effect. In order to break the dead-lock, Mazarin determined to prevent Austria from coming to the aid of Spain, and at the same time win the support of England.

He began by an attempt to secure the imperial throne for Louis XIV when Ferdinand III died in 1657. Although his agents won promises of support from the Elector of Bavaria and the Elector Palatine, the money spent on bribery was of no avail against the general suspicion of France which prevailed within the Empire. Leopold of Austria was elected unanimously, and the Habsburgs retained the title which had been held by their family since the fifteenth century. But Mazarin was not disappointed. The chief object of his negotiations had been to prevent an alliance between Austria and Spain, and the German Electors who accepted French money insisted that Leopold should remain neutral after his election, provided imperial territory was not involved. Moreover, the

MAP 6   French Gains on North-Eastern Frontier, 1643–59

election did not terminate Mazarin's interest in Germany, for in 1658 was founded a League of Rhine Princes, whom he persuaded to accept France as its protector. Led by the three ecclesiastical Electors of Mainz, Cologne and Trier, its aims were unexceptionable, unity and peace, and it proved to be a useful instrument of Mazarin's policy since it helped to ensure the neutrality of the German princes in the war between France and Spain, and provided him with a private pressure group in the Imperial Diet. One day Leopold would die, and another attempt to secure Louis's election could be made.

At first sight, an alliance with England seemed out of the question, since Louis XIV was a Catholic monarch and Oliver Cromwell a Puritan regicide. Cromwell, however, believed that war with Spain might lead to valuable acquisitions in the West Indies, and the Catholicism of France paled into insignificance when set against the Spanish Inquisition. Mazarin approached him cautiously in 1655, and he understood the English well enough to offer them first of all a commercial treaty. He also drew attention to the presence of leading cavaliers in Condé's army, and offered the tempting prize of Dunkirk if Spain were defeated. In 1657, Cromwell agreed to join France.

Mazarin's careful diplomacy secured its end, the defeat of Spain. Deprived of allies, her finances ruined and her provinces of Catalonia and Portugal still in revolt, she could not hope to survive against both France and England. When an English fleet appeared in the West Indies, and an army of 6,000 Ironsides joined with the French to seize Dunkirk and Gravelines, she gave up the struggle and sued for peace. This was the greatest moment in French history over the past hundred years, and Mazarin was determined to exploit his advantage to the very limit. The Treaty of the Pyrenees, signed in 1659, represented the full achievement of the ambitions of Henry IV and Richelieu.

(i) France agreed to deny further aid to the rebels within the peninsula, and Condé was pardoned for his treason. This was all that Mazarin would concede to Spain.

(ii) Roussillon and Perpignan; Montmédy in Luxemburg; Artois, and the Netherland towns of Arras, Béthune, Gravelines and Thionville were ceded to France.

(iii) England was given Dunkirk.

(iv) Spain recognised all French acquisitions in the Peace of Westphalia.

(v) Louis XIV was married to Maria Theresa, the Spanish Infanta.

The marriage alliance was the most important clause in the treaty, since Philip IV had no sons at that date and Maria Theresa was heiress to the entire Spanish empire. Mazarin's diplomacy, therefore, paved the way for a dramatic extension of the policies of his predecessors. France was content no longer to think in terms merely of limiting the power of Spain but rather of absorbing it altogether within a new French empire which would bestride the world. Philip IV understood Mazarin's purpose only too well, and he insisted that his daughter renounce her claim to the Spanish throne. At this juncture, however, Mazarin's able negotiator, Hugues de Lionne, demonstrated the talents which were to make him the greatest diplomat of the seventeenth century. He secured the inclusion of a clause by which Maria Theresa's renunciation was made dependent upon the payment of her dowry. Spain was bankrupt but, as Lionne realised, her rulers were too proud to admit that the dowry might never be paid; they could not, therefore, object to Lionne's proviso.

Soon after this crowning achievement of his life's work, Mazarin died in 1661. France owed him much, and it was from him that Louis XIV inherited, not only a firmly established throne, but a vision of two empires, the Imperial and the Spanish, which might conceivably lie within his grasp.

IV

The Rise of the Dutch Republic

The Nature of the Provinces in 1609

Rebellion against the encroaching authority of a central administration was a common feature of the sixteenth century, but successful rebellion was almost unknown. The Dutch Revolt was therefore a rare phenomenon, made even more unconventional by the republican character of the Dutch constitution at a time when monarchy was an unquestioned institution in Europe. The Dutch were not dismayed to be so out of fashion. For forty years they had struggled to be free of Spanish control, and their institutions were hallowed by success when Philip III agreed to a truce, and thus to an admission of their independent status, in 1609.

At first the seventeen provinces in the Spanish Netherlands had risen in protest at the destruction of their ancient liberties by Philip II. Essentially a conservative reaction, doomed to failure so long as it sought to restore the customs of a day that could never return, the movement was then revolutionised by the irruption of Calvinism in the northern provinces. The Calvinists were few in number but they seized positions of authority, and, broadly speaking,[1] it was they who saved the day by the uncompromising determination of their resolve to fight until independence had been won. The southern provinces, embarrassed by the religious and political radicalism of the north, eventually compromised with Spain and sank into obscurity. The northern provinces, banded together in the Union of Utrecht, renounced Spain altogether and rose to the rank of a first class power.

The Union of Utrecht had been forged under the pressure of war. It was not a natural union of provinces based on ethnic or economic

[1] The causes of Dutch success were many: their natural lines of defence, the growing wealth of their cities, the leadership of William the Silent, and the difficulties which beset Philip II, contributed to a great extent, but the differentiating factor between the success of the north and the failure of the south seems to be the presence or absence of Calvinism.

MAP 7   The Rise of the Dutch Republic

foundations, but the fortuitous combination of seven states prepared to accept the leadership of William the Silent and to subordinate their private interests in the common struggle for survival against Spain. Individually, the states were very different in character. Friesland, a maritime province, was governed by an assembly of free peasantry; Overyssel, Groningen and Gelderland, very similar to their neighbours in Germany, were continental in outlook, dominated by the nobles and their semi-feudal followers; Utrecht was ruled by the Protestant canons who had secularised the diocesan estates. Far different were Holland and Zeeland, where lay the real power and prosperity of the Dutch Republic. Here the nobility had been overwhelmed by a wealthy merchant class, and townsmen outnumbered country-dwellers by two to one. The war with Spain had stimulated the economy of both these provinces, especially of Holland: her ships outnumbered the combined mercantile marines of England, Scotland, Spain and France; the Bank of Amsterdam controlled the flow of capital not only in the provinces but even in northern Europe, and her trading companies had established bases around the globe. In the great towns of Haarlem, Dordrecht, Delft, Leyden, Rotterdam and Amsterdam, a commercial oligarchy controlled local government and selected from its own class the representatives to the Estates of Holland, and to the States-General of the Union.

Long before the revolt the practice of oligarchy had become almost universal in Holland. In 1445, for example, the charter granted to Delft had allowed the 'wise and rich' citizens to choose forty, 'the wisest and richest, most honourable, notable and peaceful', from whom the duke selected the regents of the town. This represented the traditional system of government, in which the leading burghers dominated affairs under the general direction of their sovereign, a count, duke, king or emperor, according to the town, the province and the period. It was to defend this system that the revolt against Philip II had originally begun, and the only change it brought about was that, within this closed circle, the sovereign was removed while the urban patriciate consolidated its position. The burghers were extremely fortunate in this, for rebellion breeds a ferment of ideas, unleashing new social forces, and it is rare that one class, and a small one at that, predominates both before and after a successful revolt. The greatest danger had come from the growth of Calvinism which, organised on democratic lines, won the support of the discontented and unfranchised, who discovered in it a path to salvation and an opportunity for political gain. Though Calvinist regents took the place of Catholics in the towns which fell to Calvinist troops, the new officials came from the same group of families as the old, and their aims were identical: opposed to the intolerance of the ministers, and hostile to the democratic and radical ideas of the Calvinist congregations, they sought to retain the inviolability of their class. By this astute conversion they preserved their monopoly of power.

The federal assembly of the United Provinces, the States-General, was not a sovereign body. The deputies were not free agents but merely the spokesmen of their provinces, and their unanimity was necessary before any action could be authorised. This situation, entailing as it did the constant reference by deputies to their local Estates, could have led to paralysis in the administration; in fact, the tradition of unanimity, observed at all levels of the government, had given rise to another tradition by which the dissentient voices to a majority decision were won over by the chairman of each committee or assembly.[1] Moreover, as Holland contributed more than half of the Republic's income, and most of its navy, her policies were frequently adopted by the other provinces, and her administrative officials became the chief functionaries of the federal government. It was Jan van Oldenbarneveldt, Advocate of Holland, who convoked the States-General, directed its deliberations, saw to the execution of its decrees, recorded its affairs and corresponded on its behalf with foreign powers. Significantly too, the States-General met at The Hague, the capital of Holland, in the same building as the Estates of Holland.

The regents of Holland, who thus dominated the States-General, read their Livy and compared their state to that of republican Rome, but there was another important factor in the political life of the United Provinces, the House of Orange. William the Silent had been the hero of the revolt; Maurice of Nassau, his son, and William Louis, his nephew, added to the family's reputation by the skill which they displayed in the war against Spain. Both Maurice and William Louis planned their manœuvres with the aid of lead soldiers, trained their men to dig their own positions, and rehearsed them in mock battles during the winter months. In addition to studying Roman methods of warfare, they paid great attention to the inventions of their own day. Maurice, perhaps the first general to use a telescope to study his enemy's position, equipped his cavalry with firearms in place of the lance, introduced the hand grenade, and employed the mathematician Stevin to make surveys for his fortifications. Brilliant in the theory of war, he excelled in action and his routing of the Spaniards at Turnhout (1597) and Nieuport (1600) won him recognition as one of the greatest soldiers of his age.

In order to secure unity of action, William the Silent had been appointed captain-general of the Republic's army, and stadtholder[2] in each of the separate provinces. Maurice succeeded him

[1] Sir William Temple, an astute English observer, commented on this practice: 'In these Assemblies, tho' all are equal in voices, and one hinders a result; yet it seldom happens, but that united by a common bond of interest, and having all one common end of public good, they come after full debates to easy resolutions . . . so as the smaller part seldom contests hard and long what the greater agrees of. . . .'

[2] Stadtholders had formerly been the representatives of the crown in each province, responsible for defence and good order. After 1579 their office was retained, along with its traditional dignity and prestige, but the appointment was controlled by the Estates.

as captain-general and was elected stadtholder in five of the provinces, while William Louis held the other two. This concentration of power in the hands of one family was regarded with great suspicion by the regent class, who had no wish to see the Republic fall under the control of an Orange dynasty. The stadtholders, on the other hand, were not content to act solely as the commissioned officers of the Estates, to be put on half-pay when the war ended. The Truce of 1609 made a conflict between the two groups inevitable. The House of Orange urged the need for central direction and control, the regents championed the sovereign rights of the individual provinces. In reality, however, the issue was less a matter of rival principles than a struggle for power. If the Republic accepted the creation of a strong, central executive then the princes of Orange would claim the leadership for themselves; if the separation of powers between the provinces was retained then the regent class of Holland would impose its own policies upon the Republic through its commanding influence in the States-General.

The Truce of 1609 and the Arminian Controversy

In the struggle for power within the United Provinces, Maurice of Nassau could invoke the memory of his father and the record of his own brilliant achievements in the field, while the princely splendour of the stadtholder's court gave him immense prestige among the lower classes. The regents of Holland, however, produced an equally formidable opponent in Jan van Oldenbarneveldt, Advocate of Holland and the senior official of the federal administration. As a result of his diplomacy, statesmanship and industry, the separate provinces which had agreed to accept William the Silent's leadership in 1579 had survived both internal dissension and external attack in the years after William's death, to emerge as an independent state in 1609. So highly was he esteemed, so indispensable were his services considered, that, in a country where Calvinism and patriotism had almost become identical, he was permitted to remain a Catholic.

The Truce with Spain (1609) was Oldenbarneveldt's personal triumph. Since 1600 neither side had made much headway against the other, and although a Spanish recovery of the northern provinces seemed most improbable, Oldenbarneveldt knew that a Dutch conquest of the south was equally out of the question. Dutch resources had been heavily taxed by nearly thirty years of warfare, Spinola was successfully holding strong defensive positions against Maurice, and the Catholics of the south hated the Calvinism of the north. In 1608, therefore, he began negotiations on behalf of the States-General, finally securing the two concessions which, in his view, satisfied the most important demands of the Dutch: Spain agreed to consider the Dutch as independent for a period of twelve years, and to allow them freedom of trade in the East Indies.

The Truce was not well received by certain groups within the Republic; yet it was neither the conflict this provoked, nor the rivalry between the House of Orange and the regents of Holland, which, on the surface, occupied the attention of the Dutch after 1609. It was a theological controversy which revived in a Calvinist setting the old problem of free will.

Calvin had taught that God had predestined the fate of all men, and his followers comforted themselves with the assurance that they alone were destined for eternal bliss. Arminius, a Calvinist theologian of remarkably liberal and humane views, questioned whether a God of love would predestine a man's soul to the horrors of hell. This, he argued, conflicted with the notion of a merciful God and paradoxically made God the author of sin.[1] He was mild, indeed hesitant, in publishing his opinions, and there was no opposition to his appointment to a chair of theology at Leyden in 1602; here, however, he was immediately challenged by a fellow professor, Francis Gomarus, whose exile from Bruges in the Catholic south had made him a fiery champion of Calvinist orthodoxy. At first the issue was confined within the lecture halls of the university, but when it touched upon political affairs a wider public joined the debate. If there was no predestined company of the Elect, if Christ in fact died for all men, then the Spanish Catholic and the Dutch Calvinist were both offered the same opportunity of salvation; this was a doctrine which savoured not only of heresy but, in the tense years before the Truce, of treason.

Arminius died in 1609, but his followers secured the protection of Oldenbarneveldt, who found their doctrine congenial to his own tolerant spirit. He had always hoped to see a state church established on broad foundations, and Arminianism was an opportune development since it served to gloss over the many differences between the Calvinist and Catholic faiths. Moreover, Arminius had

[1] See Chapter I, page 79.

followed Luther in accepting the right of the state to control the affairs of the Church, a notion particularly welcome to the regents of Holland, who had good reason to suspect the Calvinist clergy of fomenting political discontent among the lower classes. Eager to strengthen their authority over the clergy, and to encourage the formation of a more broadly based church, the Estates of Holland therefore gave approval to a formal declaration of Arminian doctrine, the *Remonstrance*, which had been drawn up and published at Gouda in 1610.

At this, Gomarus immediately mobilised support for a *Counter-Remonstrance*, reaffirming the strict tenets of Calvinism, to which most of the clergy subscribed. The controversy threatened to become so violent that the Estates of Holland, despite their sympathy with the Arminians, ordered both parties to exercise restraint in matters, 'which are, God help it, all too much in dispute'; but this intervention by a political authority only provoked the clergy to greater indignation. Every Calvinist congregation became a centre of disaffection, from every pulpit Oldenbarneveldt and his class were denounced, and, oblivious to the fact that the southern provinces had deliberately chosen to remain Catholic rather than ally with the Dutch, a war of liberation was demanded to release them from the yoke of the Spanish Inquisition. The Truce, so beneficial in its effect, was condemned as a compact with the forces of evil, the war extolled as a crusade untimely thwarted in its course by Arminian heretics in the pay of Spain.

It was unfortunate for Oldenbarneveldt that his critics lacked his clear vision of the realities of the situation. He saw that the German Protestant princes were unwilling to champion a Protestant crusade after Henry IV's death in 1610,[1] and realised that it was impossible for the Dutch to act on their own. The Truce, in short, provided an opportunity for consolidation rather than expansion. As a result Oldenbarneveldt attempted to preserve good relations with Henry IV's successors, despite their *rapprochement* with Spain, and refused to intrigue with the Huguenot leaders who were planning rebellion. Moreover, he insisted on remaining neutral throughout the Jülich–Cleves crisis. When Spinola seized the Rhineland fortress of Wesel, a Protestant stronghold near the Dutch frontier, Oldenbarneveldt allowed Maurice to take possession of other frontier posts in Cleves

[1] See Chapter II, page 112, for an account of the German situation and of the Jülich–Cleves crisis.

but not to engage Spinola in person lest the Truce with Spain be broken. His policy, however, only served to confirm the prejudiced views of the Counter-Remonstrants, who attributed his inaction to his private adhesion to Catholicism.

As the conflict expanded from the question of Free Will to embrace the issues of war and peace, the quick minds of the Amsterdam merchants awoke to the opportunity for profit which would be afforded by a renewal of hostility with Spain. The burghers of Amsterdam reserved their loyalty to the interests of commerce alone, and, despite their close links with the other regents of Holland, they had opposed the Truce of 1609. The commercial primacy of their city[1] was established by the blockade of Antwerp during the Revolt, and, although the Truce left the Scheldt in Dutch hands, the merchants of Amsterdam were not yet satisfied that their rival was beyond recovery and had sought additional security by continuing the war. Moreover, with appetites enlarged by the success of the East India Company, they dreamed of the still greater profits to be expected from the creation of a West India Company to promote piracy and trade among the Spanish islands. Oldenbarneveldt had forestalled them by making peace with Spain, and there were many disgruntled burghers who chose to believe that the Advocate did not want to see a rival to the East India Company, with which he was closely connected. As a result, the city of Amsterdam openly came to the support of the Counter-Remonstrants by demanding the dismissal of Oldenbarneveldt and an end to the Truce.

The Fall of Oldenbarneveldt

The crisis produced by the Arminian controversy was too good an opportunity for Maurice to miss. Denied since 1609 the opportunity to win further renown and threatened with the prospect of retirement as a soldier, he had cautiously set about the destruction of Oldenbarneveldt and the reversal of his policies. Caution was necessary since the Dutch, for all their admiration of his military exploits, remained generally republican at heart; an open campaign to establish the leadership of the House of Orange might well have failed. The *Counter-Remonstrance*, however, immediately appealed to him as a means to take him to the very heart of the enemy. Indifferent to the theological subtleties of Gomarus, dis-

[1] See below, page 199.

dainful of the profit-hungry merchants of Amsterdam, Maurice realised their value to himself as enemies of the Advocate. To their side he added the weight of his own authority, his known desire to ally with the Huguenots, and the support of the petty nobility from the inland provinces who led his army. In all, it was a strange company which banded together in defence of predestination.

Oldenbarneveldt was outnumbered in the States-General by enemies who extolled the House of Orange as the sole guardian of true religion within the provinces. In Holland, however, despite opposition from Amsterdam, he retained his supremacy. In 1616 he applied Holland's veto to a proposal for convening a National Synod — a patent device of his enemies to silence Arminianism — and, alarmed at the danger of the situation, he took steps to defend his province against Maurice's army. The Estates were persuaded to enlist a force of militia, the *Waardgelders*, responsible solely to the Advocate and his fellow regents, while orders were given to all regular troops stationed in Holland to co-operate in its defence. Not only was this defiance of Maurice's authority a timely reminder that such authority was held by virtue of the Estates' commission, but the levying of *Waardgelders* represented a threat of secession from the Republic, since the Union could not survive such unbridled insistence on the sovereign rights of its members.

A lesser enemy might have come to terms, but Maurice was aiming at nothing less than the control of the United Provinces, and he was confident of public support, as a flood of scurrilous pamphlets portrayed Oldenbarneveldt as the Judas Iscariot of his time. Maurice went first to Brill, a Calvinist stronghold and the first town in Holland, to call upon his father to lead the rebels in 1572. It was a private visit, simply the captain-general reviewing one of his garrisons, but it had its effect. The town council, overawed by his presence, decided not to enlist *Waardgelders*. Encouraged by this success, Maurice made a royal progress with his army through Gelderland and Overyssel, provinces which traditionally were jealous of Holland's predominance in the Union. Each town in turn made open declarations of loyalty to him, and dismissed all regents suspected of Arminianism. In August 1618 his supporters put a resolution before the States-General for the disbanding of local levies. Holland alone exercised her veto; but verbal retaliation could not halt Maurice's triumphal progress, and the separate cities of the province hastily disbanded their *Waardgelders* as he approached. Oldenbarneveldt alone refused to submit, remaining at The Hague until August 29th, when he was taken prisoner by a troop of the prince's bodyguard.

So far the *coup d'état* had been bloodless, and socially it changed nothing. Maurice was not the enemy of the regents as a class: he wanted to make them subservient to his direction, not to destroy their privileged position. Just as Catholics had been replaced by Calvinists during the Revolt, so the supporters of Arminius and Oldenbarneveldt were removed to make way for others more sympathetic to the *Counter-Remonstrance* and to Maurice himself; but new and old were of the same class as before. The high hopes of the Calvinist congregations for innovations in the urban constitutions were disappointed; their petitions, graciously received by the prince, were then quietly ignored. Nor did the *coup* put an end to Holland's important position in the Union. Indeed, the new regents appointed to rule Holland revealed a characteristic trait by insisting that the majority of the judges appointed by the States-General to try Oldenbarneveldt should be elected by their province.

Maurice was determined to secure the recognition of his own position as the embodiment of the Union of Utrecht, and Oldenbarneveldt, the resolute opponent of his ambition, had to be broken to symbolise its achievement. In March 1619 a political trial was staged in which the Advocate was found guilty of opposing Maurice's assumption of sovereignty, of fostering Arminianism, and of favouring the East India Company at the expense of others. But the victory was not complete. Maurice desired not his death but his submission, and would have gladly spared his life if he had sued for a reprieve; but Oldenbarneveldt was determined to make no move that might be interpreted as an admission of guilt. Rather than acknowledge the authority of the House of Orange, he chose to accept death.

If Maurice's victory was to some extent qualified by Oldenbarneveldt's courageous refusal to compromise, the triumph of his allies, the Counter-Remonstrant clergy, was sealed by the summons of a National Synod to Dordrecht in 1619. Although it concealed its purpose by inviting foreign delegations to attend, the Synod was clearly intended to destroy Arminianism. Its doctrine was condemned by the Confession of Dordrecht, Remonstrant clergy were ejected from their livings, and the teaching staffs of Leyden and other universities were purged. More important, perhaps, was the freeing of the church from interference by the regents in matters of doctrine. Further steps were also taken against the Catholics, who still remained numerous in the Provinces. They were permitted to worship privately, but their priests were forbidden to enter the Republic. These measures, rigorously enforced over the next few years, confirmed that the religion of the United Provinces was to be unmistakably Calvinist.

War with Spain, 1621–48

The demand for war with Spain had been a principal feature of the campaign against Oldenbarneveldt, and indeed the only aim which his enemies had held genuinely in common. Nevertheless, even had the Advocate survived, it is doubtful if the Truce could have been extended. The outbreak of the Thirty Years War in Germany and the flight of the Elector Palatine to The Hague[1] were events to encourage the Dutch to take a more active part in the defence of their faith. The Spaniards, too, had become more belligerent, refusing to renew the Truce unless the Dutch evacuated the East and West Indies and allowed complete toleration to the Catholics within the Provinces. These terms were rejected, the mass of the population endorsing Maurice's declaration of war in 1621.

Maurice, who had found the years of peace so irksome, was eager to achieve fresh triumphs, planning to overrun the Spanish Netherlands and to restore the Elector Frederick to his Palatinate. It was a personal tragedy for him, and very nearly a national disaster for the Dutch, that his ambitions were rudely checked by Spinola. The Spanish commander had worked fifteen hours a day throughout the Truce to prepare his army for the recovery of the northern provinces, and by his intervention in the German conflict he had gained control of the Rhineland. In 1622 it was he, not Maurice, who seized the initiative by attacking Bergen-op-Zoom. In old age, and already nearing his end, Maurice was unable to recover his former skill; the town was relieved by his German ally Mansfeld, and his successive attempts on the Spanish defence lines failed. In 1625 Spinola counter-attacked by laying siege to Breda.

Maurice was dying as the siege began, and his immediate concern was to establish the succession of Frederick Henry, his half-

[1] For this, and for subsequent references to events in the Thirty Years War, see Chapter II, pages 120–36.

brother, to his titles and position in the United Provinces. Unlike Maurice, Frederick Henry had few enemies. After the *coup* of 1619 he had shown sympathy for the defeated party, withdrawing from public life rather than oppose Maurice to whom he was devoted, and his accession was therefore expected to inaugurate a period of greater toleration. Moreover, as the last of William the Silent's sons, he was assured of undivided loyalty from the supporters of his House. His marriage to Amalia von Solms enhanced his popularity, and her buxom charms appeared to even better effect through her position as maid of honour to the most popular refugee in the United Provinces, the Elector Palatine's wife.

Frederick Henry proved himself an able soldier, if less spectacular than Maurice. He failed to relieve Breda but he prevented the Spaniards from advancing further north, and by skilful deployment along the eastern frontier he regained the initiative. Oldenzaal, well-stocked with supplies and ammunition, fell to him in 1626, Wesel, the important fortress controlling the Rhine crossing in Cleves, was recovered from the Spaniards who had seized it in 1614, and by 1629 he had advanced into Brabant and captured Hertogenbosch. At last a base had been secured in Spanish territory, and the inhabitants of the southern provinces were so demoralised by their government's failure to defend them that they considered uniting with the Dutch. Negotiations were in fact begun, only to be cut short by news of the harsh treatment received by the Catholics in Hertogenbosch. A Spanish official in Brussels noted, 'If the Prince of Orange and the rebels were not kept by their fanatical intolerance from granting liberty of worship and from guaranteeing churches and Church property to the priesthood, then a union of the loyal provinces with those of the North could not be prevented.' As in 1576,[1] the hatred between Calvinist and Catholic proved an insurmountable obstacle to the unification of the Netherlands; consequently the Dutch renewed their campaign by seizing Maastricht in 1632.

The breakdown of the negotiations was particularly welcomed by Frederick Henry, who had a vested interest in keeping the war going. Indeed, he hoped to extend the scope of its operations by allying with Spain's other enemy, France, with whom he had long sought a closer entente. There were personal as well as strategic reasons for this since his mother, Louise de Coligny, had brought

---

[1] The occasion of the Pacification of Ghent.

him up as a Frenchman in all but name, but a Catholic monarchy and a Calvinist republic were strange companions and the Dutch were suspicious of his plan. They had criticised Oldenbarneveldt in the past for allying with France after Henry IV's death, and in 1627 they had forbidden Frederick Henry to assist Richelieu with naval support at the siege of La Rochelle. However, so great was their alarm at the arrival in Brussels of Cardinal-Infante Ferdinand, victor of Nördlingen, that the Dutch reluctantly consented to the alliance with Richelieu in 1635. The French were so hard pressed at first[1] that they could do little more than to draw the enemy's fire, but, whether or not by coincidence, the Dutch proved to be victorious from that time onward. Frederick Henry established his reputation in Europe, and restored confidence in his leadership at home by the brilliant recovery of Breda in 1636; and, three years later, the Dutch won a momentous victory over the Spanish navy at the Battle of the Downs.

Although Frederick Henry enjoyed, in addition to his other offices, the title of admiral-general, the fleets of Holland and Zeeland were commanded in fact by Maerten Tromp, a man of vast naval experience. In his youth he had twice been captured by pirates and made to serve in their ships, and later he had fought the privateers of Dunkirk for control of the North Sea. He left the sea in 1634, intending to enter the church, but so great was his reputation that the Dutch recalled him to introduce radical reforms in their navy. His efforts were spectacularly rewarded in the autumn of 1639. The fall of Breisach in the previous year[2] had cut the overland route from Milan to Brussels, and the Spaniards, in their desperate need to reinforce their garrisons in the Netherlands with both men and bullion, were compelled to make the attempt by sea. An armada of 75 sail, commanded by Oquenda, left Corunna to sail up the Channel, just as another ill-fated armada had sailed against England in 1588. Tromp had received intelligence of the Spanish plan, but when he encountered the fleet off Beachy Head he had only 13 ships with him. Nevertheless, he attacked with such skill and vigour that Oquenda, for all his numerical superiority, hastily sought the protection of neutral waters by taking shelter in the Downs. For the hard-pressed Charles I of England this was an opportunity not to be wasted: demanding £100,000 from Oquenda

[1] See Chapter III, page 176 for the 'year of Corbie' in French history.
[2] See Chapter III, page 177.

as the price of English protection, he sent a squadron to prevent a Dutch invasion of his territorial waters. Tromp patrolled outside the Downs with a fleet that daily increased in size until, after a month of waiting, he decided to ignore English neutrality. Taking advantage of a sea mist on the morning of October 24th, he fell upon the Spanish fleet with such devastating effect that the Dutch broadsides destroyed all but seventeen of the enemy, leaving the English squadron, covered with ignominy, disconsolately protecting the charred remnants of the Spanish navy.

Spain never recovered from the destruction of her naval power in the Downs, and the growing vitality of the French armies in Europe made it impossible for her to redeem her prestige on land. As a result, a strong party began to form among the regents of Holland demanding an end to the war on the grounds that Spain no longer endangered the Republic's security. Indeed, the more far-sighted of them interpreted the French triumph at Rocroi (1643) as proof that their ally had replaced their enemy as the strongest military power in western Europe. Increasingly their suspicions were directed against Frederick Henry, the man who had insisted on the French alliance and who, patently, would derive no benefit from peace with Spain. Once again a conflict broke out between the regents of Holland and the House of Orange.

Frederick Henry had lost a great deal of his early popularity. Military success had induced an autocratic manner, and his temper and tact were the worse for recurrent attacks of gout and jaundice. Moreover, Amalia proved to be a restlessly ambitious woman, constantly urging her husband to strengthen his dynasty by the acquisition of greater authority and of more honourable titles. After his successful invasion of the southern provinces he had secured the consent of the States-General to an Act of Survivance, which declared that his offices were held, not by commission, but by hereditary right. This enabled him to assure the succession of his son to his own pre-eminent position as stadtholder in six of the seven provinces,[1] and as captain-general and admiral-general of the Union's forces. The marriage alliances, too, which he and Amalia arranged for their children were a further indication of their dynastic ambitions. In 1641 William was married to Mary, daughter of Charles I of England, and, a little later, Henrietta Louise to the Elector of Brandenburg.

[1] Friesland was held by a cousin.

The regents began to fear for their republican traditions and looked for an early end to the war to restrain the influence and prestige of their leader, who was then in resolute pursuit of the Spaniards. Opposition to his policy came to a head in 1645 when his capture of Hulst and Sas van Gent opened the way to Antwerp. This did not please the Dutch merchants at all, since, if Antwerp fell into their hands they would no longer be justified in blockading the Scheldt: rather than restore the old port and banking centre to its former eminence as a rival to Rotterdam and Amsterdam, they preferred to leave it derelict and abandoned under Spanish control. Worse still, Frederick Henry's dynastic alliances led him to propose Dutch intervention on the side of Charles I in the English Civil War. The regents refused to support his plans and succeeded in carrying the States-General with them. The cost of the war, the dangers of the French alliance, the open ambitions of their prince, the possible recovery of Antwerp and, finally, the proposal to support an Arminian monarch against Puritan rebels, were too great a price to pay for further successes against an enemy which no longer threatened their security.

One thing made possible a settlement with Spain, the opportune death of Frederick Henry in 1647. As Spain was at last convinced that she had no hope of defeating the Dutch, and as her prime concern was to concentrate her forces against the French, she purchased Dutch neutrality by accepting their demands at Münster (1648). The United Provinces were recognised as independent, the towns seized by them during the war were retained, their merchants were permitted to trade in the East and West Indies, and the closure of the Scheldt was confirmed. William II, the new prince of Orange, bitterly opposed the treaty but, at the moment of his accession, he was unable to challenge the desires of the States-General. For him the peace celebrations threatened long years of personal unimportance and inactivity; for the Dutch, however, they were not only the triumphant conclusion to The Eighty Years Struggle but the beginning of a new era as a major power in Europe.

THE COMMERCIAL BASIS OF DUTCH POWER

The Dutch Economy

The commercial supremacy which the Dutch achieved in Europe owed much to the frugality and perseverance of their people, for their country was a small one, with a small population, lacking natural resources.[1] 'Whence do the merchants' profits come except from his own diligence and industry?' wrote Calvin, and the habit of thrift, no doubt encouraged by the spread of Calvinism, came naturally to a race which waged a continuous struggle for survival. High tides threatened to breach the dykes and to inundate the polders; storms and pirates took their toll of the herring fleets and merchantmen, and the Spaniards endangered their political liberties for more than eighty years. Nothing came easily for the Dutch; their wealth was achieved by their own labour, by dint of persistent effort and careful husbandry.

If thrift provided the moral basis of Dutch prosperity, its economic foundation was the fishing industry. From June to December, the Dutch followed the herring shoals along the English coast from Shetland to the Thames Estuary. It was an arduous task, made more difficult by English competition, but one 'whereby many thousands of Households, Families, Handicrafts, Trades and Occupations are set on work';[2] one-fifth of the population earned its living from an industry which produced 300,000 tons of salt fish every year. It was the experience and the profits derived from the herring fisheries which stimulated the art of shipbuilding and made possible the beginning of the coastal trade. By rigid economy in maintaining their ships and crews the Dutch were able to offer the lowest shipping rates in Europe, the modest profits they secured being cautiously reinvested to promote further ventures. The energy and courage they displayed in the war with Spain appeared also in their search for markets and commissions; it was the spirit recalled by Joost van den Vondel, the poet of Dutch expansion.

'Wherever profit leads us, to every sea and shore
For love of gain, the wide world's harbours we explore.'

Danish records of 1578 revealed that of all the ships paying dues in the Sound one half were Dutch, who jealously guarded the Baltic trade against interlopers from France and England. They monopolised the trade between Russia and western Europe; they carried Polish corn to Italy, French wines to Scandinavia and north Germany, and Baltic naval stores of timber and hemp to their own

[1] The population of the Provinces was about 2,500,000 compared with 4,500,000 in England and 16,500,000 in France.
[2] Thomas Mun, *England's Treasure by Fforraign Trade*.

shipyards in Holland. The Dutch looked for trade even with their enemy, and controlled the import of grain into the Spanish peninsula. Efforts were made to discover new trade routes, but the expeditions of Barents in 1594 to find a north-east passage past Novaya Zemlya, and of Hudson, a decade later, to penetrate the inlets of North America, both ended in failure. The Dutch found it more profitable to seek the ports of their rivals than to explore uncharted seas. In 1615, for example, the complaint was raised in France that for every ten or twelve French ships in a French port, there were sixteen to twenty-four Dutch ones, usually manned by French crews.

Trading profits were reinvested in the trading companies, the banks and the schemes for land reclamation rather than in industry, with the result that there was insufficient production at home to supply the export trade. There were, of course, particular cities specialising in industrial manufacture: Rotterdam refined sugar, Amsterdam produced silk, Delft became famous for its pottery, Leyden for woollens, Haarlem for linen, and the Republic generally for its printing, diamond cutting and the making of optical instruments. However, the Dutch differed from other countries since the hinterland of Germany provided what was, in effect, the equivalent of home production, as the English were compelled to recognise in 1668 when they modified their Navigation Acts accordingly.[1] Moreover, Dutch wealth depended less on the sale of exports than on the transport of goods between other countries. Provided there was no lack of capital, such trade could continue indefinitely until challenged by another maritime power.

At Antwerp, in the great days before the revolt, the merchants had inscribed above the entrance to the Bourse the motto *Ad usum mercatorum cuiusque gentis ac linguae*. A similar spirit informed the commerce of the United Provinces. Toleration was offered to men of all creeds and races who came to Holland on business, provided that they practised their religion in private; and Amsterdam, where 5,000 ships, half the entire marine of the United Provinces, found their home berths on the river Amstel, was especially famed for its freedom.

'God, God, the Lord of Amstel cried, hold every conscience free;
And Liberty ride, on Holland's tide, with billowing sails to sea,

---

[1] See Chapter VIII, page 331.

And run our Amstel out and in; let freedom gird the bold,
And merchant in his counting house stand elbow deep in gold.'[1]

Toleration, despite occasional outbursts of protest from the strict Calvinist clergy, paid dividends, but it was not only freedom from persecution that the Dutch had to offer. In order to attract a flow of capital into the Republic and to encourage the agents of foreign firms to place their commissions there, the government left the bankers and merchants remarkably free of state control. The economy was sustained by, indeed depended upon, ruthless competition, and there was nowhere else in Europe where the principle of *laissez-faire* was so firmly established. In this commercial society, based on contract, commission and credit, the Bank of Amsterdam held a privileged position. As its deposits were guaranteed by the city council it attracted foreign investment on such a scale that it became the principal money market in Europe, and it served as a clearing house for bills of exchange, a centre of commercial intelligence and a source of cheap credit. Its loans, frequently advanced at less than 5 per cent, enabled the city to bear the heavy taxes imposed upon it by the States-General during the war, and the great trading companies to equip their fleets for operations around the globe.

Free of restriction and provided with a ready fund of capital, the city of Amsterdam was the ideal headquarters for the East and West India Companies, whose worldwide commitments lay behind the great expansion of trade achieved by the Dutch in the seventeenth century.

The East India Company

Dutch interest in India was first aroused by the writings of Jan van Linchoten, a Haarlem man who had been employed by the Portuguese Archbishop at Goa. His *Itinerario*, published in 1595, had an immediate effect: Cornelis van Hautmann, relying solely upon the information it contained, set sail from Gouda and returned with such profits from the sale of silks, muslins and spices that others wasted no time in following his example. In 1598 more than twenty-five great galleons made their way to India, and some even

---

[1] Joost van den Vondel. Cf. the less enthusiastic couplet by Andrew Marvell:

'Hence Amsterdam, Turk, Christian, Pagan, Jew,
Staple of sects and mint of schisme grew.'

MAP 8 Dutch Expansion in the Far East

reached the Spice Islands (Indonesia). But such expeditions by private adventurers ran great risks. The journey was long, the seas hazardous, and the Portuguese showed no mercy to interlopers who challenged their monopoly of the spice trade. Such dangers apart, the capital required to finance a voyage that might last from two to three years was beyond the means of most men. The English faced the same problem by forming a joint-stock company[1] under royal charter in 1600, and within two years the States-General encouraged the formation of a similar company to trade between the Cape of Good Hope and the Magellan Strait, authorising it to make treaties with local rulers. Other Dutch traders were rigorously excluded from this field, and, unlike the English company, private trading by company servants was forbidden.

The administration of the company was as oligarchic as that of Holland itself, and in both cases power was in the same hands. The directors came from the regent class, vacancies on the board were filled by nomination, accounts were rarely published and private shareholders were given little opportunity to air their opinions; however they had little cause for complaint since the company

[1] See Chapter I, page 15 for discussion of joint-stock companies.

declared annual dividends of about 35 per cent throughout the first thirty years of its history. The company resembled the government of Holland still more by virtue of the influence exerted upon its operations by the city of Amsterdam. She held eight of the seventeen seats in the College, the policy-framing body, her leading families produced twenty-three of the seventy-three directors, and her Bank had provided the equivalent of £250,000, almost half of the company's capital.

The directors' aims were commercial rather than colonial, and their agents were ordered 'to keep in view the necessity of peaceful trade throughout Asia from which is derived the smoke in the kitchens here at home'. Nevertheless, like its English counterpart, the company was compelled to defend itself against both European rivals and native rulers; and the ambitions of its more vigorous servants could only be fulfilled by military action. One of the greatest of these servants was Jan Pieterszoon Coen, appointed as Governor-General in 1618. Before his arrival the Dutch, whose purpose was merely to import silks and spices to Europe, had established bases and factories in piecemeal fashion from the Cape of Good Hope to Indonesia. Coen, however, believed that still greater profits were to be had by monopolising the carrying trade of the Indian Ocean and the South China Sea: to this end he planned to establish a suitable entrepôt and to destroy all European and Asian competition. In this second point he was too ambitious since the Dutch had neither sufficient ships to cope with the vast extent of the carrying trade between Japan and India, nor the men to establish and safeguard the necessary bases; the expulsion of the English from Amboina, when ten of their number were executed in 1623, was one of the few results of his aggressive policy. He did succeed, however, in his search for an entrepôt, selecting Jakarta on the north coast of Java. He renamed it Batavia, saved it from an English attack in 1619, and died in its defence against the Javanese in 1629.

Of Coen's successors, Anthony Van Diemen (1636–45) and Rijkloff Van Goens (1658–63) were among the more vigorous and successful. Their lives might be spent among the heady odours and aromatic perfumes of Batavia but their calculating minds remained as coldly practical as though their offices overlooked the chilly waters of the Amstel. The discoveries of New Holland (Australia), New Zealand and Van Diemen's Land, through faulty navigation in sailing from the Cape to Batavia, opened up a prospect of empire to entrance and bemuse less practical men, but the company and its agents paid scant attention to such unprofitable coastlines. Of greater value to them was Van Diemen's capture of Malacca and Formosa, his elimination of Portuguese competition, and his introduction of restrictive practices in the Moluccas to keep down the production of cloves in order to maintain their price in Europe. Nevertheless by mid-century the company had reduced its dividends to a beggarly 10 per cent. The cost of defending its bases mounted with every year as the native rulers of Indonesia became more difficult to control. The only solution, which in turn created new problems, was the outright destruction of all rivals and the creation of a Dutch empire from Malacca to the Moluccas, which was the task undertaken in the second half of the century by Cornelis Speelman.[1]

Although the Dutch were ultimately destined to rule Indonesia while India fell to the English, the Dutch company in the early seventeenth century regarded both areas with equal concern. But whereas it had been comparatively easy to expel the Portuguese from Indonesia because their numbers were small, in India they had established colonies rather than bases; Van Diemen reported that 'the greater number hold India for their fatherland, thinking no longer of Portugal; they trade thither little or not at all, living and enriching themselves out of the treasures of India as though they were natives and knew no other fatherland.' The Dutch attack was none the less vigorous and effective. From the Malabar coast to Malacca they harassed the Portuguese, seizing their shipping on the high seas and raiding their bases: Goa was blockaded on no less than nine occasions by Van Diemen. Van Goens drove them from Malabar and Coromandel, and in Ceylon he took possession of the cinnamon-producing lowlands. Indeed he almost altered the course of Indian history by proposing the complete conquest of Ceylon and the establishment of the company's headquarters at Colombo instead of Batavia. It was, perhaps, fortunate for the English that his directors rejected the plan.

The West India Company

In 1609 the East India Company's directors employed Henry Hudson, one of the finest navigators of his day, to discover a north-

[1] See Chapter VIII, page 350.

west passage to their eastern bases, but on his failure they abandoned all further interest in the American continent. Neither his
favourable report on Manhattan Island nor his cargo of deerskins
held any attraction for men accustomed to Spice Islands and
Indian silks. Other merchants, however, were interested in
America. In Amsterdam a powerful group demanded the formation
of a West India Company in order to colonise the North American
coastline and to challenge Spain for control of the West Indies.
The colonial project was taken seriously by few, the founders of
the company being more interested in the prizes to be anticipated
from warfare with Spain than in the profits of legitimate commercial activity. Founded in 1621, the year in which war was
renewed with Spain, the company was essentially a piratical
venture. It won approval by the States-General because its military
enterprises, designed to intercept the flow of bullion from America
to Spain, were of strategic value; and the States-General agreed to
provide a fleet of twenty warships to protect the company in its
operations.

Piet Heyn, one of the most colourful rogues in the Caribbean,
brought off a spectacular coup in 1624 by seizing Bahia, capital of
Brazil. The surprising thing was not the ease of Heyn's victory but
the unusual speed with which the Spanish government reacted;[1]
within ten months a relief force, 12,000 strong, took the Dutch
unawares and compelled them to surrender. The failure of its first
great venture almost reduced the company to bankruptcy, but its
agents excelled at privateering and so long as there was plunder to
be seized the directors were able to pay rich dividends. In 1628, for
example, Heyn took captive the entire Spanish silver fleet in
Matanzas Bay (Cuba), an occasion which his employers celebrated
by declaring a dividend of 50 per cent. The profits derived from
this and similar exploits enabled the company to equip an ex-
peditionary force of 8,000 men, to be transported across the
Atlantic in 65 ships; a military venture far greater than anything
ever attempted by the East India Company. Their objective was
Recife in Pernambuco,[2] centre of the richest sugar-producing region
in America. Recife fell easily, but its capture was of no value
without the sugar plantations of the hinterland, and for six years a

---

[1] Until 1640 in effect, though officially until 1668, Spain administered
the Portuguese empire.

[2] At the present time Recife itself is also called Pernambuco.

bitter conflict was waged against the Portuguese settlers who defended their estates with great determination. By 1637 Dutch control was finally established, and the arrival of John Maurice of Nassau, a great nephew of William the Silent and governor of the colony, inaugurated *il tempo dos flamingos*, the years of Dutch power in Brazil.

John Maurice was confronted with many problems: Recife was overcrowded, the rents were six times as high as in Amsterdam, everything save sugar and mahogany had to be imported at great cost from Holland, and the Portuguese settlers remained sullen and uncooperative, awaiting their opportunity to drive the Dutch into the sea. Nevertheless, so great was his determination to make the colony prosperous and secure that nothing could discourage him. With great skill he successfully defended a coastal strip a thousand miles in length between the Amazon and São Francisco rivers, destroying both a Spanish-Portuguese army sent against him from Bahia and a fleet from Europe. He enlarged Recife and constructed a new town, Mauritstadt. He also did much to win the loyalty of the Portuguese. By unfailing and deliberate acts of courtesy he assuaged their pride; by a display of toleration unusual in a convinced Calvinist he allowed them freedom of worship; above all, by reviving the production of sugar he benefited all, Dutch and Portuguese, Calvinist and Catholic. Loans were made to the planters for the repair of their crushing and refining machinery, largely destroyed during the Dutch conquest, and a fresh supply of slaves to work the plantations was secured by seizing the Portuguese bases in West Africa. While John Maurice governed Recife sugar exports rose sharply and relations between the two races were at least friendly. His departure in 1644 was regretted by the whole colony.

The collapse of Dutch power in Brazil which soon followed was not altogether the result of John Maurice's departure. His successors indeed lacked his ability and tact, but they were given little opportunity to reveal their inadequacy. In 1640,[1] John IV of Portugal had proclaimed his independence of Spain and sought the reclamation of his ancestor's empire. Because he proved a most valuable ally in the war with Spain the Dutch were sympathetic, but they had no intention of relinquishing Pernambuco which they pretended to regard as Spanish territory and thus fair conquest. In

[1] See Chapter V, page 220.

the event they lost it involuntarily: a local revolt in 1645, assisted by troops from Bahia, led to the loss of all but Recife itself. Within the United Provinces opinion was divided, some urging the despatch of a relief force, others demanding a peaceful settlement with Portugal to ensure the free importation of salt from Setúbal, so vital for the herring trade. This clash of interests resulted in deadlock. For eleven years the Dutch, because of their maritime supremacy, were able to safeguard Recife itself from attack, but no steps were taken to recover the hinterland. In 1654, however, during the Anglo-Dutch war, the Portuguese seized an opportune moment to attack Recife from the sea, and the Dutch were expelled.

Meanwhile, the Dutch had been active on the high seas. Since the capture of treasure fleet in 1628, commerce raiding had served the company well. By 1636, 547 vessels and their cargoes had been seized, and one of the directors wrote in 1644 that 'with scant power and at small burden to the community, by means of the contributions of a small number of the inhabitants of this state, the operations of the company have been carried out so successfully that the pride of Spain has not been able to withstand them'. But the loss of Pernambuco, effective from 1645, was rapidly followed by another disaster for the company when peace with Spain, effected by the States-General in 1648, abruptly ended its heydey. Piracy being forbidden by the Treaty of Münster, the shareholders had to be content with profits derived solely from legitimate trade.

This was still possible. The company's articles of incorporation were something more than letters of marque accredited by the States-General, and provision had been made for the planting of a colony on the North American coast. In 1624 and 1625 the Dutch had established settlements on the Hudson, Connecticut and Delaware rivers, from which a large and powerful colony might have been created. The one thing lacking, however, was numbers, and the company failed to realise that the English colonies with their growing population would find it easy to engulf the Dutch. Another serious fault lay in the company's choice of governors, as one critic complained: 'I told the Secretary that I was surprised the West India Company sent such fools to the country who knew nothing but how to drink themselves drunk. In the East Indies they would not be allowed to serve even as assistants. . . . For in the East Indies they appoint no one commander, unless he has done long subordinate service, so that they can see he is capable . . . and they promote them further according to merit. But the West India Company sends out straight to posts of great authority over people men who have seen no command in their lives. And therefore it will end in ruin.' There was much truth in this. Van Twifler was an easy-going toper; Kieft, a furious little despot, had provoked an unnecessary and disastrous war with the Algonquin Indians; Stuyvesant, the last Governor, had had some experience as Governor of Curaçao, but the problem was already beyond remedy. He showed some spirit by destroying a small Swedish settlement in Delaware Bay, but from both north and south the English were closing in. In 1664 an expedition, two thousand strong, sent by the Duke of York, appeared off Manhattan Island. Stuyvesant had one hundred and fifty trained men, and, as for ammunition, his master gunner reported 'were I to commence firing in the morning, I should have used up all by noon'. New Amsterdam became New York, and the last of the West India Company's ventures ended in failure.

In 1600 the Dutch had faced the enmity of Spain in Europe, and the rivalry of both Spain and Portugal in the West and East Indies. By 1650 the situation was entirely changed. France had emerged as the strongest power in Europe, dangerously close to Dutch territory, while England was beginning to challenge the Dutch for supremacy, not only in America and in the East, but even in the European parts where they plied for cargoes.

V

The Decline of Spain

THE AFTERMATH OF A GOLDEN AGE, 1598–1665

The Inheritance and the Heirs, 1598–1621

The failure of the Spanish Armada and the success of the Dutch rebels have been so prominently displayed in the image which English historians have created of Philip II that it is difficult to envisage the king as his own subjects remembered him in 1598. They, indeed, honoured him as *El Prudente* and proudly rehearsed his successful exploits as the champion of Spain and the Catholic Church. The Turks, defeated at Lepanto (1571), had been forced to relax their hold upon the western Mediterranean, and a crushing blow had been dealt at the legend of Ottoman invincibility; a heretic had been denied the throne of France until his conversion, and heresy expunged within the borders of Spain; royal authority had been strengthened throughout the separate kingdoms of the peninsula and dramatically extended in 1580 by the inclusion of Portugal and her overseas empire. The Dutch Revolt had been a serious blow yet Philip's control of the southern Netherlands had been intensified, and the vital lines of communication between Brussels and Milan enabled the Spaniards to harass the vulnerable frontier of France at a dozen different points from Amiens to Lyon.

Entrusted by God with pre-eminence in Europe and with an empire encircling the globe, furnished by His munificence with the dazzling riches of the Americas, sustained by the witness of His saints, Theresa and Ignatius Loyola, and endowed with such a king as Philip II, for the Spaniard it had indeed been a Golden Age.

Unhappily the burden of such greatness imposed too great a strain on the physical reserves of one man and the economic resources of one nation. Philip II had never discovered any means of financing his undertakings other than by amassing debts on the security of his American mines. The flow of treasure was so assured, his commitments so numerous and so costly, that nothing

MAP 9   Spain and Portugal

appeared more straightforward than the contraction of loans, until
the payment of interest on the public debt became itself the most
important item of expenditure. Periodically, when too many ventures coincided, when too many bankers simultaneously demanded
satisfaction, Philip repudiated the debt or secured its compulsory
conversion. On each occasion further credit was temporarily denied
him and the great undertakings had to be abandoned or postponed
until new creditors, demanding higher rates of interest by way of
insurance, were discovered. Another weakness of Philip's government was his determination to supervise everything himself; his
responsibility being to God alone, he dared not compromise it by
delegating it to lesser men. Therefore, from his councils, from all
the agents of his administration, he demanded detailed reports to
be considered in the privacy of his room. No one knew his mind.
No action might be taken without his express authorisation. In an
empire so vast, in an age so badly provided with means of communication, such a system of personal bureaucracy involved delay,
encouraged inefficiency and in the long run threatened administrative collapse.

While such a man as Philip II was king — able, industrious and
prepared to devote superhuman efforts to the task of government —
while the supplies of bullion arrived with sufficient regularity to

reassure the royal creditors, then the fundamental weaknesses of the Golden Age remained concealed; but perennial bankruptcy and a system of personal bureaucracy were fatal legacies to bequeath to heirs who had no capacity to deal with either. This was the contingency for which Philip's faith in autocracy had failed to provide: 'God who has given me so many kingdoms to govern has not given me a son fit to govern them.' Philip III (1598-1621), who so closely resembled his father in appearance, was wholly incompetent to suceeed him. The progressive deterioration of mind and body, the result of generations of Habsburg inbreeding, was already apparent in him. Spectacularly prodigal of money, he exhausted his emotions too by intermittent bouts of frenzied gaiety and fits of religious melancholia. Ultimately honoured as an example of piety, he performed his daily devotions with an automatic regularity that dispensed him from the necessity of thought. Unfortunately, he could not so easily fulfil his political duties. The arduous task of exercising the highly centralised powers of the Spanish monarchy was far beyond his capabilities, and he immediately abdicated his authority into the hands of his court favourite, the Duke of Lerma.

Lerma's administration, though unexpectedly moderate in the conduct of foreign affairs,[1] proved to be disastrous in the internal history of Spain. An experienced minister, and there were many who had served Philip II, might possibly have saved the day, but Lerma was not a man to share authority with those more talented than himself. Such men he dismissed from their posts, to burden the administration with relatives as self-seeking as himself. His uncle was appointed Inquisitor-General and Archbishop of Toledo, and a brother-in-law Viceroy of Naples, but this was not the worst of it; as Lerma stood to Philip III, so Rodrigo Calderon stood to him, and the succession of parasites, each with its own family of relatives to cater for, grew to infinite proportions. With no understanding of the economic weaknesses of Spain and seduced into believing that all expenditure could be covered by American bullion, Lerma set an example of extravagance and peculation which aggravated the collapse of the economy.[2] Occasions for ostentatious display were exploited to the full, and the court

---

[1] See below, page 224.
[2] The economic collapse of Spain, and Lerma's part in this, is described below, in pages 212-16.

became three times as expensive to maintain as in Philip II's day. Offices and titles were created by the king and sold to fill the pockets of his favourites, the currency was debased to procure a quick profit and the resources of the state were ransacked in an attempt to satisfy insatiable appetites.

When public protest at the unbridled corruption of the administration mounted so high that even the court took cognizance of it, Lerma prepared to jettison the more unpopular of his hangers-on to safeguard his own position. Several councillors of finance were arrested in 1609, the most notorious being Pedro Franquesa, whose house was discovered to be so full of treasure that it took three days to transfer it all to the royal treasury. This public display of the profits to be derived from high office merely served to whet the appetites of the envious, who redoubled their intrigues to discredit Lerma with the king. Their success was largely due to the ambitious Count of Olivares, who won the goodwill of the future Philip IV, and, strangely enough, of Lerma's own son Uceda, in whom greed was stronger than filial devotion. In 1614 the cabal secured the arrest of Calderon; by 1618 Lerma found it politic to retire from court to the dignity of the cardinalate, and with a fortune rumoured at 44,000,000 *ducats*.

The unhappiest incident of Lerma's administration was the expulsion of the Moriscos, the baptised descendants of the Moors who had been overrun in the fifteenth century. Since 1492 the government had tried in vain to assimilate them into the Spanish population. Christian to all appearance, many were suspected of performing Moorish rites and ceremonies within their houses, and despite all the laws they clung obstinately to their traditional dress and language. Denied civil equality with the Spaniards, barred from the professions and forbidden to own land, the 500,000 Moriscos, living mainly in Valencia, formed a separate, underprivileged and unpopular community amidst the seven or eight million inhabitants of Spain. The Valencian landowners, from whose class came Lerma, regarded them with jealousy and hatred. Whatever they did was criticised: their tradition of early marriages and large families betrayed improvidence, their frugality a device to cheat the government of its purchase taxes, and their capacity for unremitting toil the fruit of avarice. Not even the high rents which the Moriscos were compelled to pay for their lands could reconcile the Spaniards to so nonconformist a group. In an age which set such store by uniformity they were hated simply for being different.

It was not Valencian prejudice alone which prompted Lerma's decision to expel the Moriscos, but fear. Philip II had expelled them from Granada because of their intrigues with the Barbary pirates who raided the coast, and by 1609 there was convincing proof of their negotiations with both the sultan and the king of France. Assimilation had failed: massacre and mutilation were rejected as unnecessarily cruel, and there apppeared to be no other alternative but expulsion to Morocco. In fact, a more efficient government and one less blinded by prejudice, might well have isolated the ringleaders and left the majority to live in peace; but this was not to be. The Moriscos of Valencia were deported in 1609, and the remainder from other kingdoms followed in 1610. For these last the expulsion was particularly cruel. Being few in number they had been more easily assimilated into the Spanish population and were generally practising Christians: to expose them to the Moslems of North Africa was a ghastly crime, mitigated only by the inefficiency of the administration to ensure the expulsion of all 500,000 Moriscos.[1] Many remained behind, perhaps to the number of 350,000, scapegoats to the bitter end since to them is sometimes attributed the scepticism and anticlericalism of many present-day Spaniards.

Lerma's retirement did not leave power in the hands of his son for very long, for in 1621 Philip IV became king at the age of sixteen. Cultured, generous and elegant, with a fine taste for the patronage of arts, he was the ablest of Philip II's descendents. Responsive to a strong sense of duty he rarely failed to evince the best intentions in the world; rarely, however, did he succeed in implementing them. His virtues were powerless against his vices. Sensual and self-indulgent to a degree associated more popularly with the Orient than with Europe, his dissipation and debauchery provoked periods of morbid self-condemnation and remorse. He attributed the disasters befalling Spain to the judgement of God upon his sins; 'for no matter how adequate may be the remedies that I adopt, our sins suffice to condemn all our affairs to the most miserable state imaginable'. This fatalist acquiescence in the doom of Spain was to some extent offset by his employment of Olivares as

---

[1] So unmerciful an act was naturally supposed to bring its own retribution. The economic effects of the expulsion are discussed below, page 212.

H

chief minister,[1] but it was Spain's tragedy that when a man was found capable of directing the administration of her empire, the long ignored economic weaknesses, aggravated by Philip III's reign, should have nullified his efforts. In that respect, Philip IV's fatalism was to be justified.

The Destruction of the Economy

In 1597 the Castilian Cortes reported to Philip II on the economic situation: 'No one has either money or credit, and the country is completely desolated. Any money that is made is hidden away and the owner lives poorly upon it until it is gone. Trade is killed by taxation. In the principal cities most of the houses are closed and deserted.' Every allowance must be made for the exaggerated sentiments of a body which sought to avoid further taxes by a plea of poverty, but the report is of interest in that what was so gloomily exaggerated in 1597 had become so unhappily true by 1665. Royal bankruptcy and a general deterioration of the economy were indeed the most prominent characteristics of Spain during the reigns of Philip III and IV. The extent of the decline may be in dispute, and Protestant historians may have been a little over eager to associate Catholicism with bad economics, but the existence of the decline is beyond question.

One self-evident feature of Spanish decline was the fall in population from 8,000,000 to under 6,000,000, variously attributed to emigration, to the entry of thousands of young men into the monasteries and to the expulsion of the Moriscos; three useful scapegoats on which to blame not only the decline in numbers but the collapse of the economy itself. Monks and emigrants, however, had probably been more numerous in the previous century, and neither could have had as devastating an effect on the population as, for example, the epidemics which swept the peninsula in 1599–1600 and again in 1648–50. As for the expulsion of the Moriscos, the greater number evaded it, some areas were relet to eager Spaniards from less fertile areas, and, as there was no sudden change in the price of Valencian farm produce[2] it is fair to deduce that there was no sudden fall in production.

One fact, however, was indisputable, that the flow of bullion into Spain was dwindling rapidly. Already by 1571 the proportion

---

[1] See below, page 216.
[2] See E. J. Hamilton, *American Treasure and the Price Revolution in Spain.*

of gold to silver and copper had fallen to 2 per cent, and every succeeding year witnessed a reduction in the total value of the bullion imports, from approximately £4,000,000 in 1600 to £1,500,000 in 1650.[1] Outside Spain there were many who liked to believe that this was the result of daring raids by their sea-dogs (French, Dutch or English) but in fact it was due to the exhaustion of the best mines and to the growing population in America. As numbers increased there, more and more of the bullion was traded for food, clothing and luxuries, and, since Spain was so unproductive, these supplies had to be sought elsewhere, the greatest single drain on the colonists' reserves of bullion being the trade with China and the Philippines.

The real tragedy of Spanish history was that she had never learned the proper use of her bullion imports, great or small: as the Castilian Cortes complained to Philip III, 'the treasure immediately goes to foreign kingdoms leaving this one in extreme poverty'. One reason for this was the unprecedented cost of her commitments in Europe. In the reign of Charles V Spaniards had subsidised the emperor's policies whether these directly concerned Spain or not: Philip II considered himself the heir to his father's ambitions if not to his imperial throne and resolved to attain them at whatever cost. German heretics, Dutch rebels, French armies, Ottoman navies, alike demanded the expenditure of vast sums,[2] and when the march of Spanish troops could not wait upon the arrival of American gold, recourse was made to the banking houses of Germany and Italy. As the century progressed, an increasingly large proportion of the annual import of bullion was despatched to pay the interest on long-forgotten loans, until what remained was often insufficient for the immediate needs of the day. On six occasions between 1557 and 1647, 'mile-stones in the retreat of Spanish power', Spain repudiated her debts.[3]

More than half the bullion imports passed into private hands, but this too failed to enrich the economy since, if the royal share was despatched abroad to pay the interest on accumulated debts,

[1] See C. H. Haring, *Trade and Navigation between Spain and the Indies.* The estimated value of the bullion in English currency was made before 1939.

[2] The Armada, for example, cost £5,000,000 and the Dutch Revolt drained away £1,000,000 every year.

[3] G. N. Clark, *The Seventeenth Century.* The occasions were 1557, 1575 1596, 1607, 1627, 1647.

the rest soon followed to pay for goods. The Spaniard had fallen into the fatal error of confusing wealth with bullion, and of failing to understand that the true source of a nation's prosperity lay with its industry and trade. This was a point readily comprehended by the Venetian ambassador, who had remarked of the Spanish Netherlands in 1552: 'These are the treasures of the King of Spain, these are the mines, the Indies, which have sustained Imperial ventures for so many years.' Antwerp, a clearing house for European finance and the centre of international trade, had become the market for American bullion while Spain herself remained an economic backwater: its sack in 1576 and subsequent blockade was therefore of greater significance in the decline of Spain than any check to her supply of bullion.

Deprived of her vital entrepôt, there still remained her commerce with America, a jealously guarded perquisite of the Castilian crown which had controlled it with painstaking thoroughness through the office of the *Consulado*. Like most such perquisites, however, it had been pawned to finance the great undertakings of the sixteenth century, and the monopoly of American trade thus passed to a small group of merchants in Seville. The massive regulations of the *Consulado* forestalled both initiative and innovation but the fact that they also prevented competition made them invaluable to the monopolists. For them it was of little concern that by 1640 three-quarters of the goods in Spanish ports were delivered in Dutch ships and that the volume of trade declined with each decade: the fewer the goods the greater the price, a trend which the crown encouraged since it benefited from the *alcabala*, a sales tax of 10 per cent. The waters of trade, being thus confined and reduced, might yet have burst their banks had Spain been able to produce manufactured goods in sufficient number and quality to attract foreign buyers; but the governments of Philip III and IV not only failed to encourage industry, they accelerated its decline by their incompetent monetary policy.

Unhappily for Spain there was no one with the insight to realise, as Colbert did in France, that industry was, 'a most fertile source of a kingdom's prosperity.'[1] Indeed, had Spain secured the services of such a man his proposals would have won scant attention from Lerma and his successors, whose prime concern was to make fortunes for themselves. In the meantime they tried various

[1] See below, Chapter VI, page 268.

clumsy expedients which, designed to stave off royal bankruptcy, sufficed to destroy the nation's economy. The taxes they doubled and redoubled bore most heavily on the peasantry, which therefore had little left to spend, while the commercial classes, on whose activity the economy depended, were handicapped by the *alcabala*. The taxes were not the worst of it, for in the seventeenth century there were means of evading their incidence: there was no escape from the disastrous effects of the government's tampering with the *vellon*, a bulky coinage containing silver and copper. Finding his revenues for 1599 and 1600 pledged in advance, Philip removed the silver; in 1602 the weight of the copper in each coin was reduced by half, on the pretext that the coins would be easier to handle; in the following year the debased coinage was called in to be stamped at double its value, a device repeated in 1618, and again in 1640.

Instead of the steady price rise in the previous century which had stimulated investment and production, the sudden and varied fluctuations in the value of money produced similar variations in the price of goods, with disastrous effect. The capitalist was unable to estimate the costs of future production, the worker could never tell from one year to another the true purchasing power of his wages, and Spain began to purchase abroad the manufactured goods and even the foodstuffs which she was no longer able to produce for herself. The weaving of the fine cloths in Andalusia, for example, was replaced by the export of raw wool, later to be repurchased from France and Italy as finished cloth. Such imports, instead of furnishing the raw materials to stimulate production, were immediately consumed and the demand was as quickly renewed: 'Spain became the distributor of precious metals to Europe, and since she produced little and manufactured less she performed this function with an efficiency which startled even the Spaniard.'[1] This was the plight into which Spain had fallen; not the unhappy result of inherited disabilities nor the unkind working of blind fate, but dramatic retribution for the short-sighted expedients of those who reaped an immediate profit at the cost of ultimate ruin.

Away from the ports and industrial centres the story of decline was repeated in the countryside where the *Mesta*, one of the wealthiest institutions in Castile, suffered heavily. An association of sheep farmers, it controlled the migration of their flocks every

[1] Haring, op. cit.

six months along special routes, called the *cañadas*, between the mountains and the plains. In return for heavy tolls imposed along the *cañadas*, the crown had given the *Mesta* extraordinary powers to protect its members, its sheep and its pasture grounds; so much so that its agents, the *entregadores*, exercised a jurisdiction similar to that of the forest courts of medieval England, punishing trespass, damage and enclosure. Local authorities resented the intrusion of the *Mesta*'s courts into their areas, and the decline of royal authority in the seventeenth century exposed the *Mesta* to attack. Challenged at all levels, from the Cortes, which contested its jurisdiction, to the local farmer, who encroached on its lands, it exhausted its fortune in litigation and bribery, which alike proved fruitless. Its flocks, estimated in the sixteenth century at four million sheep, were more than halved, to the delight of the Cortes which repeatedly claimed that the weakness of Castilian agriculture was due to the encroachment of sheep. The decline of the *Mesta*, however, was not signalised by a return to arable farming. On the contrary, that too appears to have deteriorated.

The cost of commitments in Europe, the destruction of Antwerp's pre-eminence, mistaken notions of the proper use of bullion and the true worth of industry, together with the ruinous expedients adopted by the governments of Philip III and IV, brought about the economic collapse of Spain. Perhaps, too, she suffered from intellectual isolation. The proud possessor of thirty universities she was nevertheless ignorant of the philosophic and scientific ideas which were revolutionising human thought elsewhere in Europe. Piety and conservation insulated her schools from novelty and ensured the continued study of Aquinas and the medieval text of Aristotle. In painting and literature Spain indeed produced men of inventive genius,[1] but in every other field orthodoxy and tradition were valued so highly that originality of thought was at a premium, and as Holland could bear witness, freedom of thought was sometimes a powerful stimulant to trade.

Olivares, Spain and Portugal, 1621–41

From 1621 to 1643 both Spain and Philip IV were dominated by Gasper de Guzman, Count of Olivares. A masterful man, his portrait by Velazquez reveals his physical strength, his powerful shoulders, broad bearded chin and fierce black eyes; his contem-

[1] See Chapter I, pages 105–7.

poraries bore witness to his overbearing manner and violent temper. His restless spirit was well suited to the pursuit of power at court and he proved adept at intrigue and conspiracy: he assisted in the downfall of Lerma only to betray the son, Uceda, by winning for himself the affection of Philip IV. Superficially he appeared to be yet another court favourite, dancing attendance on his master, pandering to his vices and exploiting his idleness to make himself indispensable. In fact, he proved the most energetic and competent of Spanish administrators in the seventeenth century.

Like Richelieu, whom in many ways he resembled, Olivares loved power and ruthlessly eliminated his rivals: Lerma forfeited much of his fortune to purchase an uninterrupted retirement, his unhappy protégé Calderon was executed, and his son Uceda lived out his life in prison. By-passing the many royal councils, Olivares obtained information and executed policy through special committees, *juntas*, responsible to him alone. In addition to ministering to his self-importance, the *juntas* served a valuable purpose since the administration was in poor shape. The sale of offices, combined with the lack of alternative pursuits in commerce and industry, simulated in Spain a passion for official employment, with the result that the administration was burdened with incompetent and superfluous officials. Olivares forbade the teaching of Latin in small town grammar schools to reduce the number of qualified applicants; but this was to handle the problem at the wrong end, since by greater economy, by a firm refusal to resort to expedients, the sale of offices could have been checked immediately. However, the renewal of Spain's military commitments in Europe, proved so costly that by 1631 a new expedient made office holding even more attractive. In return for *la media anada*, a payment of half the first year's salary, the crown guaranteed to the office holder not only security of tenure but also the right to treat his office as a private possession, to be sold at will or transmitted to heirs. Senior posts alone were excluded from the scheme.

Inefficiency and irresponsibility in the civil service were not peculiar to Spain alone for *la paulette* in France produced a similar effect, but Olivares faced problems which were more pronounced than those, for example, that confronted Richelieu. The particularism to be found in the outlying provinces of all European countries was encouraged to a fatal degree in Spain by the mountains and plateaux which divided the peninsula so effectively that no one city had good access to the other parts of the kingdom. Furthermore, Spain was in reality a union of separate kingdoms and principalities, Portugal, Aragon, Valencia, Catalonia, Navarre and the Basque, which were virtually independent of each other. In each area the Cortes, the assembly of the Estates, accepted the sovereign of Castile as its own ruler on terms which guaranteed its traditional liberties, or *fueros*. Philip II at his greatest had found it impossible to govern Spain as a unit, and only in Castile had he enjoyed extensive powers of jurisdiction and taxation. Even here, by 1620, the Cortes was recovering some spirit and successfully fought the crown over the separate jurisdiction of the *Mesta*.[1] In every other kingdom and principality the Cortes stood firmly by its *fueros*, resisting all attempts to impose a more centralised administration. There was much to justify this attitude: centralisation tended to involve subordination as much to Castile as to the king, and the administration of Castile, itself highly centralised, was notorious for its delays and inefficiency, as a Neapolitan viceroy remarked, 'If death comes from Spain we shall be immortal.'

Contempt for Castilian practice and jealousy of her pretensions combined to make Olivares's task particularly difficult. His efforts to break down barriers of prejudice and provincialism by proposing a common legal system and by employing officials of one kingdom to serve in another were interpreted as mere devices to establish Castilian supremacy. Moreover, like Richelieu, he looked upon the extension of royal power as a necessary but ancillary step to the greater task of intervention in Europe. Unfortunately the internal problem was too complex to be subordinated to any other: indeed, it was his determination to undertake foreign wars, and the need to finance them by seeking money from the very Cortes whose *fueros* he hoped to abolish, that impeded and ultimately destroyed his work.

The traditional, and therefore inadequate, contribution voted by each Cortes was rarely augmented to finance the king's commitments abroad. Since these were generally considered by the Cortes to be undertaken in the interests of Castile alone, it was their view that Castile, proud possessor of the Indies and of the Americas, should provide the money. Olivares aroused great opposition by his contention that, 'when any of the states was at war, the rest

[1] See above, page 216.

should be obliged to come to its aid and defence'. In 1626 he urged Philip IV to appeal in person to the Cortes of Aragon, Valencia and Catalonia. Aragon rejected outright the suggestion that she had any duty to aid the king, refused to raise troops for his European campaigns, but reluctantly consented to increase her contribution by one million *ducats*, the sum to be spread over ten years. Valencia, after a very spirited resistance, also agreed to a subsidy, but Catalonia was adamant, insisting that Philip repaid all the loans made to the crown in the past before any new supplies were voted. Olivares tactfully withdrew Philip to Madrid without pressing the point. In 1632 he renewed his request to Catalonia for aid. Again it was rejected. Self-regarding and obstinate in all matters, and closer in spirit and culture to Provence than to Castile, Catalonia was the one province Olivares most wished to break.

When the French invaded Roussillon in 1639,[1] Castilian troops were welcomed into Catalonia to serve in its defence. As soon as the French had been driven back, Olivares decided to exploit the presence of his army to destroy Catalonia's 'provincial pettiness'. In addition to billeting Castilian troops on a population which regarded them as foreign as the French they had beaten, he ordered the raising of Catalan levies, not so much to safeguard the frontier as to demonstrate his power to compel obedience. His Viceroy confirmed his purpose in passing on his orders: 'This is no time to beseech, but to command. The Catalans are naturally fickle, sometimes they will and sometimes they will not. Make them understand that the welfare of the nation and the army must go before all laws and privileges.' The combination of looted billets, forced levies and Castilian interference proved insupportable to the Catalans. In 1640 they revolted. The rebels massacred the Viceroy and other Castilian troops and officials, and declared their state to be an independent republic. Most dangerous of all from Spain's viewpoint, they accepted an offer of support by Richelieu and recognised Louis XIII as Count of Barcelona.

In the same year the Portuguese revolted. Their kingdom had passed to Philip II in 1580 with the strictest provision for the maintenance of its liberties and self-government, but Olivares persistently treated it as an apanage of Castile. Employing Miguel Vasconcellos, himself a Portuguese, to further his plans, he had filled the country with Castilian officials. They sat in the

[1] See Chapter III, page 177.

Council of Portugal, inspected the treasury, held Portuguese bishoprics and acquired Portuguese estates. Indignation at the daily violation of their liberties was intensified by anger at Spain's failure to provide an adequate defence for their colonial empire, and the Portuguese looked to their greatest noble, the Duke of Braganza, for a sign. Evading all efforts by Olivares to lure him to Madrid where he might safely be arrested, and undeceived by Olivares's subsequent attempt to win him over by appointing him to command the army in Portugal, Braganza was nevertheless hesitant and shrank from any positive act of rebellion.

In 1636 Olivares ordered the collection of a 5 per cent tax on property, a tax hitherto confined to Castile. This provoked a rebellion, but without Braganza's leadership it was so disorganised as to be easily suppressed. Olivares and Vasconcellos were therefore encouraged to pursue their plans further. In 1640 they proposed to abolish the Portuguese Cortes, to enlist the nobles into the Castilian army, and to absorb the kingdom wholly into Castile. So great was the fury that within three hours of the proclamation a revolutionary group had murdered Vasconcellos, seized control of Lisbon and called upon Braganza to become king. In this crisis the decisive figure was Braganza's wife. Coming from one of the proudest families in Spain, her brother was the Duke of Medina Sidonia and Captain-General of Andalusia, her impetuous ambition had long struggled to overcome the inborn timidity of her husband. The news from Lisbon gave renewed vigour to her attack, and before the day was out Braganza had proclaimed himself King John IV of Portugal. As a further stroke, the Queen persuaded Medina Sidonia to raise his own standard in Andalusia and to proclaim his province's independence of Philip IV.

The Years of Rebellion, 1641–65

Within six months the work of twenty years was destroyed. Olivares learned of Medina Sidonia's treason in time to effect his arrest and to save Andalusia for the crown, but he could make no headway against the rebels in Catalonia and Portugal. Philip IV, in a rare moment of inspired leadership, marched out in 1642 to suppress the Catalans, only to give up when he learned that French troops had reinforced Barcelona and were advancing into Aragon. His only solace was to dismiss Olivares, who died insane with grief at the collapse of his ambitions.

Olivares's ambitions in essence had been those of his great contemporary Richelieu: why then did he fail so dramatically where Richelieu succeeded? The difference in character between the two men was in fact of far less importance than the difference between their countries. The kingdoms of Spain were not *pays d'état*; and the Estates of Languedoc, for all the trouble they caused Richelieu, were never so independent nor so powerfully united in the defence of their traditions as the Cortes of Catalonia. Moreover, the Spanish economy was collapsing and royal bankruptcy had become commonplace. Whereas Richelieu was able to send effective aid to the rebels in the peninsula, Olivares found it impossible to assist the Duc de Rohan's rising in 1629.[1] Spain, unlike France, could no longer sustain the burden of her commitments. Above all, she could not afford to be ruled by Olivares, and it is a point of some significance in her decline that while inefficient and unimaginative government merely aggravated her weaknesses, an able and energetic one utterly destroyed her by demanding too much from her depleted resources.

Olivares was succeeded as chief minister by his nephew, Don Luis de Haro. If ability in the seat of government had led Spain into disaster, the appointment of a mediocrity could not reverse the trend, and the government's persistent lack of money compelled it to adopt measures which provoked further outbreaks. In 1646 the French seized the island of Elba, whence they launched attacks on Naples. Arcos, the Viceroy, was ordered to prepare a counter attack, but to finance his expedition he had to impose duties on the sale of fruit, hitherto the one untaxed commodity. Since fruit, however, was all that the poor could afford to eat, rioting immediately broke out in the city.

Masaniello, a young fisherman whose mother had been punished for smuggling corn, put himself at the head of the rioters, retaining their loyalty by acts of violence which daily redoubled their intensity. He led them into Arcos's palace and terrorised the Viceroy into rescinding all taxes imposed since the reign of Charles V. He broke open the prisons, emptied the armouries and attacked the houses of the tax collectors. For ten days the mob was inspired to a frenzy of pillage, arson and murder while its leader, driven insane by the gratification of his lust for power, dressed himself in cloth of gold and executed all whom his demented mind

[1] See Chapter III, Page 155.

suspected of disloyalty. Suddenly, he too was assassinated, and his funeral provoked scenes of even greater excitement, for it was believed that his severed head miraculously joined itself to his trunk and, thus united, he solemnly blessed the assembled crowd before he was committed to the grave.

Other leaders sprang up, including the Duc de Guise, who claimed the Neapolitan throne, but despite the violence and anarchy which prevailed throughout the winter the rioters never became rebels. Unlike the Catalans and the Portuguese their protest was the protest of poverty. Tradition and centralisation were meaningless concepts to a hungry mob, as the new Spanish commander, Don Juan of Austria[1] was quick to realise. He exploited the differences between the local leaders, and held the nobility firm in their loyalty by threatening to abandon them to the mob. Moreover, French interference was temporarily suspended because of the Fronde. With his limited forces Don Juan skilfully held the ring until the violence of the poorest classes had exhausted itself in its wild career, and then restored Spanish control within the city.

The recovery of Catalonia was not achieved so swiftly. A royal army succeeded in reaching the walls of Barcelona at the end of 1650, and, with naval support from Don Juan, compelled it to surrender after a siege of fifteen months. Its citizens were granted an amnesty by Philip IV, whose chief concern was no longer to enforce the policies of Olivares but to secure the recognition of his authority. Once this was realised by the Catalans the work of recovery was eased, though the French troops, whose presence the Catalans were beginning to find as burdensome as that of the Castilians in 1640, remained in the principality until the Treaty of the Pyrenees (1659).[2]

In order to embarrass the Portuguese in their struggle for independence, Philip IV persuaded the pope to withhold recognition from John IV, secured the exclusion of Portugal from the peace negotiations of 1648, and, in making peace with the Dutch, encouraged them to seize what they could of the Portuguese empire. Less honourably, John's brother, serving with distinction

---

[1] An illegitimate son of Philip IV who revealed remarkable ability in government and war: see below page 229. In 1647 he had been appointed captain-general of the fleet.

[2] See below, page 227.

in the Austrian army, was kidnapped and assassinated, and an attempt on John himself was discovered only at the last minute. The Portuguese, however, remained defiant. Indeed, Spain's military strength was so fully extended by the combat with France that the rebels launched an impudent attack into Spain itself, laying siege to Badajoz in 1658. In the following year the Treaty of the Pyrenees deprived them of official support by France, but Charles II of England came to their rescue in 1661 when Catherine of Braganza brought him a dowry of £800,000, along with Bombay and Tangier. By dispensing with imperial outposts they could no longer defend the Portuguese saved their homeland, and the alliance was well purchased. Schomberg, an experienced marshal of France though the son of an Englishwoman, was granted an English peerage, and with French connivance sent to Portugal.

Upon his shoulders rested the kingdom's security, since Don Juan, the ablest Spaniard of his generation, had been transferred from his naval command to lead the troops who, after 1659, were no longer needed in Italy and the Netherlands. Don Juan came close to victory in 1663 when Lisbon seemed to be at his mercy, but his men had tasted victory so rarely during the past twenty years that success merely demoralised them. Driven back to the frontier, they were decisively routed by Schomberg at Ameixial. This failure, with the loss of 8,000 men together with the baggage and artillery, led to Don Juan's temporary disgrace, though his successors met with no better fortune. At last Philip IV, in a desperate effort to restore unity to the peninsula before death claimed him, raised every available soldier in his empire and put 23,000 men in the field. At Montesclaros in 1665, in what proved to be the last and the fiercest battle of the war of liberation, Schomberg broke the Spaniards after eight hours of hand to hand fighting. Portugal's independence, though not formally recognised until 1668, was thus assured, and news of the defeat killed Philip IV.

Spain in Europe, 1598–1659[1]

Philip II had dominated his age by land and sea; and if modern historians can see the administrative and economic weaknesses

---

[1] Events in the Thirty Years War, the Franco-Spanish War 1635–59, and the Dutch War 1621–48 are described in Chapters II, III and IV respectively. Few references will therefore be made to these chapters by footnotes.

behind the façade of power he bequeathed to Philip III, contemporary statesmen did not consider the power of Spain to be illusory. Indeed, by a fortunate turn of events, the countries at war with Spain in 1598 were eager to come to terms. With England and the United Provinces the war had reached the stage at which neither side could inflict serious harm on the other, and as both James I and Oldenbarneveldt[1] had their own reasons to desire a peaceful settlement, Lerma was able to conceal Spain's urgent need of one. In 1604 with England, and in 1609 with the Dutch, he conceded only what had already been lost in Philip II's day, and thus created an impression that Spain had ended the war in a position of strength — an impression to some extent confirmed by the resolve of the English and Dutch governments to avoid any action that might affront or provoke her. Henry IV of France, however, had made peace in 1598 only to prepare for war in the future, and his decision to fight over Jülich–Cleves in 1610 would have exposed Spain to the stresses of a major war a generation earlier than in fact occurred. His assassination, whether or not it saved France from disaster, certainly proved opportune for Spain's reputation, since his widow, Marie de Medici became flatteringly attentive to Spanish counsel and married her daughter to the future Philip IV, and Louis XIII to the Infanta, Anne of Austria.

Fostered by Lerma's sensible diplomacy, the illusion of Spanish greatness, to which perhaps the Spaniards themselves also fell victim, was a factor of importance in the Thirty Years War. Though the central theme of Spanish policy throughout the war was essentially defensive, intervention became a necessary act, not so much to assist the emperor nor to advance the Counter-Reformation, as to safeguard the lines of communication which on land and on sea were dangerously exposed to attack. In this the Spanish government showed wisdom, since the French had also realised that unless Spanish troops could freely march from Milan to Brussels, and Spanish ships sent to Genoa and to Dunkirk, the collapse of Flanders, Luxemburg and Franche Comté would soon follow.

Spinola, who commanded the army in Flanders, was particularly alive to this point. During the Jülich–Cleves crisis he had exploited

---

[1] See Chapter IV, page 186. Oldenbarneveldt: James I was by nature averse to war, particularly to an expensive one which had not been of his making.

the general confusion to take Wesel, which strengthened his hold on the lower Rhineland; and he seized upon the Bohemian war as a unique opportunity to destroy the most dangerous Protestant outpost along the Rhine, the Palatinate. When Philip III hesitated, wondering if he could afford to assist the emperor in Germany with the Twelve-Year Truce with the Dutch about to expire, Spinola successfully demonstrated that the only way to defeat the Dutch was to strengthen the lines of communication. While 8,000 men were sent to Bohemia in 1620 as a token of Spanish support, no less than 30,000 under Spinola overran the Rhenish provinces of the Palatinate. In the same year the Catholic inhabitants of the Val Telline, linking Lombardy and the Tyrol, rebelled against their Swiss overlords, the Protestant Grisons, and the Governor of Milan lost no time in coming to their aid by occupying the pass with his troops.

The Spanish position in Europe was therefore encouraging when Olivares came to power with the accession of Philip IV in 1621. Moreover he shared Spinola's strategic grasp of the situation and recognised that his chief task was to preserve the lines of communication. Unfortunately, Olivares was over-optimistic. Believing that the fortunes of Spain were again in the ascendant, he rushed into action before he had succeeded in consolidating royal authority within the peninsula, unlike Richelieu who avoided open warfare with Spain until he had first won control of France. The result was that at home and abroad he failed dismally, though the first years yielded little portent of disaster. James I was gulled into neutrality by the prospect of a Spanish match for his son Charles, Breda was seized in 1625 by Spinola, Richelieu failed to recover control of the Val Telline for the Grisons, and a Dutch fleet was destroyed off Gibraltar. To destroy the Dutch in the North Sea, especially after England's declaration of war,[1] Olivares realised the need for bases on the German coast where his naval squadrons might refit without making the long voyage back to Spain. His scheme, a brilliant one in conception, was to win the alliance of the Hanseatic League and to secure the use of its ports at Lübeck, Stralsund, Hamburg and Bremen. The League had been crippled by competition from the Dutch, English, Danes and Swedes, and Olivares offered naval protection and commercial

[1] In 1625, after Charles had discovered, by a personal visit to Madrid, that the Spanish marriage was nothing more than a diplomatic ruse.

privileges in the Spanish empire as a lure. Meanwhile, he urged the Emperor to despatch Wallenstein to take possession of West-phalia and the Lower Saxon Circle in order to dominate the area. Wallenstein duly carried out the plan during the Danish War of 1626–8, until Sweden intervened to save Stralsund and to prevent Habsburg control of the coastline.

Other setbacks coincided with the collapse of the Baltic plan. In 1627 Spain suspended the payment of interest on her debts; in 1628 Piet Heyn seized the silver fleet in Matanzas Bay; in 1629 Frederick Henry broke through the Spanish defences in Flanders and overran Brabant; in 1629 also, the disputed succession to Mantua and the fortresses of Montferrat and Casale menaced the security of the garrison in Milan. Spain, which had unfailingly supported the empire for over a century, was at last reduced to appealing to the emperor for aid. Ferdinand, however, had neither the troops to save Mantua from the French, nor the influence to sway the German princes against the Dutch. In the circumstances a peace settlement was the only cure for Spain's ills, but when a chance came during the lull following the death of Gustavus Adolphus in 1632, Olivares refused to consider the idea. He believed, in fact, that Gustavus's death made the continuation of war all the more necessary, on the grounds that Sweden's defeat would result in a revival of Habsburg power and that this in turn would ease the recovery of the United Provinces. The Cardinal-Infante Ferdinand was divested of his clerical robes and sent at the head of an army through the Val Telline. At Nördlingen he met his brother-in-law, the Archduke Ferdinand, and together they crushed the combined forces of the Heilbronn League.

Nördlingen was the last great victory to be won by Spain in Europe. It led directly to a French declaration of war, and in such a war the political stability, the material resources and the firm government of France gave her the advantage. She survived the 'year of Corbie' (1636) when the Habsburg armies made their bid to seize Paris, and thereafter the years of war proved disastrous for Spain. The fall of Breisach in 1638 blocked the overland route to Flanders, the ignominious defeat of the Armada in the Downs in 1639 confirmed Dutch supremacy in the Channel, and the victor of Nördlingen was thus deprived of supplies. With the Catalans and Portuguese in revolt during 1640, and the French armies victorious in north Italy, in Roussillon and at Rocroi in 1643, the collapse of Spain was patent. By making a separate treaty with the Dutch in 1648 she relieved herself of one enemy, but the French too were released from their German commitments by the Peace of Westphalia; and their gains of Pinerolo, Breisach, Philippsburg and the principal fortresses of Alsace and Lorraine, reinforced their stranglehold on Spain's lines of communication.

The Fronde provided an unexpected respite for Spain and an ally in the Prince of Condé, who held his own against Turenne in Flanders, beating him decisively at Valenciennes in 1656. The entry of England into the war, however, signalised by the fall of Jamaica and the Anglo-French victory at Dunkirk, decided the issue. Spain had no option but to accept Mazarin's terms in the Treaty of the Pyrenees, which was formally drawn up in 1659:

   (i) Roussillon and Perpignan; Montmédy in Luxemburg; Artois, and the Netherland towns of Arras, Béthune, Gravelines and Thionville were ceded to France. Dunkirk was given to England.

  (ii) All French gains at the Peace of Westphalia were recognised and confirmed by Spain.

 (iii) The French withdrew their support from the Catalan and Portuguese rebels.

 (iv) The Infanta, Maria Theresa, was married to Louis XIV.

This last clause was to prove the most important in the treaty, since, after the reign of Charles II (1665-1700), it led to the Bourbon succession. Spain might well have been happier if the interval of Carlos's reign could have been foregone.

THE SPANISH SUCCESSION, 1665-1714

Carlos II. The Last of the Spanish Habsburgs, 1665-1700

Three generations of royal marriages between cousins and nieces[1] produced their dreadful legacy in the pitiful form of Carlos II. Grotesque in appearance, deformed in body and backward in intellect, he seemed barely human: 'He has a ravenous stomach', reported Stanhope, the English ambassador, as though

---

[1] Of 56 of Carlos's maternal ancestors, 48 were ancestors of his father. Carlos's own grandfather was also his mother's; his parents were uncle and niece.

describing some strange Iberian creature, 'and swallows all he eats whole, for his nether jaw stands out so much that his two rows of teeth cannot meet; to compensate which, he has a prodigious wide throat, so that a gizzard or a liver of a hen passes down whole.' The Spaniards, ignorant of genetics, looked upon their divinely appointed leader with dismay and declared him to be in the grip of diabolical spirits, an explanation all the more tragic for being accepted by Carlos himself, so that the anguish of his physical infirmity was increased by nameless fears which denied him sleep unless his confessor and two friars lay in his chamber.

The elaborate administration which had been built around the person of the king collapsed into worthless wreckage since Carlos was unable to play any part in the business of government. Fifteen minutes' work, signing state papers, was reputed to be the most he could do in a day, and the interminable delays for which Spain was already notorious became even more pronounced: 'No head to govern, and every man in office does what he pleases without fear of being called to account' (Stanhope). The blight, 'so thick', wrote a Frenchwoman in Madrid, 'that it can be seen, smelt, touched', which settled upon the court and the civil service speeded the progressive deterioration of the economy. The *Mesta*, the *Consulado*, the great Fairs of Castile and all other public and official organs of trade and industry, declined with every decade, and there was little indication that their losses were in any way recouped by gains among private traders and individual farmers. The value of *vellon* continued to fluctuate wildly, with even more disastrous effect after 1680 when the government tried to restore it to its value as in Philip II's day. 'Commerce is in no better state. With the exception of Castilian wool, which foreigners buy, there is no merchandise or manufacture to attract money. The king has no ships now to protect trade and his subjects none to trade with, so that all commerce is done by strangers, and two-thirds of the money from the Indies goes direct abroad, and the other third gradually follows it in payment for goods.'[1]

Material decay found a counterpart in the mood of pessimism which spread throughout Spain, inducing acquiescence and inhibiting self-help. The race which had dominated Europe and opened up a new continent overseas became listless and apathetic,

---

[1] From *Mémoires de la Cour D'Espagne*, a brilliant and detailed commentary by de Villars, the French ambassador.

so that the physical degeneration of the royal family merely epitomised the more fundamental deterioration of the national spirit. The single-minded crusading zeal which had once been characteristic of the Spaniard gave way to an exaggerated and dangerous version of the Quietist docrines of Miguel de Molinos,[1] whose emphasis on the withdrawal of the soul from the world to lose itself in adoration of God, was perverted to encourage the utter abandonment of all interest in church and state, in favour of the passive, endless waiting for illumination by God.

The political history of Spain after 1665 resolved itself into two successive conflicts, namely to control the king while he lived and to determine the succession before he died. In the first of these Don Juan played a prominent part since his campaigns in Naples, Catalonia and the Netherlands had made his name deservedly popular. He hoped to exploit the marriage of Maria Theresa and Louis XIV to establish closer alliance between their countries, and thus to save Spain from further warfare. Undoubtedly Don Juan was right in his policy and his able qualities clearly marked him out for the direction of affairs. Unfortunately for Spain, both he and his policy were bitterly opposed by Carlos's mother, Mariana of Austria. As an Austrian she wanted to use Spain to protect her own country from Louis XIV: as a mother she was acutely aware of the contrast between the strong soldier and her own feeble infant, and she feared lest Don Juan seize the crown. No doubt Spain would have benefited had he done so, but the principle of legitimacy was not easily set aside. Philip IV, indeed, had wanted to legitimise him, but the jealous Mariana forbade it, and finally he was merely given formal recognition as a royal bastard, an honour denied to the other thirty or so children of Philip's mistresses.

In consequence it was Mariana who secured the direction of affairs on behalf of her son, while Don Juan retired to Aragon. In 1669 he marched on Madrid, and to the delight of the people, cleared the court of the queen's Austrian favourites. More than this, however, he could not do without expelling Mariana herself, and once again he went into retirement. He returned eight years later after Mariana had scandalised the country by taking a lover and making him chief minister. This time Mariana was removed from the court and Don Juan kept control of the king. For two

[1] See Chapter I, page 80.

years he enforced his policies against the intrigues of the Austrian faction, and the opposition of the fickle mob which blamed him for Spain's defeats in the war with France (1672-9), undertaken against his advice and one which he was quick to terminate. His triumph was the betrothal of Carlos to Marie Louise, Louis XIV's niece, but his death in 1679 restored Mariana to the court. Although the French princess became queen, her influence with the king was never allowed to challenge that of the queen mother and when she died a second marriage was arranged with the emperor's sister-in-law to confirm the triumph of Mariana and the Austrians. For the luckless king, however, the last years of a miserable existence were made even more intolerable by the presence of a vicious shrew.

The struggle for the control of Carlos II was barely won before it became necessary to determine the succession. Carlos had no children and, whatever the niceties of the genealogical tables, the legality of renunciations and the partition treaties of interested powers,[1] the choice before Spain lay between a French and an Austrian prince. Austrian domination at court, which in Vienna was taken to presage the nomination of the Emperor's son, had an unforeseen result: 'The general inclination to the succession', wrote Stanhope, 'is altogether French, their aversion to the Queen having set them against her countrymen.' The lead was taken by Cardinal Portocarrero, who, with powerful support from the grandees, worked actively in alliance with the French ambassador. He played upon Carlos's dislike for his second wife, comparing her unfavourably with the French princess whose short-lived gaiety had charmed the king and whose memory still lived with him. More astutely, he persuaded Carlos to change his confessor, an Austrian accomplice, for one of the French party. Out of all the intrigue there was one thing the unhappy monarch could apprehend: his empire was threatened with partition, and France alone had the power to guarantee its security. A month before his death in 1700, Carlos made the only significant decision of his life by naming Philip of Anjou as his successor, on condition that he preserved the empire from the indignity of partition at the hands of Europe.

Spain's survival in the face of continual aggression by France is one of the most startling aspects of the seventeenth century. It was

---

[1] See Chapter VII, page 306, for an account of the international negotiations preceding the War of Spanish Succession.

not, however, the result of her own doing for she was saved, in the first place, by her possession of the Spanish Netherlands. In view of the frequency with which these provinces were invaded by the French in the wars of 1667–8, 1672–9, 1684–5 and 1688–97, this may appear to be a paradox; but the advisers of Charles V in the previous century had always stressed the importance of Flanders as 'a citadel of steel, a shield which enabled him to receive the blows of England, France and Germany, far away from the head of the monarchy'. This appreciation was still valid, and Louis XIV's attacks on the Netherlands not only distracted him from Spain itself but also aroused against him a series of European coalitions. The other powers, but lately combined to destroy Spanish hegemony, found it vital to their interests to prevent the extension of French power in Europe. Spain's late enemies, therefore, rushed unasked to her defence. Secondly, Spain was saved by the chronic illness and infecundity of Carlos II; another paradox, perhaps. If Louis had not been attracted by the lure of the Spanish succession for his sons, Spain would have suffered more severely from his armies. Instead, though many conquests were made, by 1700 France had retained only Franche Comté and a line of garrisons in Flanders. The Partition Treaties, whether with the emperor in 1667 or with William III after the Peace of Ryswick, were in fact a guarantee of Spain's integrity while Carlos II lived.

Philip V and the War of Spanish Succession[1]

On learning that Carlos II had left his empire to a French prince, the Austrians straightway invaded the Spanish possessions in north Italy in the name of the Archduke Charles. Philip V was confident of victory since he could rely upon the support of Louis XIV, but unfortunately it was Louis's rash actions which drove England and Holland, along with most of the German states, into the Austrian camp. When Louis ordered Philip to grant the *Asiento*[2] to the French Guinea Company; when he expelled the Dutch from their barrier fortresses, in Philip's name but with French troops; when he declared that Philip retained his claims to the throne of France, then the spectre of a universal monarchy, dominating the frontiers of the old world, monopolising the trade

---

[1] See Chapter VII, pages 311–20.
[2] A valuable concession to foreign merchants, enabling them to supply the Spanish-American empire with Negro slaves.

of the new, impelled the creation of the Grand Alliance. Guiltless though he was of Louis's blunders, Philip V could not escape their consequences, and his accession was marked by thirteen years of warfare.

The Spaniards welcomed Philip, a cheerful and handsome seventeen-year-old whose determination to fight for his throne induced a new mood of optimism and awakened a sense of purpose among his subjects. Lethargic though he could be on occasion, and too often inclined to give up in the face of difficulties, he nevertheless provided a remarkable contrast to his predecessors. When the war began in Italy he remarked that Philip II had lost Holland by not leading his armies in person, and added, 'If I lose territories it shall not be for that reason.' During his absence his fifteen-year-old wife, chaperoned and directed by an experienced old Frenchwoman, won the hearts of Madrid by reading out her husband's despatches from the balcony of the palace. Such examples of royal leadership took Castile, at least, by storm; its citizens named Philip *el animoso*, 'the spirited', and fought loyally for him throughout the war.

In any conflict with Spain the English were wedded to the sea-dog tradition of Elizabeth's reign, believing that victory was to be achieved by raids on Cadiz and the West Indies, and by intercepting the treasure fleet. Indeed, Admiral Rooke's expedition of 1702 did this with some success, since he terrorised the citizens of Cadiz for a whole month and seized half the treasure fleet in Vigo Bay. None of this, however, was likely to drive Philip from Madrid and the adoption of a more rational strategy owed much to the skill of Prince George of Hesse-Darmstadt, the Austrian agent in London. He knew Spain well; he had helped to defend her against the French in 1695, and had served as viceroy of Catalonia until the accession of Philip V. His first *coup*, brilliantly devised to suit the Austrian cause, was the completion of the Methuen Treaty in 1703: it secured the use of Lisbon as a military base in the peninsula, it won Portugal from her nominal alliance with France, and it committed the Allies, whose main concern was the defeat of Louis XIV, to an open avowal of the Archduke Charles's claims to Spain. Rooke and Hesse-Darmstadt brought Charles to Lisbon in 1704, along with 10,000 English and Dutch troops. From there they sailed round the peninsula to attempt a landing in Catalonia, where Hesse-Darmstadt had been very popular as viceroy. The expedition failed, however, since the Catalans were not prepared to jeopardise their *fueros* by rebelling against Philip V until they had received some firm guarantee of Allied support. Hesse-Darmstadt accordingly won a promise from the English government to secure the Catalans 'a confirmation of their rights and liberties from the King of Spain'; and he reappeared in 1705 bringing the Archduke Charles with him. This time the province rose against Philip, and only the citadel of Barcelona made resistance.

In the successful attack on Barcelona, Hesse-Darmstadt lost his life, but his work had ensured that Portugal and Catalonia, the two areas of the peninsula most hostile to Castile, and most easily reinforced by sea, were won for his master. The Allies could thus exploit their mastery of the sea to launch attacks with equal facility from opposite sides of the peninsula. In 1704, before Charles had been transported to Catalonia, an Allied army under Galway had moved eastwards from Lisbon with 20,000 Portuguese in support. French reinforcements led by Berwick,[1] however, blocked its advance, and Philip enjoyed an exhilarating if short-lived invasion of Portuguese territory. Galway returned to the attack in 1705, to be repulsed at Badajoz, but Philip had then to withdraw most of his troops to cross the peninsula in order to face Charles in Catalonia (1706). While his troops were marching across the difficult terrain, the Allies were able to reinforce Charles from the sea, and it was the arrival of the English fleet at a critical moment of the battle for Barcelona which brought about Philip's defeat. Since Aragon too had declared for Charles, Philip's only way of escape lay across the Pyrenees. In great humiliation he abandoned his artillery and supply trains, crossed into France and returned to Madrid through Navarre. Galway, however, had realised that Philip's western front had been denuded for the invasion of Catalonia, and his advance was so swift that, within a fortnight of Philip's return to his capital, Galway had seized it, and the king was again a fugitive.

The occupation of Madrid, the culmination of a hundred years of disasters, produced an unlooked-for response among Philip's subjects in Castile and Andalusia. Accustomed as they had become to the ignominious record of defeat, and dulled by a fatalist refusal to believe in the possibility of recovery, they were none the less

---

[1] An interesting point: Galway was a French Huguenot while Berwick was an Englishman, an illegitimate son of James II.

galvanised into action by the sight of English and Portuguese troops triumphant among their native sierras. At one stroke they discovered alike their self-respect and a talent for guerrilla warfare. Sea power was of no avail to the Allies at this juncture, and Galway's long lines of communication across the Estremadura were harassed and broken. When Berwick's men were reinforced from Navarre, Philip was restored to his capital after an absence of only four months.

In Germany, Flanders and Italy the Allies were victorious: in Spain there was deadlock. The frontier between Castile and Aragon, the historic divide in Spanish history, lay between Philip and Charles, with Aragon, Valencia, Catalonia and the Balearic Islands in Austrian hands. At Almanza in 1707 Philip defeated the Allies but could not consolidate his victory since Louis XIV recalled many of his troops for the defence of France. Charles, on the other hand, was freely reinforced from the Austrian bases in Italy, but his incursions into Castile, and even the seige of Madrid in 1710, availed him nothing, since, as Stanhope remarked, 'We are not masters in Castile of more ground than we encamp on.' The deadlock was resolved by events outside Spain. By 1710 Marlborough's successive efforts to invade northern France and to take Paris had failed, and the Allies began to weaken in their resolve. In England the Whig cry of 'No peace without Spain' was repudiated by the Tory majority in the new Parliament; while the sudden death of Charles's brother, the Emperor Joseph, resulted in his own accession to the imperial throne. The spectre of universal monarchy suddenly appeared two-faced; and Philip's timely renunciation of his claim to France induced a general suspicion in Europe of Habsburg rather than of Bourbon pretensions. The Grand Alliance broke up, the Austrians evacuated the peninsula and England defaulted on her guarantees to the Catalans.

By 1714 the final touches had been put to the peace settlement, which affected Spain in the following particulars:

(i) Philip V renounced his claim to the French throne, and was recognised as ruler of Spain and the Spanish-American empire.

(ii) Charles, now Emperor Charles VI, was given the Spanish Netherlands, and the Italian provinces of Milan, Naples and Sicily.

(iii) Sicily passed to the King of Savoy, who at the same time gained his royal title.

(iv) England retained possession of Gibraltar and Minorca, seized in the war; and her South Sea Company was granted the right to sell slaves in the American colonies.

The Aftermath of the War

Spain at last was to be ruled by the man whom Carlos II had chosen. Though the empire had been rudely partitioned, the loss of Flanders and Italy was a source of relief to a government which had found them increasingly impossible to defend; and, if European leadership was denied her, Spain was at least free to enjoy less burdensome privileges, among them the creation of a more efficient administration. The position in 1700 had not been a happy one: 'Extreme confusion reigns in all affairs; it would appear as if the monarchs of Spain had tried by their bad conduct to destroy their realm rather than to preserve it. Thus disorder has grown so much in the last reign that it may be said that there is now in Spain no government at all.' Such was the contemptuous opinion of Louis XIV, a ruler who prided himself on his *métier du roi*, and who had no illusions about the task before his grandson. Accordingly he sent men such as Orry, whose experience of French administration was of great value to a country where there had been no bureaucrat of note since Olivares. Success depended on two factors, the king's control of the peninsula and French control of the king.

The first was assured by Austria's defeat in Spain, since the adherence of Aragon and its attendant provinces to the Archduke Charles was used as an excuse to destroy their *fueros*. The powerfully entrenched liberties of Aragon, which Philip II himself had hesitated to challenge, were abolished outright by Philip V at the head of a victorious army. Catalonia, abandoned by Charles and betrayed by England, held out for thirteen months in a vain endeavour to stave off the final reckoning. Its new constitution made no mention of its *fueros*, which survived only in the memory of the people, since no defeat could destroy the independent spirit of the Catalan race. For the first time in Spain's history, therefore, the unity of the realm was no longer personal and dynastic, but constitutional and administrative. The Cortes became an assembly of representatives from each province, with no power to defy the crown, and the Council of Castile was established, as Olivares had once dreamed, as the controlling body within Spain.

Philip V, for all his good qualities, had not been trained to direct affairs of state: indeed, his education had encouraged a quite different quality. 'Younger brother of a violent and excitable prince', wrote Saint-Simon, 'he was bred up in a submission that was necessary for the repose of the royal family.' In Spain he revealed this trait by his emotional dependence upon masterful women, a dependence so great that whenever he was separated from his wife he fell into a torpor of inactivity and indecision. While Marie Louise lived, Philip was dominated by her, while she in turn was generally open to influence from France. Galling though it was to Spanish pride, the chief posts went to Orry and his countrymen, who tightened up the administration and secured many economies in the treasury.

In 1714, however, Philip married Elizabeth Farnese of Parma. Reputed to be docile and amenable to French direction, she took Philip by storm and expelled the French from the court. Thereafter Spanish policy, temporarily diverted from subservience to France, was directed once again to the pursuit of power in Italy, where Elizabeth looked to establish her children's fortunes. The prospect of peace and retrenchment proferred by the terms of Utrecht thus soon proved illusory.

VI

Louis XIV: A Study in Absolutism

Louis XIV: his métier du roi

Her territories compactly joined, her land fertile and her population[1] the largest of any European state, France was held back from pre-eminence in Europe only by the recurrent civil war and rebellion that had plagued her since 1559. Bodin[2] in 1577 had been the first to comprehend the need for an absolute monarch to save France from disorder, and since his time the French had learned from experience to discredit all theories of a monarchy tempered by constitutional checks and balances. The tempering had too often been at the hands of overmighty subjects.

The English in 1660, the French in 1651, alike had welcomed the return of their kings to their capitals; but whereas the English retained with undiminished powers the Parliament that had defeated Charles I, the French, condemning the bitter feuds that had jeopardised the prosperity, the security and the prestige of their country, entirely repudiated the action of the Frondeurs. This popular instinct towards absolutism found formal utterance in the writings of the clergy, notably in those of Bossuet whose *Politics based on the very words of Holy Scripture* repeated the political maxims of the day and reinforced them with the sanction of biblical authority: the king was God's *vive image* upon earth, his authority was absolute and he answered for his actions to God alone. The lawyers too acclaimed the power bestowed upon kings by invoking the precepts of Roman law most apposite to their brief, and all alike owed much to Hobbes's brilliant anatomy of Leviathan,[3] despite his disreputable status as an atheist and an Englishman.

Ready as they were to accept the theory of absolutism, the French only awaited a monarch capable of practising it. Henry IV,

---

[1] About 18,000,000 in 1660.
[2] *Six Livres de la République.*
[3] Translated into French in 1649. See Chapter I, page 17, for a more detailed analysis of seventeenth-century political theory.

of course, had been an ideal hero king, but the royal authority which he had done so much to restore had since been exercised by cardinals. 'Ci-gît l'Éminence deuxième', wrote a wit in eager anticipation of Mazarin's death, 'Dieu nous garde de la troisième.' Louis XIV delighted his subjects by taking the wit at his word. When, after Mazarin's death, the Archbishop of Paris and the principal secretaries asked the king to whom they should report for instructions, they received the terse reply, 'À moi'. In two words Louis determined the destiny of France for the next sixty years.

'It was the moment for which I had waited', wrote Louis in the *Mémoires* he compiled for his son's instruction, 'and which I had dreaded', he had the honesty to add, for he knew he was wholly lacking in experience. No great tutor had supervised his formal education: his political education, however, was provided by the Fronde. The humiliation he then suffered as a child, and the dangers which beset the court, left him with a lifelong distaste for the Parisian mob and for theories of government which did not exhalt the absolute sovereignty of the king. Moreover, he was well equipped by nature for the role of king. John Evelyn, the English diarist who witnessed his return to Paris after the Fronde, described him as 'a young Apollo . . . a prince of a grave yet sweet countenance'. He was well built, toughened by long hours of hunting, with a dignified bearing and a keen eye which commanded respect. Though he lacked a sense of humour he could yet be lively and charming; and if he took himself too seriously, if he positively savoured the formality of court etiquette, this was no disadvantage in a king who was resolved to show himself to his subjects as no ordinary mortal but as God's *vive image* upon earth.

While Mazarin still lived, Louis passed his time in amorous adventures with the cardinal's nieces, impatient though he was to enter upon his inheritance. When Mazarin died he made his dramatic *début*: 'I resolved never to appoint a first minister, nor to leave to another the function of royalty while reserving to myself the mere title.' For Louis, monarchy was a specialist occupation; he liked to term it his *métier du roi*, and he took it as seriously as any other man might undertake his own profession. Once Louis had assumed the responsibility of governing France he allowed nothing to interfere with his task. He did not abandon his mistresses, but the amusements, balls and hunting trips which had

occupied his youth became the strictly regulated relaxations of a
busy man with a crowded time-table. Bishop Burnet, an English
visitor to Paris in 1667, commented, with an implied reproof of his
own sovereign Charles II, that he was 'diligent in his own councils
and regular in the dispatch of his affairs'.

The *métier du roi* required regular attendance at the numerous
councils by which France was governed. The *conseil d'état*, later
known at Versailles as the *conseil d'en haut*, met for long sessions
on three days a week to determine policy on all the major issues of
the day: the *conseil des finances* met weekly, and the *conseil des
dépeches*, supervising the law courts and the working of the
administration, met two or three times a month. These, and many
other councils, Louis attended in fulfilment of his belief that 'the
right of deliberation and resolution belongs to the head alone, and
all the functions of the other members consist in executing the
orders given to them'. In a typical day, described by his minister
Colbert, he was in council from 10 a.m. until 1.30 p.m.; after
lunch he attended another council, devoted two hours to improving
his Latin in order to read Papal documents unaided, and was in
council again until 10 in the evening. None of this was for
Louis the mechanical performance of a tedious duty, for he not
only attended but possessed a rare faculty for active listening. The
ministers whom he inherited from Mazarin were among the most
talented administrators of the century, with a genius for planning
and innovation. In their specialist fields Louis could not rival them,
but as chairman of their discussions he revealed his own genius for
committee work and an ability to take an overall view. Whatever
the shortcomings of his education, he had an excellent memory,
and by his own capacity for sustained hard work he made himself
indispensable to his more gifted subordinates. His resolve to be his
own first minister proved not to have been an idle whim.

No one attended the councils by right of birth or office. Membership was determined by the king alone, according to the
problem in hand. The great nobles and the great churchmen who
had hitherto played a decisive part in the government of France
were replaced by men of *bourgeois* stock, Michel Le Tellier, Jean-
Baptiste Colbert and Hugues de Lionne. 'It was important', wrote
Louis, 'that the public should know by the rank of those who
served me that I had no intention of sharing my authority with
them'; and though their sons were given noble titles, they in turn

served Louis on the same terms as their fathers. Indeed, family connections were very marked. The *Maison du Roi* and the *Marine*, for example, were controlled in turn by Colbert and his son Seignelay, to be succeeded by two generations of the Ponchartrain family: Colbert's brother, Colbert de Croissy, was later to super-intend foreign affairs, in which post he was followed by his son, Colbert de Torcy. The secretaryship of war was held by three generations of the same family; Michel Le Tellier, his son Louvois and his grandson Barbézieux. Family rivalry and dependence upon the king were all to Louis's advantage, but he himself had the common sense to choose men who were not merely sycophants or squabbling rivals. Once his authority was recognised, his servants were allowed great responsibility since he valued their talents and gave them full play.

Nicolas Fouquet alone among those who had served Mazarin failed to appreciate Louis's intention. He had acquired great wealth and power from his position as *Surintendant des Finances* and had hoped to succeed to Mazarin's place, but thwarted in his ambition by Louis's resolve to be his own first minister, Fouquet brought about his own downfall by a series of foolish mistakes. It was tactless to make advances to La Vallière, the current royal mistress, and to display his wealth in prodigious *fêtes* when royal revenues were pledged in advance. It was dangerous to give prominence to his motto, *Quo non ascendam*, and to fortify his home at Belle Isle. His behaviour smacked of the irresponsible and over-mighty sub-jects who had dominated Louis's childhood, and the king decided upon his downfall. The assiduous Colbert, eager for the reversion of Fouquet's office, supplied evidence of his malversation of royal funds, and a royal court condemned him to exile. At this point Louis intervened to increase the penalty to one of life imprison-ment at Pinerolo. Fouquet's punishment served as a useful warning to his colleagues from which they did not fail to profit. When Colbert secured an appointment for his son Seignelay, he passed on the lesson which he had made his own: 'Never as long as you live send out anything in the king's name without his express approval.'

Versailles: Symbol of Absolutism

Louis XIII had built a small château at Versailles to save him-self the fatigue of returning to Paris after a long hunting trip in the

Forest of Marly. It was a simple building, a rectangular block, framed to the right and left by two wings, which Louis XIV often visited in his youth, and for which he had much affection. In 1661 he began to enlarge the gardens without altering the main building, but in 1668 he determined upon a more radical transformation: the original château was to be preserved, but around it he ordered the construction of a new palace, large enough to serve as a permanent home for the royal family. By 1682, though building continued for the rest of his reign, he had moved into residence. From that date until the Revolution, Versailles replaced Paris as the seat of government.

Louis's decision sprang from many sources. He shared his father's love of walking and hunting, but the spaciousness of Versailles satisfied more than his physical needs. The splendour of monarchy, as Louis believed in it, had not been reflected in the unhappy events of his youth. His coronation at Reims (1654), conducted in haste as a manœuvre to outwit the Frondeurs, had been an undignified ceremony at which most of those who traditionally attended upon the king, including the Archbishop of Reims himself, had been absent. The Fronde, moreover, left him with a permanent distaste for the narrow streets of Paris with their frequently erected barricades, and for the noisy mob who had once swarmed through his palace. To compensate for these indignities he sought a more splendid and more spacious environment for his court. The abode of *le roi soleil* was not to be stumbled upon around a street corner; and in revenge upon his unruly capital he removed himself from its midst. Personal gratification, however, was not the only consideration in Louis's mind. As France became the most important power in Europe he wished to epitomise her greatness, which was his own, by creating a more magnificent stage for his actions; and it was after the Peace of Aix-la-Chapelle of 1668, when the military and diplomatic success of France had stunned Europe into admiration and fear, that he finally determined to transform his father's château at Versailles.

The men who built Versailles had an excellent understanding of Louis's purpose. It was not only the Roman Church that had discovered the power of art to impress and overwhelm:[1] the Baroque style had been applied to domestic architecture, grouping façades and wings, arcades, terraces and pavilions in a manner calculated

[1] See Chapter I, page 82.

to awaken in the observer a sense of movement and of grandeur. Le Vau, the first of Louis's architects, lengthened the wings of the original château to create an impressive *cour d'honneur* awaiting the visitor from Paris; while on the garden side he built a new central block which, with its two wings, presented a massive façade. To heighten the effect he broke the façade at its centre, recessing the upper storeys to leave the ground floor covered by a marble terrace, decorated with a fountain. He was succeeded, however, by Hardouin-Mansart, who represented a different tradition to the Italian style of Le Vau, opposing the Baroque with a more severely classical style. This classical tradition accorded admirably with the requirements of order, discipline and harmony which characterised the ideal of Louis's absolution. By removing Le Vau's central recess, Mansart imposed a uniform façade on the garden side, and strengthened its horizontal line by adding two further wings, slightly recessed, which brought its overall length to 550 yards. The elevation remained the same but the whole effect was transformed: the sense of movement was destroyed and in its place was created a mood of restrained magnificence, majesty and order.

Le Brun superintended the decoration within the palace. His taste was similar to Le Vau's, and the Ambassador's staircase, no longer extant, was a masterpiece of baroque illusion, intended to astound the foreign dignitaries who called upon Louis. Around it was placed a balustrade, between the pillars of which was painted a throng of courtiers who seemed to press forward to watch the stately processions as they ascended. Later, however, Le Brun bowed to Mansart's influence and the famous *Galerie des Glaces* was designed in a more restrained fashion, following the classical traditions which Louis found more apposite to his austere sense of majesty. The gardens were laid out by Le Nôtre in a similar style. The rough terrain where sandy scrub and marshland competed for precedence was reduced to order by thousands of workmen who levelled the earth and laid pipes to supply the 1,400 fountains with water from the Seine, since there were no springs in the area. From the palace there stretched countless *parterres* of flowers, vast sheets of water, and an apparently endless succession of stately avenues. Here, where man had wrought his will upon nature, was reflected the well-ordered society of which Louis was the centre.

It mattered little that several thousand workmen died from fever and pneumonia in the work of constructing the palace and its gardens; that ten thousand courtiers and servants crowded upon each other in perennial confusion and dirt; that the great corridors resembled frozen alleyways in winter, and that the chimneys smoked because their height had been reduced to preserve the dignity of the façade. It mattered little, since the prime purpose had been so notably achieved: Versailles epitomised the grandeur of Louis XIV.

If Versailles had been designed and constructed to enhance Louis's glory, life within its walls was directed towards the same end, and the complexity and rigidity of court etiquette became the marvel of Europe. To some extent this resulted from Louis's own humourless personality; taking himself so seriously, he saw nothing strange in the highly organised society that revolved, like the planets, in stately progression around its sun. He acted his part so convincingly that it is doubtful if he ever conceived of it as a part at all. Even his moments of relaxation were conducted with ceremony and dignity: he played billiards, as one lady remarked, with the air of being master of the world. The laws of etiquette and precedence, however, had also a political value, since they demonstrated the inferior rank of all who attended upon the king. The most minute distinctions between the greatest of his courtiers, and indeed among his own family, were reflected in the degree of familiarity permitted to them.[1] The seriousness of Louis's purpose is made clear from a revealing passage in his *Mémoires*: 'About this time I learned that my brother was thinking of asking that his wife might be allowed to sit in the Queen's presence on a seat with a back to it. My friendly feelings towards him made me unwilling to refuse him anything; but seeing of what great moment this matter was, I let him know forthwith, with all possible gentleness, that I could not possibly give him satisfaction; . . . that I did not feel able to grant this which would seem to be an approach to my own elevation.'

The king's day began with the *petit lever* to which over a hundred people were admitted in six successive parties, each one a shade

[1] See for example, the English philosopher John Locke's description of a court occasion which catches the subtle gradations among even the most exalted of the court. 'At night we saw the opera of *Alceste*. The King and Queen sat on chairs with arms; on the right hand of the King sat Mme. de Montespan, a little nearer the stage, Mademoiselle, the King of England's niece; on the left hand of the Queen sat Monsieur and at his left hand Madame, and so forwards towards the stage other ladies of the court, all on tabourets, except the King and Queen'.

less select than the one before. Those of the highest rank were permitted to see the king leave his bed; the least favoured had to be content with observing the final stages of his dressing. At Mass, it was said, the king worshipped God while the court worshipped the king; dinner, *au grand couvert*, was eaten by the royal family alone, in the presence of the hushed congregation of the court; and at the *petit coucher* the favoured few, who had watched the king rise, attended him to his bed. 'Given an almanac', wrote the Duc de Saint-Simon, 'and a watch, one could always tell that the king would be doing.' This constant parade before the court demanded from Louis as much care as attendance at his councils, and never did he neglect either. Seven days before his death, the old and broken king yet managed to dine *au grand couvert*, even though he could barely sip a little liquid, to demonstrate that the life of the court still revolved around him alone.

Residence at Versailles was a costly affair for the great nobles, since their households had to be maintained in the style of sumptuous affluence to which the king was accustomed. Few indeed could secure a place in attendance at Versailles, but unless they did so they lived without hope of favours from the king's hand: 'C'est un homme que je ne vois jamais,' was Louis's coldest rejection of a suitor for preferment, and the exorbitant expense of court life ensured that once a noble had secured charity from the king he was as quickly reduced to petitioning for more. Trapped within the confines of the palace, the nobles who had ridden roughshod over the crown in the past were transformed into servile courtiers, submitting eagerly to the laws of precedence for fear of seeing someone of inferior status gain closer access to the king than themselves. To be at Versailles was in itself a privilege, to attend the more intimate ceremonies of the king's life was a peerless distinction, and the offer of holding the royal candle at the *petit coucher* reduced Saint-Simon, for one, to mute ecstasy. Petitioning for favours to stave off bankruptcy, jostling for precedence to assuage their dignity, their lives an artificially gay succession of balls, hunts, gaming and gossip, the nobility was tamed more effectively by the etiquette of Versailles than by the harsh edicts of Richelieu. To quit the court of Louis XIII had been an act of defiance: to be sent from Versailles was a shameful disgrace. 'Loin de vous, Sire', breathed a fervent noble released from exile, 'on n'est pas seulement malheureux, on est ridicule.' Unhappily for the future, the life of those at court became divorced from that of the people who worked their estates: France ceased to exist beyond the borders of Le Nôtre's gardens, and the dusty miles between Versailles and Paris seemed to grow longer with every year.

Yet another vital function of Versailles was to attract the services of poets, artists and musicians to enhance Louis's fame. Louis's offer was an attractive one of generous pensions, a permanent audience of the most distinguished kind, and a magnificent *milieu* from which their fame might radiate throughout the civilised world. Louis himself was no connoisseur. He had no interest in promoting the nascent talents of young men, but exploited for political ends the genius of men who had already made their name. Molière, Bossuet, La Fontaine, Le Brun, Le Vau and Le Nôtre were established before 1661 and the only great name to appear as a result of Louis's patronage was, perhaps, Racine. Moreover, he exercised strict control over their work. Adherence to the classical tradition was demanded not only of the architects of Versailles but of the poets and dramatists. Nicolas Boileau's *Art Poétique* was acclaimed a masterpiece of literary criticism because it urged the literary world to take its subjects from classical mythology and history, and insisted, for example, that in the drama the Aristotelian unities of time, place and action be preserved. Obviously this could not be imposed to the letter, but the classical tradition remained nominally as the prime source of inspiration at Versailles. Molière alone was allowed to analyse and expose the foibles of his own society without censure, since his wit and perception appealed to the king: he took care, none the less, not to direct his comic genius at the institution of monarchy.

Fénelon and La Bruyère, whose works revealed criticism of Louis's government, and Descartes and Bayle, who were suspected of atheism, did not receive bounty from the king. Patronage, in fact, was a more effective weapon than censorship; and the foundation of the *Académies* was undertaken to ensure a better control over their members. The *Académie de Peinture et de Sculpture*, for example, met monthly to discuss a work of art; from its discussions the members formulated rules to be observed so that a common spirit informed their work. As the *Académies* met under Le Brun's direction, Louis was assured that novelty, or any other trend unsuitable to an absolute régime, would be immediately suppressed, and he succeeded in his purpose. The fine arts supported and gave lustre to his political supremacy. No other court in Europe could display the talents of so many gifted men, and primacy in the arts, once the proud boast of Italy, was won for France. While other states combined to attack the armies of France, they competed with each other in adopting French fashions and in imitating the achievements of the civilisation created at Versailles.

Royal Control in the Provinces

The work of Henry IV and Richelieu had done much to extend the authority of the king throughout France, but administrative uniformity had yet to be achieved. Although the *pays d'élections* had been reduced to obedience and conformity, the *pays d'état*, which had been heartened by Richelieu's failure to defeat Languedoc, and by the temporary collapse of the central government during the Fronde, still retained particular liberties which made nonsense of Louis's concept of *l'état, c'est moi*. It would be misleading to compare the Estates of Languedoc, for example, with the Cortes of Catalonia or with the East Prussian Diet: self-regarding as they were, they did not claim a nationality separate from the rest of the kingdom nor did they repudiate the king's action in foreign affairs. Their loyalty to Louis XIV was not in question, nor did they deny his right to financial assistance. Their concern was simply to safeguard their local jurisdiction, and their pockets, from interference by the central government, and when they voted their annual *don gratuit* to the king, they jealously preserved its original meaning.

The task of bringing the *pays d'état* into line with the rest of France was entrusted to Colbert, and his treatment of Languedoc in particular will serve as an illustration of his actions in general. Sessions of the Languedoc Estates were effectively controlled by securing the election of the Archbishop of Toulouse as President. As an eminent local dignitary there could be little objection to him by the members: as one of Colbert's clientele, however, seeking to further his career by service to the central government, he was able to exercise great influence over their actions. Speakers favourable to the crown were given the floor, their opponents were cut short by operation of the closure, and the agenda was carefully supervised. Some members responded to bribery, prompting

Colbert to remark that 'perhaps ten or fifteen thousand *livres* distributed in this way might have a good effect on all other matters that might arise in the future': others were reduced to silence by the presence of Colbert's agents who, with great ostentation, made notes of their speeches. The recalcitrant few, who determined to contest this manipulation of their debates, suffered from interference in their private lives, their friends and relatives found it difficult to secure the reversion of vacant offices, and, in the last resort, their arrest was ordered by *lettre du cachet* which removed them from the public eye without the compensation of a public trial.

Brutal and ruthless, Colbert's methods were successful. By 1665 Languedoc was voting its *don gratuit* on the advice of royal intendants, and, as the king's hold tightened on the province, it became unnecessary to employ these methods further. Colbert had originally proposed to abolish the Estates outright: in the long run, however, he found them invaluable as a means of enforcing royal policy under the guise of local consent. The device was scarcely a state secret. In 1671 Madame de Sévigné attended the session of the Brittany Estates and reported that these would be short. 'They have only to ask what the king requires; no-one will say a word, and so it will be done.' The Estates on this occasion voted 2,500,000 *livres*, of which the king remitted 300,000, 'wishing to repay them for the good grace with which they obeyed him by this result of his liberality'. For the rest, 'an infinity of presents, some pensions, some repairs of roads and bridges, everlasting hospitality and gaming, eternal balls, three comedies a week; in all a magnificent show'.

Within all the provinces, however, there existed groups and individuals whose privileges, derived from custom or authorised by charter, might check the smooth running of the king's writ. The authority of provincial governors had already been drastically curtailed; Louis reduced it further by limiting their term of office to three years, thereby ensuring that the real direction of provincial affairs was assumed by intendants operating on a permanent commission from the *conseil d'état*. The *parlements*, too, became politically innocuous. After the collapse of the Fronde had dealt a death blow to their pretensions they were subsequently supervised by the *conseil des dépêches*. Cases in which the crown had a particular interest were removed from their jurisdiction, and judgements adverse to royal policy were swiftly revoked by edict.[1] 'It is no use writing about speeches made in the *parlement*', wrote Colbert to his intendant at Grenoble, 'As you know, the noises made by *parlements* are no longer in season.'

There remained the municipal corporations, invested with considerable autonomy by their charters of incorporation, but whose affairs were notoriously mismanaged by the small group of families which controlled each town. Incompetence and dishonesty in the administration of civic funds gave the crown an unimpeachable excuse for intervention — as at Saint-Quentin where the citizens had been hoodwinked into paying for the maintenance of walls which had never been constructed. In 1683 Colbert ordered each corporation to submit an annual report of its finances to his intendants, who were then charged with the significant duty of liquidating their debts. Finally, in 1692, when effective control had been firmly established by the intendants, the farce of election was abolished and civic offices were sold for life as profitable sinecures.

Throughout France the traditional system of government was thus preserved in appearance only. Governors, mayors, members of the Estates and of the *parlements* maintained the ceremonial trappings of their office and enjoyed their accustomed perquisites: the right to govern was transferred to men wholly dependent upon the king. The duties of the intendants were exhaustive, and some idea of their extent can be gathered from the *Mémoires* of Nicolas Foucault, who served successively in Montauban, Pau and Poitiers. He was variously employed in supervising the sessions of the Estates and the *parlements*; in police work, censorship and in scrutinising the activities of taxcollectors and municipal officers; in surveying roads and rivers; in superintending conscription, vagrancy, tobacco farms and industry, and in reporting to the central government on every matter under the sun, from the behaviour of Huguenots to the state of the harvest. Professionally competent and always accountable to the *conseil d'état*, the intendant served as the principal agent of Louis's absolutism.

Opposition from the nobility was no longer a force to be reckoned with. Their social status and their freedom from taxation

[1] See, for example, the case of the Widow Falempin of Amiens, below, page 269.

were left untouched, but the opportunity for service, which alone justified their privileged position, was denied them. The 200,000 nobles of France paid in full for the reckless faction of their fathers. Louis refused to employ them in the administration; the army offered a career only to those who attained to the high professional standards demanded by Le Tellier and Louvois;[1] the Church did not have enough wealthy benefices to satisfy all who sought them; Versailles opened its gates to a select few only. The laws of France and the traditions of their order combined to forbid them entry to other occupations, and, as all the children of the nobility were themselves ranked as nobles, younger sons were denied that freedom of action allowed to their counterparts, for example, in England. Commerce and industry were reserved for the *bourgeois* alone; and if there were nobles prepared to outrage their dignity by marrying the daughter of a successful business man, there were unhappily too few opportunities for such a *mésalliance*.

Isolated from the rest of society by the rigid conventions of their caste, the majority could only withdraw to their estates, where active farming of their land was discouraged not only by custom but also by the government. Land held by tenants was subject to taxation, and Colbert refused to exempt it if a noble recovered direct possession in order to work it himself. Moreover, a noble employing more than four ploughs for his personal use became liable to taxation. The *noble de province*, the squireen, the *hoberau*, became an object of scorn: 'Useless to his country, his wife and himself; often without a roof, clothing or any merit at all, the provincial noble tells himself ten times a day that at any rate he is a gentleman.'[2]

Louis XIV's government had little to fear from the 16,000,000 peasants of France, the overtaxed, underprivileged section of the community. Many differences of degree existed among them. A million or so still endured the shackles of serfdom in the eastern provinces; a million, perhaps, owned their own land; several million were landless labourers; but about half the peasants were *métayers*, paying as much as half their produce in rent to their lords. Collectively, however, the peasantry bore the brunt of the *taille* and the *gabelle*,[3] sustained the church by tithes, and the

---

[1] See below, page 275.
[2] La Bruyère, *Caractères*.   [3] See below, page 264.

nobility by seigneurial dues. Many of these dues had become nominal, but the lord could still compel his peasants to grind their corn in his mill, to bake their dough in his oven, and to crush their wine in his presses, for all of which he exacted payment. The *métayers*, in addition, paid him a tax whenever their lease was transferred by inheritance or by sale. Despite these hardships the peasant's lot was very slowly improving, since he benefited from the long period of internal peace provided by Louis's government. Only at the end of the century[1] did the burdens imposed by the government to finance the War of Spanish Succession (1701–14) prove so insupportable as to cause revolt.

The Officiers *and the Laws*

To the envious princes of Europe, Louis XIV appeared as the very epitome of absolutism. Absolutism, however, in seventeenth-century France must not be equated with totalitarianism in the present age, since its practice was limited and restrained by several factors.[2] Absolute control of the state is only possible in an egalitarian society, in which each member is equally exposed to the power of the government: French society resembled a privileged hierarchy, and, arbitrary though the *ancien régime* might be, it retained countless bulwarks against encroachment by the king. The individual was powerless before the majesty of the throne, but the class to which he belonged was hedged about and protected by time-honoured privileges which prevented radical changes in the distribution of wealth, power or social esteem. Uniformity could only be attained through social revolution, and it is significant that the Revolution of 1789 gave birth to the truly absolute powers of Napoleon.

At all the lower levels of the administration Louis's absolutism was compromised by the very servants he was compelled to employ. The intendants, of course, were endowed with unprecedented powers of direction and coercion but the *généralités* they controlled were often the size of a province. Of necessity they had to work through the *officiers* who constituted the civil service of the day, and without whose co-operation as a class nothing could be done. To the intendants, schooled by Colbert to serve the state with professional skill and utter loyalty, the body of *officiers*

---

[1] See below, page 282.
[2] See Chapter I, page 26, for a general study of this phenomenon.

represented an incubus. It was not that the *officiers* were necessarily inefficient or fraudulent but that their interests were their own rather than the king's. Having purchased their posts for profit, they were entrenched in positions of authority from which they were virtually irremovable. They could rarely be called to account, and they reflected the narrow outlook of their neighbourhood. Wise enough not to challenge the government by open opposition, they relied instead on their capacity for private or passive resistance. They exercised an informal surveillance over royal edicts, quietly ignoring those which threatened their position or offended the traditions of their locality. Months might pass before the intendant had noted and reported their offence; still more before the council's indignation was brought home to them. The *officier* merely shrugged his shoulders. The edict had never arrived, it had been lost, it had been misunderstood, it would be enforced tomorrow, and the intendant remained uncomfortably aware that the matter would again be ignored on his departure.

The stranglehold which the *officiers* exercised over the administration seriously affected the commercial and religious policies of the crown, but it is best revealed by Colbert's failure to secure a more systematised legal system. The seigneural and church courts touched upon the daily life of the subject far more than the royal courts, and these could not be abolished without serious opposition from the nobles and clergy. Colbert did not attempt to do so, especially as the crown had evolved a procedure for evoking from their jurisdiction any case in which it was interested. His concern was to remedy the confusion in the royal courts themselves. There existed, for example, two distinct areas of law, the *droit coutumier* based upon custom and precedent, and the *droit écrit* derived from Roman law, and court procedure varied from one place to another. To create a standardised code, a *droit français*, applicable to the whole kingdom and uniformly enforced in every court of justice, was a prospect to delight the tidy minds of Colbert and his uncle Pussort. As the law itself presented so great a tangle, their first step was to establish methods of procedure, which they did in 1667 and 1669 respectively when they issued the *ordonnance civile* and the *ordonnance criminelle*. The codes which followed were concerned with the laws themselves. The *Code Savory* (1673), named after the merchant who inspired it, established uniform trading and commercial practices; the *ordonnance de la marine* (1680) related to maritime cases; the *Code Noir* (1685) regulated the government of the colonies.

The total effect was to demonstrate Colbert's skill as a legislator; but whatever virtues the codes and ordonnances possessed they lacked enforcement. The magistrates, possessing to the full the deep-rooted conservatism inherent in all legal bodies, and resenting the necessity of adopting new procedure, opposed them from the first. Moreover, they had paid a high price for their positions and they knew only the traditional methods of recouping themselves. No matter what the royal councils decreed, their edicts were ignored. Passive resistance triumphed, and Pussort reluctantly admitted failure; 'France', he wrote, 'has the honour of having the most wonderful and the wisest ordinances to be found in Europe, but she has also the reputation of enforcing them more inefficiently than in any other state.'

There was only one remedy, to abolish the sale of offices and to create an entirely new bureaucracy subservient to royal direction, but this was impracticable. Though Louis XIV had never forgiven the *officiers* for their part in the Fronde and despised their *bourgeois* origins, he nevertheless had a sound respect for their strength. Moreover, to the Treasury the sale of offices was an indispensable source of revenue. 'One of the most wonderful privileges of the kings of France', wrote Desmarets, himself an *officier*, 'is that when the king creates an office, God, at that very instant, creates a fool to buy it.' It was true that the demand never slackened, but the purchasers were not fools. From the *premier president* of a *parlement* to the village bailiff and clerk, the *officiers* formed a privileged estate, and every middle-class family centred its hopes on acquiring office. It was a profitable investment since it purchased exemption from taxation and provided a means to secure valuable fees and other perquisites. 'When a villager has learned three words of Latin', ran one report, 'he at once stops paying the *taille*; he becomes a procurator, a syndic or a sergeant and proceeds to ruin his neighbours.' Not only wealth but honour awaited the successful *officier* and the highest positions carried with them a social status akin to nobility, the *noblesse de la robe*. The president of a *parlement* was received in his province with honours accorded to princes; while he lived the greatest persons gave him precedence; when he died all the church bells were rung.

So attractive was the sale of offices to the middle class and to the

Treasury, so powerful were the *officiers* themselves, that the government was unable to reform the system. The king, against whom all open resistance had ceased, and whose authority was recognised by every institution which had formerly claimed some degree of autonomy, was thus exposed to the silent opposition of the men who administered the laws in his name. The existence of the *officier* class thus explains the paradox that the most absolute ruler of the seventeenth century was so frequently disobeyed.

CHURCH AND STATE

The Gallican Clergy

To all appearances Louis XIV had the French Church well under control. As a result of the Concordat of Bologna (1516) he controlled the appointment to all abbeys, priories and bishoprics in France; and as most of the candidates for higher office were of noble birth, with little prospect of success in any other career, they made it their business to be as accommodating as possible to the king. Opposition, even on theological grounds, was a luxury they could not afford and many remained securely ignorant of theology. The Catholic revival in France[1] owed little to the leadership of such men who sought benefices by the same means as their elder brothers sought pensions and places at Versailles. Their sisters, too, joined in the struggle for preferment; and Angélique Arnauld, appointed at the age of eleven as Abbess of the convent at Port-Royal, proved a disconcerting exception to the general rule by allowing herself to be converted by a visiting preacher when she was nineteen.

In such circumstances it was not difficult for Colbert and Le Tellier, acting on the king's behalf, to build up a loyal clientele among the clergy. Colbert's brother, the Archbishop of Rouen, and Le Tellier's son, the Archbishop of Reims, could of course be relied upon implicitly, as could the de Carbon brothers, who held the archbishoprics of Toulouse[2] and Sens. There were many others, and in Harlay, appointed to Paris in 1671, they found their examplar. Sufficiently scholarly to win attention, astute enough

[1] See Chapter I, page 77.
[2] The Archbishop who performed valuable service as President of the Languedoc Estates: see above, page 246.

not to take his studies too seriously, he served Louis XIV with constant devotion and unflagging self-interest; his influence was equalled only by the royal confessor, de la Chaise, his sole colleague in the *conseil de conscience* which advised the king on Church affairs. Against their policies it was always dangerous, and generally useless, to protest, and the Church became very much a mere department of state.

There was, however, another side to the coin; one which explains why, if the clergy were so amenable to discipline, the king and his ministers were perennially concerned to ensure their co-operation: indeed, the Assembly of the Clergy was the only representative body in France to be consulted with serious intent by Louis XIV. He knew that though his clergy were anxious to gratify his wishes, they were also determined to maintain what they termed their 'Gallican liberties'. Gallicanism, in essence, repudiated the authority of the pope over the Catholic Church in France. The orthodox prelate might have hesitated to put it so bluntly; but the laymen of the *parlement*, jealous of all ecclesiastical jurisdiction, whether papal or episcopal, had sharply defined the limits of the pope's authority in France. They denied him any temporal jurisdiction, his bulls were valid only after approval by the king and his *parlements*, and his decisions in spiritual matters were capable of amendment by the councils of the Church. The Sorbonne, however, where most of the bishops read their theology, disliked this attempt by the lawyers to subject the clergy unconditionally to the crown. Accepting the general principles of Gallicanism, it interpreted them rather as a safeguard of a bishop's autonomy within his diocese, an attitude as dangerous to king as to pope. The result was that in conflict with the pope, Louis had no more devoted allies than his own clergy: it was less certain whether they would support him as readily if he invoked papal assistance to discipline one of their number.

The *cause célèbre* of Gallicanism in Louis's reign arose from the conflict between Louis and two of his bishops. Throughout most of France Louis enjoyed the right of *régale*, which allowed him to appropriate the revenues of a vacant bishopric and to make appointments within the diocese. The mounting cost of the Dutch War (1672–9) prompted Colbert to advise the king to assert his lucrative prerogative in the twenty-nine dioceses hitherto exempt. The extension of the *régale* went unopposed by all but two of the bishops, Caulet of Pamiers and Pavillon of Alet, who challenged the legality of Louis's actions. Unfortunately for themselves, they antagonised the rest of the clergy by appealing directly to Pope Innocent XI to champion their cause.[1] Pavillon died in 1673, his successor accepting the *régale*, but Caulet remained recalcitrant. He was dispossessed of his see, but the canons of Pamiers refused to elect a new bishop and the Archbishop of Toulouse ordered their prosecution. Innocent XI then intervened to condemn the extension of the *régale* and to threaten de Carbon with excommunication if Caulet were not reinstated.

To repel the attack from Rome, Louis summoned an extraordinary Assembly of the Clergy in 1681. Behind the scenes Colbert and Le Tellier mobilised their adherents, and Harlay led them into action in the Assembly. In pleading the cause of Gallicanism Louis's anxiety was not that the clergy might refuse to follow him against the authority of the pope, but that they might outstrip him and precipitate a schism: he welcomed the moderate views of Bossuet, Bishop of Meaux, who, in asserting the liberties of the French Church, nevertheless reminded the Assembly of its duty to preserve unity with Rome. In 1682, the Assembly drew up Four Articles, which gave force and clarity to opinion which had hitherto been loosely, even carelessly, defined. Their effect was to reduce the pope's authority in France to nought, and to deny his infallibility in matters of faith[2]. Trenchant though the Articles were, they raised no novel issue to complicate the *régale* crisis still further, but gave Louis the means he sought to force the pope's hand. An edict of March 1682 ordered the Articles to be registered in the *parlements*, and demanded subscription to them from all candidates for degrees in theology. Innocent was not to be intimidated. As bishoprics fell vacant he refused bulls of institution to any cleric who had taken part in the Assembly: Louis would nominate none who had not.

The deadlock was prolonged until Innocent's death in 1689, by which time thirty-five dioceses were without bishops. Only mutual compromise could avert schism, yet both sides were

[1] It is some indication of the confused politics of the French Church that it was only a few years previously that Caulet and Pavillon had joined with other bishops in support of Jansenism (see below, page 261), claiming the protection of the Gallican liberties against the pope.

[2] The Assembly, influenced by Bossuet, had actually avoided the word infallibility, stating that the pope's judgements were not *irreformable*.

reluctant to make concessions. Important though France might be to the Catholic Church, the publication of the Assembly's Articles was a grave affront to the papacy. Orthodox though Louis was at heart, he was obstinately resolved to secure the extension of the *régale*. Tension was eased at last only by a change of circumstances. A new pope, Innocent XII, was less bitterly involved than his predecessors; Louis had good reason to desire Italian neutrality in his war against the League of Augsburg (1688–97); moreover, the unwelcome views of a section of the clergy on an entirely different issue[1] offended equally both king and pope, and these could only be suppressed by effective co-operation between Rome and Versailles. Louis revoked his edict enforcing the Four Articles, and the clergy apologised to the pope, but in terms, however, which did not explicitly renounce their opinion, and in a manner so un-publicised that few outside their number were aware of it. The *parlements*, in fact, never withdrew their registration of the Articles: nor for that matter did Innocent XII give more than tacit consent to Louis's extension of the *régale*. Through the mists of compromise and secrecy which finally shrouded the issue it is at least clear that the cause of Gallicanism had suffered a set-back. Louis himself was unperturbed. He had merely used Gallicanism as a means to compel the withdrawal of papal support for Caulet, who had died in the meantime without securing a retraction of the *régale*.

Neither Gallican nor Ultramontane, neither schismatic nor subservient to Rome, Louis's interest in the Church, as in all other matters, was political, his policy opportunist. Whereas in 1682 he denied the validity of papal authority, by 1693 he was preparing to invoke that same authority to discipline a section of his own clergy. The religious history of his reign reflected the view of an absolute monarch from whose ways none might dissent, and who practised the maxim enunciated by Bossuet, *un roi, une loi, une foi*.

The Huguenots

Since the Grace of Alais had destroyed their military powers,[2] the Huguenots had maintained an exemplary record of loyalty and obedience. No longer did they cherish political ambitions: the nobles and *officiers*, whose grandparents had fought against the

---

[1] The Jansenists. See below, page 260.
[2] 1629. See Chapter III, page 155.

Catholic League, renounced their faith to seek preferment at court or in the royal administration; of their more resolute brethren, 1,500,000 at the most, many resorted to industry or commerce in which their abilities won at least the respect of those who hated their religious convictions. Louis XIV had nothing to fear, and much to gain, from their presence in the kingdom. Their freedom from persecution was a factor of great importance in winning the alliance of Protestant states against the intolerant Habsburgs, and their contribution to the economic strength of France was out of all proportion to their numbers. Nevertheless their very existence became an outrage to the government. The French clergy appealed to their unshakeably orthodox monarch against 'this wretched liberty of conscience which destroys the liberty of the true children of God'; and Louis was reminded that the Edict on Nantes[1] had been wrung from the crown at a moment when Henry IV had had no other means of silencing Huguenot opposition than by concession. What had once been granted out of weakness could, logically, be reversed from strength. Louis's concept of the state allowed no room for dissent, and the Huguenots, as a separate community within his body politic, were a blatant example of irreconcilable nonconformity.

If Louis's *Mémoires* can be trusted, he was not at first in favour of revoking the Edict of Nantes outright: 'I thought that the best way to reduce the Huguenots of my kingdom was to avoid using any new severity against them, and to maintain all the concessions which they had obtained from my predecessors, but to give them nothing more and to limit the execution even of these within the narrowest bounds that justice and decency would admit.' The Assembly of the Clergy was eager to assist Louis's definition of these 'narrowest bounds', and set up a commission to investigate the administration of the edict, construing its terms as literally as possible. So stringent were its recommendations that Colbert was forced to protest at the damage to the economy which might result from Huguenot emigration, and Louis's diplomats advised him of the concern displayed by his Protestant allies. For the moment Louis agreed to restrain the ardour of his clergy, but the respite lasted only a decade. The end to the Dutch War (1679) made it easier to ignore opinion abroad; it also gave Louvois, the military secretary, an unwelcome release from constant attendance

[1] 1598. See Chapter III, page 141.

upon Louis, and he adopted the campaign against heresy in order to bask more prominently in the warm rays of the sun-king's approval. His action was well timed. Embarrassed by his public controversy with the Pope over the *régale*, Louis was eager to demonstrate his orthodoxy by persecuting Huguenots. Moreover, he had abandoned his vivacious mistresses for the sedate companionship of Madame de Maintenon, whom he subsequently married after the queen's death. Her personal devoutness made itself felt in the improved morals of the court, and both she and de la Chaise urged Louis to atone for the sins of his lusty youth by eliminating heresy within France. 'The king is beginning to think seriously of his salvation,' she wrote. 'If God preserves his life there will soon be only one religion in this kingdom.'

After 1680 a series of edicts attacked the Huguenots at every point. Churches built since 1598 were demolished on the grounds that the Edict of Nantes protected only those churches in existence at the date of its issue; the professions were formally closed to all save Catholics; Huguenot academies were closed, and children aged seven were taken from their parents to make a 'free choice' between the two faiths. In areas where the Huguenots were most numerous, in Alsace, Picardy, the Midi and the provinces along the west coast, many of them had purchased office and were thus able to protect local congregations from the full force of the edicts. Against the *dragonnades*, however, they were powerless. The billeting of troops had been used in the past to punish the inhabitants of a region for non-payment of taxes. In 1681 Louvois ordered Marillac, the intendant of Poitou, to adopt the same device in order to 'force the Huguenots into conversion'. By looting their billets, by brutal and bestial conduct, the troops terrorised their hosts into renouncing their faith. Whole villages were 'converted' overnight, but such was the influence of the *officiers*, even of Huguenot *officiers*, who by the recent edicts should not have held office at all, that when those of Poitou protested Louis made a public show of disapproval by reprimanding Marillac and by ordering the *dragonnades* to cease. Louvois, however, understood the true wishes of his master and extended his activities. Both Louis and the court privately applauded what Madame de Sévigné described as 'the astounding success of the magistrates and provincial governors, aided by a few dragoons'.

Thirty thousand conversions were reported from Poitou alone, and Louis claimed that the Edict of Nantes was no longer relevant, 'as the best and largest part of our subjects of the so-called reformed religion have embraced the Catholic faith'. In 1685 the edict was revoked. Henceforth, Huguenot services were forbidden, all children were to be baptised by a priest, and, though the pastors were exiled, laymen who tried to emigrate were to be executed or sent to the galleys. To enforce the decrees the troops were again employed, and Louvois officially approved their excesses, 'since these people are distinguished by their refusal to submit to the king's decrees, you need not observe in their case the restraints which have been prescribed to you, nor can you make too severe and burdensome the quartering of the troops upon them'. At least 200,000 Huguenots risked their lives to flee abroad. Sixty thousand came to England, and the remainder found refuge in Switzerland, Denmark, Brandenburg and the United Provinces. Most of them were merchants or craftsmen, since the less wealthy had not the means to escape. France could ill afford this exodus of talent: her ironworks, paper-mills, tanneries and textile centres were grievously affected, and Nîmes, Lyon and Reims lost more than half their number of skilled workers. A new impetus was given to the industries of France's rivals by the influx of *emigrés* who established, for example, the manufacture of glass at Copenhagen, of lace at Nottingham, and of silk in London, Amsterdam and Geneva.

'The Revocation, without the least pretext of necessity, depopulated a quarter of the kingdom, ruined its commerce and weakened it in all parts. It authorised tortures in which thousands of both sexes died, split families in twain, drove manufacturers abroad, profited the foreigner at the expense of France and filled the country with the perjury and sacrilege of those who sacrificed their conscience to their prosperity and quiet.' Saint-Simon, of course, exaggerated and, furthermore, he wrote in secret. In public the revocation was acclaimed. 'The greatest and most wonderful thing that has ever been imagined or achieved', wrote Madame de Sévigné, and the official view was given utterance by Bossuet: 'Proclaim this miracle of our times. Send up to heaven our praises and say to this new Constantine, this new Theodosius, this new Charlemagne, it is the worthy achievement of your reign. By you heresy no longer exists.'

The forced conversion and the passive resistance of those who could find no refuge in flight, did nothing to improve the condition of the French Church, but this was beside the point. The king's absolutism had been expressed in a satisfyingly dramatic manner, and uniformity, no matter how superficial, had been achieved.

Catholic Nonconformists

During Louis XIV's minority a small but extremely devout section of the French clergy had begun to identify itself with the teaching of Cornelius Jansen, a theologian of Louvain in the Netherlands. Jansen had revived the perennial questions of Free Will, Justification by Faith and the nature of Divine Grace:[1] he taught that man was saved only through the love of God which created faith, that this love was awakened by an act of conversion, and that conversion came about solely by the operation of God's irresistible Grace. A convinced Catholic, who owed his inspiration to the writings of St. Augustine, he not only opposed the Jesuits who emphasised the value of man's own efforts towards attaining salvation, but his doctrine smacked of predestination. His followers were attracted mainly by the emphasis he placed upon the sense of personal conversion, resulting in a life of personal devotion and piety: without it, he claimed, morality became little more than the performance of prescribed duties.

Jansen died in 1638 but his close friend, the Abbé de St. Cyran, introduced his ideas into France; and before his death in 1643 he had found two loyal adherents in Angélique Arnauld, the Abbess of Port-Royal, and her brother Antoine, a doctor of the Sorbonne. In their hands Jansenism developed as a spiritual movement with a strong bias against the Jesuits, whom they accused of encouraging too worldly an attitude to religion. The Jesuits retaliated by charging them with heresy, and enlisting the support of the government. Largely due to Mazarin's intervention, five propositions extracted from Jansen's writings were condemned by Pope Innocent X in 1653, and, three years later, Antoine Arnauld was censured by the Sorbonne and deprived of his doctorate. More dangerous than the hostility of the Jesuits was Louis XIV's own disapproval of the movement. He was not a theologian but he made up in prejudice

[1] See Chapter I, page 77, for a more detailed examination both of his doctrine and of his followers.

what he lacked in understanding. The Jansenists offended him beyond measure, since, as Racine put it, 'they had dealings with many people in disgrace at court, who came to them to seek spiritual consolation and sometimes even to adopt a life of penitence'. Many of these people were former Frondeurs, among them Madame de Longueville, who had discovered at Port-Royal an austerity and a discipline which provided a welcome change from their previous life. This, though bad, was not all. By embracing a particular mode of life and by defending doctrines which the orthodox Catholic found suspect, the Jansenists stood accused of nonconformity, the very sin which Louis XIV most abominated.

The first attack, in 1661, was directed against the community at Port-Royal, where the nuns were required to sign a Formulary condemning the five propositions attributed to Jansen by the bull of 1653. Mère Angélique died just before the crisis broke, but despite her loss the nuns refused to submit to Louis's orders, and were consequently removed from Paris to confinement in the convent of Port-Royal des Champs. When the Formulary was presented to the clergy, however, Louis found it less easy to discipline his opponents. Four bishops, among them Pavillon and Caulet, declared that though the pope's condemnation of the propositions had to be accepted, his ruling that these propositions represented Jansen's teaching was only a matter of fact, and there-fore open to question. It was an ingenious distinction, made in the first place by Blaise Pascal, whose *Lettres Provinciales* had made him the most effective propagandist of Jansenism. Moreover, the bishops were on good ground in denying the pope's authority to intervene in this matter, since they could invoke in their defence the liberties of the Gallican Church. Nineteen other bishops supported their stand, and so loth was Louis to provoke a crisis in the Assembly of the Clergy that he handed the affair over to his diplomats. Lionne, in particular, was expert at reconciling diverse views,[1] and he finally secured a settlement, the *paix de l'église* (1668) which allowed the clergy to preserve a 'reverent silence' as to whether or not the condemned doctrines were in fact those of Jansen. Louis was beaten for the time being: the Formulary was withdrawn and the nuns at Port-Royal des Champs were permitted to live there freely, preserving their doctrines and even teaching them in the convent school.

[1] See Chapter VII, page 285.

For some time an uneasy truce prevailed, but the action of Caulet and Pavillon in defying the king a second time, over the *régale*, revived Louis's indignation against the Jansenists in general who, while the *paix de l'église* was prolonged, were able to grow in strength. One of their books, Quesnal's *Réflexions Morales sur le Nouveau Testament*, enjoyed remarkable success and was even approved for use in his diocese by Noailles, the influential Bishop of Châlons, who later succeeded Harlay as Archbishop of Paris. Louis could wait no longer, and, despite the thorny problem of Gallicanism, he resorted to Rome for assistance. Clement XI was as eager as Louis to suppress the Jansenists and the bull *Vineam Domini* (1705), worded with meticulous care to avoid affronting the Assembly of the Clergy, forbade any further recourse to 'reverent silence'. Port-Royal des Champs was closed and, by a petty act of vengeance which revealed the personal spite behind Louis's policy, the graves of former members were desecrated. Quesnal's book, however, had not been specifically condemned by Clement's bull, and Noailles's approval of it required an effective answer. Louis appealed to Clement yet again, and in 1713 he was rewarded with the bull *Unigenitus*, which handsomely condemned no less than 101 of Quesnal's moral reflections.

Unigenitus gave rise to such confused debate within the Assembly that, among its opponents it became impossible to distinguish Gallican from Jansenist. At first Louis tried to appease them by modifying its terms; but Clement refused to countenance any further interference with the pope's power to condemn heresy, and Noailles preferred to defy the king than to endure the humiliation of retracting his approval of Quesnal. When all else had failed, Louis used force, and the bull was accepted only after its opponents had been exiled to their dioceses. This resort to personal intimidation, in the last months of Louis's life, destroyed the working alliance he had always sought to maintain with his clergy; yet, paradoxically, it identified church and state more closely than ever since Louis had thus made himself the sole arbiter in a theological dispute. The king's will was expressed not only in law but in dogma: his absolutism extended beyond the realm of politics into the recesses of the individual conscience.[1]

[1] For yet another incident revealing Louis's obsessive hatred of religious nonconformity, see the account of Madame Guyon and the Quietists in Chapter I, page 81.

THE SOURCES OF FRENCH PROSPERITY AND POWER

Colbert and Royal Solvency

Jean-Baptiste Colbert was perhaps the most talented, certainly the most ubiquitous, of Louis XIV's ministers. He had served a long apprenticeship, first under Le Tellier, then as Mazarin's principal agent, until finally, after Fouquet's disgrace, he became Louis's chief adviser and servant in domestic affairs. Finance, industry and trade were his greatest interests, but he also proved invaluable in matters relating to the navy, the administration of justice, the control of the clergy, the dispensation of patronage and the creation of a centralised administration. To most people he seemed a colourless man, meticulous and coldly ruthless, but without the pompous idiosyncrasies of Sully or the dominating personality of Richelieu. In fact his life was filled with the endless satisfaction of directing the affairs of state from the privacy of his office. A true bureaucrat, he had a genius for planning and organisation; he loved the collation of reports, the preparation of agenda, and the compilation of instructions. He was, in short, the best type of *officier*. Like others of his class he built up a private fortune, married his daughters into the nobility and secured the advancement of his brothers and sons; but, unlike his fellow *officiers*, he devoted his energy more to the service of the king than to the promotion of his own interests. Utterly loyal to Louis, he worked unceasingly to make his master the wealthiest and the most powerful monarch in Europe.

The fiscal system was as bad as it had always been.[1] The privileges of the nobility, the clergy and the *officiers* prevented the Treasury from taxing the wealthier sections of the community, an anomaly constantly indicated by Colbert's intendants: 'Less than half the land in the kingdom is liable to the *taille*: the nobles who own the greater part of it pay nothing; the citizens of several towns who own land in the surrounding countryside are exempt by privilege, office or favour; only the miserable peasant has to pay.' The taxes, moreover, were levied at different rates in different parts of the country. If the incidence of taxation was unfair, its collection was inefficient and unreliable. In the villages it was necessary to conscript one of the peasants as tax-collector, and if he failed to

[1] See Chapter III, page 147, on Sully.

secure the full amount from his neighbours, by means of methods which could in any case only imperil his future social life, he himself was mulcted of the deficit and imprisoned. Higher up the scale, the *officiers* through whose hands the taxes then passed made a fortune by falsifying their accounts. Colbert estimated that of the 85,000,000 *livres* collected in 1661, more than 53,000,000 *livres* were lost to the crown before the remainder finally reached the Treasury.

The fundamental faults of the system could not be remedied. In an age when the civil service lacked a tradition of honesty and efficiency, and when the government possessed no effective means of speedy communication and law enforcement, Colbert's imaginative concept of a uniform fiscal system was incapable of execution; and Louis XIV was too concerned with foreign affairs to allow his minister to initiate radical changes which might result in revolution. Colbert himself recognised this, though he never abandoned his efforts to achieve some measure of reform. Each tax in turn was scrutinised in the hope that its incidence might be extended or its collection improved. Some provinces, for example, paid the *taille personelle*, a form of poll tax based on estimates of personal income, while others paid the *taille reélle*, a property tax which spared the landless labourer but in general imposed heavier burdens upon the taxpayer. Colbert attempted to make the latter universal, though first of all it was necessary to undertake an effective land survey. This he did in the *généralité* of Montauban and the increased yield from taxation was immediately apparent; unfortunately it was also clear that the organisation of a land census on a national scale was beyond the resources of Colbert's staff. It was not simply a matter of handling and interpreting the statistics: the application of mathematical techniques and principles to the science of administration, termed political arithmetic, provided no formula to account for the passive resistance to be expected from the threatened provinces.

The *aides*, too, a series of tolls and purchase taxes, suffered from the exemption of privileged groups and the chicanery of local collectors. Of the national taxes, therefore, there remained only the *gabelle*, the compulsory purchase of salt from the government's licensed retailers, which had the degree of uniformity essential for exploitation and development on a national basis. Some indication of its efficacy was afforded by the universal hatred it aroused, especially as the retailers frequently augmented their profits by wholesale adulterations: the Bordeaux peasants who rebelled in 1674 echoed the plea of thousands when they shouted, 'Vive le roi, sans *gabelle*.' Unfortunately for Colbert, its incidence varied from thirty-five to forty-eight *livres* on each hundred pounds of salt between the Somme and the Loire, the region of the *grande gabelle*, and from six to thirty in the southern provinces. Although the *pays d'état* had been compelled to accept royal direction in matters of taxation, there was nevertheless a limit to the amount which the king dared to demand. Once again, Colbert's vision of uniformity was frustrated by the entrenched privileges of the *ancien régime*.

What could not be reformed had nevertheless to be made to work. Colbert hit out at peculation by using the *chambre de justice* appointed to condemn Fouquet to investigate the activities of his subordinates. The shock administered by Fouquet's disgrace, and the obvious determination of the king to reinforce Colbert's efforts, proved remarkably salutary. By 1669 over 100,000,000 *livres* had been recouped by the Treasury from the pockets of its agents. At the same time, Colbert reduced payments on the *rentes*, which he abhorred as a parasitic growth on the Treasury since they consumed money that was needed for the king's government. In December, 1664, Madame de Sévigné recorded a rumour in Paris that 'the *rentes* were to be paid off at a rate which would send them all to the workhouse'. Her report was exaggerated, but Colbert's action was none the less severe. Some of the *rentes* were paid off at their value in 1639, others were repudiated altogether, and the interest on the remainder was revised. In all, this represented a virtual repudiation of the debt by about 60 per cent. From Colbert's point of view it was a satisfactory achievement, but the blow given to public credit was to have harmful effects later.[1]

Colbert, like Sully, compelled the tax farmers to accept rates more favourable to the Treasury, and he scrutinised patents of exemption with the result that in Provence alone he claimed to have discovered more than a thousand *faux nobles*. His intendants, the only men he could trust, were ordered to supervise the *officiers* engaged in tax collection, and an improved system of accounts was introduced in order to make peculation more difficult. Within the Treasury he kept a *registre de fonds* and a *registre de dépenses* to record the anticipated revenues and expenses of his

[1] See below, page 271.

department, while the actual payments and receipts were recorded in a daily balance sheet, the *journal*. From this he compiled an annual *état au vrai*, of which a simplified summary, the *abrégé des finances*, was presented to the king. By this means the collectors and other agents of the Treasury discovered that Colbert had established a clear idea of the sums to be expected from them. Consequently, their falsified reports had to be hastily amended to the Treasury's advantage. The system was not foolproof: Le Pelletier reported several discrepancies when he succeeded Colbert, but for this Colbert's idealism was to blame. Denied the chance to establish good order throughout the kingdom, it was some small consolation to make his books reflect an ideal statement of his intentions.[1] His achievement was none the less remarkable. Taxation in 1683, the year in which he died, produced 116,000,000 *livres* as compared with the 85,000,000 *livres* of 1661; but the significant figure which revealed the value of his work was the reduction of the amount lost in collection from 53,000,000 *livres* to 23,000,000. The reputed glory of Louis XIV's reign, the perpetual warfare to aggrandise his fame and to enlarge his territories, was thus made possible by the indefatigable efforts of an honest minister who increased the net value of a corrupt and out-dated fiscal system from 22,000,000 *livres* a year to 93,000,000.

The nature of Colbert's genius when untrammelled by vested interests is best revealed by his management of crown lands, a sphere in which he was entirely free to apply the principles of good order that delighted his imagination. First he prepared a survey of all lands, waters and forests belonging to the king, scrutinising all charters of alienation to ensure that nothing had been forfeited during periods of anarchy in the past. Then he examined the activities of his staff and prepared a comprehensive code of instructions for the better management of the royal estates. During his term of office, the value of the forests alone increased from 168,000 *livres* a year to over 1,000,000; while the other crown lands produced 5,500,000 *livres* in place of the 800,000 recorded for 1661. It is a sad comment on the *ancien régime* that no proportionate increase in revenue could be achieved in the national system of taxation.

[1] Cf. the comment of E. Lavisse, *Histoire de France*, 'Il y a l'abîme entre ce qu'il a voulu et ce qu'il a fait', a verdict which applies to so much of Colbert's work.

Colbert and National Prosperity

Colbert's comprehensive programme for the expansion of industry and trade had been formulated during his long period of service under Mazarin. As early as 1653 he prepared a statement of policy which embraced every section of the economy, and, though Mazarin had ignored it, it was to be the basis of Colbert's work after 1661: 'We must re-establish or create all industries, even luxury industries; a system of protection must be developed by means of a customs tariff; trade and traders must be re-organised into gilds; financial hindrances which burden the people must be lightened; transport of commodities by land and sea must be restored; colonies must be developed and commercially bound to France; all barriers between France and India must be broken down; the navy must be strengthened to afford protection to merchant ships.'

The plan was not designed to benefit Louis XIV's subjects so much as Louis himself, since any increase in national wealth was to result in an equivalent increase in taxation. Colbert realised the intimate connection between economic and military powers and attempted to construct an economic system geared to the needs of warfare; 'the commercial companies', he wrote, 'are the armies of the king, and his industries act as his reserves'.[1]

For a country which maintained such vast armies and paid such generous subsidies to its allies, it was natural to identify national wealth with the possession of gold: gold, moreover, was considered to be a limited commodity, and the value of trade was accordingly assessed by Colbert by its success or failure to bring bullion into France. Trade itself, he believed to be as limited as gold, and he accepted as a basic fact that 20,000 ships were all that was required for the commerce of his age. 'The Dutch have of this total 15,000 to 16,000, and the French 500 or 600 at the most.' Whether or not his figures were correct the moral was obvious; and if it was easy for historians of a free-trade era to condemn the economic theory informing Colbert's work, it is less so now in an age pre-occupied with the need to avert an adverse balance of payments.

The first task was to stimulate productivity, but curiously enough Colbert paid little attention to the essential problem of food production. A bureaucrat brought up in an urban community, he had no understanding of farming, and what he saw of it

[1] See Chapter I, page 23, for a general discussion of mercantilism.

disconcerted his tidy mind. The disastrous failure of the corn crop of 1661 served to emphasise the vagaries of nature, and he devoted his energies to industries which, as an intendant commented 'are not subject to the changes of the seasons, nor the inconstancy of the elements, but depend upon the art, industry and application of men'. Moreover, he believed that agricultural production was essentially static, in contrast to the manufacturing industries which, if handled correctly, could attain to unlimited heights of prosperity: it was these which he described as 'the fertile sources of a kingdom's prosperity'. In the event, therefore, little was done for French agriculture, and the peasant was left to fight his own struggle for existence unaided.

To revive old industries and to introduce new ones Colbert recruited skilled craftsmen from all over Europe: tapestry-makers, dyers and paper-makers from the Netherlands; silk-workers, glass-blowers, embroiderers and lace-makers from Italy; leather-workers and hatters from Spain; engineers, mining experts, engravers, iron-founders and naval constructors from England, Germany and Scandinavia. To train Frenchmen in the best techniques, Colbert envisaged a national system of technical education, but his ambitions once again outran the facilities at his disposal. Nevertheless, teams of craftsmen were despatched to demonstrate their methods in the provinces, the *Académie des Sciences* was mobilised to study techniques of production, and the *Journal des Savants* gave publicity to its findings. The experts were also employed to make detailed recommendations which Colbert embodied in a series of edicts of an exceptionally high standard. The object of his legislation was best expressed in the preamble to an edict affecting most of the textile workers, and dealing with the length, width and quality of cloths, serges and other stuffs of linen and wool: 'to render uniform all those products of the same type, name and quality, in whatever place they may be made, both to increase their sale inside and outside our kingdom, and to prevent the public from being cheated'.

A staff of inspectors was appointed to administer the edicts, penalties were laid down for all irregularities in production, and the gild system was revived, by making membership compulsory (1673), in order to establish a more effective control over the artisans themselves. As was only to be expected, Colbert's regulations were disliked by those who had become accustomed to their own traditional methods of work, and even more by the *officiers* who resented this detailed interference in their local industries. Their resistance frequently jeopardised the system, and the case of the Widow Falempin was by no means untypical. Obstinately refusing to conform to the standards required by Colbert, she was punished by the inspectors, but successfully appealed to the *parlement* of Amiens to rescind the penalties. Colbert immediately drafted a new edict to reverse the verdict, and emphasised the moral that 'if such frequent contraventions as those of the Widow Falempin, and such enterprise as her appeal to the *parlement*, were not severely repressed, the *échevins*[1] of Amiens would lose prestige, the regulations would be violated with impunity, and industry and trade would be ruined'. Colbert's words revealed perhaps a trace of hysteria, but the magistrates frequently refused to impose the penalties demanded by the industrial edicts, and it was impossible for him to interfere in each case. Moreover, there were many thousands of workers who supplemented their living from the fields by part-time spinning or weaving.[2] Scattered across the countryside, and working in their own homes, they evaded the supervision of the gilds and could ignore Colbert's edicts with impunity.

Despite Colbert's difficulties, French industry was revitalised, and the production of textiles, his favourite concern, was greatly improved. France began to produce lace of a quality which sold abroad. The Gobelins factory in Paris, one of Colbert's *manufactures royales* established to introduce new industries, became a showpiece for visitors, and its tapestries, along with those of Beauvais and Chaillot, were eagerly purchased outside France. At Arras the production of heavily embroidered fine cloths was established with the help of government subsidies, while in Languedoc half a million skilled workers were similarly employed in the neighbourhood of Carcassonne.

If industry as a whole were to expand, the transport of heavy goods had to be radically improved. Colbert, as *Grand Voyer*, reorganised the departments of state responsible for roads and bridges, provided a national freight service, and encouraged the widespread use of stone setts to make the *pavés du roi*. Once again

[1] Inspectors.
[2] In Picardy 19,000 or more worked at home, against the 6,000 officially registered in the town gilds.

he was confronted with the opposition of local authorities; indeed, there were many landowners with a vested interest in bad roads since they were lawfully entitled to all spilt merchandise. Coach travel between Paris and Orleans, a distance of 75 miles, took two days, and eight more were needed to continue the journey to Lyon: heavy transport made slower progress. Colbert therefore turned to transport by water. Great stretches of the Seine, the Loire and the Rhône were opened to navigation, and the most spectacular of his ventures was the construction of the Languedoc Canal. The engineering genius of Riquet, and later of Vauban, was employed in damming an entire valley to create a reservoir supplying water at the summit, and in constructing a hundred locks and three great aqueducts. The two ends were linked by blasting a tunnel of 180 yards, the first time that gunpowder was used for this purpose. With a depth of 6½ feet, and 32 feet wide, the canal was able to carry barges of 200 tons from the Mediterranean to the Atlantic, a feat of civil engineering which far surpassed any other since the time of the Roman Empire.

An even greater handicap to internal trade than the state of the roads was the exorbitant number of tolls and taxes levied on goods in transit across France. The *péages*, payments to local corporations or landowners, had outlived their original purpose since the collectors were no longer required to maintain roads and bridges in their area; but like so many other features of the *ancien régime* they had become the perquisite of a privileged class, and Colbert was powerless to reform them. The *traites* were government taxes, and though Colbert was free to establish a more rational system of collection, they were too lucrative to be abolished. Colbert divided France into three free-trade areas, the central provinces, the outlying provinces which ringed them, and the newly acquired towns of Alsace. By this means internal trade was encouraged, but it was still possible for the *traites* to be levied more than once in a single journey, thus making the whole transaction unprofitable.

The tariffs on goods passing in and out of France were another matter, since Colbert intended to use these to protect French industry. To begin with, the import of raw materials was encouraged by reducing the tariff, while goods manufactured abroad were heavily taxed, but a new tariff code in 1667 carried his plan a stage further. All imports of Venetian lace and glass were forbidden, and the tariffs on imported textiles were doubled; fine cloths, for example, were taxed at 80 instead of 40 *livres*, and worsted stockings at 8 instead of 3 *livres*. In this way Colbert intended not to raise revenue but to discourage foreign competition: above all, he hoped to strike a blow at the Dutch by limiting their exports into France. This, of course, was an important factor in the war which broke out between the two countries in 1672. Unfortunately for Colbert, the cost of the war, prolonged by the spirited defiance of the Dutch, made his tariff policy impracticable. The state needed money urgently, and tariffs had to be exploited as a source of revenue rather than as a means to benefit French industry and trade.

Another of Colbert's plans to stimulate production was by seeking control of markets overseas, a difficult task since English and Dutch companies were already established in this field. Colbert nevertheless believed that the formation of properly controlled companies might yet establish France as *l'arbitre du commerce*. The plan was well conceived but the companies were handicapped from the start. The middle classes could not be persuaded to invest in them. Traditionally, they preferred to employ their capital in buying offices in the administration, and Colbert's drastic revision of the *rentes* discouraged investment in government funds. The Treasury could only afford to make initial grants to the companies, and then only during the rare periods of peace. The activities of French merchants aroused the hostility of the English and Dutch governments, and commercial rivalry was an important factor contributing to the wars of 1688–97 and of 1701–14. The recurrence of warfare was the final blow, since a government preoccupied with defending its frontiers could afford time only for the most cursory attention to the well-being of its trading companies. Indeed, its sole action was to apply Colbert's regulations after his death in a rigid, mechanical way that inhibited commercial activity, whereas the companies directed by private merchants in England and Holland continued to expand their operations.

In short, none of Colbert's companies achieved anything more than partial success, and after his death in 1683 they collapsed. The Senegal Company challenged the Dutch in West Africa to good effect, but to undercut its rivals it had to forgo its own profits, and thus failed to attract the investment needed for consolidating its position. In the Baltic the French maintained so favourable a balance of trade, selling wines, textiles and West Indian sugar for naval stores, that the English and Dutch governments made it a specific feature of their policy during the war of 1688–97 to drive French shipping from northern waters. The Levant Company had a longer life: based on Marseilles it was better placed for trade with the Middle East than its rivals in London and Amsterdam, but Colbert disliked its operations since the import of silk, leather, rice and cotton had to be paid for in gold. Repeatedly he urged the Marseilles merchants to sell the fine cloths of Carcassonne, deliberately designed for export, but no amount of regulation could create any enthusiasm for them in the markets of the Levant. The most immediately successful of Colbert's projects was the West Indies Company. By its efforts the production of sugar in the islands was increased from an annual total of 12,000,000 lbs. in 1674 to 18,000,000 lb. in 1682, and twenty-nine refineries were established in France to process the entire crop. Tobacco, too, did well, until the Dutch War when the tobacco monopoly was farmed out to speculators. But while Colbert surpassed himself in re-cruiting Dutch experts to create his refineries, he failed to attract settlers to run the plantations. Indeed the men he most needed, men of independence and resourcefulness, were discouraged by his paternalist regulations and chose to live instead in the backwoods of the St. Lawrence or join La Salle in opening up the Mississippi delta.

The internal peace and security afforded by Louis XIV's reign no doubt accounted in part for the expansion of trade and industry between 1660 and 1685, but France could not have developed her economic resources so effectively without Colbert's controlling genius. He planned imaginatively on a national scale, and since he aimed so high, without the administrative means of implementing his plans, the gulf between theory and practice was made more obvious. In this respect Colbert may be deemed a failure, but the privileged nature of French society, the power of the *officiers* to resist his orders, and the persecution of the Huguenots which deprived France of thousands of skilled workers, were faults for which he was not responsible, and which he was powerless to amend. Nor can he be blamed for excessive regulation: his direc-tives, so skilfully compiled, maintained and sustained new industries and revitalised old ones. Far from stifling initiative, his watchful paternalism was all the more necessary since initiative itself was generally lacking among his fellow-countrymen. His successors, who falsely equated *Colbertisme* with strict regulation, failed to realise that his successes were achieved not by the edicts alone but by the informing genius that inspired them. The weakness of his economic policy was that while it depended for success upon the maintenance of peace, it was nevertheless compelled to subserve the military ambitions of his sovereign.

Le Tellier, Louvois and Colbert: the Army and Navy

Louis XIV's pursuit of glory depended upon the fact that his army increased in size more rapidly than that of any other state: 72,000 men were under arms in 1660; 120,000 in 1672; 300,000 or more during the critical years of the War of Spanish Succession. Recruitment on so vast a scale created unprecedented problems not only of finance and of leadership in the field but especially of administration. It was not enough to exploit every device known to the Treasury until the state fell into bankruptcy, nor to enjoy the services of such brilliant commanders as Condé, Turenne and Luxembourg: if the army were not to collapse under the weight of its own numbers an administrative revolution at the war office was necessary. This was achieved by Michel le Tellier and his son, the Marquis de Louvois, who between them controlled the army from 1643 to 1691.

Le Tellier protested to Mazarin in 1643, 'The army has become a republic with as many cantons or provinces as there are lieutenant-generals.' The Fronde made matters worse, since commanding officers disposed of their troops as they saw fit, changing sides and making treaties without reference to any authority but their own. Such a condition of anarchy derived in part from the arrogance of the French nobility before it had been tamed by Louis XIV, but its basic cause was the system of recruitment. Companies and regiments were raised by noble contractors, who then bargained with the king to determine their conditions of service, with the result that the men of these regiments owed a greater loyalty to the employers who protected their interests than to the king who had played no part in their recruitment. It was necessary therefore to destroy the independence of the contractor by reducing his status to that of a regimental officer subject to the authority of general officers and the commander-in-chief; but this could not be done overnight since it was only by the existing system of contracts that the army could maintain its numbers. The day of feudal levies was long past, and its revival in 1674 at a critical stage of the Dutch war produced so motley a force of ill-equipped and untrained men that Turenne disbanded them at once; nor was conscription a satisfactory alternative since, on the rare occasions when it was adopted, the men deserted in their thousands. Le Tellier and Louvois achieved no radical reform, but by piecemeal modification and improvement, by more stringently worded contracts, and in Louvois's case by means of a formidable, overbearing personality, they extended royal control throughout the army as relentlessly as Colbert had done throughout France. As a measure of their success, 72 of the 78 infantry regiments in existence at Louvois's death, were no longer known by their colonel's name but bore permanent titles as regular units of the royal army.

A serious fault was the dishonesty of commanders who falsified their muster rolls. Having contracted to raise a company of 60 men at a rate of 75 *livres* a month, they would often recruit less than thirty: if the company were to be inspected the remainder, popularly known as *passe-volants*, were enlisted from the streets and taverns for a day's pay. To remedy this, Le Tellier appointed *intendants de l'armée*, inferior in rank only to the commander-in-chief, whose task was not merely to check the muster rolls but also to examine the standard of training in every company and regiment. Men like Martinet, who became a household word for his stringent application of military regulations and whose name significantly was given to the twelve-thonged whip used for military punishment, did much to raise standards of discipline and training throughout the army, and by exposing the *passe-volant*, hastened his departure.

Two further weaknesses of the system were that the man who contracted to raise a body of troops inevitably commanded them, and that commissions were bought and sold like offices in the civil administration. Wealth alone was thus the prerequisite of command. Le Tellier and Louvois therefore limited where possible the advantages of wealth by keeping down the cost of purchasing commands; an infantry regiment in 1689 could be bought for 22,500 *livres*, a company for 12,000, but for a fashionable company of Guards it was still possible to pay as much as 80,000. Of greater service to the poor but talented officer was the new system of promotion, designed by Louvois to allow men to rise to the specially created rank of brigadier-general without first having purchased a colonelcy. A much more positive solution, however, was to accept that wealth was an indispensable factor but to ensure that the serving officer possessed other attributes as well.

Nine colleges were established by Louvois along the north-eastern frontier, each with roughly 500 cadets, whose professional training in the colleges was supplemented every summer by practical experience in the field. Existing officers were subjected to promotion examinations and to constant supervision, and Louvois's persistence in setting the highest standards began to produce results since none was spared his displeasure. His treatment of one offender who preferred Versailles to the camp was gleefully recorded by Madame de Sévigné for the entertainment of her daughter:

'M. de Louvois spoke very haughtily to M. de Nogaret the other day.

"Sir, your company is in very poor shape."

"Sir," said he, "I did not know it was."

"You should know," said M. de Louvois. "Have you had a look at it?"

"No," said M. de Nogaret.

"You should have done."

"I will issue some orders about it."

"They should have been given already. You must make up your mind, Sir, whether to declare yourself a courtier or do your duty as an officer." '

Despite the innate conservation of many officers, Le Tellier and Louvois successfully overcame their resistance to new weapons. The typical company of 1660 comprised two rows of musketeers, whose match-fired *mousquets* were so cumbersome that an additional row of pikemen had to be provided to protect them during the processes of reloading. By 1679 the *fusil* with its flintlock action had replaced the *mousquet*, the plug bayonet the pike. The transformation was completed in 1688 by the introduction of the ring bayonet, which made it possible for the same infantryman both to fire and to thrust, and also brought about a consequent revolution in tactics in that the infantry were no longer compelled to seek the shelter of a square but could form line to repel a cavalry attack. The *carabine rayée*, a rifle, was another innovation

K   M.E.S.C.

which Louvois adopted, when he formed a company of carbineers in 1680 to give protection to the cavalry. So successful did the weapon prove that within ten years he had created no less than 107 companies of carbineers. In other fields the work of specialisation and improvement was continued: grenadiers, bombardiers and sappers made their appearance in the army; schools of artillery were established; the commissariat was no longer left to private enterprise but directed by the government, and the value of Louvois's supply dumps was dramatically demonstrated in 1674.[1]

The total effect of the inspired efforts and the painstaking administration of both Le Tellier and Louvois was to create the first modern standing army. None the less, by modern standards it was still incredibly haphazard: not all the troops wore uniform, most of them were still sent home for the winter, and little was done to provide medical care or accommodation. Nor, for all its improved efficiency, could the army escape the horde of camp followers which still clung to its heels. The seventeenth-century army, 'had not yet lost all resemblance to a confused tribal migration'.[2]

In 1665, Colbert was appointed to control the *conseil de la marine* where he fought a single-handed struggle to expand the French navy. Louis XIV frankly disliked the sea, and his prosaic imagination could not encompass the benefits to be derived from sea power. Moreover, there was little to show for the efforts of Richelieu a generation before; few of his ships had survived, and their crews had dispersed to the merchant navy or to the fleets of England and Holland.

Colbert attacked the problem with characteristic vigour. Brest, a village of fifty inhabitants, was transformed by 1680 into one of the greatest dockyards of France with a population of 6,000. Rochefort was the next to be developed, then Toulon, and finally Dunkirk. A vast programme of shipbuilding was undertaken and nearly 300 vessels were constructed ranging from the 40 great ships of the line, with armaments of between 60 and 120 guns, to the humble but still effective Mediterranean galley. The greatest problem was recruitment. Each galley needed at least 250 men, and it was customary to use slaves, criminals, and, eventually, Huguenots to man the oars: but these men were not satisfactory

---

[1] See Chapter VII, page 296.
[2] G. N. Clark, *The Seventeenth Century*, p. 111.

material for the Atlantic fleet. In 1673, therefore, Colbert instituted the *inscription maritime*, a roster of all sailors in French ports who were required to serve with the fleet for a period of six months, and to stand by on half pay for another six months. At the end of the year they were released to seek more congenial employment in the fishing and trading fleets for two years. It was in fact a highly selective press gang with many defects and with many loopholes for evasion, but it certainly produced more men of a suitable nature for the fleet. As for officers, Colbert faced the same problems as did Pepys in England; unfortunately he administered too many other departments to emulate the patience and single-mindedness of his rival. Many naval captains used their ships for private trade, and there was bitter rivalry between those trained at sea and the so-called land admirals whose appointment resulted from royal favour or was purchased outright. In order to enforce naval regulations Colbert appointed intendants to serve with the fleet, although they were not permitted to interfere with the handling of the ships.

Though Louis XIV remained indifferent to the navy, and though its strategic importance to France was bound to be secondary to that of the army, Colbert's achievement was none the less remarkable. Within less than 20 years, handicapped though he was by lack of money and by many more onerous tasks in the government, he created a navy which succeeded in holding its own against the English and the Dutch until its disastrous defeat at Cap La Hogue in 1692.[1]

THE PRICE OF WARFARE: FRANCE, 1683–1715

The dead hand of the Administration

In the glorious aftermath of the victories of Condé and Turenne, Louis XIV conceived of Versailles as a seat of government worthy of his majesty and might, but it was the sad irony of his reign that the palace was completed only to receive the news of Blenheim, Oudenarde and Ramillies.[2] Indeed, the growing failure of French troops to hold their own against the combined forces of a hostile Europe was reflected in the malaise which afflicted the court after 1690. The younger nobles deserted Versailles for the livelier atmosphere of their hotels and *salons* in Paris, and the ceremonial

[1] See Chapter VII, page 303.   [2] See Chapter VII, pages 316, 317.

constructed around the sun king began to lose its meaning as his mortality became all too evident. 'The years pass one after the other,' wrote Louis to his grandson Philip in Spain; 'time slips by without our being aware of it; we grow old like ordinary men, and we shall finish like them.' The dauphin died in 1711, to be followed within a year by his elder son, his daughter-in-law and his grandson. Saddened by their loss, the king lived on in lonely isolation.

If Louis himself had died in 1688, at the age of 50, he might have left an unblemished reputation for majesty, power, efficiency and success. Moreover, because of his own active contribution to affairs of state he would have deserved the credit for managing the brilliant team of servants bequeathed him by Mazarin. It was his tragedy to outlive them by a generation. Lionne died in 1671, and no successor could rival his sure control of diplomacy: Colbert died in 1683, Le Tellier in 1685, and their talented sons, Seignelay and Louvois, in 1690 and 1691. Louis was either unlucky in that men of similar ability were not forthcoming during his last decades, or else he simply lacked the skill to choose them. His own efforts to fulfil his *métier du roi* never faltered. No longer diverted by love affairs and hunting excursions he spent all his time in the council chamber, save for ceremonial appearances in the court. The edifice of bureaucracy created by Colbert and Le Tellier was maintained; his writs ran unchallenged in *pays d'état* and in *pays des élections*, in *parlements* and in municipal corporations; yet the power he exercised was valueless without the ability to wield it. The practice of minutely regulating the affairs of France to benefit both king and country was succeeded by the mere habit of regulation for its own sake. The informing genius which had breathed vigour into the agencies of government was lost, and the administration congealed.

So great a burden had been imposed on the Treasury by the relatively short campaign against the Dutch (1672–9), that even Colbert had been forced to run into debt. His successors, none of whom had that minister's ability and were faced with a period of almost continuous warfare, were therefore doomed to failure. The increasing cost of financing Louis's campaigns, combined with the greater laxity of the tax collectors, led to a desperate situation shown by the following table:

	Income due from taxation	Amount received at the Treasury	Expenditure	Deficit
1683	116,000,000 livres	93,000,000	109,000,000	16,000,000
1715	152,000,000	74,000,000	119,000,000	45,000,000

Moreover, the table does not reveal the whole story. Both 1683 and 1715 were years of peace, and the figures shown take no account of the extraordinary expenses incurred during the intervening years of warfare, which increased the total deficit to 430,000,000 *livres*.

Taxes were increased, but they fell upon an ever-shrinking section of the community, on those who were too impoverished to purchase exemption, and so imminent was the danger of bankruptcy that a more effective system of taxation was attempted. During the war of 1688–97, the government introduced the *capitation*, under which the population was graded into twenty-two classes, the first to pay 2,000 *livres* a year, the lowest one *livre*. The provinces of Alsace, Franche Comté and Flanders immediately purchased their exemption, as did the clergy, and the rest of French society rushed in to be downgraded on the scale. The tax produced 22,000,000 *livres* in its first years, but it became so riddled with exemption that in 1710 it was supplemented by the *dixième*, a tax claiming one tenth of all incomes. Powerless to enforce it uniformly, the Treasury discovered that most of the revenue it produced was immediately offset by decreasing returns from the other taxes still in existence.

The government resorted to an endless variety of expedients. Leases were limited to a period of nine years so that the Treasury might secure frequent fees from their renewal; coffee, tea and chocolate joined the ever-increasing list of state monopolies; forced loans were imposed on municipal corporations, naturalised aliens, the newly nobled, and the remaining Huguenots whose wealth secured them unofficial toleration. The government sold even its personal credit: the contracts for the tax farms of 1693 were revoked after they had been purchased, and sold a second time at a profit of 10,000,000 *livres*, while bills on the *Caisse des Emprunts* were so dishonoured that they fell to 30 per cent of their nominal value. More general and more injurious in their effect, were the nine adjustments made between 1689 and 1709 in the relative values of bullion and currency, and the issue of paper money (1702), which within three years had become so inflated that royal edicts were powerless to compel its acceptance as legal tender.

Worst of all was the excessive sale of offices: 'The powers of protecting innocence,' wrote La Bruyère, 'of punishing crime and of providing justice for everyone were sold to the last penny, as though the administration were a business firm.' When legitimate posts had been duplicated beyond all measure — at Besançon, for example, a new chamber had to be added to the *parlement* to accommodate the new *officiers* — the government resorted to the creation of ludicrous ones. Controllers of *perruques* were appointed in 1706. More fantastic still was the sale of offices to supervise the registration of baptisms: in 1691 Guardians of Registers were appointed; in 1697 their work was duplicated by Controllers of the Registers, in 1706 by Controllers of Extracts from the Registers, in 1709 by Bailiffs of the Registers. Baptism became an expensive affair when each of these *officiers* demanded his fee. The device, moreover, recoiled upon the Treasury. Between 1690 and 1715 it raised over 900,000,000 *livres* by selling offices, but each new *officier* was not only exempt from taxes but had to be paid a salary. Whereas 23,000,000 *livres* were spent in salaries in 1683, the cost in 1699 was 47,000,000—and in 1715, 84,000,000.

It was the fundamental weakness of the *ancien régime* that it failed to tap the real sources of wealth within the country, and the true condition in France should not be judged by the plight of the Treasury. Nevertheless, the withering influence of the government's unimaginative policies brought about a serious economic decline. The trading companies collapsed because the government was too preoccupied with warfare to direct them efficiently; the revocation of the Edict of Nantes deprived industry of many of its skilled workers; and heavy taxation, along with the uncertainty of money values and the fluctuation of wheat prices, led to a fall in consumption and productivity. The gilds resorted to restrictive practices and the masters exploited the powers conferred on them by Colbert, not to improve the quality of their work but to discipline and to underpay their journeymen and apprentices. Strikes broke out frequently, and it was not only the Huguenots who sought refuge abroad: 4,500 Catholic weavers suffered so severely from the depressed condition of their industry in Normandy that they emigrated to England. The government's attempt at remedial action made matters worse, since it resulted in a spate of new edicts which merely parodied those prepared by Colbert. In trade and industry alike the hope for the future lay solely with a few merchants and manufacturers whose personal initiative and enterprise overcame the stultifying effect of the government's policies. Indeed, by the end of the reign, this unlooked-for development was beginning to take effect. In the *chambre de commerce* the need for a change in policy was indicated by one of its members: 'Colbert's companies', he said, 'served their purpose forty years ago; but now we need more freedom from control.' Hence, in 1715, the system of protective tariffs was modified in order to secure reciprocal trade agreements with neighbouring countries. In the hands of private individuals the outlook for the French economy was not without hope.

Colbert had done little for agriculture; his successors did less. A small group of peasant proprietors in the Ile-de-France profited from their nearness to the markets of the capital to enlarge their holdings, but elsewhere the *laboureurs* were reduced to a chronic condition of misery and poverty, which was aggravated further by the steady decline in the price of agricultural produce. Despite the periods of famine during the war years, this decline, which began about 1670, lasted well into the next century. Wine-growing districts were unable to sell their produce. The English deliberately abandoned their traditional taste for claret in order to purchase sherry and port from the Iberian peninsula, while increases in the *péages* and *traites* sent the price of a measure of Burgundy from one *sou* in Orleans to 24 *sous* in Normandy and Picardy. Where corn was produced, the failure of the harvest led to starvation: a good crop produced profits to be shared only by the distributors and the tax-collectors. 'It is the same everywhere', recorded Vauban in his *Dîme Royale*,[1] 'the strong overwhelm the weak, and things have come to such a pass that whosoever can develop his talents or has the knowledge of some skill or trade which could put him and his family in a position to live more comfortably, prefers rather to live without doing anything; and he who could acquire a few sheep and cattle with which to improve his farm and land is forced to deprive himself of these advantages in order to avoid being ruined by an increase in the *taille*, for he will not escape it if he has improved on his property or if his harvest is seen to be rather more abundant than usual'.

Rebels and Critics

Discontent among the industrial population led to strikes and

[1] See below, page 283.

rioting: In the countryside the peasants, confronted with starvation, broke out in sporadic rebellion. Troops were employed to restore order, but another bad harvest led directly to further outbreaks. More serious still was the revolt of the *Camisards*[1] among the hills and forests of the Cévennes. Here, a peasant population which had jealously preserved its attachment to the Huguenot faith, was driven to revolt by persecution and by lack of food. In 1702 a Catholic official was murdered, and the act became a signal for a general rising. The *Camisards* knew their countryside well, and, at a time when Louis XIV was at war with the rest of Europe, they maintained an open struggle against the royal troops for four years.

Risings of this sort, though a novel feature of Louis's reign, were simply the natural protests of men made desperate by poverty and persecution. Of far greater significance was the appearance in public of a reasoned body of criticism which condemned the regime as a whole for impoverishing its subjects and for encouraging persecution. Among the most distinguished of Louis's critics was Fénelon, Archbishop of Cambrai, who had been tutor to Louis's grandson and heir apparent, the Duke of Burgundy. He had suffered humiliation for his support of Madame Guyon,[2] but his opposition to the king was not a capricious act of retaliation. In place of absolute monarchy he proposed a return to an ideal form of aristocratic government, in which the nobility earned its privileges by the performance of public duties. Romantic as it was, no such ideal had ever been realised in France, but Fénelon's belief in it prompted him to attack the personal policies of the king which, he claimed, no longer satisfied the true needs of the kingdom. 'Your loyal subjects are dying of hunger,' he wrote, 'You are praised to the skies for having impoverished France, and you have built your throne on the ruin of all the classes in the state.'

Fénelon's attack on the king was justified, but his advocacy of the virtues of the nobility held no appeal for Frenchmen. A more practical solution to the abuses of the day was proposed by Pierre le Pesant, a magistrate of Rouen. In his *Détail de la France*, published in 1697, he reaffirmed Colbert's principle that the vital sources of national prosperity were production and trade, though he was more enlightened than Colbert in giving pride of place to

---

[1] So called because they concealed themselves on raiding parties by wearing nightshirts over their clothes.

[2] See Chapter I, page 81.

agricultural production. He saw that while the nobility was allowed its privileged immunity from the tax-collector, the Treasury had no option but to adopt expedients which caused damage to the whole economy. To remedy this, he proposed that all incomes should be taxed, and that the *traites* and *péages* which hampered internal trade should be abolished. Colbert himself had realised this, but he knew that such an attack on the privileged classes was politically dangerous. Chamillart, one of his successors, went so far as to grant le Pesant a sympathetic hearing but could not accept his proposals; whereupon le Pesant immediately published a *Supplément* to his original work, bitterly attacking the government for incompetence. This led in 1707 to the suppression of all his books, and his own exile from Rouen.

In that same year his views were echoed by Vauban, whose *Projet d'une dîme royale* expressed a loyal soldier's concern at the poverty which assailed him as he journeyed throughout France. 'I have come to the clear conclusion', he wrote, 'that one-tenth of the people is reduced to beggary and does as a matter of fact live by begging; of the nine-tenths remaining, five cannot give alms to the first tenth because they are very little better off; of the other four-tenths, three are in far from comfortable circumstances.' Once convinced of his case, Vauban laid siege to the Treasury as he had once laid siege to Maastricht, and the solution he sought was as methodically organised as the saps and trenches of his campaigning days. The king, he claimed, owed equal protection to all his sub-jects and therefore the privileges granted to any single class could only harm the whole state. Accordingly, he proposed the *dîme royale*, a tax of 5 per cent on the yearly produce of all land, and a gradu-ated tax on all incomes derived from other sources. The book was circulated privately among his friends in the government; but its analysis was too penetrating, its proposals too well informed, for the comfort of the king, and it was condemned by royal edict.

Louis XIV could silence criticism; he could not alleviate the distress caused by his policies. In his earlier days he had written for the Dauphin's instruction: 'In working for the state, the monarch is working for himself; the good of the one is the glory of the other; when the former is happy, noble and powerful, he who has brought this about is glorious.' France, during the war of Spanish Succession, was neither happy, noble nor powerful: by his own criterion, Louis XIV stood indicted.

VII

Western Europe, 1660–1714

Louis XIV, Lionne and French Diplomacy

The initiative in Europe had passed to France: the Dutch, powerful as they were, looked anxiously for other states with whom they might combine to provide an effective balance to French influence, but Spain was a spent force, Austria dared not relax her concentration over the Hungarian plain, Sweden was preoccupied with her struggle for Baltic supremacy, and England, after the triumphs of Cromwell, returned to her subordinate role. France, on the other hand, had seen her power confirmed by the Treaties of Westphalia and the Pyrenees, and in Louis XIV she had a king who delighted in the conduct of war. His ministers cast wide their net of diplomacy to entangle every other state in his plans, his armies marched with confidence against all comers, and for nearly thirty years his ambitions determined the course of events in Europe.

Louis had said 'l'état c'est moi,' making no distinction between personal and national ambitions; what he sought for himself he believed to be also to the advantage of France. Whereas Henry IV and Richelieu had worked to strengthen their frontiers and to weaken their enemies, Louis was concerned to satisfy a desire for fame and empire, to be the heir of Charlemagne and yet greater. The mystique of the imperial throne enthralled him. Mazarin had failed to secure his election in 1656 but Louis never abandoned his dream, always referring to his candidature in his frequent negotiations with the German Electors. 'The German Emperors', he wrote scornfully, 'are neither the heirs of the Romans, nor the successors of Charlemagne.' He alone was destined for that honour; Versailles, not Vienna, was to house the temporal overlord of Europe. It was a sad blow when Leopold lived out the century and thus forestalled the possibility of a Bourbon triumph in the Electoral College.

Mazarin had bequeathed him yet another imperial vision, that of the Spanish empire, since Maria Theresa's renunciation of her claim had been invalidated by Spain's failure to pay her dowry.[1] Louis's predecessors had sought to destroy Spain: he himself desired to gain possession of her. Occasionally he acted in the practical traditions of Henry IV and Richelieu by seizing Spanish towns to strengthen his frontier; but his persistent ambition was to absorb the empire as a whole, and thus to enjoy a power in Europe which no man had ever held before. In 1661, indeed, his hopes seemed about to be realised. On November 1st Philip IV's sole surviving son died; on the same day Maria Theresa gave birth to the Dauphin. For five days the heir apparent to the Spanish throne was, in Louis's eyes, his own son, until on November 6th the Spanish court celebrated the birth of the future Carlos II. Nevertheless, the child's sickly nature gave rise to Louis's hope that soon the Bourbons would succeed to the Spanish empire. He lived in this hope for forty years.

That Europe was so slow to recognise the serious intent of Louis's grandiose ambitions was due largely to the skill of Hugues de Lionne. International relations were no longer left to dignitaries of church and state, embarked on special embassies for particular occasions. Since the sixteenth century, when the Italians had demonstrated the value of a regular and organised corps of diplomats, diplomacy had become a specialised profession: in Lionne it found one of its most brilliant practitioners. He had acquired from the part he had played in the complex negotiations preceding the treaties of Westphalia and the Pyrenees an unrivalled knowledge of European politics, and his personal experience was daily reinforced by the systematic reports[2] he demanded from his agents in every capital city. These agents were trained not only to observe but to advise their hosts, and to impress upon them the value of a French alliance by means of the generous subsidies they had to offer. Moreover, as representatives of Louis XIV they were to reflect his majesty throughout Europe, and insults, real or imagined,

[1] See Chapter III, page 180.
[2] N.B. the comment of G. N. Clark, *The Seventeenth Century*, p. 132. 'Men like the comte d'Avaux, whose dispatches became a textbook for the next century, were not merely talented individuals, but also they had the prestige of a tradition, the style of a great school. They and the secretaries of state whom they served had devised a thoroughly efficient routine of instructions, reports, dispatches and memoranda. No other country at that time approached them in the technique of their calling.'

to his honour were not to go unchallenged. When, in 1661, Lionne learned that the Spanish ambassador in London had insisted on taking precedence over the French ambassador, despite the recent defeat of Spain by France, he advised his agent how best to retaliate. Consequently, when Charles II next rode in state, a running fight broke out between the servants of the rival embassies as they jostled their carriages to secure the place of honour. Not content with this, Lionne demanded from Philip IV an apology for the presumption of his representatives, a special audience being convened in the Louvre to witness Spain's submission.

Apparently trivial, this kind of incident served a useful purpose in augmenting Louis's prestige, and assured his agents of deferences throughout Europe. Such matters, however, were merely tactical exercises: Lionne was also a strategist on the grand scale, skilled in the art of gaining allies and in isolating an enemy. Knowing the strength and weakness of every European ruler, he could assess the probable reaction to any change in French policy. It was he who made it possible for Louis to attack first Spain and then the United Provinces, secure in the knowledge that in each case the victim stood alone.[1] After Lionne's retirement (1671) Louis became over confident and paid less heed to the value of diplomacy. He failed to recognise that without the careful management of allies, in which Lionne had excelled, the spectacle of French domination would cause Europe to forget its memory of Spain's ascendancy and to unite against that of France.

The War of Devolution, 1667–8

The 'year of Corbie'[2] (1636) had demonstrated the weakness of France's frontier to the north-east, for which the only remedy was to occupy the Low Countries: as Mazarin had said, 'they would provide an impregnable rampart for Paris which would then become the real heart of France'. Louis, though prepared to wait upon events to secure the empires he coveted, at least saw the urgency of pressing his wife's claim to the Spanish Netherlands. His case was ingenious if illogical, taking advantage as it did of the local laws of inheritance peculiar to the Netherlands. In Brabant, for example, all property devolved upon daughters by a first marriage in preference to sons of a second. When Philip IV died in 1665 Louis XIV claimed that his own wife, Maria Theresa, should

---

[1] See below, pages 287–8, 291–3.   [2] See Chapter III, page 176.

succeed in place of Carlos II, her younger stepbrother, in all provinces which observed this custom of devolution. At one stroke he thus demanded possession of Brabant, Antwerp, Limburg, Malines, Upper Gelderland, Namur, Cambrai and those parts of Hainault and Artois still unoccupied by France. In Luxemburg, local custom was not so amenable for it allowed sons to inherit two shares of the property to the daughter's one. In this case Maria Theresa with one stepbrother and one sister, was only entitled to a quarter of the duchy. In Franche Comté, where equal division was made among all the children, she claimed a third. Naturally enough, the Spaniards resisted Louis's argument that what applied to property within the provinces applied equally to the sovereignty of the provinces themselves, and Philip IV declared in his will that the Spanish Netherlands were an integral and indivisible part of Spain. He also insisted that his daughter had no claim upon any part of his estate. Louis immediately published a statement of his wife's claims and announced his determination to enforce them. As a pretext for aggression the devolution claim served its purpose, but it could scarcely be taken seriously in itself, and the lengthy justifications and refutations which streamed from the pens of French and Spanish lawyers were vain manœuvres in a battle of books. Louis had stronger weapons in readiness.

While Le Tellier and Louvois had built up the striking force of the French army, Lionne had achieved a diplomatic triumph by isolating its intended victim. Sweden, Denmark and Brandenburg assured him of their neutrality in the event of war between France and Spain, and Portugal was assisted in her struggle for independence with an annual subsidy of 2,000,000 livres. The emperor, of course, as Spain's natural ally, could not be won over, especially as his victory over the Turks in 1664 had freed his hands to some extent on the Danube.[1] To prevent his intervention in the Netherlands, therefore, Lionne approached the League of the Rhine Princes, but the League, a pliant tool of French diplomacy in the days of Mazarin, was on the point of breaking up. Moreover, its members were at that time more sympathetic to Leopold I after his repulse of the Turkish invasion than to Louis XIV, whose troops had occupied Lorraine in 1662.[2] Their fears, however, were

[1] See Chapter IX, page 362.
[2] Louis had purchased the succession to Lorraine from its ruler, Charles IV, in order to secure easier access to the Alsatian towns acquired in

ultimately allayed by lavish subsidies, and though the League itself made no official alliance, Lionne secured separate, if expensive, agreements with its individual members.

Lionne had anticipated no difficulty in winning Dutch support against Spain, but on this occasion the Dutch were alarmed by Louis's plan to advance his frontier to the Scheldt. While agreeing that France should strengthen her northern frontier by the seizure of some Spanish towns, the Dutch wanted to leave the intervening territory as a buffer state between themselves and the French. Their leader, de Witt, was handicapped in his negotiations by the outbreak of the Anglo-Dutch War in 1665, but, since both combatants were allies of France, the war also raised a problem for Lionne. He solved it by sending troops against England's ally, the Bishop of Münster, a move which assisted the Dutch without alienating Charles II, whose need for French subsidies made him receptive to Lionne's secret assurances of friendship.

As a result of Lionne's efforts not a single European state was prepared to go to the aid of Spain when, on May 20th, 1667, Turenne marched north from Amiens with 35,000 men. Against a commander of such experience, the most talented French soldier of the seventeenth century, the Spaniards had little hope of success. Possessed of great patience and tenacity, Turenne's particular skill lay in the deployment of troops against forces which outnumbered his own, but in 1667, however, these talents were scarcely to be required since the Spanish governor in Brussels had but few men to put in the field. By the end of June Turenne had seized a dozen towns, while Lille, the most important city in Flanders, fell to Vauban after the first great siege of his career. The swift advance of the French took Europe by surprise, and evoked an unexpected response from the emperor. Alarmed by the French successes against Spain and by the threat of further Ottoman attacks against his own territories, Leopold was moved by a yet deeper concern for the continuance of his dynasty. The sick condition of Carlos II in Spain, and the advice of his own doctors that the Empress was unlikely to bear him heirs, caused him to believe that the Habsburg family was doomed. In order to gain time, he offered to divide the Spanish empire with Louis on the death of Carlos, giving France the Netherlands, Luxemburg, Franche

1648. When Charles showed signs of going back on his word, French troops immediately occupied the duchy.

Comté, Naples and Milan. In return, Louis was to content himself for the moment with the towns he had already seized, or with Franche Comté. Leopold believed he was acting in the best interests of his family, but he was also conscious of betraying his cousin of Spain, and he insisted that the treaty, ratified by Louis in January 1668, should be kept secret in the safe keeping of the Duke of Tuscany. Ironically, he was to marry a second wife in 1678 who produced two sons, while Carlos survived in Spain until 1700.

At this moment of apparent triumph Louis was suddenly disconcerted to learn of the defection of England and the United Provinces: Charles II and de Witt, having made peace at Breda (1667), had joined with Sweden in January, 1668, to form a Triple Alliance.[1] De Witt, who wanted to appease Louis, maintained that the allies sought only to compel Spain to accept the loss of the cities taken by France in 1667, but it became clear that they were pledged to oppose Louis if he tried to advance further north. Louis's anger was intense, but the alliance of the three maritime powers at a time when Colbert had not yet fulfilled his plans to revive the French navy, made him circumspect in action. Diverting his attack from the Netherlands, he launched his next campaign in February against Franche Comté. This time it was Condé's turn to demonstrate the speed and efficiency of the French army. Turenne's closest rival, he waged war more passionately and had earned a reputation for impetuosity and courage. Under his spirited leadership, an army of 15,000 overran Franche Comté within three weeks and occupied Besançon, the capital.

This lightning campaign destroyed the remnant of Lionne's system of alliances and when Spain made peace with Portugal and when the German princes threatened to join the Triple Alliance, Louis at once decided to end the war. Reassured by the terms of his secret agreement with the emperor, he saw no need to antagonise European opinion by demanding territory which he expected to acquire by peaceful means in the near future. His terms, therefore, appeared to be disarmingly magnanimous. By the Treaty of Aix-la-Chapelle, May 1668, he evacuated Lorraine, restored Franche Comté to Spain, having first dismantled its fortresses, and retained only the towns seized by his troops in the

---

[1] See Chapter VIII, page 340.

Netherlands.[1] Their possession in no way strengthened his northern frontier since they lay too far inside the border, but as forward positions, threatening Ghent and Brussels, they might prove valuable in the event of further conflict.

The Dutch War and the Grand Alliance of The Hague, 1672–9

Louis regarded the formation of the Triple Alliance as an act of presumption and betrayal. His anger was especially directed against the Dutch since he had believed de Witt to be a reliable ally, a view he never held of Charles II, and in his mortification he vowed to teach the Dutch a lesson. Though such a step ran counter to the policies of Henry IV, Richelieu and Mazarin, who had always looked for support from the other enemies of the Habsburgs, Louis was able to find many reasons to justify his personal vendetta against de Witt. The campaigns of 1667–8 had demonstrated that Spain was no longer to be reckoned a major power and it seemed to Louis that Dutch opposition to his wholesale occupation of the Spanish Netherlands was likely to be more of a stumbling block than the resistance of Spanish troops in the field. Indeed the Republic's action in striking a medal depicting Joshua holding the sun in the heavens was a clear indication that it was congratulating itself upon restraining the action of *le roi soleil*. In this respect Louis's decision to attack the United Provinces was a logical development of the devolution policy.

In many ways Louis had never been able to consider the Dutch suitable allies of so eminent a sovereign as himself. Their Calvinism outraged his Catholic orthodoxy, their republicanism was an unpardonable affront to his concept of monarchy. There were other matters, too, which had rankled for some time, on which Colbert was well equipped to brief his master. Dutch ships controlled the carrying trade in the Baltic, the Atlantic and the Levant which Colbert sought to win for his own trading companies, and he denounced the evils of the Dutch monopoly which he desired so fervently for France. 'As we have crushed Spain on land, so we must crush Holland at sea. The Dutch have no right to usurp all commerce . . . knowing very well that so long as they are the masters of trade, their naval forces will continue to grow and to

---

[1] Bergues, Furnes, Armentières, Oudenarde, Courtrai, Douai, Tournai, Ath, Charleroi and Lille.

render them so powerful that they will be able to assume the role of arbiters of peace and war in Europe and to set limits to the king's plans.' Commercial warfare had in fact preceded military conflict by a decade or more. In 1664 and, more dramatically, in 1667, Colbert had altered tariffs in order to drive Dutch competitors from French ports. Refined sugar, a major French import, was virtually excluded if carried in Dutch ships, lace was taxed at 60 *livres* instead of 25, and fine cloths paid 80 instead of 40. In such a conflict the Dutch were the losers since it was difficult to discriminate effectively against the few French ships which entered Dutch ports. None the less, retaliation had to be made and new tariffs were promulgated in 1670 and 1671. Finally in 1672 when war seemed imminent in any case, the Dutch banned all French imports from their territories for a whole year.

In order to isolate the Dutch, the alliances of 1667 had to be refashioned by Lionne, a task made the more difficult by the swift successes of the French army which had to some extent alarmed Louis's neighbours. Indeed, the Archbishop-Elector of Mainz was proposing an alliance of German states to resist French aggression, and his arguments were strengthened in 1671 when Charles of Lorraine was once again expelled from his duchy. Lionne counterattacked by exploiting the habitual lack of common purpose among the German princes. With great skill he caused them to suspect each other's good faith, revived their latent distrust of the emperor's ambitions, reassured them individually that France intended them no harm, and when the moment was ripe clinched the agreement with a generous subsidy. Münster, England's ally in the Anglo-Dutch war (1665–7), was delighted to secure a more powerful ally against her traditional enemy: Brandenburg was won by the promise of assistance against the Dutch in Cleves and the Swedes in Pomerania: Bavaria was flattered by the Dauphin's marriage to the Elector's daughter: Hanover, the Palatinate and Cologne were bought outright. Since Cologne also controlled the bishopric of Liège, which ran like a wedge through the Spanish Netherlands from France to the Rhineland, Lionne had thus opened up for Louis a safe route through the Rhineland to the United Provinces. Moreover, his allies afforded some protection to the eastern frontier of France in the event of imperial intervention in support of the Dutch. Leopold, in any case, was afraid that French agents in Germany were planning to form a league against him, which in

Map legend:

- ▬ ▬ French advance 1672
- Archbishopric of Cologne
- Bishopric of Liège
- Dutch territory
- Spanish Netherlands and Luxemburg 1672
- Flooded area

Amsterdam

Utrecht

R. Yssel

R. Lek

Arnheim

R. Waal

Nijmegen

Wesel

BISHOPRIC OF MÜNSTER

Antwerp

Neuss

SPANISH NETHERLANDS

Cologne

Bonn

Maastricht

Liège

R. Rhine

Namur

Charleroi

R. Sambre

LUXEMBURG

FRANCE

MAP 10   Warfare in the Netherlands, 1672–3

addition to his perennial fear of an Ottoman attack, made him agree by the Treaty of Vienna (1671) to remain neutral.

Since the French planned to by-pass the Spanish Netherlands by advancing through Liège, Lionne did not attempt the impossible task of winning the alliance of Spain. Instead, his final act in isolating the Dutch was to destroy the Triple Alliance of 1668. Charles II, indeed, had not intended to remain for long in alliance with de Witt. His purpose had been to placate a section of his own parliament, to secure a higher price from France for his services in the future, and to pave the way for an Orange restoration by embittering relations between de Witt and Louis XIV.[1] It was not difficult, therefore, for Lionne to restore relations with England. The offer of Walcheren in return for naval support against the Dutch, the opportunity to destroy Dutch commerce, the subsidy of £166,000 with the promise of more to come, and the presence among the negotiators of the beautiful Louise de Querouelle, subsequently created Duchess of Portsmouth, were temptations which Charles found irresistible. In 1670, at Dover, he became Louis's ally. As for Sweden, her government was so seriously in debt that Pomponne had merely to double the Dutch offer of 200,000 *livres* in order to win her over. As a result of this the Elector of Brandenburg realised that France could no longer help him to clear the Swedes from Pomerania, and sold out to the Dutch. Brandenburg apart, there was no power left in Europe to support the Dutch against France. It was a fitting conclusion to Lionne's career, since he retired in 1671 to be succeeded by Pomponne.

Louvois, as meticulous and as skilful as Lionne, had meanwhile been making his preparations for war. In addition to raising 120,000 men, he established supply bases along the frontier, surveyed the route through Liège, and trained a special corps of engineers in the use of pontoons for crossing the Dutch waterways. The Dutch, in contrast, were wholly unprepared. For twenty years control of the army had been exercised by the separate provincial administrations of the Union, for fear lest the House of Orange secure control of it and thus re-establish its ascendancy. So incompetent were these local bodies that even the powder in their magazines had been sold to Louvois's agents. Ironically, there was no one to appoint as commander in 1672 but the very prince whose ambitions de Witt most feared. William of Orange, however, at twenty-one, with no

[1] See Chapter VIII, pages 340-1.

experience of campaigning, was unlikely to succeed against the French generals; and his task was made all the more hopeless since each province appointed its field deputies to control his actions and to safeguard its own contingents.

In April 1672 Louis joined Turenne at Charleroi, one of the forward bases acquired in 1668, and the army of 60,000 advanced through Liège. The Dutch foreseeing this obvious move, had strengthened the fortifications of Maastricht, which lay along the frontier. Contemptuously by-passing the city Turenne joined forces with 30,000 men under Condé and marched swiftly down the Rhineland scattering the Elector of Brandenburg's troops in Cleves as he did so.[1] When William moved his men into trenches behind the Yssel, at the point where it flowed into the Rhine from the north, Turenne smartly turned his flank. Since prolonged drought had reduced the water level of the Rhine, the French army crossed on pontoons to the south bank, marched past William, now impotent on the further bank, and recrossed the river below him at Arnheim. The Dutch were therefore cut off from their base, and William retreated rapidly to Utrecht. There the city corporation was so demoralised by the speed of the French advance that it refused to allow him entry, and he was forced to continue his flight as far as Amsterdam. The French had only to follow him for the war to be over.

Condé, with his flair for the penetrating thrust, urged Turenne to race for Amsterdam, ignoring the other towns as Turenne himself had ignored Maastricht; but the plan was too daring for Louis and Louvois, who attended the army, and they overruled it. Louis, moreover, revelled in the glory of receiving the surrender of each town in turn, and it was the long succession of these petty triumphs which lost him the opportunity to win the war. On June 18th William ordered the dykes to be breached, leaving Holland and Zeeland in temporary security behind the water line.

Like Louis, de Witt too recoiled from the daring proposals of his generals, rejecting William's appeal for a heroic stand behind the water line. As the French advance lost momentum he sued for peace, which did not suit Louvois's plans at all: eager to complete the campaign by the methodical reduction of the entire Republic, he urged Louis to demand terms so humiliating that the Dutch could

[1] After this the Elector temporarily became Louis's ally by the Treaty of Vossem.

only refuse them. This they did. Accusing de Witt of betraying
them to the enemy, an angry mob lynched him in the street, and
throughout the provinces William of Orange was acclaimed as the
national leader. The French settled down to await the coming of
winter when the flooded polders would become a frozen pathway
to Amsterdam, but the weather proved unexpectedly mild and the
enemy unexpectedly active. By 1673, Leopold found it impossible
to stay neutral any longer, and his general, Montecucculi, fought
his way across Cologne to join forces with William in the capture
of Bonn. This unexpected move threatened the French lines of
communication: the main body of the French army was withdrawn from the Dutch provinces, Turenne marching eastwards to
protect Münster, while Vauban retired southwards to capture
Maastricht in order to give the French more effective control of the
line of the Meuse. From there they repulsed an audacious thrust by
William at Charleroi.

The character of the war had altered radically. Holland and
Zeeland, far from renewing their pleas for peace, were fighting
back vigorously in company with the Imperialists, and it was the
turn of the French to be concerned with lines of communication
and defence. England, defeated at sea, made peace with the
republic at Westminster (1674)[1] and for the next six years Charles
II was to be preoccupied with the domestic consequences of the
Treaty of Dover and the Popish Plot. Pomponne was complacent
about Charles's plight: internal dissension was at least a guarantee
of England's inactivity abroad, and if Charles could no longer
assist Louis's ambitions, neither could he upset them, as in 1668.
'This perpetually agitated state of England is one which suits us
best,' he commented. There was little else, however, to suit France
in the swift turn of events. In 1674 William and Leopold were
joined in the Grand Alliance of The Hague by Carlos II, Charles of
Lorraine, and the rulers of Mainz, Trier, Brandenburg and the
Palatinate. France was threatened from every quarter.

The French army was at last put to the test and its conduct in
1674 justified the great efforts of Louvois to make it the finest in
Europe. Condé fought a successful defensive action to contain
William in the Netherlands, while Vauban and Louis occupied
Franche Comté with a speed that rivalled the lightning campaign
of 1668; but it was Turenne who outshone the others by his

[1] See Chapter VIII, page 343.

famous defence of Alsace and Lorraine against Montecucculi. Throughout the summer months he held his own against superior numbers and devastated the Palatinate in order to deny the enemy the opportunity of revictualling in the Rhineland. He then feigned retreat to lure them further into Alsace. Here, in November, just as Montecucculi was about to withdraw his troops for the winter, he equipped his own from the supply dumps prepared by Louvois and launched a new offensive. A forced march of seventeen days brought him to Turckheim, south of Strassburg, where he took the enemy by surprise and drove them across the Rhine. The advantage thus gained was maintained for the next six months until Turenne's death in battle (July 1675) temporarily demoralised his army. His pupil, Créqui, had not yet acquired the patience of his master, and an impetuous attack resulted in his own capture. At this crisis, Condé was transferred from the Netherlands to hold the Rhine, leaving Luxembourg to defend the northern frontier against William. Towards the end of the year, however, Condé was forced by ill health to resign his command, and Louis lost his second great general. The security of France after 1675 was to depend upon the abilities of Vauban and Luxembourg, and of a chastened Créqui, who was ransomed from the emperor.

Sweden, meanwhile, had met with disaster. La Gardie, the Chancellor, had never anticipated that France might call upon him for assistance; his intention had been to do nothing more strenuous than to receive the liberal subsidies of Pomponne, but the change of circumstances by 1675 compelled him to relieve the pressure on his ally by intervening in north Germany. The Swedish army, however, was defeated at Fehrbellin by the forces of the Elector of Brandenburg, which then overran Pomerania, while Denmark invaded the mainland provinces of Scania and Bleking.[1]

Throughout 1676 and 1677 the overall situation became one of stalemate. The armies of the Alliance of The Hague could not penetrate the French lines of defence; the French were unable to launch a major offensive. Louis led a sudden attack into the Spanish Netherlands in 1677, seizing Cambrai and other frontier towns, including Valenciennes which was taken by Vauban after an assault in daylight, thereby confounding the pundits who were horrified by such a venture; but there was no breakthrough to the Dutch frontier. Both sides had become mesmerised by the conduct

[1] See Chapter X, page 399.

of sieges; outright victory was clearly denied to either side, and negotiations were begun for a peace treaty. In Holland the fanatic determination of William to fight until Louis had been destroyed was overruled by a powerful group of merchants. These men were entirely unconcerned about the fate of Spanish Franche Comté, imperial Alsace or Swedish Pomerania: their one desire, now that their country's safety was assured, was to return to the conditions of peacetime commerce. So precipitate, in fact, were their efforts to end the war that their allies were denied the opportunity of exploiting their own bargaining positions. William indeed tried to undermine their negotiations with Louis by making a sudden attack on Mons in 1678, but the French refused to be drawn. At Nijmegen the terms were finally settled, and by 1679 western Europe was again at peace.

The settlement was a comprehensive one since nearly every state in western Europe had been involved in the war.

(i)   The French restored Maastricht, their sole conquest in the Dutch provinces, and reduced the exhorbitant tariffs imposed before the war in an effort to damage Dutch commerce.

(ii) The French returned their forward bases in the Spanish Netherlands, gained in 1668, in exchange for a strip of territory, 200 miles long, running from Dunkirk to the Meuse, which afforded a more effective means of strengthening their northern frontier.

(iii) Louis, abandoning his belief in the immediate death of Carlos II, retained Franche Comté, and provided Carlos with a French wife, the Princess Marie-Louise.

(iv) Charles of Lorraine refused to accept any of Louis's terms, with the result that France retained possession of his duchy.

(v)   The Emperor, owing to the haste with which his allies made peace, had no option but to agree to Louis's retention of the principal Alsatian towns.

(vi) Brandenburg and Denmark, though they were not a party to the Treaty of Nijmegen, were subsequently compelled by Louis, who threatened their Rhineland territories, to restore to Sweden the lands they had occupied since 1675.[1]

In their justifiable enthusiasm for the peace settlement, the

---

[1] See Chapter X, page 400.

French, forgetting the anxieties they had undergone, and ignoring the massive debt which burdened the Treasury, hailed their king as 'Louis le Grand'. The Dutch had yet to restore their scarred towns and flooded fields; Spain had again revealed the feebleness of her resistance; the German princes had gained nothing, and were anxious only to restore the flow of French subsidies into their depleted treasuries. Frederick William of Brandenburg voiced the general sentiment: 'In the present state of affairs, so far as human prudence can judge, it seems that no prince will henceforth find security and advantage except in the friendship and alliance of the king of France.'

Nevertheless, the Dutch had not been defeated. The motives which had driven Louis to declare war had eluded achievement, and in William of Orange the French had made an implacable enemy. Moreover, the Alliance of The Hague was an ominous indication that Europe had learned the need to unite against French aggression.

The Corrosive Peace, 1679–85

Louis's next venture was directed primarily against the German princes. Since 1648 the French had acquired piecemeal many towns and provinces along their frontiers, and Louis was concerned to integrate them more closely with France by eliminating the enclaves of other powers which separated them from each other or from the main body of the kingdom. In addition, he wished to extend his influence within the Holy Roman Empire in preparation for the day of Leopold's death: Louis renewed his treaties with the Electors of Brandenburg and Bavaria and hoped, by securing control of the Rhineland, to be able to coerce the Elector Palatine and the Archbishop-Electors of Cologne, Mainz and Trier. To achieve his purposes, Louis exploited the military unreadiness of his neighbours to blackmail them into conceding what he required. The years of peace were to be made as profitable to France as those of war. It was scarcely a wise policy to antagonise the former members of the Grand Alliance of The Hague, and Pomponne was dismissed for saying so, but with Louvois abetting him, Louis had become over-confident. In Colbert de Croissy they found a new foreign secretary who could offer them the means to achieve their ends, and they were eager to make a start.

Croissy, brother of the great Colbert, had formerly served as intendant in Alsace, and the experience he had gained there in unravelling the complex network of rival jurisdictions, which were a legacy of the Peace of Westphalia, prompted him to develop his *réunion* policy. In the first place he sought to clarify the status of towns ceded to France in the past, and thus to ensure that within their boundaries the absolute sovereignty of Louis XIV was universally recognised. In Alsace, for example, the towns acquired in 1648 had retained their immediacy to the Holy Roman Empire, a term which had been invented in order to reconcile the emperor to their loss. Croissy proposed to break this tenuous link, and to enforce the recognition of Louis's *supremum dominium*. This was reasonable enough, but his second step was to examine the archives of all the towns ceded to France along with their dependencies, another ill-defined term employed by the peacemakers of Westphalia, to ascertain what these dependencies were in order to appropriate them. By this means he hoped to extend the boundaries of each of these recently acquired towns and provinces until they formed a coherent frontier, embracing all positions of strategic importance.

The *réunion* policy, in short, was nothing less than a calculated gamble that the German princes would sooner accept the loss of some territory than risk another war with France. In 1680 Louis appointed *chambres des réunions* at Besançon, Breisach and Tournai with jurisdiction over Franche Comté, Alsace and Flanders respectively, and a fourth chamber at Metz to investigate the duchies of Bar and Lorraine and the bishoprics of Metz, Toul and Verdun. Their decisions were swiftly made, and as swiftly enforced by the French army, so that by 1681 the frontier from Dunkirk to Grenoble had been strengthened by the systematic annexation of towns and villages which were deemed by Louis to have been formerly dependent upon France. Since it controlled a Rhine crossing of great importance, the most valuable single acquisition was the free city of Strassburg, which had previously been in the anomalous position of owing a degree of loyalty to both Louis and the emperor. In addition, the French seized Casale, the capital of Montferrat, though this was less of a *réunion* than an act of outright confiscation.[1]

Europe was outraged, but none of Louis's neighbours dared to

[1] See Chapter II, page 127, for an account of Montferrat's value to France in controlling Spanish troop movements in north Italy.

challenge the legality of his action by resorting to war. The German princes had no option but to submit; Sweden was unable to defend her Rhineland base of Zweibrücken, and Spain was powerless to recover Casale. It was not until French troops marched into Luxemburg to enforce their claims there (1682) that the victims of the *réunions* made some show of protest. Led by William of Orange, Louis's most resolute enemy in Europe, many of the lesser German princes, particularly those of Franconia and the Rhineland, met at Laxenburg to seek an alliance with Sweden, Spain and Austria, in an effort to halt the course of French expansion. Louis deemed it wise to withdraw for the moment, announcing that a new Turkish threat to Austria made it necessary for Europe to remain at peace, an ironical term to describe the condition of Europe after 1679. Louis indeed offered to assist at the siege of Vienna,[1] but the emperor refused his aid since its acceptance would have implied his own tacit consent to the *réunions*. As soon as Vienna had been saved, but before Leopold was free to intervene in western Europe, Louis renewed his assault on Luxemburg (1684). Spain, unable to countenance this final blow to her dignity, attempted armed resistance, but without the support of allies her efforts were ineffective. The Laxenburg powers had evolved no plan of military action: William's plan to support Spain was overruled by the States-General: Leopold could do nothing. Thus, after the French had taken Luxemburg, bombarded Genoa and invaded Catalonia, the Spaniards had no option but to make peace in 1685. By the Truce of Regensburg (Ratisbon), they recognised for a term of twenty years all Louis's acquisitions since 1679.

'After 1672', wrote Leibniz in his effort to stir up German feeling against Louis XIV, 'the French decided that the king no longer needed to justify his enterprises to the world.' The immediate fruits of Louis's aggressive policy gave him a position of unrivalled power in western Europe: their long-term effect in provoking the opposition of all his neighbours was to prove less advantageous.

THE EUROPEAN COALITIONS AGAINST FRANCE, 1685–1714

The War of the League of Augsburg, 1688–97

The ruthless exploitation of his military power since 1679 had

[1] See Chapter IX, page 372.

left Louis XIV without the support of allies. Worse still, his victims were becoming accustomed to combining against him, and the habit of regular opposition to French expansion was producing a new sense of solidarity in western Europe. Louis remained insensitive to it. To celebrate his triumphs he commissioned a monument which inconsiderately displayed the rulers of Sweden and Brandenburg as his chained vassals; and the revocation of the Edict of Nantes despatched a thousand fervent embassies throughout the Protestant states to confirm the growing legend of an arbitrary and irresponsible monarch. In 1686 the princes of Franconia and the Rhineland entered into a defensive league at Augsburg; within two years they had been joined by Brandenburg, Bavaria, Saxony, Spain, Sweden, Savoy, the United Provinces and the emperor. That such a coalition, on the scale of the Grand Alliance of The Hague (1674), could be formed in peace-time was a significant indication that Louis's disregard for European opinion had been carried too far, and that the initiative in Europe was slowly passing to his enemies. Moreover, the emperor was at last becoming free of the Ottoman threat to his territories which had paralysed his previous attempts to limit the expansion of France. In 1687 the Turks were defeated at Mohács,[1] Transylvania and Hungary were cleared, and by 1688 Belgrade was once again in European hands, for the first time since 1521.

When Louis tried to extend still further his control of the Rhineland, a European war became inevitable. In 1685, on the death of the childless Elector Palatine, William of Neuburg claimed the succession. As a member of the League of Augsburg, and as father-in-law to both Carlos II and the emperor, he was in Louis's eyes an undesirable neighbour, so the French put forward a claim on behalf of the former Elector's sister who had married Louis's brother. While the dispute was being referred to the Diet, there fell vacant another Rhineland throne, the archbishopric of Cologne, which, like the Palatinate, possessed not only a position of great strategic value but also a vote in the Electoral College. Louis resolved to secure this too by proposing the Bishop of Strassburg, Cardinal Fürstenberg, in whom he had implicit confidence. Unfortunately, the Bavarian Electors had long been accustomed to look upon Cologne as a family possession, to be used as a lucrative refuge for younger sons: a Bavarian candidate was therefore put

[1] See Chapter IX, page 375.

forward, but since he was a minor and had not yet been admitted
to holy orders, the pope was required to adjudicate in the matter.
Louis considered that he had shown uncommon restraint in
accepting a resort to arbitration in two cases which so closely
touched his interests: he was, therefore, all the more indignant
when both the Diet and the pope decided against him, and straightway reverted to those stronger measures which had so often stood
him in good stead. In 1688 he installed Fürstenberg by force in
Cologne, and invaded the Palatinate.

No diplomatic preparation, no husbanding of allies, preceded
this stroke, save for a published *Mémoire des raisons qui ont obligé
le roi à reprendre des armes*, a piece of empty rhetoric to lay the
blame at Leopold's door. Louis, in fact, intended nothing more
than a simple *coup* such as he had recently become accustomed to,
and did not believe that his action would result in a general conflict; but Europe sprang to arms with surprising speed. Leopold
planned a march on the Upper Rhine, while Saxony and Brandenburg advanced upon its lower reaches, and the defensive League of
Augsburg was transformed into an offensive coalition at Vienna.
The invasion of the Palatinate, moreover, by diverting Louis's
troops from the Dutch frontier, enabled William to sail for
England;[1] before the year was out, James II was an exile at
Versailles. As soon as Louis realised that he was committed to a
war in which all his frontiers were threatened with invasion he
abandoned his forward position in the Palatinate, ordering its
devastation in order to deny its use as an enemy base. The work
was done with systematic brutality. Turenne in 1674 had been
content to destroy the crops but Louis destroyed the cities too.
Heidelberg, Mannheim and Speyer were sacked and their fortifications razed; several thousands died at the hands of the troops
and from starvation, and many more fled to recount their pitiful
tale among the member countries of the Vienna alliance. Louis had
thus succeeded, where every emperor had failed, in creating a
unanimous body of German opinion hostile to France.

At sea the French immediately seized the initiative. It was
indeed remarkable that their navy should be prepared to challenge
the acknowledged naval might of England and the United Provinces, and it was due to the devoted efforts of Colbert, before his
death in 1683, that they were able to do so.[2] De Tourville landed

[1] See Chapter VIII, page 346.   [2] See Chapter VI, page 276.

James II in Ireland with a small force to lead the Irish rebellion against William, but a repulse at Bantry Bay compelled him to abandon his plan to establish control of the Irish Sea. In consequence, the English transports conveyed William's army safely to Ireland, there to inflict a crushing defeat on James at the Battle of the Boyne in 1690. On the very day of William's triumph, however, de Tourville scattered both the English and the Dutch fleets off Beachy Head, one of the gravest disasters in British naval history. For two years he retained mastery of the Channel until defeated by the English admiral, Russell, at Cap La Hogue. The loss of fifteen ships of the line so weakened the French that subsequent operations in the Atlantic were left to the privateers, like Jean Bart, who raided allied merchantmen from the fortified harbours of Dunkirk, St. Malo and Dieppe. So successful were their attacks that the French government leased them naval vessels and stores on easy terms; thus equipped, squadrons of privateers ranged the Atlantic from the North Sea to West Africa. England, Holland and Spain were peculiarly vulnerable to this kind of attack, and their losses were heavy. In 1693 over a hundred merchantmen of the Smyrna convoy were captured off Lagos, and in 1697 an audacious raid as far afield as the Caribbean led to the capture of Cartagena, the entrepôt of Spanish-American trade.

On land the French remained secure behind frontiers which had been strengthened, not only by the *réunions*, but also by the hand of Vauban. In the south they invaded Catalonia, and would have taken Barcelona but for Russell's timely relief of the city by sea. In 1697, however, de Tourville escaped from an allied blockade of Toulon to assist a second, and successful, campaign against Barcelona. French troops also crossed the Alps and defeated Victor Amadeus of Savoy at Stafforda in 1690. The Savoyards then rallied under Prince Eugène and invaded Dauphiné. Eugène had spent his youth in France, but when Louis XIV who wanted to make a churchman of him refused to give him a military command, Eugène took service with the emperor and soon demonstrated his talents as a soldier. So invaluable were his services that Leopold recalled him in 1692 to drive off a Turkish counter-attack in the Danube; deprived of his leadership the Savoyards collapsed, being defeated at Marsiglia in 1693 by Catinat, who held the Alpine passes with ease for the rest of the war. In the Rhineland, though the French lost Mainz and Bonn, the allies were unable to force

Legend (on map):
- — · — Frontier of Spanish Netherlands 1648
- French acquisitions by 1688
- Bishopric of Liège
- United Provinces

Map labels: UNITED PROVINCES, CLEVES, Ostend, Bruges, Antwerp, Dunkirk, Furnes, Ghent, Calais, Ypres, Oudenarde, Brussels, JÜLICH, Cologne, Menin, Courtrai, Neerwinden, Maastricht, Bonn, Lille, Tournai, Steenkirk, Ramillies, Liège, Denain, Mons, Fleurus, Charleroi, Namur, Malplaquet, Cambrai, FRANCE, Luxemburg

MAP 11   Warfare in the Spanish Netherlands, 1688–1714

their way into Alsace and Lorraine. The three great natural barriers of the Pyrenees, the Alps and the Rhine had proved insurmountable.

It was in the Netherlands that the allies launched their main attack, but the campaign was predestined to a form of stalemate since both sides held firm lines of defence, the allies the rivers and waterways, the French the fortresses of Vauban. The armies became accustomed to a sluggish crawl from one siege to another, although Luxembourg showed himself a lively successor to his tutor, Condé. At Fleurus in 1690 he defeated the Dutch, preventing them from joining with the Brandenburg army in Cleves, and held the ring while Vauban reduced the fortifications of both Mons in 1671 and Namur in 1692. In this latter year William launched a surprise attack on the French at Steenkirk, but his plans were badly made, and the French, leaving their quarters *en déshabille*, routed him; this victory was celebrated at Versailles by the ladies who adopted a new hairstyle, dishevelled *à la Steenkirk*. Luxembourg triumphed again in 1693 at Neerwinden where he took 15,000 prisoners and sent so many standards in triumph to Paris that he was named *le tapissier de Notre-Dame*. William had realised already that the allies could not attain their aims and that peace talks would have to begin; but he caused something of a sensation by recovering Namur in 1695. It was rare indeed for a fortress defended by Vauban to fall, and its capture provided some solace for the man who was fast earning a reputation for being the most defeated commander in Europe.

France had more than held her own against the rest of Europe, but her display of military virtuosity was to no good purpose since it was clear that Louis could never secure Cologne and the Palatinate. Meanwhile, the cost of fighting on all fronts had driven the Treasury to adopt one desperate expedient after the other, in addition to which a succession of bad harvests had caused widespread distress. If France had victories to celebrate, she had little to celebrate them with: in Voltaire's words, 'she was perishing to the sound of Te Deums'. By 1696 Louis had lost Louvois and Croissy, the ministers who had urged the war, and Luxembourg, the one general capable of winning it. Fortunately, in Colbert de Torcy, Croissy's son, he had a diplomat of sufficient skill to see how to secure peace. His first step was to neutralise north Italy by concluding a separate treaty at Turin with Victor Amadeus of Savoy. Since the French already occupied most of his territories he had little to gain by continuing the war, and Torcy won him over by conceding Pinerolo and Casale. The Treaty of Turin in 1696 paved the way for a general settlement. William was aware of opposition in England to the 'King's War', as it was termed; and both he and Leopold were as anxious as Louis to end the conflict when they learned that the death of Carlos II, so frequently anticipated, was at last imminent. The problem of determining his heir made it imperative to end the deadlock in Europe.

The terms of the Peace of Ryswick in 1697 did not altogether reflect the true course of events of the war:

(i) William of Neuburg secured the Palatinate.

(ii) Prince Clement of Bavaria became Archbishop Elector of Cologne.

(iii) Louis recognised the accession of William as King of England, and promised to withdraw his support of James II.

(iv) Lorraine, after more than thirty years of French occupation, was restored to the grandson of Charles IV.

(v) Luxemburg, Charleroi, Mons, Courtrai and Barcelona were restored to Spain.

(vi) Territories gained by the *réunions* were restored to their original rulers, with the exception of Strassburg and the towns of Lower Alsace.

(vii) In addition, by a private treaty, Spain allowed the Dutch to garrison a series of frontier towns, including Ypres, Menin, Courtrai and Luxemburg, to act as a barrier against future French aggression.

Louis thus renounced all the acquisitions, save Alsace, which he had made since 1679, and also gave up Lorraine and Pinerolo whose occupation had been of longer standing. His most difficult obligation was to recognise his most persistent enemy as king of England, since this involved the repudiation not only of his ally James II but also of his whole concept of monarchy and divine right. Nevertheless, the burden of waging a prolonged war was proving too great for France to bear, and Louis was prepared to accept the losses of 1697 in order to realise his dream of peaceably acquiring the Spanish Empire, which, at long last, seemed to be within his grasp.

The Problem of the Spanish Succession, 1697-1702

Louis, for once, had learned something from his mistakes. The arbitrament of war had proved to be too uncertain a means of securing his aims, both against the Dutch and in the Rhineland, and its brief moments of glory were overshadowed by its excessive cost. Moreover, the emperor's reconquest of Hungary, confirmed by the Treaty of Karlowitz in 1699, and William's accession to the throne of England, made it all the more difficult for France to ride roughshod over Europe. If Louis were to secure the Spanish Succession then it could only be by negotiation and diplomacy.

It was clear that the Dauphin had a good claim to the Spanish throne since his grandfather and his father had married the elder daughters of Philip III and Philip IV, but the prospect of one prince inheriting both Spain and France was one which appalled not only the rest of Europe but the Spaniards themselves. Louis wisely instructed his ambassador in Madrid that the Dauphin would renounce his claim in favour of his younger son, the Duke of Anjou, 'in order to remove all grounds for fearing that Spain and France might ever be united'. Leopold, too, could urge a strong claim on behalf of his family: both he and his father had married

Genealogical Tree showing the Descent of the Three Chief Claimants (shown in capitals) to the Spanish Throne.

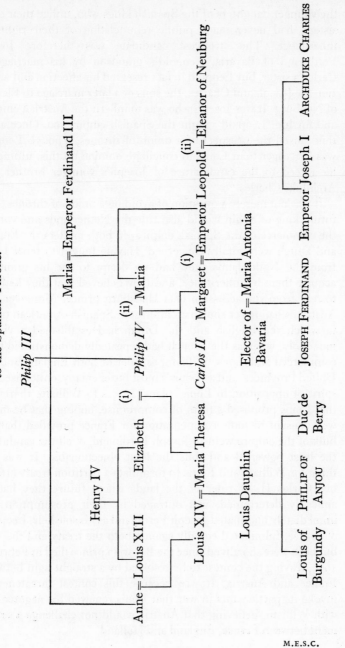

the younger daughters of the Spanish kings who, unlike their elder sisters, had never made public renunciation of their rights of inheritance. The strongest candidate was therefore Joseph Ferdinand of Bavaria, Leopold's grandson by his marriage to Carlos's sister, but Leopold in fact reserved his affection and ambition for Joseph and Charles, the sons of a later marriage to Eleanor of Neuburg. It was Joseph who was to inherit the Austrian empire, and for him Leopold sought the Spanish empire too. Once again this caused the prospect of a union of thrones. Though Leopold was less eager than Louis to conciliate opinion on this, ultimately he agreed to the candidature of Joseph's younger brother, the Archduke Charles.

It was not merely a question of avoiding a union of thrones. The future king of Spain would also rule the Netherlands and control the commerce of the Spanish empire: in both matters the English and Dutch were vitally concerned. Having fought to repel Louis from the Netherlands they had no desire to see his grandson acquire them by inheritance, and they believed that they had less to fear from the accession of a Habsburg prince. Moreover, the Austrians had never shown an interest in Spanish-American trade, in which the English and the Dutch had established a virtual monopoly, whereas the French had repeatedly demonstrated their commercial ambitions. William, as ruler of both England and the United Provinces, and as Louis's most bitter enemy, epitomised the spirit of opposition to Louis' plans. It was to William, therefore, that Louis proposed a form of compromise, hoping that he might well consent to some compensation for France provided that the bulk of the empire went to Joseph Ferdinand, of all the candidates the least powerful and thus the least objectionable. It was one thing for William and Louis to formulate a partition treaty (1698), but Carlos II, as ruler of the lands whose future they had so amicably determined, was outraged by their presumption and immediately nominated Joseph Ferdinand as his sole heir. Leopold, of course, fulminated equally against both the treaty and the will, but both were shortlived since the Bavarian prince died in February 1699, leaving the contest to be resolved by a straight fight between France and Austria. It was because this contest threatened to invoke its participants in war that Louis renewed his negotiations with William, believing that Austria would not challenge a settlement between France, England and Holland.

Louis's hand was strengthened by the fact that the English Parliament was busily cutting down the size of William's army. Thus William was in no position to threaten war on behalf of Archduke Charles; on the other hand he could scarcely fail to negotiate lest Louis abandon the idea of partition and seek the entire inheritance for France. The second partition treaty in fact favoured Archduke Charles without in any way benefiting Austria, since he was assigned the throne of Spain on condition that he renounced all ties with Austria; Louis was to be compensated by the acquisition of Spanish territory in Italy, though, to reassure Leopold, he promised to give Milan to the Duke of Lorraine, and to take his duchy in exchange. Despite the Milanese clause, despite the assurance of his son's accession, despite William's signature, Leopold condemned the treaty outright, and his refusal to sign it destroyed the basis of Louis's policy, since Louis's object had been to compel Leopold to accept a settlement of the problem before Carlos II died. It was Carlos himself who finally exposed the unreality of the negotiations. In a last spirited effort to preserve the unity of his empire he drafted a new will in October 1700 naming Philip of Anjou as his heir, on condition that he renounced his claim to the French throne. While his choice of the French prince owed much to the influence of Louis's ambassador in Madrid, it was also a recognition of the fact that only a prince supported by the might of France could hope to preserve the Spanish empire from partition.

One month later Carlos died, leaving Louis with the choice of rejecting the will or of repudiating the partition treaty. The Dauphin, Torcy, Ponchartrain and the Duc de Beauvilliers were summoned to a historic meeting in Madame de Maintenon's rooms. Beauvilliers urged Louis to stand by the treaty: it was guaranteed by the governments of both England and the United Provinces, and it assured to France the permanent acquisition of Lorraine, Naples, Sicily and the Tuscan ports. The will was defended by Torcy and Ponchartrain, for if Philip refused his inheritance the Spaniards would offer the empire to Archduke Charles; it was unlikely in such an event that William would be willing to join France in a war to enforce the treaty; moreover, though Philip's accession offered France no territorial gains, there were many commercial and strategic advantages to be derived from it. In short, since Leopold would certainly contest both the will and the treaty, Louis should fight for the greater gains offered by the will. To this argument both the Dauphin and Madame de Maintenon assented, and Louis informed the Spanish ambassador that he might acknowledge Philip as his new king. The decision was undoubtedly correct, since the treaty had already been rendered worthless by Leopold's refusal to sign it.

William expressed his anger in a letter to Heinsius, the Grand Pensionary of Holland: 'I never relied much on engagements with France but I must confess I did not think they would on this occasion have broken in the face of the whole world a solemn treaty before it was well accomplished;' but he was also compelled to admit 'I am troubled to find that nearly everybody prefers the will to the treaty.' His Parliament was indeed already pursuing the impeachment of those who had negotiated the partition treaty, and though Leopold had launched a campaign in north Italy on behalf of Charles, the neutrality of both England and the United Provinces seemed assured. There were only two things to guard against, as Louis was warned by his ambassador in London: 'Your Majesty cannot take too great pains to exhort the Spaniards not to make any changes in their commercial relations with England and Holland, nor to behave too circumspectly with regard to the security of the Low Countries.'

At this crisis of his reign, when the prize he had sought for forty years was in his hands, Louis lost his nerve. His anxious seeking out of William's support for the partition treaties had already revealed his fear that Europe would never permit the accession of Philip of Anjou. Having then chosen to accept the will he yet betrayed his irresolution by a tragic series of miscalculations and blunders which brought upon him exactly that hostile coalition of Europe he had striven to avoid.

In February 1701 he reaffirmed Philip's rights of inheritance as third in line to the French throne, an unnecessary act which foolishly drew attention to the close links binding the French and Spanish crowns. In the same month he sent French troops into the Spanish Netherlands in order to seize the barrier fortresses held there by the Dutch. Since the States-General had not yet recognised Philip as King of Spain there was some justification for Louis's action, but the cavalier use of French troops in a matter relating to Spanish territory provoked a universal suspicion that Louis, not Philip, was to be the arbiter of Spain's fortunes. In

August he secured from Philip the right for French companies to trade in the Spanish colonial empire. If this was intended to coerce the English then Louis had badly miscalculated: from this moment William was assured of support from the powerful merchant houses of London and Amsterdam. When news came that Eugène had driven the French and Spanish troops from Lombardy, the English and Dutch governments were emboldened to ally with Leopold in the second Grand Alliance of The Hague (September, 1701).

The allies agreed that none of them should make a separate peace with Louis; the French and Spanish thrones were to be kept separate; French trade in the Spanish empire was to be forbidden; Leopold was to acquire Italy and the Netherlands; the English and Dutch were to seize what territory they could in the West Indies and America. Significantly, no mention was made of Spain herself, though Leopold's determination to place his son in Madrid was understood if not acknowledged. The maritime powers in fact were concerned to fight only for commercial advantage, leaving Leopold to pursue his dynastic ambitions as best he could. With the allies so divided in their aims, Louis might still have won the neutrality of England and the United Provinces by repudiating his actions of the past months. Instead, he committed his most disastrous indiscretion: on the death of James II he recognised James's son as James III of England. No doubt he was concerned to safeguard James's position as much at Versailles as in London, since an unrecognised pretender had few claims to precedence in the rigid hierarchy of court life. Moreover, William was dying and the possibility of a Stuart restoration could not at least be ignored. Yet in England, Louis's action was regarded as a flagrant violation of the Treaty of Ryswick, and for Englishmen the War of Spanish Succession became a war to protect the Protestant succession at home. William, in his last months, recaptured the wholehearted support of his subjects for the first time since his arrival among them in 1688, and his death in March 1702 did nothing to prevent a declaration of war on France.

The War of the Spanish Succession, 1702–14

In 1702 France possessed none of the advantages she had enjoyed at the outset of her previous wars. Of her allies, Portugal and Savoy were on the brink of defecting to the Grand Alliance, and Philip V ruled a kingdom which had proved so incompetent in defending its territories that it was more of an incubus than an ally. Louis's sole diplomatic triumph was an alliance with Maximilian of Bavaria and his brother the Archbishop of Cologne, whose appointment Louis had contested in 1688: in return for their support, Maximilian was to receive the Spanish Netherlands of which he had been governor since 1695. As a result, Louis secured a useful foothold across the Rhine, and the compact *bloc* of Spain, France and Bavaria gave him the advantage of interior lines of communication. In every other respect, naval, military and financial, France was inferior to the combined strength of the Grand Alliance. Against her were ranged the maritime powers of England and the United Provinces; the Elector of Brandenburg, who hoped to secure the title of king in Prussia by loyal service to the emperor; Leopold himself, his Danubian provinces secured from Turkish attack; the Elector of Hanover, an experienced imperial general whom the English had named heir presumptive to Queen Anne; the king of Denmark; and almost all the minor German princes. In all, the Grand Alliance could muster more than 200,000 men, several thousand more than the French, while in Marlborough and Eugène it possessed two generals who were to prove their outstanding brilliance. Marlborough too was an astute diplomat who well understood the petty jealousies which continually threatened to disrupt the Grand Alliance, and whose winter visits to the allied capitals did as much to hold the allies together as his summer campaigns against the French. At sea the fleets of England and Holland were supreme, and the wealth they derived from commerce ensured the financial stability of the alliance. France, in contrast, was virtually bankrupt.

Despite their advantages, the allies achieved little success in 1702, and it was the French who seized the initiative in the Netherlands. Advancing through Liège and Cleves, their plan of campaign so closely resembled that of 1672 that the Dutch were thrown into a panic, until Marlborough adroitly halted the invading force by a swift attack on its lines of communication in Liège. His action revealed his revolt from the static pattern of limited marches and perpetual sieges which Vauban had imposed upon his age. He sought to meet the enemy in the open, to ignore the scattered garrisons beleaguered within their own earthworks, and to deliver a series of penetrating thrusts into the heart of France.

His very training of the infantry indicated the adventurous role he had evolved for them. Equipped with the new flintlock and the ring bayonet, they were no longer condemned to huddle in defensive postures, repriming their clumsy matchlocks while the pikemen protected them from marauding horse, but were trained to advance in the open as aggressively as the cavalry. As soon as it was clear that the French invasion of the Netherlands had failed, and their army was withdrawing in confusion, Marlborough planned to exploit his advantage by invading France up the Moselle valley: unfortunately the Dutch field-deputies who accompanied him were slow to abandon their traditional outlook on war and could only think in terms of defence. The opportunity to catch the French at a disadvantage was thus forgone, and it was many years before the allies were again in so favourable a position for striking at Paris.

Elsewhere in 1702 the French held their own. In Italy, where fighting had begun in the previous year, Eugène captured Marshal Villeroi, whose failure to halt the Imperial advance caused the French to celebrate his loss as a victory, but he was unable to drive Vendôme from the Alpine passes of Piedmont. The support of Bavaria made it easy for Louis to repel attacks in the Rhineland, and the only dramatic gain for the allies was the destruction of a Spanish fleet in Vigo Bay.[1]

Secure in their control of the Atlantic, the English were badly in need of a naval base in the Mediterranean, and planned to seize Toulon. The French were already weakened in that area by the revolt of the Camisards,[2] and when Victor Amadeus had been persuaded to join the Grand Alliance in 1703 and to allow the Imperialists to march through Savoy, the project seemed feasible. In the event Leopold was too suspicious of Victor Amadeus's ambitions in north Italy to co-operate satisfactorily with him, and an Anglo-Dutch fleet bombarded Toulon to no effect. Of greater importance was the Methuen Treaty with Portugal in the same year, by which the harbour at Lisbon was opened to the allies. In return, England and the United Provinces undertook not only to expel Philip from Spain and to install Archduke Charles in his place, but also to pay and equip half the Portuguese army. The English and Dutch were therefore pledged to assist Charles in Spain, a point which had been avoided during the formation of the

[1] See Chapter V, page 232.   [2] See Chapter VI, page 282.

Grand Alliance, but England at least had no immediate cause for worry since the military treaty was followed by a commercial one, granting her valuable concessions in the export of wool to Portugal. The Dutch on the other hand gained nothing: moreover, they had further cause to be restive since, by agreeing to England's policy of prohibiting all trade with France, they were causing themselves a great deal of hardship. England, it seemed to them, was becoming far more dangerous as their ally than as their enemy. Not surprisingly their field deputies forestalled Marlborough's plan to seize Ostend: caring nothing for its strategic value, they knew only too well that with such a base in his hands Marlborough would equip his army direct from England instead of via the Dutch ports. In any case, the field deputies still distrusted Marlborough's plans of invading France, although one of them made an astonishingly handsome confession of his own faults in the campaign of 1702: its success was, 'solely due to this incomparable chief, since I confess that serving as second in command I opposed all his opinions and proposals'. His colleagues remained obdurate, and throughout 1703 Marlborough's only conquests were Bonn and Spanish Gelderland.

If anything the advantage in 1703 lay with France. Not only did the allies fail to cross her frontiers but she herself launched a new offensive in Germany, using Bavaria as a base from which to advance down the Danube. Eugène was held in north Italy; Hungary rose in revolt; Regensburg fell to Villars and the Elector of Bavaria, and the way was open to Vienna. The Elector, however, was more interested in the future of Milan, and wasted five months in an unsuccessful attempt to secure control of the Tyrolean passes. Villars, denied the opportunity of acting independently of his wayward ally, could only await his pleasure, occupying himself meanwhile in keeping the Imperialists at bay and in the taking of Augsburg. When, in September, the Elector returned, Villars urged upon him that there was yet time to take Vienna. The Elector demurred, and a violent quarrel between the two commanders led to Villars's recall in disgrace. In this manner France lost not only one of her best generals, but also her best opportunity of ending the war.

During the winter Eugène was recalled to Vienna where he turned the general panic to good account by making himself president of the council of war. He was desperately short of men with

MAP 12 Marlborough's Danube Campaign, 1704

which to face both the Hungarians and the French in the campaigns
of 1704, and appealed to his allies for aid. Though it was no new
thing for the Imperialists to operate several hundred miles from
their base, the English and Dutch governments had no experience
at all of campaigning in central Europe, and the prospect appalled
them. Nevertheless, to his great credit, Heinsius, Grand Pensionary of Holland, comprehended the danger of the situation and
persuaded a reluctant States-General to allow Marlborough to
leave the Netherlands in a bold but dangerous venture to save
Vienna. How he was to do this no one knew: Marsin, Villars's
successor, had already joined forces with the Bavarians, and while
Tallard protected his lines of communication across the Rhine,
Villeroi stood guard against Marlborough in the Netherlands.

In the event Marlborough deceived both friend and foe by one
of the most brilliantly planned marches in history. Leaving Jülich
in May 1704, he advanced up river along the west bank of the
Rhine, and tricked Villeroi into anticipating an attack from
Coblenz up the Moselle valley. Villeroi in consequence was

mystified on learning that Marlborough, far from leaving the Rhine at Coblenz, had merely crossed over to the farther bank, there to continue his march up river. Suspecting a ruse, Villeroi dared not abandon his position in the Moselle, and Marlborough made his way safely to Mainz. His appearance there brought Tallard back from Bavaria to the French side of the Rhine in order to cover Alsace, which allowed Marlborough to slip away to the south-east, across the Main, up the Neckar and over to the Danube, arriving at Donauwörth by the end of June. He had completed what was virtually a flank movement across the enemy front; it was a fine example of what was considered one of the most impudent manœuvres in warfare. As a piece of reckless improvisation, its success would have been startling, but, astonishingly, every detail had been deliberately planned in advance, from the timing of the marches to the supply of new boots for the army at Mainz from barges which had followed Marlborough up the Rhine. The march alone, however, could not save Vienna: Tallard and Villeroi were swiftly converging on Marsin's forces, and the combined skills of Eugène and Marlborough would be taxed to the utmost if Bavaria was to be seized from the French.

The issue was decided when Marlborough and Eugène took the enemy by surprise as they were breaking camp on the morning of August 17th. Marsin, Tallard and the Elector had the advantage of numbers and of position, but the determined attacks by Eugène on their left flank, and by the English guards on their right at Blenheim, succeeded in containing forces which outnumbered their own, and prevented the French from shortening their front. Marlborough was thus assured of local supremacy in the centre, where he launched a series of attacks in which the infantry, true to his training, ran into battle behind the cavalry to take advantage of the breaches made in the enemy line. Marsin and the Bavarians were driven off into the hills, and Tallard was taken prisoner in Blenheim. As a result of this, the most crucial engagement of the war, Vienna was saved, Bavaria occupied and the legend of French invincibility destroyed. Elsewhere the allies were only moderately successful in 1704: Rooke beat the French fleet off Malaga, and captured Gibraltar and Minorca, but the attempt to land Archduke Charles in Catalonia was repulsed.[1]

In 1705 a second attempt was made to establish Charles in

[1] See Chapter V, page 233.

Catalonia, but its success was overshadowed by Marlborough's failure to invade France in that year. France appeared to be secure behind her frontiers, and the allies were faced with the prospect of a long conflict against the loyal population of Castile. Moreover, the Emperor Leopold had died and his successor Joseph showed more interest in his Danubian territories than in his brother's ambitions in Spain. Marlborough sensed a weakening of purpose within the Grand Alliance and resolved in 1706 to restore its morale by a second great victory. Louis too wanted a victory to strengthen his hand before negotiating for peace, and sent Villeroi to meet Marlborough with the troops of the *Maison du Roi*, the cream of the French army. The armies met at Ramillies. A vigorous attack on Villeroi's left wing succeeded in drawing his reserves from the centre, at which Marlborough withdrew half his attacking force behind the cover of a ridge of high land and sent it, without Villeroi's knowledge, to strengthen his other wing, an example not only of tactical skill but also of perfect timing and control. The allied left, thus reinforced, outflanked the French and drove them from the field. The towns of the Spanish Netherlands, in revulsion against the warfare which ravaged their territories, declared for Archduke Charles, and the allies gained immediate control of Brussels, Antwerp, Ghent and Bruges. Meanwhile, the year of victory was crowned by Eugène's swift campaign in north Italy. Although the emperor refused to withdraw troops from Hungary, Marlborough persuaded the German princes to send contingents to Eugène's support, and his victory at Turin not only saved Savoy from occupation by the French, but ensured allied control of the Alpine passes.

Blenheim, Ramillies and Turin loosened the French hold in Germany, the Netherlands and north Italy: it was less easy to penetrate the frontiers of France herself. After a year of fruitless campaigning (1707), Marlborough defeated the French again, at Oudenarde in 1708, but his subsequent capture of Lille, the first French city to fall to the allies, was achieved only at a cost in casualties five times greater than those at Oudenarde. Louis judged the moment ripe to appeal for peace. He had every reason to believe that France could no longer sustain the burden of war, and he tried desperately to conciliate the allies: England was to have Newfoundland and his guarantee of the Protestant Succession; the Dutch were to acquire a formidable range of barrier fortresses in the Netherlands; the emperor was to have Strassburg; Charles was to inherit Spain and Philip would be denied French support. The allies, however, replied by raising their terms too high. They had suffered too much from Louis's aggression in the past to believe in his good intentions in 1709 and interpreted his offer as a diplomatic trick to split the Grand Alliance.[1] Marlborough too led the allies to believe that in one more campaign they would enter Paris in triumph. Consequently they demanded of Louis that he join them in expelling Philip from Spain, a demand which he rejected with dignity, 'While I have to make war,' he said, 'I prefer to fight my enemies than my grandson.'

To his own people Louis made a spirited appeal against the conduct of the allies: 'Though I love my people as much as I love my own children; though I share in all the evils which the war has brought upon my faithful subjects; though I have shown how sincerely I desire to give them the blessings of peace; I am persuaded that they themselves would refuse the terms which are offered, as contrary to justice and dishonourable to the French name.' Short of repudiating Louis altogether, the French had no alternative but to stand by him in the defence of their country; and in the event their resistance was to bear fruit. Marlborough, in pursuit of his promised victory, invaded France in 1709, to be met at Malplaquet by Villars with an army mainly composed of recruits. Although the French were driven from the field, the allied losses exceeded those of the French, who, moreover, retired in sufficiently good order to re-group between Marlborough and Paris. Meanwhile, in Spain, Philip's army had defeated the allies at Almanza in 1707. The allies, though they did not yet fully realise it, had shot their bolt. The English Tories, who shared none of the Whig determination to establish a weak naval power like Austria in control of Spanish commerce, repudiated the cry of, 'No peace without Spain,' and came to power in the general election of 1710. Their hostility to Charles's candidature was reinforced in 1711 by the death from smallpox of the Emperor Joseph and the accession of Charles to the Austrian and imperial thrones. There was no good reason to prolong the war in order to secure for him a third crown, especially as Philip had made himself master of all but Barcelona. Marlborough was recalled and disgraced: Ormonde, his

[1] See Chapter VIII, page 348 for the crisis which resulted in Anglo-Dutch relations.

successor, was ordered by an infamous memorandum to co-operate as much with the French as with Eugène, who was thus exposed to defeat at Denain in 1712.

From 1710 the movement of diplomats took precedence over the

MAP 13   French Territorial Expansion, 1643–1715

march of armies; and the allies, encouraged by England's example, betrayed each other's interests in order to secure their own. Their confusion of purpose resulted in a series of treaties, negotiated at different places, at different times and between different parties, and not infrequently between the allies themselves; however the main clauses were finally ratified at Utrecht in 1713 and at Rastadt in 1714.

(i) Philip V, confirmed in Spain, renounced his claim to the French throne and ceded the Netherlands, Lombardy, Naples and Sardinia to the Emperor Charles.

(ii) England acquired Gibraltar and Minorca from Spain, along with the right to import negro slaves into the American colonies; from France she gained Newfoundland, Hudson Bay, St. Kitts and recognition of the Hanoverian Succession.

(iii) The Elector of Bavaria was reinstated in his territories.

(iv) The Elector of Brandenburg, already rewarded by the emperor with the title of king in Prussia, acquired Spanish Gelderland.

(v) Victor Amadeus of Savoy recovered Nice and acquired Sicily — subsequently to be exchanged with Charles for Sardinia.

(vi) Louis XIV ceded his conquests along the east bank of the Rhine, but was confirmed in his control of Alsace, Franche Comté and the Flanders line of 1679.

(vii) The Dutch secured a new barrier treaty from the emperor, and control of the mouth of the Scheldt.

Not one of Louis XIV's wars achieved the ends for which it was fought. Though Louis in 1714 secured terms far better than those denied him in 1709, this was small consolation for what might have been achieved in 1702. He had failed, not by attempting to fulfil great ambitions, but by an overbearing arrogance which had antagonised every vested interest in Europe. Had it not been for this basic weakness in his character, the dawn of the eighteenth century might have seen Europe under the domination of a Bourbon dynasty, secure in both France and Spain.

VIII

The Dutch Republic

The Eclipse of the House of Orange, 1648–51

Led by Andreas Bicker, Burgomaster of Amsterdam, the regents took advantage of Frederick Henry's death in 1647 to overrule the protests of his successor, William II, and make peace with Spain.[1] The conclusion of the Eighty Years War was undeniably in the best interests of the republic, but William knew that the regents would exploit the peace to destroy his position, and his only solution was to renew the war as soon as possible.

France was still at war with Spain, and William listened eagerly to Mazarin's proposals for an alliance. Moreover, the execution in 1649 of his father-in-law, Charles I, prompted him to consider an attack on the regicide government in England. Bicker, however, countered his aims by calling for a reduction by two-thirds in military expenditure. It was an astute move since it attacked William at his most vulnerable point by appealing to the thrifty nature of the Dutch taxpayers, who were already perturbed by the growth of the public debt and who could easily be persuaded that the cost of maintaining a standing army in peace-time imposed unnecessary strains upon the economy. 'There is no need to have a garrison in every town', wrote one pamphleteer, 'to pay salaries to military governors, colonels and innumerable other officers; it is unnecessary that the military should go about in clothes plastered with gold and silver while the common people have to eat dry bread.'

William retaliated by undertaking a tour of the chief cities of Holland, accompanied by over four hundred troops, in an attempt to intimidate the town councils into withdrawing their support for Bicker's proposals. His action deliberately paralleled that of

---

[1] See Chapter IV, page 196, for fuller details both of the political situation in the Dutch Republic and of the conclusion of the war with Spain in 1648.

Maurice in 1618,[1] but history did not repeat itself. The public was weary of war, and there were few outside the prince's entourage who stood to gain by its renewal; nor was there any religious controversy in 1649 to cloud the issue and inflame the passions. William was coldly received: a few of his more outspoken opponents were removed from office as a result of his visitation, but the demands for a reduction in military expenditure were not withdrawn. The tour ended in humiliation at Amsterdam, where Bicker closed the gates and denied William access to the city. To add to William's discomfiture the regents followed up their efforts to diminish his military power by attacking his constitutional authority to determine the republic's policies. The stadtholder — and William held this office in six of the seven provinces — was in their view nothing more than the servant of the estates whose commission he held. A Dordrecht member went further and declared in the Estates: 'In peace, at any rate, there is no need for a stadtholder.'

Since the threat of force had failed to have effect, William resorted to active violence by imprisoning at Loevestein six prominent members of the Holland Estates, and by ordering his nephew, the Stadtholder of Friesland, to seize Amsterdam by a surprise attack. For reasons which have never been explained his nephew's troops lost their way as they crossed the Hilversum Heath by night. In the early hours of the morning the driver of the Hamburg post coach came across them jostling about in confusion in a wood, and arrived in Amsterdam in time to give warning of their approach. On their arrival they found the drawbridges up and the walls manned by the civic guard. Opposed as the regents were to William's policies, however, they were not prepared to follow Bicker into a civil war with the prince, and negotiations were begun to secure a peaceful settlement. In August 1650 William released his prisoners from Loevestein, Bicker resigned his office in Amsterdam, and the Holland Estates agreed to modify their proposals for reducing the army.

William had won a respite if not a victory, but in November his efforts were dramatically nullified by his sudden death from smallpox. Though his widow was pregnant, there was no immediate heir to succeed to those offices reserved to the Orange family by the Act of Survivance,[2] and the the regents celebrated their good

[1] See Chapter IV, page 190.   [2] See Chapter IV, page 195.

fortune by striking a medal inscribed: 'The last hour of the prince is the beginning of freedom.' At the Great Assembly of 1651 they confirmed their control of the republic: William's activities of the past two years were condemned, the regents deposed by him were restored to office, and, on the advice of a member who said, 'Let us not be so foolish as to hurt ourselves twice on the same stone', the post of captain-general was abolished. Furthermore, since the House of Orange had imposed its leadership by controlling the federal institutions of the Union of Utrecht, the regents affirmed that sovereignty resided with each individual province.

Jan de Witt and The True Interests of Holland

The principle of states sovereignty was a useful device to forestall any resumption of power by the House of Orange, but the necessity for securing the unanimous assent of seven sovereign states to each decision of the States-General would have led to anarchy had not the regent class of Holland succeeded in imposing their own direction over the republic's affairs; this they did by virtue of the commanding position enjoyed by Holland as the chief contributor to federal funds, and by securing the appointment of their own leader, Jan de Witt, as head of the federal administration.

Jan de Witt was an outstanding example of the best type of regent, devoted to the interests of his country and tireless in its service. His high forehead and long face, its length accentuated by the downward thrust of a powerful nose and chin, made him seem both restless and ascetic in comparison with the cheerfully complacent appearance of his fellow citizens. A man of simple tastes, he sought no private fortune from his public service, and foreigners were astonished to see him walking home through the streets of The Hague accompanied only by a servant carrying state papers in a cloth bag. The state papers, indeed, were never far from his thoughts. At 8 a.m. he began the day by meeting the Standing Committee of the Holland Estates: from 9 to 11 he attended either the States-General or one of its committees, reporting back to another session of the Standing Committee before lunch. Throughout half the year his afternoons and evenings were occupied by the Holland Estates meeting in full session. In all these committees and assemblies de Witt was the presiding officer, preparing the agenda and reporting the debate, and when all was done it was his responsibility to administer the policies which had been agreed upon. This last task alone imposed upon him the burden of a vast correspondence with local officials and foreign agents, his tireless industry being reflected in the official registers of correspondence where the number of entries during his term of office was four times greater than in any other equivalent period.

A superb civil servant, de Witt was also a skilled politician who directed the republic's affairs from the obscurity of a committee room by means of family connections and personal influence. He belonged by birth to the exclusive oligarchy of the regent class: his grandfather had represented Holland in the States-General; his father had served as pensionary of Dordrecht, and his fame as one of the Loevestein prisoners had eased the son's rise to power. In 1650, at the age of twenty-five, Jan de Witt was appointed pensionary of Dordrecht, and within three years had become grand pensionary of Holland. Subsequently, by his marriage to Wendela Bicker, he became associated with her uncles, Cornelis Bicker and Cornelis de Graeff, both prisoners with his father at Loevestein, who controlled the city council of Amsterdam. Such family ties assured de Witt of supremacy in Holland, but the regents of the other states, jealous of the sovereign powers assured to them by the Great Assembly of 1651, were as suspicious of the leadership of Holland as they had been of the House of Orange. De Witt overcame this by persuading the States-General to delegate much of its work to committees endowed with plenary powers. In these, surrounded only by the seven representatives of the separate provinces, de Witt's personal influence was exerted at its greatest. He overawed his colleagues by his extensive knowledge of the issues which they debated, he flattered their sense of importance in being at the centre of affairs, he exploited by his brilliant chairmanship the ancient tradition of arriving at unanimous conclusions,[1] and, finally, when all else failed, he forced them to recognise that Holland's demands, backed by her financial contribution and her naval power, could not be resisted without dire consequences for the future of the Union as a whole. In the event, the republic, preserving the form of provincial separatism, was run as effectively as a centralised monarchy.

'Jan de Witt', wrote d'Estrades, the French ambassador, 'is the most important person in the whole state, through the power of

[1] See Chapter IV, pages 184–5.

Holland over the other provinces, and that which he possesses over the ten or twelve leaders of the governing party.' None the less, it was not an easy task to maintain his position. The Orange party was powerful in Overyssel and Zeeland, and in Holland itself there was jealous opposition from de Witt's fellow regents to the dominant influence of the 'Loevestein faction', the family compact of de Witts, de Graeffs and Bickers, whom they charged with exploiting the downfall of the House of Orange for their own advantage. De Witt survived because his services were indispensable to the republic, but there were to be occasions when even his personal influence was insufficient to overrule policies which he opposed.[1]

The charges of self-interest levied against the 'Loevestein faction' drew substance from the fact that de Witt tried to fill all positions of importance in the administration with his relatives and friends. This of course was true, but the sincerity of the charges could be discounted since they merely reflected the frustrated ambitions of men who themselves wanted to do the same thing. De Witt, moreover, sought power to benefit the republic as a whole, his policies being given public expression in 1661 by Pieter de la Court in *The True Interest of Holland*. Here, with the title displaying the author's naïve belief that what was good for Holland was good for the United Provinces, de la Court provided a sober account of the principles which underlay de Witt's administration.

Hostility to the House of Orange pervaded the book. Its members were accused of gambling with the republic's security in order to further their dynastic ambition, and, heedless of the benefits to be derived from commercial expansion, of seeking to perpetuate their military power by denying the fruits of peace to their subjects. William II's activities were singled out for special condemnation. The regents, who drew strength and comfort from the literature of republican Rome, were quick to see a parallel between their own experiences and those described by Tacitus under Caesar Augustus, who 'raised himself by degrees, grasping into his own hands the business of the senate, of the magistrates, and of the laws, while nobody dared to oppose him, for the stoutest were cut off either by being sent to the army or by proscription'. In contrast, de la Court claimed that the regents encouraged commercial prosperity

[1] See below, page 329, on the Act of Seclusion and page 340 on the Triple Alliance.

to everyone's advantage: 'The inhabitants under this free government hope by lawful means to acquire estates, to sit down peacably
and use their wealth as they please, without dreading that any
indigent or wasteful Prince or his courtiers and gentry, who are
generally as prodigal, necessitous and covetous as himself, should
on any pretence whatsoever seize on the wealth of the subject.'

In the years immediately following de Witt's rise to power there
was little to be feared from William's posthumous son, the future
William III, but in 1654 the Holland Estates debarred him by an
Act of Seclusion from succeeding to his father's appointments.
Though de Witt had not prompted the Act, which had been passed
more to appease Cromwell than to weaken the Orange family,[1] he
issued a *Declaration in justification of the Act of Seclusion*, which
rehearsed the main charges of the regents against the House of
Orange. To ensure that the point was well taken he also prepared a
more pithy version, the *Deduction*, for popular consumption. The
exclusion policy, however, had a fundamental weakness in that it
endangered the military defence of the republic. Though each
province controlled its own forces, confusion had been avoided in
the past by entrusting the separate provincial commands to a
single captain-general from the House of Orange. Since these
princes had subsequently exploited their military authority to
establish control over the provinces which had commissioned
them, the regents were resolved to prevent a recurrence of this.
'The sword of war in the hands of a captain-general is always
sharper and reaches further than the sword of justice in the hands
of political or civil rulers and judges', wrote de la Court. De Witt
stated the case even more succinctly in the *Deduction*: 'And have
we not seen with our own eyes that the late deceased captain-
general of the States endeavoured to surprise the capital and most
powerful city of the land [Amsterdam] with those very arms which
the States entrusted to him?'

Not only did the regents deny military employment to the
Orange family, they also destroyed the army's central organisation
for fear that the officers, who provided the main strength of the
Orange party, might use it as a cover for planning a *coup*. The
result was that seven different military organisations existed, each
under civilian control. Holland pretended that there was no need
for concern since the navy was run in the same way, and the

[1] See below, page 329.

strength of Dutch naval power was universally accepted; but since Holland's own fleet was virtually the republic's fleet also, the analogy broke down. In the event, the provinces, even those with the most to fear from land attacks, failed to maintain effective military establishments, with disastrous results in 1672.[1] *The True Interest of Holland* was for once at variance with the policies of the regents, and de Witt, as the one man most able to centralise the administration of the republic, deliberately did nothing to improve the organisation of the army. This, of course, stemmed from his belief that it would never be employed: France and the Rhineland princes were his allies and England was his sole enemy.

The Anglo-Dutch Wars

'There is more to be gotten by us in a time of peace and good trading', wrote de la Court, 'than by war and the ruin of trade'; but though the regents pursued a policy of peace typified by this attitude, de Witt came to power at a time when the Dutch were at war with England. Memories of the Amboina massacre and of Maerten Tromp's victory in the Downs[2] still rankled in England, conspicuous examples of a long-standing conflict in which the English claimed the sovereignty of the Narrow Seas and the right to free trade elsewhere, while the Dutch insisted on the doctrine of *mare liberum* in home waters and that of *mare clausum* throughout their commercial empire. The execution of Charles I had so shocked the Dutch that the murder of the Commonwealth's ambassador at The Hague by English exiles went uninvestigated, but it was the Commonwealth's Navigation Act of 1651 which finally brought about the war since it forbade the import of foreign goods unless carried in British ships or in those of the country of origin. This threatened the Dutch carrying trade so effectively that, as an act of defiance, the States-General sent Tromp to enforce Dutch freedom of navigation from Gibraltar to Denmark. When his fleet encountered an English force and refused to salute the flag, the war began.

The advantage lay with England. Between 1648 and 1651 the English had doubled the size of their fleet, whereas the Dutch had reduced theirs after making peace with Spain. Dutch shipping, moreover, had to run the gauntlet of English attacks in the Channel, or seek the stormy routes round Scotland and still risk an

[1] See below, page 342.   [2] See Chapter IV, pages 194–5.

encounter in the North Sea. Tromp hoped to keep the sea open for merchantmen by inflicting a series of crippling defeats on the English fleet, but, since neither Blake nor Monk would accept the challenge to a pitched battle, he failed to achieve his purpose and was replaced by Cornelis de Witt, the pensionary's brother. De Witt had proved his administrative ability in the Admiralty, but he was no naval captain as the seamen on both sides knew: with a mutinous fleet he was attacked and routed by Blake off the Kentish Knock in October 1652. The government hastily reinstated Tromp, who succeeded, since Blake's victory had made him over-bold, in engaging the enemy off Dungeness in December. Blake was defeated, and the victory not only restored Tromp's reputation but saved his son Cornelis from court martial for losing his own ship on service in the Mediterranean. Taking advantage of the Dutchman's celebration of St. Andrew's Eve, an English cutting out party from Leghorn had seized his ship, and Van Tromp had only avoided capture by diving from his cabin into the sea. However, escaping disciplinary action because of his father's victory, he then redeemed himself in the following March by a great victory at Leghorn which restored Dutch naval supremacy in the Mediterranean.

The set battles, for all their drama, had little effect on the most serious aspect of the war since, whether the Tromps won or lost, the lifeblood of the Dutch economy continued to be drained away by the daily loss of merchantmen. England was still primarily an agricultural country and could withstand the temporary dislocation of her foreign trade; not so the Dutch, who had everything to lose from warfare with a rival who could deny them access to the herring shoals and prohibit the passage of their transports through the Channel. Maerten Tromp tried to save the day by a system of convoys, but the intransigent independence and ill-discipline of the civilian captains made convoy duty a nightmare, and a fruitless one since, when Monk or Blake attacked, the merchants scattered in a disastrous attempt to save their own cargoes, and thus delivered themselves into the enemy's hands. At the end of February 1653 Tromp fought a magnificent rearguard action from Portland Bill to Calais Roads in an effort to safeguard a homeward bound convoy of 150 ships, but on the third day his formation was broken and the battle lost. In June he lost again, at the Battle of the Gabbard, when his own naval captains abandoned him, half of them taking refuge in the Texel, the rest in the Maas. Though

Monk pressed home his advantage by a blockade of the coast, Tromp ultimately succeeded in reuniting the two halves of his fleet, only to be defeated in August at Ter Heide where he himself was killed.

Such a succession of defeats brought discredit upon the new administration led by de Witt: 'Responsibility for the disasters', he wrote, 'is generally attributed to the bad conduct of affairs by the regents; certain men are fishing on the troubled waters and inspire the commonalty with the idea that an eminent chief is needed to save the country.' The only 'eminent chief' in 1653 was still a baby, but it was clearly unwise to allow the Orange party further opportunities of making capital out of the government's defeats, and as there was no chance of winning victories de Witt sensibly appealed to Cromwell for peace. Indeed, the threat of an Orange revolt alarmed Cromwell nearly as much as it did the regents since the restoration of the House of Orange would have provided Charles II with an excellent base and willing allies. By harping on this fact de Witt finally beat down Cromwell's more extreme demands; the English project for a union of the two states in preparation for a Protestant crusade was dropped, and in February 1654 de Witt secured terms which inflicted little lasting harm on the Dutch. By the Treaty of Westminster they agreed to recognise English sovereignty in the Narrow Seas, to pay for the privilege of fishing in English waters, to make compensation for the massacre at Amboina and to deny assistance to Charles II.

One further clause, known as the Act of Seclusion, to debar all members of the House of Orange from holding the office of stadtholder, was demanded by Cromwell as a further precaution against an Orange restoration. When de Witt convinced him that the clause would never secure the unanimous consent of the States-General, Cromwell agreed to withdraw it from the public treaty provided that de Witt secured its acceptance by the Holland Estates. This was finally done, unenthusiastically, and more as a means to end the war and return to trading than as a deliberate attack on the Orange party; but the States-General discovered the secret and ordered the Dutch agents in London to send back all secret documents in their possession for perusal. De Witt as pensionary was powerless to alter the decisions of the States-General, but, in passing on its orders in code, he sent a letter to the one agent he could trust, telling him to hand the secret papers to

Cromwell before the official instructions could be decoded. Once Cromwell had ratified the treaty the protests of the States-General were in vain, since none of the provinces was prepared to advocate a return to war.

The peace did not last long: as an English hemp merchant remarked to Samuel Pepys, secretary of the Admiralty: 'the trade of the world is too little for us two; therefore one must down'. When the Duke of York, allowing his interests as a director of the Royal Africa Company to prompt his action as Lord High Admiral, sent a naval force to drive the Dutch from Goree, de Witt swiftly despatched de Ruyter in pursuit. This encounter off the African coast was the occasion for the renewal of war in 1665.

This time the Dutch were in a better state of preparation. De Witt and his brother Cornelis had reorganised the Admiralty and strengthened the navy, and though English public opinion was jubilant at the news of war, Cornelis's opposite number, Pepys, confided his fears to his diary: 'We all seem to desire it [the war] as thinking ourselves to have advantages at present over them; for my part I dread it.' In fact the war began well for England. New Amsterdam fell,[1] the Bishop of Münster invaded Overyssel as Charles II's ally, and at Lowestoft in June 1665, the Dutch commander Opdam, having held the weather-gauge for two days to no advantage, lost it on the third, together with the battle, his flagship and his life. The survivors were rallied by Cornelis Van Tromp, who fought a skilful rearguard action to bring sixty sail back to the Texel. Despite his youth, the government rewarded him with the command of the fleet, but at this moment de Ruyter returned from his successful mission to Goree and superseded him. This caused much bitterness and resentment though the two served together well enough in the famous Four-Day Battle of June 1664. On this occasion the English, fearing that a French fleet was on its way to join the Dutch, attacked prematurely against superior numbers; even so, the Dutch victory was not easily come by. Van Tromp bore the brunt of the attack, moving his flag so frequently as one ship after another under his command was disabled that the English asked 'whether there were five or six van Tromps in the Holland fleet or no'. In addition, he won the unique honour of capturing an English admiral, Sir George Ayscue, in a battle at sea.

By 1667 the Dutch were confident of victory but de Witt desired

[1] See Chapter IV, page 206.

to end the war quickly to restore the flow of peace-time trade into Dutch harbours as well as to strengthen his position against Louis XIV, whose army had just invaded the Spanish Netherlands.[1] To do so he planned with de Ruyter one of the most daring and effective naval *coups* of European history. Since the English fleet was laid up at Chatham, because Charles II had no money to put it to sea, de Ruyter sailed up the Thames and the Medway to the dockyards, where he held his position for two days and nights, destroying much of the fleet and making off with its latest acquisition, the *Royal Charles*. The humiliating effect of the raid on a public demoralised by the great plague and the fire, and on a government already bankrupt, was wholly devastating. 'Thus in all things,' wrote Pepys, 'in wisdom, courage, force, knowledge of our own streams, and success, the Dutch have the best of us and do end the war with victory on their side.' In the Treaty of Breda, 1667, de Witt wisely refrained from provoking the English by imposing further humiliations, especially since he had an eye to an alliance with them against Louis XIV. He accepted the loss of New Amsterdam and the right of the English to a salute in the Channel; but in the important matter of the Navigation Act he won a vital modification by the recognition of Germany and the Spanish Netherlands as a sort of Dutch hinterland for the purpose of importing goods from there into England in Dutch ships.

Culture and Society in the Golden Age

The middle years of the seventeenth century constituted a golden age for the Dutch. As the tension of the war years was eased by victory the nation became a self-confident society in which commercial success induced a mood of mellow affluence, and even the social dictates of a narrow Calvinist creed could not prevent the cheerful enjoyment of material prosperity.

The freedom allowed to commercial activity brought other freedoms in its wake. The Dutch presses were notoriously prolific; there were forty in Amsterdam alone in 1664, and their freedom from government control was a great attraction to writers wishing to escape the censorship of their native country. Galileo, for example, could publish his study of mechanics only in Holland, and frequently the authors themselves followed their manuscripts. Descartes moved to Holland to publish his *Discours* and the

[1] See Chapter VII, page 288.

Meditationes, to be followed later by many fellow countrymen, including the Huguenots and the atheist *philosophe* Bayle. English victims of the political crises between 1640 and 1690 fled to Holland to await better times and it was fitting that John Locke should follow in their tracks to write his *Letter on Toleration* in the most tolerant society in Europe.

Refugees were welcomed for what they could contribute, but the Dutch were not dependent on the stimulus of foreign imports, least of all in the arts and sciences where they produced men of international repute. The microscope of Leeuwenhoek and the telescope of Lippershey led to some of the most important developments in seventeenth-century science, making possible the accurate calculations of men like Huygens, whose researches in astronomy and the study of light and motion ranked him with Galileo and Isaac Newton.[1] With the practical sense typical of his countrymen Huygens applied his inquiry into the calculus of probabilities to the study of annuities, and his results were used as the basis of de Witt's legislation on the matter. Simon Stevin, another great mathematician and the inventor of the decimal system, applied his talents to military engineering and book-keeping, assisting not only in the fortifications of the republic but in reforming the accounting system of the States-General. In the older disciplines of law and philosophy, the Dutch produced two men of outstanding merit; Grotius,[2] whose *De Belli et Pacis* proved to be one of the most influential studies of international law but whose political association with Oldenbarneveldt led to his own exile, and Spinoza, who rivalled the achievements of Descartes, Locke and Leibniz. The Dutch were less fortunate in literature since their authors were tied by their language to a public of less than three millions: whereas Spinoza and Grotius, writing in Latin, won international reputations, only the Dutch themselves could know of Jakob Cats, whose mastery of the language made him one of the most influential figures in Dutch literature until the twentieth century; of Hooft the lyric poet; of Joost van den Vondel, whose poetry immortalised the daily life of his society and expressed the excitement of a nation conscious of its expansion overseas.

The greatest outburst of creative activity was in the arts and in a

[1] See Chapter I, page 51.
[2] See Chapter I, pages 18–20 and 63–64 for reference to Grotius and to Spinoza.

manner which accurately reflected the nature of Dutch society.[1] There was little sculpture, save for a few statues of soldiers and sailors, since the Calvinist aversion to graven images had struck root in the national consciousness. It was also a characteristic of the Calvinist to be uneasily self-conscious, even afraid, of the human body with which sculpture is concerned; the more so since sculpture, unlike painting, is pre-eminently an art of the public place. So too is architecture, which gave the Dutch a concrete image of their own ideals. It was essentially domestic. Innate thrift, Calvinist reticence and the deliberate rejection of monarchy by the Dutch, made it inconceivable for the prosperous merchant to build himself a palace. Even the civic buildings, like the Mauritshuis at The Hague, and the castle at Amsterdam, where civic pride in any other country might well have found expression in a façade of Baroque magnificence, remained unpretentious but dignified, reflecting the solid, domestic character of the men who commissioned them.

It was above all in painting that the influence of the social environment was most apparent. The revolt had at one stroke removed the Catholic Church and the monarchy, the twin pillars of the artists' world: no longer able to make a living from aristocratic or clerical commissions, the artist had to paint for a very different market. The result, if initially disconcerting, was ultimately liberating, since the market he found was that same vigorous yet frugal, revolutionary yet respectable, middle-class community to which he too belonged. In working for his fellow citizens he was working for himself; he shared their limitations, he reflected their greatness. It was not a patrician aristocracy but an ever-growing body of merchants and farmers who thronged the markets to buy his works on a scale which took the foreigner by surprise: 'We arrived late at Rotterdam,' reported John Evelyn, the English diarist, 'where was their annual mart or fair, so furnished with pictures that I was amazed. . . . The reason of this store of pictures and their cheapness proceeds from their want of land to employ their stock, so that it is an ordinary thing to find a common farmer lay out two or three thousand pounds in this commodity. Their houses are full of them, and they vend them at their fairs to very

---

[1] The main concern here is to trace the relationship between Dutch art and Dutch society; see Chapter I, pages 81–107, for a more general survey of European art and architecture.

great gains.' But it was not a desire to invest mere surplus capital which prompted this unprecedented demand for pictures. It was an heroic age: no people could have been more self-consciously proud than the Dutch in their years of victory, or have taken more delight in their country and in themselves. Before their ardour cooled, before life was reduced once more to terms of profit and loss, they sought the artist to show them themselves, to immortalise the present. The great age of Holland thus found eternal expression in the great age of Dutch art.

Naturally the Dutch were practical and unsophisticated in their demands: they wanted a picture which would fit conveniently into their rooms; one which could easily be moved from room to room, from house to house, and as easily be sold again. Nor did they want to be perplexed. They wanted pictures which related to their own experience of life, with which they could feel at home. Having no knowledge of classical mythology and history, nor of the conventions of academic painting, they looked for something immediately comprehensible, a realist portrayal of familiar scenes, a mirror to life. It was not commercial cynicism which led the Dutch artists to satisfy these demands, since these demands were also their own. Their work displayed a genuine and serene contentment with the ordinary world about them, a world of grey seas and flat fields, of domestic virtues and solid respectability. Never was the sober spectacle of daily life so lovingly portrayed, nor such prosaic material illumined by such affection. In one respect only did the nature of the market, and the competition of several thousand painters, influence the work of individuals. Since it was intensely satisfying to the patrons of art to associate one artist with certain constant characteristics in his work, the artist himself, once established as a painter of landscapes or still life, was encouraged to specialise within that genre, to an unprecedented degree.[1]

'The result of these endless pursuits seemed a hitherto unknown revelation of microcosmic life in all its facets.'[2] What saved the Dutch from becoming trivial, or stultified by the narrow limits of

[1] Of the 3,000 known artists of seventeenth-century Holland, more than 600 are immediately recognisable by their characteristic treatment of a specialised genre.

[2] Professor R. Wittkower, p. 166, of the *New Cambridge Modern History* vol. V — see also, on the same page, a summary list of the varieties of genre painting.

their specialisation was their intense love for what they painted and their superb gift of observation. The mirror they held up to life was astonishingly accurate, too much so for adherents of the French School whose views eventually triumphed in Holland. Lairesse, in his *Art of Painting*, published in Amsterdam in 1707, wrote scornfully, 'These painters imitate life just as they see it', whereas in his view derived from France, nature should be painted, not as it ordinarily appears, 'but as it ought to be in its greatest perfection'. But the painters of the Golden Age were not so artless as Lairesse implied. No matter how realist his school, the visual impression the artist received of the world he wished to portray could never be wholly comprehensive. He had to select, and by selection he reveals his individual genius.

This is immediately apparent in the work of Frans Hals. Portrait painting was a popular field of specialisation since it was a source of great pride to the middle-class citizen to see himself immortalised on canvas, especially in the company of his fellow citizens. The artist was merely required to make an accurate representation of his patrons, each one paying according to his position in the group, so that the occasion might be suitably preserved for posterity. Thus, for the most part, the group portraits are as sober, patient and unspectacular as the men who commissioned them. Yet it was exactly in this prosaic work that Hals, and men like him, discovered opportunities to release the imaginative forces of their genius. Hals's greatest talent was to catch the fleeting expression of his sitters — the artless informality concealing the most skilfully contrived effects; and by his mastery of grouping and movement to give coherence to the crowded scenes of archers and musketeers whose intense pride in their achievements in the war with Spain was celebrated in a succession of convivial portraits. His first great success was such a portrait, *The Civic Guard at Haarlem*; in subsequent studies, however, the problem of transforming the solid groups of impassive faces into an exciting, satisfying whole began to tease his imagination so that finally the individual sitters were resolved into an organic unity by the invention of complex patterns of light and shadow. The result did not always please his patrons. Genius is not invariably recognised for what it is, its power to generalise can be disturbing, and the burghers were increasingly perplexed by the image which Hals offered them of themselves. In consequence they turned to other, lesser artists to satisfy their needs and Hals died comparatively poor.

Vermeer's genius, in contrast to Hals's, did not disturb but rather enhanced the expectations of the patron. The prosperous burgher was as eager to purchase paintings of his house, his rooms, his pots, pans and kitchen tables, as he was to secure a portrait of himself. These things were a source of pride, they evinced his attainment of comfortable prosperity, and above all they were an integral part of his life. Dutch standards were domestic; the Dutchman would not have recognised himself in any other setting. So too the miraculous cleanliness and tidiness which pervades these Dutch interiors were not the creation of the artists but accurate reflections of life itself. These houses were furnished as museums, indeed as temples since within these rooms were enshrined both the burgher's treasurers and his heart: consequently they were scrubbed and polished to such a degree that no one dared to live in them. 'Even the kitchen was too fine a place for daily use; food was cooked there once a week; on the other days it was heated up in the small oven in the recess behind the kitchen where the family dwelt throughout the winter. When better weather returned, the family went to live outside on the pavement.'[1] In painting interiors such as these Vermeer gave to domesticity a universal significance. Unlike Hals, who appears to be excited by his subject, he seems detached. His paintings are still-lifes with human beings: the cook, caught in the act of pouring milk into a bowl, the lady seated at the virginals, are at one with the objects around them, not in the sense that they are lifeless, but that life itself has been momentarily suspended to permit its meaning to be interpreted with loving precision.

Vermeer developed a technique of floating on the paint so that no trace of brushwork betrays his hand. The surface is translucent, suffused with light, and, indeed, the treatment of light is a common factor in all the genres of Dutch painting. Light radiates from velvet drapes and warm brick, it floods their interiors and permeates their landscapes. No part of Europe, save East Anglia, possesses so much sky as the low-lying Netherlands, and the Dutch were the first to discover the beauty and the variety of its moods. This gave their landscapes a freshness of observation whose power to charm and to astonish is universal. In the canvasses of Albert Cuyp the mood of perennial high summer, with contented cattle

[1] Dr. D. G. Renier, *The Dutch Nation*, p. 99.

browsing in lush grass, is imparted by a golden glow, an effect he learned from the Frenchman Claude. With Van Goyen the horizon is set low, the river estuaries and mud flats merge in a distant haze, there to blend with the watery skies. More sombre, more consciously dramatic, were the landscapes of Jacob Van Ruisdael: the light gleams across the desolate dunes as the sun breaks fitfully through the cloud; it falls upon a clustered copse, exposing the twisted gnarls, making the shadowy paths mysterious. Ruisdael's love of light and shadow, the poetry he discovered in evening skies, lone trees and castle walls, evoked a romanticism alien to his age and his work was only fully appreciated by later generations.

It is the paradox of genius, and perhaps its explanation, that for all its universality it yet epitomises its own immediate environment. Though the artist never loses his community of interest with his neighbours, he discovers realities of which these neighbours are indistinctly aware. No one was more Dutch than Rembrandt; where he excelled was in his power to take everything that was so patently Dutch and to give it universal significance. His first success was a group study in 1632 of the Amsterdam Guild of Surgeons, *The Anatomy Lesson of Dr. Tulp*, which was followed by a prosperous decade of fashionable portraiture. Like Hals, however, Rembrandt could not paint to a formula; what had once proved acceptable could not be mechanically repeated since his paintings were stepping stones in his continuous discovery of himself and of mankind. As this developed, the emotions which drove him became increasingly more powerful. In 1642 a company of local defence volunteers in Amsterdam commissioned a group portrait. The result, *The Company of Capt. Frans Banning Cocq*, better known as *The Night Watch*, was a work of tremendous tension and emotion. So overpowering is its effect that its modern custodians at the Ryksmuseum in Amsterdam found it too overwhelming when hanging in a small room and were compelled to set it apart on a separate wall in the largest hall of the gallery. The men who commissioned it were also disturbed since it showed them themselves in a relationship which they could not comprehend.

Commissions were less frequent after this, and until his death in 1669 Rembrandt became more or less dependent on his family. It was during these years, however, that he produced most of the work upon which his subsequent reputation rests, none more famous, and none more illustrative of his genius, than his studies of the life of Christ. In these the figures, the faces and the countryside are those he might have seen from his own doorstep, but their universal significance springs from the insight with which they are interpreted. No less vital a factor in the success of these studies was Rembrandt's integrity, a technical quality, a guarantee of craftsmanship as it were, and a moral sense which repudiated deception of any kind. No one has ever revealed himself with greater candour than did Rembrandt in the series of self-portraits which immortalise the separate moments of his life and which stand for all time among the most brilliant and most sensitive works of autobiography. Few have looked so directly and so honestly upon the figure of Christ. Baroque artists[1] presented a set of idealised concepts which had been adopted almost as the official iconography of the Counter-Reformation; Rubens's *Descent from the Cross* in Antwerp Cathedral expresses and enhances the divinity of Christ by the portrayal of His physical perfection. Rembrandt reflects the Calvinist spirit of the northern provinces by insisting upon making his personal comment. For the first time since Giotto the common humanity of Christ and His disciples is emphasised, as for example in the etchings of the Crucifixion where the mood is one of in-dividual human suffering. Sympathetic insight is thus matched with the uncompromising integrity of the Calvinist in a manner which is wholly Dutch.

THE RECESSION OF DUTCH POWER, 1667–1714

The Triple Alliance and its Aftermath

De Witt's achievement in bringing the second Anglo-Dutch war to a successful conclusion in 1667 had been only one of his many services in the conduct of the Republic's foreign policies. The imperialist ambitions of Charles X of Sweden[2] had been as dangerous to the Dutch as the commercial rivalry of the English, since they threatened the Dutch monopoly of Baltic trade, the mainstay of the economy. On Charles X's invasion of Poland in 1655 de Witt remained unmoved by the fate of inland cities such as Cracow and Warsaw, but when Swedish troops laid siege to

[1] See Chapter I, page 96, on Baroque art.
[2] See Chapter X, pages 395–7, for an account of Charles X's Baltic campaigns.

Danzig, a city significantly referred to by the Dutch as their 'breadbasket', he promptly despatched a squadron to its aid. His action served its purpose, though a more serious situation developed in 1659 when Charles inflicted a crippling defeat on the Danes and compelled them to deny passage through the Sound to ships of any country hostile to Sweden. When warfare broke out again between Charles and Denmark in 1660 de Witt persuaded Mazarin and Cromwell to join him in blockading the Sound, denying to either belligerent the opportunity of striking at the other, until a firm peace had been imposed. In this final settlement, the Peace of Oliva, de Witt ensured that the Dutch were confirmed in their freedom of access to the Baltic.

In order to discourage Portuguese attacks on the West India Company in South America,[1] de Witt ordered a blockade of the Portuguese coast in 1657, but as nothing could save the Dutch in Brazil from ultimate ruin, he wisely came to terms in 1661. Though the treaty put a formal end to the company's activity in South America, it none the less made provision for Dutch merchants to trade freely in Portuguese territories, an agreement which in the long run was more profitable to the Dutch.

Above all de Witt could rely on the friendship of Louis XIV, whose ambassador, d'Estrades, had orders to support the administration of the regents against the intrigues of the Orange party. Nevertheless, Louis's friendship could be embarrassing when it involved de Witt in his ambitions to seize possession of the Spanish Netherlands. *Gallicus amicus sed non vicinus* was no doubt a sound maxim for de Witt to adopt, but there was little he could do to apply it. He offered to accept French occupation of the southern provinces provided the northern ones were given independence, his especial purpose being to keep Antwerp away from the French lest they tried to revive its commercial power; but while his attentions were concentrated on the defeat of England in 1667 Louis invaded Brabant.[2] There was nothing for it but a rapid realignment of Dutch policy: if the French were to be halted before they reached the Dutch frontier, de Witt had to win the support of Sweden and England, the only powers strong enough to

---

[1] See Chapter IV, pages 203–4, for a description of the West India Company's activities in South America.

[2] See Chapter VII, pages 286–94, for a detailed account of Louis XIV's foreign policy as it affected the Dutch 1668–72.

make Dutch resistance effective. Spain, as de Witt remarked, was 'a broken reed', the Empire 'a skeleton, the parts of which are held together not by sinews but by iron wires without natural movement'; and though England and Sweden were recent enemies of the Dutch, de Witt secured their co-operation against France in the Triple Alliance of 1668. As a partial consequence of this, Louis transferred his attack from the Spanish Netherlands to Franche Comté, and in the same year, made peace at Aix-la-Chapelle, retaining only a few towns in the southern provinces.

For all its apparent success the Triple Alliance did not turn out as de Witt had wanted. His intention had been to confront Louis XIV with nothing more than the possibility of military opposition from England, Sweden and the Dutch Republic unless he moderated his claims upon the Spanish Netherlands. He had no thought of denying Louis the southern provinces nor of abandoning the French alliance for an English one: as he informed the English ambassador, 'the States-General would think it like to prove too sudden a change of all their interests, and that which would absolutely break them off from so constant a friend as France, to rely wholly upon so new and uncertain a friend as England had proved'. The frankness of his words revealed de Witt's honesty of purpose. He merely wanted an entente with both Sweden and England in order to strengthen his hand in discussions with Louis XIV. Only if Louis refused to compromise was de Witt prepared to consider the possibility of war. The English, however, from the start insisted on a formal alliance with secret clauses relating to the precise military action to be adopted if Louis were obdurate, and it was some indication of the limited powers of de Witt as pensionary that he was unable to prevent the States-General agreeing to the English proposals. The more he opposed the treaty the more the Orange party exploited the general alarm at French expansion to secure its ratification.

De Witt was not alone in suspecting Charles II's intentions: Pomponne, Louis's foreign secretary, also had his doubts. 'I shall not say what intentions motivated England on this occasion, nor whether, at the time when she appeared to enter more deeply into the sentiments of the States-General and to second more sincerely their ardour for the Triple Alliance, she had in mind vengeance upon them or upon France.' There is no doubt that Charles II was seeking not only to placate his Parliament and perhaps to compel

Louis to buy him out of the Triple Alliance, but also to embroil de Witt with Louis to the advantage of Charles's relatives, the House of Orange. It is significant that the secret clauses of the Alliance were discovered by French agents not at The Hague but in London, and it was this revelation which ruined Franco-Dutch relations. De Witt, in apologising to d'Estrades for his part in signing the Triple Alliance, had explained that his hand had been forced and that there was nothing in the treaty to give offence to Louis. His assurances were accepted until Louis discovered the full story, when, to Charles II's delight, the United Provinces, and de Witt in particular, became the principal object of Louis's hatred and indignation.

In these circumstances the celebrations marking the Peace of Aix-la-Chapelle rang hollow in de Witt's ears. His government commissioned a medal, 'After having made the laws secure, reformed religion, reconciled kings, maintained the freedom of the seas and established peace in Europe, the Council of the Netherlands has caused this medal to be struck.' It read ominously like an epitaph. From this moment, in fact, de Witt was engulfed by forces over which he had no control. He was reappointed as grand pensionary at twice his former salary but the bases of his power were weakening. Every time he made an appointment the disappointed candidates joined themselves to the increasing number of his enemies. In Groningen and Zeeland there was open hostility, and even in Amsterdam he could no longer secure the election of a friend as pensionary of the city. As the regent party lost its cohesion, the House of Orange grew in strength. Popular support for the young Prince William was becoming more apparent, and de Witt's device of treating the boy as a 'child of state', in order to supervise his education, only served to emphasise his special position. Though the Estates of Holland secured the acceptance of the other provinces to a Plan of Harmony to prevent a captain-general from holding administrative office, it was clear that agreements of this sort would have no effect if the public found it necessary to demand the strong government of a prince of Orange. The time was not long coming: in 1672 the French invaded the United Provinces.

The Revival of the House of Orange

Louis's act of vengeance had been well prepared. De Witt could not prevent the governments of England and Sweden selling out to France, and it was too late to organise an effective defence force after the years of provincial indifference and separatist control.[1] Not even a prince of Orange could save the Dutch at such short notice, and it was the French themselves, by their failure to make a swift thrust to Amsterdam, who gave William time in which to breach the dykes. Holland and Zeeland were thus safe for the time being, and William prepared to use the respite to reorganise the army for an attack on the invaders. De Witt, however, sued for peace. His offers of both territory and money met only with renewed claims, until finally Louis demanded the cession of all territory occupied by his army, the removal of all restrictions on French trade, and freedom for Catholics to hold office and worship freely in the United Provinces.

In Dutch history the year 1672 is referred to as *Drukjaar*, meaning not only 'year of stress' but also 'year of printing', since, in this crisis, the administration of the regents was subjected to an intense attack of broadsheets and pamphlets. De Witt was singled out for special abuse, and his opposition to the military clauses of the Triple Alliance, his willingness to negotiate with France, and his failure to secure terms were all cited against him as evidence of his treachery. In the Estates of both Holland and Zeeland the Orange party carried the day and conferred sovereign power on William III. The population, appalled by the success of French arms, demoralised by unscrupulous propaganda and perplexed by the swift change of government, began to panic. The respectable middle classes swelled the ranks of the wild mobs of the poor and the unemployed; on August 20th, 1672, one such mob, the Civic Guard of The Hague, tore to pieces in the street Jan de Witt and his brother Cornelis.

The shock of de Witt's murder steadied the Dutch. Nerved by the crisis and invigorated by the leadership of William III they rose to resist the French, whose army was held in check only by a few square miles of water.[2] Luck favoured them with a mild winter, but it was their own determination in the spring which led them to recover Naasden and to strike at the long lines of communication which supplied the invading army. Spain and the Empire, moreover, declared themselves their allies, Cologne was invaded by both Imperialist and Dutch forces, and, in the Grand Alliance of

[1] See above, page 326.   [2] See Chapter VII, page 295.

The Hague, William revealed his diplomatic skill as the architect of the first great European coalition against Louis XIV. As far as the war on land was concerned the Dutch were safe.

At sea the Dutch faced the English in their third encounter of the century. Charles II had returned to the haven of French subsidies in 1670, and from that moment the English had revived their traditional disputes with the Dutch. In March 1672 they attacked a convoy homeward bound from Smyrna: in June they joined the French in an attack upon the Dutch coast. Though both these ventures failed, the Dutch were none the less in great danger and William III's first act was to effect a reconciliation between Cornelis Van Tromp and de Ruyter, the one a zealous Orangist, the other a friend of de Witt, in order to restore unity to the fleet. In the event the two rivals combined to defeat the English in a series of naval battles in 1673. Accordingly, since Charles II was bankrupt and the English Parliament was alarmed by the consequences of his alliance with Catholic France, the Dutch secured peace in 1674, when the Treaty of Westminster virtually renewed the clauses decided at Breda in 1667.

William's refusal to seek English mediation, at the price of substantial commercial concessions and the loss of Walcheren, had confounded not only the anticipations of his uncle Charles II, who had eagerly desired his accession, but also the forebodings of the regents who had opposed it. They were not to know that at the moment of domestic triumph William had found another goal, the defeat of Louis XIV. To free his country from invasion was not enough: the invader himself and his allies must be crushed. This became the obsession of his life. Normal men could not have harboured so lasting a grudge; but nature had equipped William for single-mindedness, compensating for the deformed back, and for the body wracked by asthma, with an indomitable spirit which made him independent of the affection and support of others. Trained by the circumstances of his childhood to practise unnatural restraint, he remained ascetic and aloof, and in his unimaginative mind the simple concept of defeating Louis XIV became the all-consuming passion of his lifetime.

William's triumph at home, though accompanied by widespread rioting against the regents, did not result in victory for the lower classes who had traditionally identified their cause with that of the

House of Orange. Many of William's appointments among the new pensionaries and civic officials were merely regents who had been dismissed or excluded by de Witt, and many more were de Witt's own supporters who had hastened to acclaim William. Typical of these was Caspar Fagel, the new grand pensionary, an able diplomat who had served de Witt well until 1672, when he went over to William, believing that only the prince could save the regents from the lower classes, and all of them from the French. William tacitly accepted the bargain. Throughout both Holland and Zeeland his sovereign authority was proclaimed, and subsequently enforced to restore the regents to their monopoly of power in cities like Haarlem and Rotterdam where, in the excitement of the *Drukjaar*, other classes had taken control. The Calvinist congregations, the lesser merchants, the farmers and the artisans, who had imagined William to be their leader in a far-reaching social revolution, were abandoned for the class which had sought to exclude him from power. The decision was not a difficult one to make. The traditional antagonism of the regents and the House of Orange was being resolved in a new synthesis in which both sides at last recognised a cardinal principle of their conflict that whichever won or lost, no third party was to benefit.

William in fact acted as de Witt had done. Using his powers of patronage to fill key positions in the government, in the East India Company and in the consistories of the Church, he built up a powerful following in Holland, and, in the States-General, where de Witt had exploited Holland's overwhelming wealth, William exploited the jealousy aroused by this wealth among the other provinces. When the French began to withdraw from Utrecht, Gelderland and Overyssel, the two maritime provinces, Holland and Zeeland, attempted to secure their readmission to the Union as subordinate members only. William's intervention not only forestalled their design but secured the loyalty of the regent administrations in the liberated provinces. Unlike de Witt, William could always fall back on force, though, as his father had experienced,[1] it was a double-edged weapon and he avoided its use. Far more radical, however, as a move to end for ever the internal conflicts of the republic, was his attempt in 1675 to secure recognition of his house as the royal family of the Netherlands. It came about when the Estates of Gelderland offered him the title of

[1] See above, page 322.

duke: this created a paradox in that William as the commissioned servant of the United Provinces was to become hereditary sovereign of one of them. The solution which William desired was for all the others to follow suit; accordingly he sounded the opinion of the provinces as to whether or not he should accept Gelderland's offer. The crucial decision lay with Holland. The nobility cast their vote in the Estates in favour, together with Dordrecht and four other towns; Rotterdam, however, and three other towns gave only reluctant approval, and the remaining eight were either opposed or observed a studied neutrality. William accepted the mixed verdict as a defeat. It was clear that the Dutch, while accepting him as stadtholder of the separate provinces and as captain-general of them all, would never receive him as their monarch.

William III and Louis XIV, 1678-1714

The limitations of William's position were revealed most clearly in 1678. Once the French had ceased to menace Dutch territory, and the burden of the war had passed to the republic's allies, the regents decided to make peace in order to restore the full flow of trade through their ports. William opposed the suspension of warfare, inspired as much by his consuming determination to defeat Louis XIV as by fears that his authority might subsequently be reduced. He failed to halt the negotiations, however, and not even a last-minute attack on Mons when the French were off their guard believing the war to be over, stopped the Peace of Nijmegen, which represented a real victory for the regents whom he had saved.

The merging of interests between himself and the regents was none the less too valuable to both sides to be permanently disrupted by conflict over the peace treaty, and the following years were marked by the close co-operation which developed between the prince and the grand pensionary. Fagel stood by him in 1684 when the city of Amsterdam threatened to withhold supplies if William joined the Spaniards against Louis XIV, and, though neutrality was preserved, informed opinion among the regents began to accept the fact that William's belligerent attitude towards France was justified. Anthony Heinsius, a former opponent of William who succeeded Fagel in 1689, became a convert to this view when he was sent on a mission to Versailles in 1683. There he was struck by the arrogance of Louis's ambitions and from that moment became one of William's most fervent supporters.

It was this close understanding which had grown up between the prince and the regents that made possible William's invasion of England in 1688. His wife, James II's elder daughter, was heir-apparent to the throne, and her staunch protestantism had already encouraged many an Englishman to suggest her immediate accession backed by William's army. Though the acquisition of England as a second base from which to prosecute his crusade against Louis XIV was an attraction of prime importance, William made no move until he had received firm assurances of English support. That the Catholic policies of James II were unpopular was obvious to everyone; that the people would rise against them was uncertain, and, unlike the ill-fated Monmouth, who had landed in 1685 to be welcomed only by peasants, William was not to be lured into action by vague promises. In June 1688 he received as specific a guarantee of support as any invader could require, signed by seven of the most influential politicians in the land: 'If the circumstances stand so with your Highness that you believe you can get here time enough, in a condition to give assistance this year sufficient for a relief under the circumstances which have been represented, we, who subscribe this, will not fail to attend your Highness upon your landing.'

William began immediately to raise German troops for the invasion force, and, when their presence in Holland could no longer be concealed, took the Estates into his confidence. The *réunions* of Louis XIV and his revocation of the Edict of Nantes gave point to William's argument that France was daily becoming more dangerous, and though the States-General feared for the future if William were to rule in London it ultimately agreed to take into public service the troops which William had privately raised. The last restraint was the fear that once William was at sea the French might invade, and this was removed in September 1688 when Louis attacked the Palatinate.[1] Straightway an unwieldy fleet of 200 transports, protected by 49 warships, exposed itself to the hazards of the Channel. Vulnerable though it was, it was swept on its way by a 'Protestant' wind, a steady north-easterly which penned the English navy in the Thames while sweeping the Dutch triumphantly round to Torbay. William was joined there by all who had invited him, the royal army deserted piecemeal as he

[1] See Chapter VII, pages 302–6, for an account of this, and of the war of the League of Augsburg which followed.

advanced upon it, James II fled to France, and on December 25th William entered London without having fired a shot.

The Revolution Settlement which followed, vital though it was to the English, was only one side of the bargain so far as William was concerned. He had not risked everything in a dangerous venture merely to bring constitutional monarchy to England, and though the English protested at what they termed 'Dutch William's War', they were compelled to fight alongside the Dutch in the War of the League of Augsburg. The Dutch for their part shared William's hostility to Louis and supported him loyally but, wiser than him in this respect, they were prepared to settle for a secure frontier instead of outright victory. The quest for a barrier against French expansion was to dominate their foreign policy for nearly a generation, and the Peace of Ryswick (1697) took them one step towards its attainment by granting them the right to post garrisons in the Spanish Netherlands, at Ypres, Namur and Menin.

William's absence in England produced little change in the administration of the United Provinces where Heinsius served as a kind of viceroy. So close in fact were the prince and the pensionary that William's death in 1702 passed without crisis: his titles were inherited by an obscure cousin, his policies by the regents. One legacy, however, bequeathed by him, the War of Spanish Succession, was to cause the Dutch considerable distress. Heinsius had approved the declaration of war since the future of the Spanish Netherlands and of Spanish trade touched the Dutch as closely as it touched the English, but the circumstances of the war itself imposed too great a strain on the Anglo-Dutch relations at a time when William was no longer alive to act as mediator. In part the trouble sprang from misunderstanding. The field deputies who hamstrung Marlborough's efforts in the opening campaigns[1] could not be expected to understand tactics which were entirely novel, especially as the French attack of 1672 had had so devastating an effect upon the Dutch that they dared not risk exposing themselves to a second invasion. More serious was the deliberate policy of the English to confine the Dutch to a purely military role, reserving to themselves the command of naval expeditions. Naval supremacy, as both countries knew well, led to commercial supremacy, and the Dutch

[1] See Chapter VII, pages 311–20, for an account of the War of Spanish Succession.

had further reason for complaint in the Methuen Trade Treaty of 1703 which gave them no advantages at all.

As allies of the English the Dutch began to lose not only the primacy in overseas trade which they had preserved through three wars with England, but also, since they ceased to be masters of their own destiny, their status of a first-class power. Even over the vital question of the barrier they were shamelessly betrayed. With the occupation of the Spanish Netherlands, for which the Dutch had contributed half the cost and half the troops, they insisted on the right to garrison the principal towns at the expense of the local population. The emperor, who expected to acquire the Spanish Netherlands after the war, refused to approve the plan, but the English, for fear lest the Dutch make a separate peace with Louis XIV, guaranteed, in the Barrier Treaty of 1709, Dutch possession of eighteen towns and also a share in Spanish-American trade. Thereafter, a General Election in England resulted in a new government which, far from trying to keep the Dutch in the war, was itself resolved to back out at almost any price.

Heinsius should have made his own peace with the French, but he adhered loyally to the Allies' policy of 'No peace without Spain', even when it was no longer viable. In addition, he failed to understand the significance of the Tory victory in 1710 and continued to correspond with the Whig leaders as though they were still in power, instead of facing impeachment as in fact they were. His gaffe gave the Tories an excuse to betray the pledges of 1709, and it was ironical that a peace conference from which the Dutch were virtually excluded should have been held at Utrecht. The paltry concession of seven barrier fortresses was a public demonstration that France, Great Britain and Austria no longer considered the Dutch Republic as an equal.

The Economic Position of the Dutch

Political decline was not immediately marked by economic stagnation or decay. The English had indeed expanded their commerce at the expense of the Dutch, especially in the Mediterranean, yet the Dutch retained their hold on the trade with France in which England showed little interest. Far more dangerous than English competition had been the Swedish attempt to create a *dominium maris balticae*[1] which had threatened the main artery of

---

[1] See Chapter X, *passim*.

MAP 14   The Dutch East Indies

Dutch commerce, but the attempt failed after 1707 and the Dutch showed remarkable resilience in recovering their position there. In any case, so great had been the extent of Dutch commerce at its height, amounting to a practical monopoly of European trade, that it could not be overthrown in a generation. It was not until the middle of the eighteenth century, and perhaps later still, that the economic decline of the Dutch became evident.

Moreover, though the English had begun to outstrip the Dutch in the struggle for markets overseas, and though the West India Company had collapsed, the East India Company had continued to expand throughout the second half of the seventeenth century. While other nations found that trade with the east merely drained them of their precious metals, the Dutch had overcome this by monopolising the entire carrying trade between Ceylon, 'the cinammon garden,' Malabar, the centre of a flourishing cloth industry, and the spice islands of the Moluccas. This, however, necessitated not only the driving out of European interlopers, as Van Diemen and Goens had succeeded in doing,[1] but also the defeat of the Indonesian princes who themselves engaged in competition with the Dutch or gave succour to their rivals. The

[1] See Chapter IV, pages 201-2.

Company's rules forbidding territorial expansion had been well observed: Batavia on the island of Java was the only settlement of any size, and this was merely a small enclave wedged between the kingdom of Mataram and the sultanate of Bantam. Elsewhere, apart from Ternate, which was governed through puppet rulers, the Company owned nothing more than trading stations. In 1666, however, Jan Maetsuycker, the governor in Bantam, decided that the Dutch would never monopolise the spice trade of the Moluccas unless they occupied Macassar in Celebes, since its ruler not only patronised Portuguese and English interlopers but encouraged his own people, a race of bold seafarers, to attack Dutch shipping.

Command of the expedition was given to Cornelis Speelman, one of the most lively Dutchmen of the century, whose riotous life in the east reflected nothing of the strict environment of his native Rotterdam. A hard drinker and a man of boundless energy, he made a fortune by lending money to Chinese and Indonesian merchants, and begot countless illegitimate children. Since he was able to apply his energies equally as well to the public service as to his private pleasures he was of great use to the Company. To compensate for lack of soldiers he won the support of the Prince of Boni, a minor ruler in Celebes, whose Buginese warriors were to play a major part in his subsequent conquests. By 1669 Macassar had been reduced, whereupon the European interlopers sought refuge in Bantam and Mataram. Speelman appealed in vain to Maetsuycker to repeat his breach of the Company's rules by taking over the whole of Java. In 1678, after civil war in Mataram, when the legitimate prince was defeated and appealed to the Dutch for assistance, Speelman advocated the cause of intervention so eloquently that Maetsuycker dryly commented, 'the only objection I miss in your letter is that perhaps even the sky will fall down from heaven and destroy the whole human race'. Nothing, however, could be done until Maetsuycker's death in the following year, and Speelman's appointment as his successor.

Speelman raised a force of Buginese troops in Celebes and with their help restored the legitimate prince, under Dutch control, to Mataram. He then turned on his other Javanese neighbour, the Sultan of Bantam, who sought to make his country the entrepôt of the spice trade by encouraging the settlement of English merchants. In 1681 a dispute over the succession gave Speelman an opportunity to intervene, and though he died before the war was over the

Bantam Treaty of 1684 secured the aims for which he had fought: the Dutch gained full control of the pepper trade and all other foreigners were expelled. The unification of Indonesia under Dutch rule had thus been forwarded, and a commercial system founded from Japan and Formosa to India and Persia. So valuable did this inter-Asiatic trade prove to be that the profits from it exceeded those derived from the cultivation and export of spices to Europe, and made it possible for the Company to accumulate in Bantam a reserve fund of over twenty million gilders.

Within the Dutch Republic itself the pattern of the economy was changing, and it was perhaps natural for contemporaries to interpret the symptoms of change as indications of economic decline. They pointed to the stagnation of the textile industry in Holland, to the increasing number of the poor, to the falling off in trade as witnessed by the fall of customs' receipts, and to the collapse of shipbuilding, so marked that in 1727 the city of Amsterdam had to send to England for shipwrights. Yet contemporaries are rarely the best judges of their own plight. Industry declined in Holland only because the textile manufacturers transferred their business to Dutch Brabant where they were free of urban guild restrictions; the poverty of the lower classes was matched by the greater fortunes of the rich who began to turn from trade and industry towards the land and foreign investment. The Dutch became a race of commission agents, and the Bank of Amsterdam retained its primacy in Europe, supported by the private fortunes of its stockholders and growing rich on the interest of the enormous loans which helped to finance the wars against Louis XIV. Whatever disasters the eighteenth century was to hold for the Dutch, the bases of their economy were still sound in 1714.

IX

The Creation of the Danubian Monarchy

Austria and Western Europe

In the eyes of western Europe the decline of the Austrian Habsburgs in the seventeenth century seemed to be as obvious a fact as the decline of their cousins in Spain. The Peace of Westphalia appeared to have exposed their position in Germany as nothing more than the nominal leadership of the loosest and most impotent federation in Europe. Their position in Germany, however, was not the result of the Thirty Years War, since the Holy Roman Empire was not and had never been in the least like a nation state. Ferdinand I's acceptance of the Augsburg principle of *cujus regio, ejus religio*[1] was proof that real power had passed to the princes long ago.

What gave the Thirty Years War its special importance in this respect was that from 1619 to 1629 Ferdinand II had successfully overcome the limitations which had crippled his predecessors. His imperial projects, like the creation of a military force independent of the German princes, the conquest of north Germany, and the restoration of secularised lands to the Catholic Church, were destroyed, not by the German princes who proved utterly unable to make their protests effective, but by the intervention of France and Sweden. Consequently, though the Peace of Westphalia recognised that the revolutionary plans of Ferdinand II had failed, the authority of Ferdinand III and Leopold was neither more nor less effective than that of Matthias, Rudolf and Ferdinand I. Moreover, if the ambitions of the emperors were buried in 1648, so were the attempts of many protestant princes to transform the empire into an aristocratic republic in which the emperor's role would have been nominal, a view which had gained much publicity in 1640 through the writings of Martin Chemnitz [Hippolithus] who claimed that sovereignty was an attribute of the princes and not of the emperor.

[1] See Chapter II, page 108.

Of far greater importance than the effect of the Thirty Years War was the fact that other developments were taking place which made it all the more unlikely that any future emperor might imitate the action of Ferdinand II. Not only were the princes following the pattern of the age in claiming to be the independent and absolute sovereign of their territories; some of them were becoming too great to be confined within the archaic structure of the empire. Since his accession in 1640, Frederick William of Brandenburg had begun the long process of integration which was to transform his territories, scattered between Poland and the Rhineland, into a powerful kingdom of two million subjects.[1] Equally significant was the growth of Saxony, Bavaria and Hanover, each with a population of 1,500,000, whose dynastic ties with Poland, France and Great Britain respectively were to encourage them to act outside the framework of the empire. The lesser princes followed suit by forming regional groups, such as the League of the Rhine Princes, which treated independently with foreign powers.

As the German states looked beyond Germany to satisfy their ambitions, and as Sweden and France intruded their own disruptive influence by controlling Pomerania and Alsace, the empire lost cohesion. The Diet continued to deliberate imperial affairs, and in 1663 it was even transformed from an occasional assembly of no fixed abode into a permanent one meeting at Regensburg, but its discussions were rendered pointless by the envoys who wrangled interminably over precedence and who, if an occasion for decision should arise, merely referred the issue back to their princes: 'Those who are unacquainted with the proceedings of this assembly would wonder that, where so many ministers are met and maintained at so great a charge by their masters, so little business is done, and the little that is so slowly. . . .'[2] Moreover, the traditional concept of the Holy Roman Empire as a metaphysical ideal to which the institutions of Germany ought to approximate, a model as it were for their behaviour, was being overthrown by the new philosophy of the scientific revolution,[3] which denied the independent existence of all metaphysical ideals. The empire, far

---

[1] See Chapter X, pages 402–13.
[2] 'The Letterbook of Sir George Etherege', quoted in *New Cambridge Modern History*, vol. v, p. 447.
[3] See Chapter I, page 54.

from being an idea in the mind of God, was reduced to the level of a mere contractual association, with the obvious implication that what could be once made could later be broken.

Austria's failure to control the destinies of Germany was not the only indication of her decline: contemporaries were even more impressed by her feeble resistance to French aggression. Whereas Charles V, for all his domestic problems, had contained the French attempts to cross the Rhine and to break through into Italy, Leopold I proved remarkably ineffectual in restraining the ambitions of Louis XIV. Indeed, the advance of French power seemed to be the measure of Austria's decline. Leopold did nothing in 1667 to prevent the invasion of the Netherlands, and his subsequent attempt to buy off Louis with the promise of partitioning the Spanish empire was nothing more than a confession of weakness.[1] It was true that he sent Montecucculi to invade Cologne in 1673 and thus gave dramatic and invaluable aid to the Dutch at a critical moment in their history, but this was an unexpected occasion. In general he played the part of a reluctant enemy, submitting even to the *réunions* rather than openly challenge Louis for the mastery of Europe, which was a role he preferred to leave to William III.

After 1697, however, Leopold confounded the prophets of Austria's doom by showing unwonted determination in urging the succession of his sons to the Spanish empire. Not only was Austria the first power to declare war on the Bourbons, not only were her armies more continuously engaged against the French than those of any other member of the Grand Alliance, but she gained possession, if not of the Spanish empire, at least of the Netherlands, of Lombardy and of Naples and Sicily. In addition, if Leopold no longer had authority to order the armies of the German princes, as the most important leader of the Germans against French aggression, his influence within the empire was increased immeasurably.

This dramatic reversal of Austria's role in the west was not fortuitous. Leopold in fact had achieved so little in reviving Imperial power in Germany and in halting the advance of Louis XIV because he had deliberately chosen to fulfil his great ambitions in the east. It was a wise choice: the defeat of the Ottoman Turks[2] was an event of the utmost importance to Austria, compared with

---

[1] See Chapter VII, page 288.
[2] This is described below, pages 370–6.

MAP 15   Austrian-Habsburg Territories in 1630

which the loss of imperial sovereignty in Alsace and the indignities
suffered at the hands of Louis XIV were of little consequence. The
recovery of Hungary and the creation of the Danubian monarchy,
by which the peoples of the upper Danube valley were restored to
the community of Europe, was not only of considerable value to
Austria, enabling her to play a much more commanding role in
western Europe after 1697, but ranks as one of the greatest events
in the history of Europe in the seventeenth century.

The Austrian Empire

The Austrian Habsburgs ruled over a fragmented empire,
the chance result of two centuries of marriage contracts; its
separate territories, stretching from the Alpine valleys to the
middle reaches of the Danube, were dissimilar in race, language,
religion and custom. Austria alone comprised the two separate
duchies of Upper and Lower Austria, each with its own Estates
and traditions, and each with Protestant minorities entrenched
amid the Catholic population: the only common factors they
shared with each other, and with the duchies of Carinthia,
Carniola, Styria and the Tyrol, were the German language and a

habit of regarding Vienna as the capital city of the Habsburg family. Utterly different in every way were the kingdoms of Hungary and Bohemia which had been more recently acquired, and in which the practice of elective monarchy made uncertain the continuous succession of Habsburg rulers.

It was clear that the Habsburgs could not achieve pre-eminence in Europe until they had consolidated their diverse possessions into an effective administrative unit. The first step was taken when the practice of allocating these possessions among the younger members of the family was checked by Matthias; the next occurred in 1665 when the Tyrol escheated to Leopold I who thus became the first Habsburg ruler to exercise personal control over the entire Austrian empire. It was Matthias who began to extend his authority in Upper and Lower Austria by undermining the traditional privileges of the Estates, and by attacking the Lutheran communities whose nonconformity had political as well as religious implications. The young Archduke Ferdinand was meanwhile performing a similar task so effectively in Styria that he was selected by Matthias to succeed him in 1619. It was Ferdinand's great achievement to weld the non-Germanic kingdom of Bohemia to the bureaucratic system directed from Vienna.[1]

This system was never so efficient as that of France, for example, since Louis XIV could raise taxes at will whereas the emperors could only augment an inadequate income by bargaining with the separate Estates. The idea of a States-General for the Danubian territories as a whole had been proposed, but the Habsburgs decided that such an assembly would only aggravate the problem of disunity by revealing the fundamental differences between the representatives. Nevertheless, without a central legislature to override the authority of the local Estates the task of centralisation was made all the more difficult for the civil servants who had, by 1600, created the nucleus of an imperial administration. With a privy council (*Geheime Konferenz*), a war council (*Hofkriegsrath*), an imperial treasury (*Hofkammer*), and a chancellery (*Hofkanzlei*), the division of powers seemed to be well organised, but in practice the separate departments were not equally effective. The *Geheime Konferenz* was an advisory rather than an executive body. The *Hofkriegsrath* had no control over the recruitment of troops within the Habsburg empire, and could only suggest quotas which the

[1] See Chapter II, pages 119–20.

local authorities might or might not fulfil. The *Hofkammer* controlled only mineral rights and indirect taxes; the assessment and collection of direct taxes was jealously preserved by the Estates. In the long run the importance of the departments was determined less by the tasks assigned them than by the character of the men who staffed them, and it was the administrative genius of the 'cameralists', as they were called, which transformed the *Hofkanzlei* from a legal and judicial body into the most active force in the creation of the Danubian monarchy, and ultimately its administrative centre.

The work of the cameralists was impeded by the local nobility who had little comprehension of the arguments of chancellery officials, and who stubbornly defended the validity of their franchises, immunities and traditions. Such opposition to bureaucratic centralisation was common to the rest of Europe, but in the Danubian territories it was all the stronger since the entire character of local government was coloured by the existence of serfdom. This was no antique survival from past centuries but an economic necessity for landlords who sought to exploit their demesne lands in an age of rising prices.[1] The relation of landlords to serf was reflected in local law and local institutions, and made it impossible for any but landlords to control local government. All the cameralists could do was to reinforce the landlords' authority by applying the principles of Roman law, which made a harsher distinction between bond and free than did customary law, and to expect in return a greater degree of co-operation. It was, in short, an extremely cautious policy whereby local institutions were not destroyed but fitted into the loose framework of the centralised administration; and had it not been for special, extraordinary circumstances the work of one century would scarcely have been completed in three.

The Bohemian revolt, so dangerous in its initial stages, was ultimately to prove beneficial to the Habsburg monarchy. In the years before 1618 the *Hofkanzlei* had made little headway in its efforts to establish a centralised regime: indeed, the Letter of Majesty in 1609[2] had given formal protection to the disruptive forces of nationalism, separatism and heresy. Attempts were made by Lobkowitz, the most able of the cameralists, to whittle away the terms of the Letter but he could do nothing radical until the

[1] See Chapter I, page 3.   [2] See Chapter II, page 114.

election of Ferdinand II as Matthias's successor in 1617. It was then that he secured the appointment of two fanatical Catholics, Martinitz and Slavata, to lead the council of regency in Bohemia. The consequences of his action were greater than he had intended. The immediate effect was to provoke rebellion, during which the Estates of Lower Austria were also emboldened to make their own demands for toleration and autonomy; but because the rebels failed and because the rebellion was engulfed in the larger issues of the Thirty Years War, Ferdinand II was free to impose his own terms upon Bohemia. Returning to Prague at the head of a triumphant army there was no need to placate nor to win the support of any section of the community. He ruined the gentry by confiscating their lands, the townsmen by deliberate inflation, and the Protestants by proscription. Advised by Lobkowitz he then created a new class of Roman Catholic and mostly German landlords, who depended upon him utterly for protection in their new titles and estates, and who ruled as his agents in occupied territory.

By 1627 it was safe to summon the Estates in order to give the appearance of popular consent to a new constitution which destroyed the traditional liberties of the Bohemians. The monarchy was declared to be hereditary in the house of Habsburg; Austrian legal customs and administrative practices were to be adopted throughout the kingdom; the Bohemian chancellor was to accompany the king at all times. In short, the government of Bohemia was to be determined henceforth in Vienna. It remained for Ferdinand II's successors to achieve a similar result in Hungary.

The Ottoman Turks

Hungary presented a challenge which the cameralists of the *Hofkanzlei* were not equipped to meet: it was not that the privileges of the Magyar nobility were protected by the Golden Bull,[1] a document so far reaching in its concessions that it made the Letter of Majesty seem innocuous by comparison, but that most of Hungary was occupied by the Ottoman Turks.

Since their conquest of the former Byzantine empire, straddling the Balkans and Asia Minor, the Ottoman Turks had expanded not only into Egypt and Persia, but also further into Europe. Until 1521 they had been held back at the line of the Danube and the Save, but in that year they had seized Belgrade, standing at the

[1] See below, page 368.

junction of the two rivers, and burst northwards into the Hungarian plain. From that moment the fortunes of the Habsburgs became indissolubly bound with those of the Turks, as became evident in 1526 when the Turks routed the Hungarians at Mohacs and killed their king. His widow, a Habsburg princess having no children of her own, secured the election of her brother Ferdinand to the thrones of Hungary and Bohemia. Important as this was to be for the future the immediate course of events made Ferdinand's election seem pointless since the Turks then overran the whole of Hungary and, in 1529, besieged Vienna.

Fortunately for Europe the siege was abandoned after twenty-eight days, and though other attacks were launched on later occasions the walls of Vienna proved to be the high water mark of Turkish expansion into Europe. Ottoman lines of communication were too dangerously extended to permit of a long campaign in Austria, and the largest section of the army, the Spahis,[1] insisted on being free to return home at the onset of winter. Moreover, the Turks had to undertake a long series of campaigns against the Persians which prevented them making anything more than sporadic attacks up the Danube. In the event, as was recognised in the Treaty of Sitva-Torok (1606), the line of effective Turkish occupation lay midway between Buda and Vienna, which left to the Habsburgs a strip of Hungary varying in depth from forty to eighty miles, constituting barely a quarter of the kingdom, for which they paid tribute to the sultan.

Occupation by the Turks was not so intolerable for the Balkan peoples as western observers believed. The Turks had inherited the culture of the Seljuks, of the Arabs and of Islam; moreover, both as neighbours, and later as conquerors, of the Byzantine empire, they had learned much from Hellenistic civilisation. The capture of Constantinople, therefore, 'was not a victory of barbarism but rather of another and not undistinguished civilisation. The four slender minarets that the Turks added to the Church of Santa Sophia may be, for the Christian, a desecration. They are not a defacement.'[2] Though the Turks were capable of occasional acts of great cruelty, and though they conscripted a fifth of the young

[1] The *Spahis*, a feudal levy of cavalry, numbered about 130,000 though not all would serve at the same time: the regular standing force of highly trained infantry, the *Janissaries*, was only 12,000.

[2] 'Europe and the Turks: the Civilisation of the Ottoman Empire.' Bernard Lewis, *History Today*, October 1953.

men every five years for the army, their rule had its compensations. The records of registers and travellers alike testify to the steady increase in wealth and population, for the people could live in peace, their frontiers protected by the Ottoman army. Things were not so satisfactory in Hungary where frontier warfare continued for nearly two centuries, but the estimated decimation of the population[1] was caused more by a combination of plague, emigration and starvation resulting from the inadequate cultivation of poor soil, than by Turkish brutality. Many Hungarians were Protestants and thus enjoyed a greater measure of toleration, no matter how capriciously withdrawn on occasion, than they could expect to receive from the Habsburgs, their self-appointed liberators. Above all, since the seigneurial jurisdiction of the Magyar nobility was replaced by that of Ottoman fief-holders who demanded taxes but not forced labour, the peasantry had no cause to envy the serfs of central Europe.

The Turks were nomadic warriors and the basic character of their empire remained that of an army on the march, so that whenever their advance had reached its limits they lost their vigour. The periods of consolidation and settlement which have marked the history of other empires were denied to the Turks. They occupied vast tracks of territory but never settled in them. They exploited but never assimilated their subject races, and none save the conscripted Janissaries could identify themselves with their conquerors as men in the Roman empire had proudly done by winning Roman citizenship. The military nature of the empire left all power in the hands of the sultan. If he were gifted the empire prospered, if he were insane or feckless there was no other authority to direct events and the empire fell into decay. Apart from Murad IV (1623-40) the only ruler of the century to reveal any ability, the sultans exchanged their imperial responsibilities for the intrigues of the harem, or gave way to a life of debauchery so excessive as frequently to induce insanity. The effect upon the empire was disastrous: the efforts of the wives to secure the succession for their own favourite son caused faction in the army, the fief-holders grew independent, the Janissaries relaxed their rigorous standards of discipline, and the frontiers began to contract. Shah Abbas the Great of Persia drove the Turks from Azerbaijan, Georgia and Kurdistan, the Poles recovered Moldavia, and in

[1] See *New Cambridge Modern History*, vol. v, p. 479.

Transylvania, among the Carpathian mountains of eastern Hungary, George Rackoczi set up an independent Magyar kingdom.

The accession of Murad IV in 1623 restored the efficiency of the empire since he proved to be a successful soldier; so successful that it was fortunate for Europe that he chose to fight against Persia instead of intervening in the Thirty Years War. Shah Abbas was a powerful opponent but Murad triumphed in 1638 when, after the fall of Baghdad, the Peace of Sehab re-established Ottoman rule in Mesopotamia. The moral effect of military success was startling. The army abandoned its political intrigues to become once again the well-drilled agent of the sultan's conquests, and the feudatories returned to their obedience. Though his successors were inept, Murad's death in 1640 did not lead to disaster since an astute Albanian, Mahomet Köprülü, came to power in the next reign as Grand Vizier. Köprülü recognised that only by constant warfare could the disintegration of the empire be averted, and he was fortunate enough to win the ear of the sultan's mother. Knowing that her son, Mahomet IV, was incapable of anything but hunting and debauchery, she drew up a contract with Köprülü which virtually gave him absolute authority within the empire provided that he maintained efficient government and waged war effectively. Köprülü did both. Credited with ordering the execution of 60,000 dishonest tax-collectors, officers and soldiers, he was obeyed as no grand vizier had ever been before, while the armies renewed their conflict with Europe. They seized Tenedos and Lemnos from the Venetians in 1657 and then, having driven the Rackoczi family from Transylvania, began a long campaign to subdue the local nobility who still clung to their independence.

Köprülü died in 1661, to be followed by his son Ahmed, the finest Ottoman soldier of the century. By 1663 Ahmed had defeated the Transylvanian nobles and sent 80,000 Christians into slavery; he then advanced on Austria. The great fortress of Neuhaussel, the proud creation of Ferdinand I to guard the Waag valley north of the Danube, fell in November, 1663, but its spirited resistance and Montecucculi's brilliant rearguard action ensured that the main Turk attack was delayed until the following year. Nevertheless, many detachments broke through to the north to raid Moravia and Silesia. Immediately the Ottoman Turks ceased to be the private problem of the Habsburgs: Pope Alexander VII called for a Holy

League and a cosmopolitan force assembled for the defence of Austria. As a result of experience gained in the Thirty Years War Europe at last was no longer inferior to the Turks in cannon and cavalry, and in 1664, at St. Gotthard in the Raab valley, the Turks were defeated on European soil for the first time.

The Habsburgs derived little positive benefit from their victory. Their allies withdrew as soon as it was clear that Europe was no longer in danger, and Montecuccoli advised Leopold that there were not enough men to make possible the recovery of Hungary. Moreover, since Louis XIV was preparing to enforce his devolution claims upon the Spanish Netherlands, Leopold decided to purchase a respite in the Danube. By the Treaty of Vasvár (1664) Ahmed Köprülü agreed to a twenty-year truce.

Poland

Poland in the seventeenth century was the sick man of Europe. Its territories, sprawling across the continent from Silesia to Kiev, from the Baltic to the Balkans, were coveted by aggressive and expansionist neighbours against whom Poland was singularly ill equipped to defend them.

Since the fifteenth century when the Ottoman Turks had captured her ports on the Black Sea, and thus disrupted the overland trade routes to the Baltic which had invigorated the commercial life of the inland cities, Poland had become a kingdom dominated by the nobles. They alone had wealth, exporting grain, flax and timber from their estates by shipping them down the Vistula; they alone had political power, electing their sovereigns and imposing upon them whatever conditions they wished. The *pacta conventa*, a formal statement of the concessions he was willing to make, was signed by the elected candidate before his coronation, and the nobles held him to his promises by threat of rebellion. Unlike the rulers of other states, the kings of Poland were unable to influence their assemblies to make laws of benefit to the crown since the dissentient voice of one representative alone was enough to prevent the passing of any measure. No matter how successfully the kings played off one group against another or employed the arts of intimidation, flattery and bribery, there always remained the obstinate opponent whose resistance could not be overcome by the votes of the majority.

Occasionally a king was elected whose vigour and military skill,

MAP 16   Poland and her Neighbours

if they did nothing to strengthen the monarchy, at least helped to
stave off the endless succession of invaders. Such a man was
Sigismund III (1587–1631). His greatest victories were against the
Turks, who had won control of Moldavia by 1618 and who then
seized Chotin on the Dniester. From there they threatened to
overrun Podolia, the narrow corridor between the Dniester and
the Bug along which Poles and Turks had fought for more than a
century. Inspired by Sigismund's leadership, the Poles made such
valiant resistance that they recovered Chotin in 1621 and secured
the restoration of Christian rulers to Moldavia, so that the principality might lie as a buffer state between themselves and the
Turks. Against his other enemies Sigismund was less successful.
He failed to defend Kiev against the Russians and could do nothing
to prevent the triumphal progress of Gustavus Adolphus through
Livonia and Courland.[1] Fortunately for Poland, Gustavus was so
eager to intervene in north Germany that he allowed his French
allies to negotiate the Truce of Altmark (1629), by which he withdrew his troops in return for control of the Baltic ports.

[1] See Chapter X, page 384.

Sigismund's elder son, Ladislau IV (1631–48), was elected to succeed him, and so effectively did he wage war against the Russians that his army entered Moscow in 1634. There he compelled the tsar to renounce his claim to White Russia and Little Russia, to the areas surrounding Smolensk and Kiev respectively, which the Poles had seized from Russia in the Middle Ages.

The achievements of Sigismund and Ladislau were all the more striking when set against the disasters of John Casimir's reign (1648–68). John Casimir was Ladislau's brother, and so little expectation had he of ascending the throne that he had entered the church as a Jesuit priest. In the year of his election he was awaiting appointment to an altogether different seat in the College of Cardinals. He was not the man to deal with the Cossack revolt which broke out within a few months of his accession.

The Cossacks of the Dnieper were Russian in race, language and religion, though they enjoyed their position as nominal vassals of Poland since it left them free to practise piracy on the lower reaches of the Dnieper and brigandage along its banks. Fierce and warlike, they might have served Poland well, especially against the Turks, if the Poles had not regarded them with suspicion, disliking both their independent behaviour and their loyalty to the Russian Orthodox Church. Attempts were made during Ladislau's reign to convert them to Roman Catholicism, and intendants had been appointed to strengthen royal authority in their territory. By 1648 the Cossacks were near breaking point. Finally, when their leader, Bogdan Chmel'nyckyj, left home to protest to John Casimir against the tyranny of the intendants, one of these raped his wife and killed his son, and thus provoked the most serious rebellion of the century in Poland. Foreign invasion was dangerous enough but civil war was far more so since the Polish nobles, who rarely lacked courage in facing an invader, behaved then at their most factious for fear of strengthening the crown. Even when the Cossacks seized Lwow with ease, they made no move to support John Casimir, who was compelled to appeal to Vienna, pleading his cause as a Catholic crusader against heretics of the Orthodox Church. With Austrian aid he defeated Bogdan Chmel'nyckyj's army in 1651, but, in their desperate stand along the Dneiper, the Cossacks too could call upon allies, the Russians, who were eager to avenge their defeat of 1634. The Russians had soon occupied all Polish territory east of the Dnieper, and in 1656 they overran

Little Russia, seized Lwow and advanced as far as the ⸮
reaches of the Vistula. In that same year Rackoczi, the Ca⸲
ruler of Transylvania, crossed the Carpathian mountains to invade
Poland from the south, while Charles X of Sweden[1] attacked from
the north, captured Cracow and Warsaw and compelled John
Casimir to fly into Silesia.

It was only the fact that Poland's invaders were so bitterly
opposed to each other which saved her from immediate partition.
In the event the consequences were severe though not disastrous.
Sweden gained nothing since the Dutch intervened to save Danzig
and a Danish invasion of his homeland caused Charles to withdraw
in haste from Poland; the Turks under Mahomet Köprülü chose
this very moment to drive Rackoczi from Transylvania; the Great
Elector of Brandenburg exploited the crisis to win full independence of Poland for his fief of East Prussia; Russia, after a further
decade of warfare, was confirmed in possession of Kiev and
Smolensk with their surrounding territory by the Treaty of
Andrussovo (1667).

No sooner had the Russians been bought off than Poland was
again torn by civil war, as a result of Louis XIV's ambitions to
win the kingdom as a permanent ally against the Habsburgs. John
Casimir, who had married a French princess, and who sought to
retire to the calmer life of a rich benefice in France, undertook to
secure the election of the great Condé's son as his successor. To
strengthen his hand he appointed Jan Sobieski, who too had
married a French wife and who supported Louis's ambitions, as
commander-in-chief of the army. Sobieski had previously betrayed
John Casimir to Charles X during the Swedish invasion, but
French influence had subsequently effected a reconciliation
between them. This support was well worth having: not only could
he supply the entire army from his own estates, but, by pledging
these, he could if necessary raise sufficient money to pay the troops
himself. His appointment provoked the opponents of the French
party into civil war, and when in 1668 John Casimir gave up the
struggle by abdicating, the crisis was resolved by the election
of Michael Wisnowiecki. A native Pole, Wisnowiecki had
the advantage of being tied to no party, but he was wholly
lacking in ability and leadership, qualities which were

---

[1] See Chapter X for this and subsequent references to Sweden and
Brandenburg.

sorely needed four years later when the Turks again invaded Poland.

Since the defeat at St. Gotthard had halted his plans of conquest on the Danube, Ahmed Köprülü knew only too well that his retention of office depended upon the achievement of military success elsewhere. For some years he fought in Crete to expel the Venetian garrisons, but he looked for some more dramatic occasion to silence his detractors. This presented itself in 1671 when the Cossacks west of the Dnieper, who were still under Polish control, again rebelled and appealed to the Turks for assistance. Ahmed championed no cause but his own in this tangled conflict along the Dnieper, and he exploited the crisis brilliantly. Within a few months (1672) he had taken Lwow and Kamenets Podolskiy, overrun Podolia and laid claim to the Ukraine. Michael Wisnowiecki, himself incompetent and unable to discover ability in others, ceded all these conquests without dispute, and by his supine acquiescence in defeat stung a large section of the nobles into doing what they might well have done before. Under the leadership of Jan Sobieski, whose factious refusal of support had been partly responsible for the recent humiliations, they raised 40,000 men and in 1673 routed the Turks at Chotin. Michael Wisnowiecki died on the eve of this great victory and so great was the enthusiasm for Sobieski that he was elected king. Thereafter he harried the Turks between the Dniester and the Bug until much of Podolia had been cleared, drove them from Lwow, and, finally, in the Treaty of Zurawno (1676) forced them to cede all their conquests save Kamenets Podolskiy, the capital of Podolia, and its surrounding districts.

The campaigns of 1673–6 brought about a great change in Sobieski. The factious noble, the tool of French diplomacy, became obsessed with a desire to crusade against the Turks. Louis XIV, who had welcomed his election as a triumph for France and who had offered to secure the recovery of East Prussia from Brandenburg if Sobieski would assist the Magyar rebels in Hungary,[1] stood condemned in Sobieski's eyes as the unofficial ally of the sultan, and it was to Leopold I that he offered his alliance. His determination to drive the Turks out of Poland was clearly of political value, since it enhanced his prestige and assured him of the support of the nobles; but when he dreamed of something

[1] See below, page 369.

greater than the recovery of Kamenets Podolskiy, greater even than the reconquest of Moldavia and the Black Sea ports, he subordinated the true interests of Poland to the achievement of his private ideals. Sobieski, of all Poland's kings, might have exploited his military skill and prestige to strengthen his country's defences and to improve its administration: he might have recognised that Poland, threatened as she was on all sides by powerful and aggressive neighbours, was in no condition to undertake a crusade. To all this he remained blind. His determination grew, 'to give the barbarian conquest for conquest, to pursue him from victory to victory over the very frontiers that belched him forth upon Europe, in a word, not to conquer and curb the monster, but to hurl him back into the deserts, to exterminate him, to raise upon his ruins the empire of Byzantium; this alone is noble, chivalrous and wise.' Noble and chivalrous, in terms of the medieval world which Poland still inhabited, but in terms of seventeenth-century politics it was scarcely wise.

LEOPOLD I AND THE RECONQUEST OF HUNGARY

Habsburg Hungary

On the death of his elder brother in 1654, the future Leopold I was hastily snatched away from his theological studies in Spain in order to prepare himself for the task of succeeding his father. Three years later Ferdinand III died and Leopold, at the age of sixteen, became head of the Austrian empire. Intellectually he was well equipped and he had a clear sense of his vocation and his duties. He admired and envied the style of monarchy established by Louis XIV, and he likewise announced his intention of being his own first minister, but he lacked both Louis's commanding appearance and his ability to command. The lolling jaw which disfigured the Habsburgs merely gave physical emphasis to Leopold's characteristic irresolution, for while he enjoyed the task of administration, the burden of decision was too great for him. For such a ruler, faced with so many dangers from both east and west, this was a serious failing, scarcely remedied by implicit reliance upon divine intervention: 'If I were permitted to say so,' wrote the Papal nuncio, 'I would personally wish that the emperor's trust in God were a bit less, so that he might deal with somewhat more foresight with those dangers which threaten, and when he has decided, act.' None the less, unfitted though he seemed to be, it was left to this self-conscious prince, who longed for glory but distrusted his ability to attain it, to determine the relationship of Hungary to the growing unity of the other Habsburg possessions.

Habsburg Hungary was little more than a frontier province where the Habsburgs fought a double battle against Turkish aggression and domestic disaffection. A few German officials held posts in Pressburg, the capital, but the country was in reality controlled by the Magyar nobles whose privileges had been preserved intact since their donation in the Golden Bull of 1222. Irresponsible and ungovernable, they paid no taxes and claimed the *jus resistandi* or right of insurrection. As a result of a great missionary campaign undertaken by Cardinal Pázmány early in the century most of the landlords were Catholics, but total conversion had been denied because of the assistance given to the Protestants by the Calvinist rulers of Transylvania. Moreover, so suspicious were the Hungarians of all things Austrian that it was almost a point of honour for many of them to be heretics. The Protestants tended to fear the Ottoman pashas in Buda less than the Catholic emperors in Vienna, but Ahmed Köprülü gave them a rude shock when he sold 80,000 Christians into slavery after his conquest of Transylvania (1663). This act assured Leopold of unanimous support from the Hungarians at the battle of St. Gotthard, but the ensuing Truce of Vasvar merely increased his problems. Excited by the prospect of a campaign to release the rest of Hungary from Turkish control, the Magyars felt betrayed: on the grounds that Leopold had not first consulted the Hungarian Diet, they denounced the Truce which they interpreted as a device to win for Leopold twenty years of peace in which to do to Hungary what his grandfather had achieved in Bohemia. The construction of a new fortress at Leopoldstadt, which was allowed for by the Turks in the treaty, was seen not as a bastion against the enemy but as a citadel from which to subdue the local champions of Hungarian independence.

In 1666, when one of the leading nobles married into another prominent Magyar family, the celebrations were organised on so lavish a scale that the nobility attended in great numbers. It was not surprising, therefore, that the innocent occasion of a wedding became the setting for conspiracy. Nor was it surprising that though the conspirators shared a common aim they were wholly lacking in unanimity. The intransigent independence of the Magyars, which so frequently led them into rebellion, made rebellion itself too often ineffective since none would discipline himself to serve under another. Suspicion of Leopold was of too recent a growth to overshadow the more ancient rivalries of one family with another, and for three years the conspirators pursued a confused course of treachery, cowardice, delay and deceit. Moreover, they failed to win support abroad. Louis XIV, who alone might have given them practical aid, was at that time negotiating a partition treaty with Leopold[1] and judged the moment inopportune to embarrass him.

Lobkowitz, the man who had used the failure of the Bohemian revolt to destroy the liberties of the Letter of Majesty, waited until the conspiracy had worn itself out in futility and struck in 1669. Detachments of the Austrian army marched into Pressburg to augment the local forces, and a series of arrests was swiftly carried out. Four of the most prominent rebels were executed straightaway, and a fifth, Stefan Tokoli, was killed as he defended his castle against Imperialist troops. As in Bohemia, the punishment of treason was made an excuse to extend royal authority: 'The Magyars rebelled and therefore have lost all their privileges,' wrote one of the cameralists. 'Henceforward they must be treated as *armis subjecti*', or, as Lobkowitz put it, 'the Hungarians were to be put into Czech trousers'. A new governor, Caspar van Ampringen, was appointed to reduce Hungary to obedience by a reign of terror. The Magyars were not easily intimidated. Many fled into the northern valleys to fight under Imre Tokoli, Stefan's son, who combined the advantages of courage with those of birth, being related to all the victims of 1669. Within a few years it became clear that Tokoli was unlikely to be suppressed, especially since the issues confronting Leopold were not confined to Hungary alone. Because he had intervened in the Netherlands to save the Dutch in 1673 the French had declared their support for Tokoli and sent agents to recruit on his behalf in Poland, though in the event they did little harm as Sobieski was becoming increasingly obsessed with his vision of a crusade. More serious were the indications of a renewed Turkish attack which prompted Pope Innocent XI to take the lead in reconciling Leopold and Tokoli. As

[1] See Chapter VII, page 288.

neither side could triumph over the other, they wisely agreed to a truce in 1679.

Peace was bought at a high price since Leopold was compelled to recall van Ampringen, declare an amnesty for both rebels and Protestants, and withdraw all German troops from Hungarian soil. Worst of all, he agreed to accept the decisions of a Diet held at Oldenburg in 1681, which gave new life to the time-honoured forms of Magyar government and administration, and freed the council in Pressburg of all control from the cameralists in Vienna. Leopold was to some extent playing for time, and Imre Tokoli was not deceived. Boycotting the Diet of Oldenburg and opposing Leopold's choice of officials, he appealed to the Turks to recognise him as king of Upper Hungary in place of Leopold. In January 1682 the Turks accepted his proposal: the destiny of Hungary was thus once again thrown into the balance.

The Defeat of the Turks, 1682–1721

The decision to support Tokoli was taken by Kara Mustafa who had succeeded his brother-in-law, Ahmed Köprülü, as Grand Vizier in 1676. The most ambitious of the Köprülü family, his contempt for Europeans blinded him to the possibility of defeat, and in his determination to outshine his predecessors by the capture of Vienna he made his plans with cavalier disregard for what the enemy might do to prevent him. When he heard of Tokoli's rebellion he decided not to wait upon the expiry of the Truce of Vasvar but to make immediate preparations for attack. In the spring of 1683 he mustered the Rumelian *spahis* at Adrianople, along with the professional Janissaries, and marched northwards collecting local levies as he went until finally he arrived with 250,000 men at Gran on the frontiers of Habsburg Hungary. Leopold was unready to meet him. Unwisely he had relied upon the Truce of Vasvar to secure him immunity until 1684, and had it not been for Montecucculi's foresight in retaining 30,000 men after peace had been made with Louis XIV at Nijmegen in 1679, the Austrians would have been entirely defenceless. Montecucculi himself had just died and it was Charles, the exiled duke of Lorraine, who faced Kara Mustafa's vast horde. After playing with the idea of striking the first blow by attacking Gran, he decided that it was his prime duty to keep his small army in being by not taking risks. In consequence, though he fought a creditable

MAP 17 Ottoman Frontiers, 1606-1718

Habsburg Hungary
1606

Transylvania
1606

Ottoman frontier 1699
Ottoman losses by 1718

Kamenets Podolskiy

R. Pruth

R. Dniester

Chotin

MOLDAVIA

R. Danube

WALLACHIA

TRANSYLVANIA

R. Theiss

R. Maros

O T T O M A N

H U N G A R Y

R. Waag

Leopoldstadt

Pressburg

Parkany

Gran

Budao Pest

Vienna

Wiener

Gunso

Vasvar

St. Gotthard

Mohacs

R. Drave

R. Save

TEMESVAR

Zenta

R. Theiss

Karlowitz

Salankemen

Belgrade

Passarovitz

E M P I R E

SERBIA

BOSNIA

HERZEGOVINA

CROATIA

ADRIATIC
SEA

N

M.E.S.C.

delaying action up the Danube, the harsh fact emerged that whatever he did nothing could stop the Turks reaching Vienna.

Leopold quitted his capital on July 7th, leaving the Count of Starhemberg to defend it as best he could, and its capture would have been assured if the Ottoman army had stormed its walls within the week; but Kara Mustafa made slow progress. He arrived on the 17th and then rejected the idea of a direct assault in favour of reducing the city by attrition, thus preserving its value when taken. It was the wrong decision, though Kara Mustafa very nearly succeeded. By attempting to starve the city into submission he imposed considerable strain on his own army, whose lines of communication were stretched to their utmost, and whose commissariat, though the best in Europe, was scarcely capable of supplying a quarter of a million men for two months. The besieged, of course, were in a worse plight. They had over three hundred cannon but very little ammunition, and bread but little else; by the end of August dysentery and near starvation had seriously reduced their power of physical resistance. On September 12th the last stage was reached in a complicated series of sapping operations, and within twenty-four hours the explosion of the mines would have given the Turks access to the city.

While Charles of Lorraine used his small force to the full to defend Pressburg from attack by Tokoli and to harass the Turkish lines, a powerful army began to assemble under his direction behind the Wienerwald, the Alpine spur to the south-west of Vienna, overlooking the foothills and the plain which stretched to the city walls. The Elector of Saxony came in person with 9,000 men, the Elector of Brandenburg with 10,000, and the Circles of Franconia and the Upper Rhineland sent 9,000 more; most valuable of all was the arrival of 27,000 Poles under Sobieski. For him it was the fulfilment of his dream of striking a dramatic blow at the Turks, and since the February of 1683, at a time when the emperor was still refusing to take the Turkish threat seriously, he had been raising troops, corresponding with Charles of Lorraine, and denouncing the opposition of the French party in Poland. When news of Vienna's danger reached him he moved swiftly to its defence across three hundred miles of country with few roads and no bridges. To him Charles surrendered command of the army.

The Turks were well aware of this concentration of more than

70,000 men in the Wienerwald and a council of war on September
9th urged Kara Mustafa to attack it before it could reach the plain.
Kara Mustafa rejected the advice: the city would fall within three
days, and his contempt for European troops made him over-
confident of success. Thus the relieving force was able to approach
with no greater hindrance than the terrain it covered. Working
from the map alone, Sobieski had imagined a gentle continuous
slope from the Wienerwald down to Vienna, only to discover that
the foothills were covered with woods and terraced vineyards; his
plan of a swift dash by the cavalry had therefore to be laid aside
and it was not until the critical day of September 12th that his
army was in position for the final attack. At 4 a.m. the Austrians,
led by Charles of Lorraine, advanced along the Danube while the
Germans in the centre awaited Sobieski's final manœuvres to
bring his cavalry over the last of the foothills on the army's right.
The army, stretching from Sobieski in the west to Charles in the
north, thus formed a wide arc which began to close in upon Vienna
throughout the morning, until Sobieski gave his cavalry the signal
to charge. The effect of 20,000 horse impetuously bearing down
upon the Turkish lines was too much for an army which had done
little but dig trenches for the past two months. Moreover, having
turned to face the attack, the Turks were immediately harassed by
sorties from Vienna itself, and by late afternoon their front was
broken. Kara Mustafa was swept away in the headlong flight of his
troops down the Danube valley, and the relieving army burst into
Vienna.

For three days the allies and the Viennese celebrated their
triumph, but by September 14th when Leopold arrived for the
thanksgiving service the expressions of gratitude were beginning to
wear thin. The Poles complained that they were denied fodder for
their horses, the Germans claimed that the Poles had fought the
least and seized the most, and the Elector of Saxony withdrew his
men immediately after Leopold's arrival on the grounds that his
Protestant troops were ill received by the Catholic population.
Sobieski retired to sulk in his tent when Leopold, far from giving
him the praise and gratitude to which he felt entitled, and the hand
of a Habsburg princess for his son, received him coldly and
snubbed his son at their official meeting on the 17th. Jealous that
Sobieski should have won the great victory that had always been
beyond his own reach, Leopold had listened too intently to false

rumours that the Polish king, who had after all been a French agent in the past, was seeking to win Habsburg Hungary for himself.

Dissensions of this sort prevented the allies from exploiting their advantage until the 18th when the chase was at last taken up. With the capture of Gran in early October, European troops entered a fortress which had been held continuously by the Turks since the first siege of Vienna in 1529. After this the coming of winter prevented any further campaigning and the armies went home. Meanwhile Kara Mustafa, having executed all those whose counsel he had foolishly rejected, was himself put to death by the sultan's orders.

The winter months gave Leopold time in which to come to a crucial decision: he could either abandon western Europe to Louis XIV in order to recover Hungary from the Turks, or he could settle for a truce with the Turks, like that of Vasvár, in order to return to the struggle against France. It was a complex problem: to attempt the conquest of Hungary meant accepting the *réunions* and the sacrifice of Spain to France; against this, Austria might become more of a match for France if her territories were united and her eastern frontier settled. In a historic decision Leopold agreed to all Louis XIV's demands in order to secure the Truce of Regensburg, and ordered Charles of Lorraine to renew his campaign in the Danube. One factor of great importance in nerving Leopold to a decision was the support of Innocent XI who formed a Holy League in 1684 in order to raise funds to recruit troops and, especially, to keep Poland in alliance with Austria. This was particularly important since Louis XIV had intensified his efforts to isolate Sobieski, a task made all the easier by Leopold's treatment of the Poles after the relief of Vienna. Innocent's appeal to Sobieski, however, kept that gallant crusader in the field, and even reconciled him, two years later, to making formal recognition of Russia's control of the left bank of the Dnieper, in order to win another ally against the Turks.

In the subsequent campaign Charles of Lorraine ignored the Turkish and Hungarian fortresses which commanded the numerous river valleys running down to the Danube since these were too strongly sited to be taken with ease. Instead he sought to hustle the Turks down the Danube valley itself and thus disrupt the lines of supply without which the fortresses could not long subsist. For four years (1684–8) the campaign went well. Buda, the ancient capital of Hungary, was taken in 1686 after a ten-week siege, and Tokoli, after successive defeats in the north, was expelled from the kingdom. In 1687 the nobles of Transylvania made their submission, and in a great victory near Mohacs Charles of Lorraine avenged the Hungarians who had been slain there in 1526: where the first battle of Mohacs had resulted in Hungary's conquest, the second was followed by its liberation. Finally, in 1688, Belgrade was taken by the Elector of Bavaria, its capture being singularly opportune since in that year Louis XIV invaded the Palatinate,[1] an act of aggression which Leopold as a member of the League of Augsburg could not overlook.

Since he had to strip the Danube army of its best men and commanders, leaving Louis of Baden hard-pressed to retain control of Hungary and Transylvania, it was a wise move for Leopold to assure himself of Sobieski's continued co-operation by at last offering to provide his son with a Habsburg princess and to guarantee that Moldavia, when liberated, should return to Poland. Once again Sobieski's determination to destroy the Turks proved of service to Austria, for the years during which Leopold had to turn against Louis XIV were marked by the rise to power of Mustafa Zadé, yet another member of the Köprülü family and the brother of the famous soldier Ahmed. Recovering Belgrade in 1690, Mustafa Zadé sent Tokoli into Transylvania to raise the Protestant nobility and seemed about to drive the Imperialists out of Hungary. In the late summer, however, the Poles won a major battle in Moldavia, and though Sobieski was not able to exploit his victory for lack of reinforcements from the emperor, Louis of Baden profited from this diversion to drive Tokoli from Transylvania. Finally, at Salankemen, the Turkish revival was abruptly ended by the death of Mustafa Zadé and the defeat of his troops by Louis. Unhappily for Sobieski his inability to follow up his Moldavian victory forfeited him support at home where he was fatally hampered by the influence of his wife who returned to her old love for her native country and who revived French intrigues among the nobility. In any case, it was only too obvious that Sobieski's efforts against the Turks, invaluable though they had been, had benefited Austria rather than Poland: Austria had been saved and had gained Hungary, whereas Poland had nothing more to show than the recovery of Kamenets Podolskiy. Sobieski died in 1696 without

[1] See Chapter VII, page 302.

again taking the field against the Turks, and his disappointment at the results of his crusade was heightened by the Diet's refusal to elect his son as his successor. In his place it chose Augustus, Elector of Saxony.

Curiously enough, this too was of benefit to Austria rather than to Poland since Augustus had succeeded Louis of Baden in command of the Danube army and had proved his incapacity as a soldier. Leopold, hesitant to dismiss him on account of his importance in Germany, seized the opportunity of his election to the Polish throne to replace him by Prince Eugène. Eugène's decisive victory at Zenta in the Theiss valley completed the work of reconquest begun after 1684, and with Imperial troops marauding as far afield as Bosnia and Herzegovina, Leopold called a halt in 1699. Well satisfied with the recovery of his territories, his mind was urgently occupied with the problem of the Spanish succession; accordingly, before the Turks were ready to counter attack, Leopold offered them terms at Karlowitz. This proved to be a general settlement:

(i) Transylvania and Hungary, with the exception of Temesvar, a small province in the south-eastern corner of the kingdom, was recognised as Habsburg territory, the new frontier being drawn along the lines of the Save and Theiss rivers at their junction with the Danube.

(ii) The Turks recognised the recovery of Kamenets Podolskiy by Poland.

(iii) Russia gained Azov in the Crimea.[1]

The Turkish empire was not destroyed but its existence was no longer a threat to Europe. Little attention was paid to it during the War of Spanish Succession, but once it was over Leopold's son, Charles VI, sent Eugène down the Danube in a successful bid to recover Belgrade (1717). The Treaty of Passarovitz which followed reaffirmed the terms of Karlowitz and added Tesmesvár, western Wallachia and parts of Bosnia and Serbia to the Habsburg dominions. The Danubian Monarchy had at last been established.

The Integration of Hungary into the Danubian Monarchy

The Danube campaign was of paramount importance in the extension of Habsburg administration to Hungary since every

[1] See Chapter X, page 423.

defeat of the Turks was also a defeat for Tokoli and his followers. When the kingdom was occupied by an army of 44,000 Leopold became ruler by right of conquest and, as had happened in Bohemia, election promises and coronation oaths were powerless to protect the cause of local liberties. As early as 1685 when the relief of Vienna had demonstrated that the Turks were occasionally fallible, but when there was as yet nothing to presage their whole-sale expulsion from Hungary, Leopold had none the less appointed a special commission to investigate means of effecting the integration of Hungary with his other territories. Significantly, its leaders were two experienced cameralists, Stratmann and Kinsky, the chancel-lors of Austria and Bohemia; men who regarded traditional liberties as concessions to anarchy, and feudal immunities as obstacles to effective administration, and whose recommendations were certain to favour the supremacy of Austrian bureaucracy.

A most difficult problem was the one of religion. Leopold's devotion to the Catholic Church precluded him from freely granting toleration to heretics, and it was an inescapable fact that the Holy League against the Turks should also be opposed to Protestantism. Moreover, the association of dissent and treason in Hungarian history was too close to be ignored. The cameralists, however, urged caution. They planned first to create an effective bureaucratic system which, having overriden political non-conformity, would then be able to eliminate heresy: until the first stage had been achieved, any precipitate attempts at conversion might cause rebellion. Consequently commanders were ordered to restrain their men from destroying Protestant churches, and the promises of 1681[1] were not broken outright.

By 1687, before the kingdom had been altogether cleared of Turks, the political plans of the cameralists reached fruition, and a Diet was summoned to Pressburg to receive their decisions. The Golden Bull of 1222 was amended by the abolition of the *jus resistandi*, and the monarchy was declared to be no longer elective but the hereditary possession of the Habsburg family: to symbolise this, Leopold's nine-year-old son, Joseph, was brought to Hungary and formally crowned. Though Hungary was thus reduced to the provincial status of Bohemia, the administrative revolution was carried through with caution and without the brutality which had occurred in the latter. Leopold desired to make his settlement

[1] See above, page 370.

acceptable, and since he could not liquidate the Magyar nobility he made them what few concessions he could. Though a Hungarian section was established in the *Hofkanzlei*, and though the fiscal administration too was reorganised to assess contributions in proportion to the kingdom's wealth, within the kingdom itself the administration of the edicts was left in the hands of Hungarian officials, and the nobility were confirmed in their social and economic privileges as landlords.

Transylvania, where traditions of independence died hard, was allowed further concessions. By special arrangements drawn up in 1690 and 1691 the country was not merged into Hungary but governed directly from Vienna, which meant in practice that the local nobility retained their political pre-eminence, and the coexistence with the Roman Church of the various Protestant denominations was allowed to continue.

There was of course opposition to the ascendancy of Austria, no matter how moderately exercised. The new tax assessments were naturally unpopular, and the Protestants feared that the period of toleration was of uncertain length. Thus, when Francis Rackoczi led a rebellion to restore the guarantees of the Golden Bull he did not lack for recruits, and the government had to maintain 30,000 troops in Hungary in order to contain the insurgents until the War of Spanish Succession had ended. From that moment Rackoczi was doomed, though both Joseph I (1705–11) and his brother Charles VI (1711–40) were determined to pursue the policies of their father by avoiding undue violence. Rather than crush the entire rebel army, Charles won over the rebels individually until Rackoczi had been isolated. He was then allowed to escape into exile.

The final stage in the creation of the Danubian monarchy was reached in 1713 when Charles VI declared, in the Pragmatic Sanction, that the German, Bohemian and Hungarian possessions of the Habsburgs were to be regarded as a single state. The problems of the diversity of race, religion and culture persisted long after this date, indeed they were never solved, but the political structure of the empire had been established. The Austrian Habsburgs, no longer condemned to the impossible task of rejuvenating the obsolete Holy Roman Empire, emerged as a major European power whose diverse territories had been organised into one administrative unit. They had defeated the Turks; they had contained, and finally had helped to destroy, the French attempt to establish a Bourbon hegemony in Europe; they won possession of Milan, Tuscany, Naples and the Netherlands; and from the dangers and confusions of both the Thirty Years War and the war with the Turks they survived to create the great Danubian monarchy.

X

The Struggle for the Baltic

---•---

THE CREATION OF THE SWEDISH EMPIRE, 1611–60

The Rise of Sweden to 1611

Since 1397 Sweden had formed part of the kingdom of Denmark-Norway and though many attempts were made to win independence, the Danish kings had suppressed them with savage strength. But violence only gave rise to violence. The Blood Bath at Stockholm in 1526, when the Danes executed more than ninety nationalist leaders in one day, far from intimidating the Swedes provoked a new and more widespread movement; and as the leaders had all been killed at Stockholm it was a young and unknown noble, Gustavus Vasa, who assumed their place at the head of the free peasantry. He also won valuable support from the north German towns of the Hanseatic League which resented Denmark's control of the Sound and the tolls she levied on their shipping. Though Gustavus was successful in Gotland and Svealand, the area around the lakes of the central plain and northwards along the east coast, Denmark retained possession of the mountain ranges along the Norwegian frontier, of all the southern and western provinces, and of the island of Gotland from which the east coast could be controlled.

The revolutionary character of the new kingdom was symbolised in 1527 by Gustavus Vasa's adoption of Lutheranism. Not only did he give the nobility a stake in the rebellion by restoring to them all the Church lands which their families had donated since 1430, but he strengthened the crown by taking the remainder for himself. In addition, he compelled the Lutheran clergy to buttress royal authority by subservience to his direction. Two brilliant churchmen, Petri and Andreas, who successfully achieved a doctrinal reformation, the necessary sequel to Gustavus's appropriations, were sentenced to death in 1539 for resisting the king's interference within the Church. Their subsequent release and pardon in no way diminished the effect of their trial and condemnation, and the Church became a valuable department of state.

MAP 18   The Swedish Empire in the Baltic, 1610–60

Under the pressure of Denmark's hostility, Gustavus Vasa and
his sons sought safety in expansion along the northern and eastern
shores of the Baltic. Finland was their first conquest and then, in
1561, they leaped the Gulf to occupy Estonia and its off-shore
island of Dago, where their success brought upon them the
enmity of the Russians. Nor was this all, for when Gustavus's
second son, John III, married a Polish princess he brought up his
son Sigismund as a Catholic, and secured his election to the
Polish throne in 1587: his accession in 1592 to the throne of
Sweden led to a Protestant revolt in which the third of Gustavus's
sons, Charles IX, seized the crown. The Protestant character of
Sweden was thus confirmed, and its national spirit, the sensation
of being different, was considerably strengthened. Poland, how-

ever, was added to the growing number of Sweden's enemies in the Baltic, and when Charles IX died in 1611 Sweden was at war with the Danes, the Russians and the Poles.

Far more dangerous to Sweden were the symptoms of internal dissension. The nobles, many of whose families had suffered in the Stockholm Blood Bath, considered themselves the natural leaders of Sweden, and their representatives sat by right of birth in the council of state, the *rad*, which daily determined royal policy. Affronted by Gustavus Vasa's assumption of royalty in 1523, their jealousy was not allayed by his gifts of Church land. They argued that the monarchy should be elective, and the subsequent depositions of Gustavus's eldest son Eric XIV, and of Sigismund I, the one for being insane, the other for being a Catholic, gave practical force to their theory. Against them the Vasas could only appeal to the *riksdag*, the assembly of the Estates in which the nobles were outnumbered by the clergy, the townsmen and the free, tax-paying peasantry: the latter were passionately loyal to the Vasas, the townsmen preferred monarchy to noble oligarchy, and the clergy were essentially civil servants. But the *riksdag*, however willingly it endorsed the king's wishes was of limited value to the crown since it met rarely and had no power to initiate legislation.

As disaffection grew among the nobles, many returned to their Danish allegiance, others chose to follow Sigismund, while the remainder determined to withhold allegiance from Charles IX's son when he should succeed his father, unless he agreed to guarantee them a monopoly of power both in making policy and in administering it.

Gustavus II Adolphus, 1611–32

Unlike his father, Gustavus II Adolphus did not lack sympathy for the nobles' demands. For all his self-conscious royalty he respected their desire for important posts in the administration, and though he was not a man to be readily intimidated he recognised that Sweden was too small a country to withstand the secession from public service of so important a section of the community. In order to bring the nobles back into responsible political activity he disarmed them by wholly conceding to the demands presented by Axel Oxenstierna, their leader. They were given employment beyond their expectation in a civil service which was reorganised into five colleges, or departments, under the admiral, the treasurer, the high steward, the marshal and the chancellor. The nomenclature was that of medieval government, and so were the sources of revenue, since the administration was maintained by the produce of crown lands assigned to the separate colleges; but because of the co-operation between king and nobles the system worked admirably, withstanding the burdens of perpetual warfare, of assimilating conquered territories and of governing in the absence of a king whose reign was spent with the army.

Since the nobles thus gained responsibility and power, their privileges, especially their exemption from taxation, were not, as in France or Spain, the residue of anachronistic traditions but the fruits of their own labours in the state. Being trusted, the majority proved trustworthy, and in Axel Oxenstierna the best qualities of public service were personified. Gustavus appointed him chancellor, responsible for co-ordinating and directing the work of the other colleges, and it was owing to his efficiency and his loyalty that Sweden survived the crisis of the King's sudden death in 1632.

Oxenstierna was an admirable foil to the volatile king, being practical, cautious, diplomatic and a gifted bureaucrat: when Gustavus complained, 'If we were all as cold as you we should freeze,' he retorted, 'If we were all as hot as your majesty we should burn.' Gustavus was indeed a fiery monarch, and it was his personality rather than his concessions which transformed a jealous nobility into a body of loyal officials. A big, clumsy man with tawny beard and hair, *il re d'oro* to the Italian mercenaries, immensely strong, with the fierce temper, the easy manners and the blunt directness of an infantry officer, he inspired others with his boundless self-confidence: 'He thinks the ship cannot sink that carries him,' wrote the English ambassador. But self-confidence and a manly gait were not all. His father had prepared him well for the task of kingship, training him in military skills, making him fluent in five languages and able to understand four more, and instilling in him a respect for the institution of monarchy as intense as his devotion to the Lutheran Church. In addition to his education, Gustavus possessed natural powers of leadership which made him a national figure, able to win the nobles back into public life without forfeiting the affection of the other estates. The nobles followed him despite themselves because, like Henry IV of France, he commanded both loyalty and affection. Like Henry, too, his deliberate appeals to the peasantry succeeded because they sprang as much from genuine concern as from calculation: 'My wish for the common man and peasantry is that their meadows may be green and their fields give a hundredfold, so that their barns may be filled and that they may all grow and increase in prosperity, and so that they might cheerfully and without murmur perform their duties and exercise their rights.'

Secure at home, it was a wise decision of Gustavus to deal separately with his enemies abroad and to clear the field a little by negotiation. The most dangerous threat came from the Danes who had broken through from their provinces on the west coast of Sweden to recover the district of Alvsborg, but they were handicapped by the cost of their campaign, and by the local peasantry whose opposition made their conquest valueless. In consequence they were glad to restore it by the Treaty of Knared (1613) in return for an annual subsidy, and Gustavus was left free to face his opponents in the eastern Baltic. There fortune favoured him since the Russians had been distracted by a series of civil wars, known as the Time of Troubles. The new tsar, Michael Romanoff, had no means of withstanding Gustavus and, after a mere show of resistance, was content to make peace at Stolbova (1617), where he recognised Swedish possession of Carelia, Ingria and the island of Kexholm. These acquisitions had a double value to Sweden since they provided not only a territorial link between her possessions of Finland and Estonia, but also a barrier to repel any future attempt to revive Russian ambitions in the Baltic.

Gustavus was free to campaign against his remaining enemy, the king of Poland. In part his purpose was the defensive one of safeguarding his dynasty from the Polish claimants, in part imperialist. Gustavus did not want more tracts of territory but, since rivers were the arteries of trade in northern Europe, and a rich source of revenue from customs, he sought control of the Polish ports and river mouths. In a series of disjointed episodes between 1617 and 1629 the Swedes leapfrogged from one estuary to the next. Riga, Memel, Pillau and Danzig fell to them, and with them the river mouths of the Duna, the Niemen, the Pregel and the Vistula. Sigismund of Poland was too preoccupied with his campaigns against the Turks and the Russians[1] to be able to check Gustavus's marauding raids, and in the Truce of Altmark (1629)

[1] See Chapter IX, page 363.

officially ceded possession of these ports to Sweden for a period of six years.

The negotiations preceding the Truce of Altmark owed much to the diplomacy of Richelieu[1] whose agents were eager to disentangle Gustavus from Poland in order to embroil him in the Thirty Years War. Already Wallenstein's irruption into north Germany, his capture of Rostock and Wismar, his assumption of the title 'Admiral of the Baltic', had compelled Gustavus to assist at the relief of Stralsund in 1628 in order to prevent the emergence of a new force in the struggle for Baltic supremacy. Wallenstein's military ambitions were the more ominous since the Habsburg emperor who employed him was both a champion of the counter reformation and an ally of Poland. His victories in north Germany had been exploited to enforce an Edict of Restitution: it was not too fanciful to suppose that further victories in the Baltic might presage a restoration of the Catholic Vasas to the Swedish throne. Oxenstierna later recorded, 'It is certain that had his late Majesty not betaken himself to Germany with his army, the emperor would today have a fleet upon these seas. And if the emperor had once got hold of Stralsund, the whole coast would have fallen to him, and here in Sweden we should never have enjoyed a minute's security.'

No doubt Gustavus would have invaded Pomerania whatever the circumstances in Europe, since logically it was the necessary consequence of his possession of Livonia and the Polish ports. With the Oder and the Elbe under his control the Baltic would be his, and the perceptive Wallenstein, as early as 1627, had tried to delay the inevitable by sending 1,000 cavalry to strengthen Polish resistance. Nevertheless Imperialist victories gave urgency to Gustavus' action while French diplomacy determined its timing. The Truce of Altmark ending one stage of Sweden's expansion was immediately succeeded by the Treaty of Bärwalde which began another: for 20,000 imperial thaler, to be paid by Richelieu every six months, Gustavus undertook to make war upon the Austrian Habsburgs.

Gustavus's prime objective was to drive the Imperialists from the Baltic ports, to seize possession of these for himself and to establish a permanent base in Pomerania. Beyond this he no doubt hoped to support the Lutheran princes in their struggle to withstand the

[1] See Chapter II, page 129.

Edict of Restititution. Perhaps he may have intended to drive the
Habsburgs entirely from north Germany. Perhaps he even
imagined himself at the head of a crusade to liberate Protestantism
throughout the empire. 'If we should conquer,' he said in council,
'it will be in our power to do as we please.' If, as is possible, his
words were deliberately vague in order to evade precise definition
of his ambitions, it is none the less true that once launched upon his
campaigns[1] these ambitions fed upon success. The victory at
Breitenfeld and the triumphal progress through the Rhineland
transformed his desire for security to a demand for satisfaction.
The saviour of north Germany required payment. It was no longer
Pomerania alone but Magdeburg too. Moreover, as the Rhineland
cities fell to his onset, south Germany beckoned alluringly. But if a
crusade through the south were to result in permanent and substantial concessions from the Catholic powers entrenched there,
then these powers would have to be so thoroughly defeated that
peace could be imposed, as Oxenstierna put it, 'with our foot on
their neck and a knife at their throat'. To do this the Protestant
powers would have to co-ordinate their resources more efficiently
and to find a leader to direct their march.

By 1632 Gustavus had no doubts about his mission to dominate
Germany. Continued success brought out in him the autocratic
streak and the arrogant conceit of the presumptive world
conqueror. Justly perhaps, he scorned the military ability of the
Lutheran princes, and compelled their assent to treaties of contingent federation, a form of subsidiary alliance which gave
him full control of their armies. If any protested the right, as
an ally, to be consulted he was brusquely informed that his lands
were already at Sweden's mercy by right of conquest. It required
a special mission by Oxenstierna to smooth the ruffled vanities of
his sovereign's allies; but there was more at stake than vanity. The
treaties of contingent federation could too easily become stepping
stones to a political federation with Sweden, a *corpus bellicum et
politicum* which Gustavus actually proposed when encamped at
Frankfurt. Though Sweden's supremacy in such a federation was
never openly admitted, its creation would involve the repudiation
by the German princes of the emperor's authority, and thus leave
the field clear for a recognition of the Swedish king's. Since neither
Saxony nor Brandenburg would submit to this, Gustavus had a

[1] See Chapter II, pages 131–2 for an account of Gustavus's campaigns.

further reason to invade south Germany where the dangerous plight of the Protestants might make them more devoted to his cause. At Lützen, however, his life, together with his vision of empire, was abruptly ended.

If Gustavus's aims have perplexed posterity, his dramatic successes astonished contemporaries. Contrary to the legend, embroidered by later ages, of blonde Nordic giants fighting with matchless valour for their king and their faith against the mean-spirited mercenaries of north Germany, the Swedish army was as polyglot as its rivals, and differed from them in only two respects. One important feature was the military genius of its generals, of whom the greatest was Gustavus himself. A great admirer of Maurice of Nassau[1] he learned from him to adopt new tactics and to develop new weapons: indeed, where Maurice had armed his cavalry with pistols in order to fire into the enemy and wheel away to reload, Gustavus trained his to charge with the sabre after discharging their firearms. His greatest achievement was to revive the role of the infantry who had become accustomed to scrumming together in massive formations, whether in defence or attack. Gustavus regrouped them in smaller units and thus enabled them to change front and to move their ground with speed and efficiency, as was well demonstrated at Breitenfeld when the Saxon army fled exposing the Swedish flank. Since the smaller units were more exposed he provided groups of cavalry to defend them, and equipped them with light artillery. His famous 'leathern gun', a three-pounder with a very thin bronze barrel, bound with rope and mastic enclosed in a sheath of hard leather, was developed by him before 1627, though its successor in 1629, an all metal four-pounder, proved rather more effective. The value of these guns was that they were easily portable and, relatively speaking, quick-firing. Three men were enough to transport and to operate one in the battlefield, and it was the possession of forty-two of these at Breitenfeld, against Tilly's ponderous twenty-four pounders, which helped to give the Swedes their victory.

A recruiting officer could offer nothing more attractive than the prospect of being on the winning side, unless it was the certainty of regular pay; and it was this second feature of the Swedish army which reconciled a mercenary to its harsh military code. Discipline was more easily acceptable to promptly paid troops who did not

[1] See Chapter IV, page 185.

have to plunder so frequently on their own account in order to stay alive. The Swedish army existed like any other on the subsidies of allies and the contributions enforced from occupied towns, but unlike its rivals it was not dependent on these. Sweden was increasing in wealth. Her cities were growing in size; Stockholm was already established as a commercial and financial centre, and Gothenburg, by reason of its position west of the Sound, was supplying timber and hemp to the dockyards of England and Holland without having to pay dues to Denmark. More important was the possession of the ports and river mouths which gave Sweden the power to impose duties on all trade within the Baltic. In addition there was the income from the crown lands specifically assigned to maintain the army. All this, however, would not have sufficed to sustain the vast expense of Gustavus's wars: in the last analysis it was Sweden's mineral resources which maintained them.

With the assistance of Dutch engineers and mining experts the production of iron was raised from 5,000 tons in 1620 to 20,000 by 1630. More valuable still was the extraction of copper. In the Stora Kopperburg Sweden enjoyed possession of the largest deposit of copper in Europe, at a time when every government needed copper urgently for the manufacture of coinage and artillery. In 1613 the mine was appropriated by Gustavus in order to pay to Denmark the indemnity required by the Peace of Knared. From that time its production of 3,000 tons a year, until its exhaustion after 1648, gave Sweden a unique advantage over her enemies since it enabled her to procure on the Amsterdam market a constant supply of foreign exchange to pay her continental armies.

The Regency and the Reign of Queen Christina, 1632–54

Although it was well known that Gustavus always fought alongside his men in battle and thus incurred the risks which beset the humblest soldier, Sweden was utterly unprepared for his death in 1632. Everything had depended upon him; the collegiate structure of the administration had no other title to existence than his will, while the direction of the war had been solely in his hands. No plans existed for the formation of a regency government despite the fact that his daughter Christina was only five years old. Fortunately, in Axel Oxenstierna, Gustavus left a man with the ability and the power to form an effective government. The *riksdag*, summoned by him to receive the news of Gustavus's death was so stunned that the Estates so far forgot their habitual suspicion of the nobility as to authorise the *rad* to govern in Christina's name. This virtually committed the government into the hands of Oxenstierna: within the *rad* he was supreme; as chancellor he held the most important office in the administration, and of the four other great offices, one was held by his brother, another by a cousin.

Oxenstierna's loyalty to the memory of Gustavus and the immediate interests of Sweden alike determined that he should continue the German war, since to withdraw unilaterally would have been to forfeit Pomerania. The Heilbronn League,[1] despite the unwelcome predominance of the French in its councils, was useful enough to hold the Habsburgs in check while Sweden regrouped her forces after Lützen. After Nördlingen, however, Oxenstierna began to follow an independent line. Sharing none of Gustavus's imperial ambitions he believed that Sweden's interests lay solely in the Baltic. In the Baltic, moreover, the expiry of the Truce of Altmark in 1635 deprived Sweden of her lease of the Polish ports, a loss of great financial and strategic importance. There was enough for Sweden to do, therefore, without becoming involved in Germany and, for this reason, Oxenstierna maintained that Denmark rather than Austria was the most dangerous of Sweden's enemies: 'We find that Denmark is not less inimical to us than Austria, and the worse enemy because she is nearer.' When Christian IV of Denmark increased the duties to be paid by Swedish shipping in the Sound, Oxenstierna regarded this a more acute *casus belli* than any German issue.

Swiftly and without warning, the Swedes invaded Holstein from Pomerania in December 1643: by January they had overrun the Danish mainland and stood expectantly along the shore of the Little Belt, awaiting the winter frost to afford them a safe passage across to the island of Fyen. When the waters failed to freeze Oxenstierna sent thirty-two Dutch ships, raised privately by Swedish agents, to transport his troops for an assault on Copenhagen. Christian IV, however, led his own fleet in a spirited counter attack at the Battle of Kolberg Heath and foiled the Swedish plan. If the Imperialist general, Gallas, who had had the wit to chase northwards behind the Swedish army while it was preoccupied in Holstein, had also had the sense to keep sober, the Emperor might well have recovered his influence in north Germany; but it was in

[1] See Chapter II, page 133.

a drunken stupor that Gallas directed his assault, and his men failed to dislodge the Swedes from their grasp of Holstein. In addition, the ships which escaped from Kolberg Heath joined with a second fleet to seize the Danish island of Bornholm. The result was a form of stalemate. If the Swedes had restored their position they were doubtful if they could renew their original attack: if the Danes had won a respite, few of them believed they could withstand a second attack.

Into this mood of hesitancy intruded the personality of Christina, perceptive, imperious and uncomprisingly determined to end the war, not merely with Denmark but with all Sweden's enemies. She was convinced that war served no other purpose than to justify Oxenstierna in excluding her from the direction of a purely masculine occupation. In September 1644 she came formally of age on her eighteenth birthday; and with the termination of the regency came an end to the war. In one respect, however, her strictures on the futility of the war were unfair, since the campaign against Denmark resulted in important gains for Sweden in the Treaty of Brömsebro, 1645:

(i) Denmark ceded the provinces of Jemteland and Herjedalen along the frontier between Norway and Sweden;
(ii) Denmark also ceded the islands of Gotland and Osel, both of strategic value in the Baltic;
(iii) Sweden was exempted from the payment of Sound dues, and in pledge of this was to occupy the province of Halland on her south-western coast, for a period of thirty years.

These acquisitions, obtained after eighteen months of relatively minor warfare, were of much greater value to Sweden than the territories gained four years later at Westphalia.[1] It was not that Sweden had won the mainland provinces which were to be hers for ever while the German territories acquired in 1648 were held only temporarily — only later generations were to discover this — but that despite seventeen years of expensive, continuous warfare, she gained less in 1648 than Gustavus II Adolphus had held at the end of 1631, even before he succumbed to imperialist delusions. Sweden was refused an electoral title, nor could she gain a permanent voice in the Imperial Diet. Instead, as an alien conqueror, she was grudgingly confirmed in her possession of Western

[1] See Chapter II, page 137.

Pomerania, of Stettin, Stralsund and Wismar, and of the offshore islands of Rügen, Usedom and Wollin. In addition, the secularised bishoprics of Bremen and Verden gave her control of the river mouths of the Weser and the Elbe.

The ending of the war went almost unnoticed in Sweden where the country was swiftly moving to the brink of civil war, as a result of the wholesale alienation of crown land which had taken place since 1632. The departments of the administration depended on the produce of the royal estates assigned to them, but as rents in kind were sometimes difficult to convert into negotiable currency — salted hides and bales of corn were scarcely liquid assets — Oxenstierna had decided to alter the fiscal system. He began by giving land outright in lieu of payment for good service in the army or in the administration, or by selling it to raise immediate capital. His next step was to recoup the administration by providing it with a more efficient source of revenue from indirect taxation. Unhappily for Sweden, Oxenstierna lost control of his colleagues in the *rad*, who became so excited by the opportunity afforded them by the disposal of royal estates that they ignored the second, essential part of his plan. From 1632, without Gustavus's physical presence to overawe and to inspire them, the nobles forgot their recent conversion to the ideal of public services, and, brushing aside the protestations of Oxenstierna, began to plunder Sweden with the irresponsible selfishness of triumphant mercenaries. Twenty-two of the most influential families obtained lands worth one-fifth of the ordinary revenue of the state, their lesser colleagues gaining less in proportion to their status. With land they also sought honours and titles, the number being more than doubled during the Regency: where three men had held the title of count, twenty were to glory in the honour, and the barons increased from seven to thirty-four.

The consequences for the peasantry, a vigorous and self-reliant estate, were serious. Those living on crown lands, who had enjoyed a position of virtual independence under an absentee and generally tolerant landlord, were subjected to the mercy of a profit-minded noble in their midst, anxious to exploit his investment. Worse still, and much more frequent, was the sale not of land but of the tax revenues from the freeholding peasantry, since the nobles who thus collected these taxes for themselves fell very easily into the habit of treating these freeholders as though they were their tenants. The threat of degradation to the status of servile labourers, made all the worse by the seigneurial habits acquired by the nobles from their experience of serfdom while on service in Germany, brought the peasantry very close to rebellion. At the same time, the administration began to founder without its accustomed revenues: offices in the civil service went unpaid, and the army had to plunder to survive. When the *rad* at last took up Oxenstierna's proposals for indirect taxation it could not introduce these without the *riksdag*'s consent, and on this issue the peasantry, the clergy and the townsmen were united in opposition: 'When the nobility have all the peasants subject to themselves, then the Estate of Peasants will no longer have a voice at the diet, and when the Estate of Peasants goes under, Burghers and Clergy may easily go under too.'[1] The *riksdag* demanded *reduktion*, the restoration of all crown lands, and when the *rad* refused to surrender its gains, the *riksdag* refused to pass the indirect taxes.

In this impasse the decision lay with Christina, a woman of such intrepid self-assurance that it was unlikely that she could stay out of any controversy for long. In many ways she resembled her father; physically tough, capable of great endurance, trained to diplomacy and the command of foreign languages, she was as autocratic and self-willed. Her ebullient mind extended beyond the confines of statecraft and war: these alone bored her, and she looked for companionship to men of letters and philosophy — she patronised both Grotius and Descartes — delighting in the excitement of intellectual debate. Unlike Gustavus, Christina had no concept of duty: if ruling Sweden should prove tedious then with wilful disregard of the consequences she was ready to give it up: if ruling Sweden meant that she would have to provide an heir, she was too imperious to submit to the servitude of marriage and chose rather to abdicate. Moreover, her restless spirit, ever prone to novelty and the seizure of forbidden fruit, was leading her by secret debates and private communications into the fold of the Roman Church. Her choice therefore lay between abdication and expulsion.

For the moment her secret desires remained her own, and with some finesse she set out in 1650 to win the *rad*'s assent to the nomination as heir to the throne of her cousin Charles who had

[1] Archbishop Lenaeus, quoted by M. Roberts, 'Queen Christina and the General Crisis of the 17th Century', *Past and Present* July 1962.

commanded Swedish troops in Germany. It was a difficult task since the nobles could see no reason why Christina should be in so much haste. Moreover, they sought to impose conditions upon their recognition of Charles which would subject him to the *rad*'s control. In any case, the prospect of another vigorous soldier on the throne was not comforting. If Christina were to win she required some powerful weapon: she thus decided to champion the *riksdag*'s demand for *reduktion*, despite the fact that she was as guilty as the *rad* in alienating royal land. Since her formal accession in 1644 she had made no attempt to remedy the finances of the crown she was preparing to abdicate, and with precipitate abandon, originating from a combination of generosity, irresponsibility and recklessness, increased the flood of donations. Of all the lands alienated by the crown, more than half were lost by Christina after 1648. Indifferent to the effect of her acts upon the administration, she was as blind to the consequences for the peasantry, until in 1650 she discovered in their readiness to revolt a weapon with which to coerce the *rad*.

In that year the failure of the harvest, the worst of the century, brought peasant discontent to a head. The *riksdag* met for the unprecedented period of four months in one year, and the speeches of the lower estates, in conjunction with the demonstrations of hungry villagers, caused consternation among the nobles. Oxenstierna confessed that he was afraid to visit his country house, and another noble drew an unhappy parallel with events elsewhere: 'They all want to do as they have been doing in England, and make us all as like as pig's trotters.' The more the nobles panicked, the more they played into Christina's hands. Cynical though she was of the *riksdag*'s demands, she incited it to attack the nobility and pretended to embrace the cause of *reduktion*. At this the nobles had no option but to capitulate: Christina, in return for withdrawing her support from the campaign for *reduktion*, won acceptance of Charles as Hereditary Prince.

Christina's remaining years as queen were spent in filling in the details of her abdication. She was determined to live as lavishly in retirement as she had done on the throne, and, by one of the ironies of her reign, compelled the *rad* to recover certain crown lands in order to assure her of a fixed income. Occupied also in preparing for her spiritual comfort, she entertained in secret a succession of priests through whom she was received into the Roman Church. In May 1654 she abandoned her throne. Christina's romantic vision of herself as an exiled queen holding literary court in Rome before the astonished eyes of Europe was not fulfilled. After the initial shock people found her merely absurd. Her punishment was to live to an old age, ignored by her former subjects and bored by her friends.

Charles X, 1654-60

Charles X, at the age of thirty-two, was ill-equipped to adapt himself to any problems but those of warfare. His life had hitherto been spent in camp and the complexities of Swedish government eluded him. The threat of bankruptcy, however, was plain for even him to see: the administration was unable to pay its servants, the navy lacked provisions, and the royal horses had no hay. The revenues from Baltic ports were not enough, the Stora Kopperburg was almost exhausted, and there was nothing left but *reduktion*. This of course would have solved the financial crisis and delighted the *riksdag*, but as the nobles had only accepted Charles in order to avoid *reduktion* its introduction would have caused rebellion. Charles settled for a compromise: royal estates deemed 'indispensable' to the running of the administration, along with one quarter of all other lands, were restored to the crown, a gain of roughly 3,000 farms and homesteads. In return, permanent possession was guaranteed the nobles of all the other crown lands they had acquired.

This limited *reduktion* while pleasing none was grudgingly accepted by all classes in Sweden, but the social conflict of the previous years had produced tensions which were less easily resolved. As a soldier, Charles had only one solution to offer, war. The thrill of victory or, equally, the determined response to defeat might serve to unite the nation as in Gustavus II Adolphus's day. In any case, the crown was so poor that the only way to maintain its army was by waging war abroad where the troops could keep themselves alive by plunder. 'Other nations make war because they are rich,' said one Swede sadly, 'Sweden because it is poor.' It was not difficult to find an enemy. Denmark was the traditional opponent, and Charles had married into the ducal house of Holstein-Gottorp in order to assure himself of a base from which to harass the Danes; but in 1654 he chose to fight Poland. John Casimir, the Polish king, had not only recovered control of the lucrative Prussian ports ceded in 1629, but had revived his family's claim to the Swedish throne, though he was scarcely in a position to make it good.[1] Poland was being overrun by Russians, Cossacks and Magyars; but if John Casimir's plight made Swedish intervention easy, it also made it necessary, for if the Russians gained the Prussian coastline they might well attack the Swedes in Livonia and Estonia.

The invasion of 1655 was both swift and successful. The Polish army could not withstand simultaneous attack from four quarters, and there were many disaffected nobles, Sobieski among them, who welcomed Charles's approach and recognised him as king. Within a few weeks Charles entered both Warsaw and Cracow, the joint capital cities, and John Casimir fled into exile. A tentative move by the Elector of Brandenburg to sneak advantage from the Swedish invasion by gaining full independence for his duchy of Prussia, a Polish fief,[2] was firmly checked by Charles at Königsberg in January 1656 where the Elector was compelled to recognise Charles as his overlord, to supply him with troops and to pledge him half the revenues of his duchy. By this time, however, the situation in Poland was turning against Charles. His ultimate purpose in invading Poland is hard to discern, and, having conquered western Poland, he showed no notion of what to do with it. Perhaps he intended to incorporate the coastal provinces with Sweden, protecting them by the creation of dependent principalities inland, but if so the project was chimerical. There were not only insufficient troops to control the population against its will; their behaviour ensured that their presence would never be voluntarily endured. As Charles had intended they lived off the country but, in addition to their depredations, their deliberate desecration of Catholic churches roused the peasantry to hysterical revolt. Charles plunged blindly into the interior in a vain attempt to buttress his control of the north. By February 1656 he arrived as far to the south-east as Lwow, while behind his back the Russians poured into the Baltic Provinces and John Casimir recovered Warsaw.

If Charles had been anything more than a soldier he would not so stupidly have imperilled his army; if he had been less of a

---

[1] See above, page 381 for deposition of John Casimir's father Sigismund; see Chapter IX, pages 364–5, for details of Poland's position.

[2] See below, page 407.

soldier he could never have extricated it so easily. With the countryside vociferous for the return of Casimir and with nearly 500 miles between himself and his base in Pomerania, he skilfully brought his army to the coastline, where he promptly laid siege to Danzig. This immediately raised yet another enemy against him, the Dutch, who at once despatched a squadron to prevent the centre of their Baltic trade falling into the hands of Sweden.[1] The emperor too began to send aid to Casimir; and the Elector of Brandenburg, who daily became increasingly reluctant to fulfil his treaty obligations to Charles, was retained as an ally only by granting him full sovereignty in Prussia. If the situation should worsen Charles would have nothing left to bargain with.

The decisive action was taken neither by Charles X nor by the states then at war with him, but by Frederick II of Denmark, who could no longer hold back from an opportunity to exploit Charles's predicament and to recover the losses of 1645. Whatever its dangers Frederick's declaration of war in June 1657 at least gave Charles an excuse to abandon a position which was rapidly becoming untenable, and to demonstrate again his excellence in attack. Within eight weeks he brought his army by forced marches across Pomerania to the shore of the Little Belt, separating the Danish mainland from the island of Fyen. But unless he could win control of the sea the point of his swift campaign would be lost, and a Swedish fleet which ventured into the Little Belt in September was driven back by the Danes. Charles's subsequent conquest of Jutland won him no advantage: as a show of force it made no impression upon Frederick who knew he was perfectly secure in Copenhagen, and who drew confidence from the news of Casimir's restoration in Poland and of Brandenburg's desertion of Sweden.[2] Poised on the brink of the sea yet impotent to cross it, Charles became daily more exasperated until at last a desperate opportunity offered itself. In January 1658 the waters of the Little Belt froze and the Swedish army marched across to Fyen, losing two squadrons of horse and the royal carriages through the ice. More dangerous than the crossing was the situation it created, for Charles had merely isolated himself in Fyen instead of in Jutland and once the ice melted there would be no escape. But the cold held, and intensified until the Great Belt too was frozen. For seven days, in a thrilling race against the thaw, Charles with 5,000 men and his

[1] See Chapter VIII, page 338.   [2] See below, page 407.

artillery, leaped from one island to the next until he arrived on Zealand with Copenhagen at last at his mercy. Frederick, betrayed by the elements, could only surrender.

The Treaty of Roskilde, concluded in February 1658, was the most important in Swedish history since it established the boundaries of modern Sweden. Whatever Charles's faults of judgement the result of his military escapades was to expel the Danes once and for all from the Swedish mainland. Halland, pledged to Sweden for twenty years in 1645, was ceded in perpetuity along with the coastal provinces of Scania, Bleking and Bohus. In addition the Danes surrendered Trondhjem in Norway and the island of Bornholm. By losing Scania the Danes lost control of the Sound, which could thus be closed only by the two countries acting in co-operation. Charles X immediately demanded that it be closed to Dutch armaments, in revenge for Dutch intervention at Danzig, but Frederick refused to commit himself. He was playing for time in which to find allies, and he wasted no opportunity to inform the Dutch of his efforts to preserve their access to the Baltic. Charles X was not given to patient negotiation. The difficulties and delays prompted him to teach the Danes a sharp lesson, and no doubt he considered the advantages of deposing Frederick in order to take for himself the triple crown of Scandinavia. Moreover, the reversion to peace merely revived his original problem of what to do with the army. He dared not dismiss it for fear of his Baltic rivals, yet he could not maintain it in idleness. Consequently, within five months of the Treaty of Roskilde his forces landed again on Zealand.

This time the Danes in Copenhagen resisted him so strongly that instead of the swift success upon which he had reckoned he was forced to undertake a siege which promised to be both long and bloody. Simultaneously the inhabitants of Trondhjem and Bornholm rebelled against their change of ruler. Most serious of all was the sudden blockade of the Sound by the navies of France, England and the United Provinces, acting in rare concert. Their trade with the Baltic was too lucrative to depend upon the whim of a Swedish king, and indifferent though they were to his quarrel with Denmark they could not permit him to control both banks of the Sound. Charles was thus unable to defeat Denmark, but neither could he be defeated. The impasse was only resolved by his death from camp fever in 1660.

In the Peace of Oliva Charles's successors restored Bornholm and Trondhjem to the Danes and abandoned the attempt to close the Sound to other states: in every other respect the Treaty of Roskilde was confirmed. At the same time, in a series of separate settlements, John Casimir renounced his claim to Sweden, the Elector of Brandenburg won general recognition of his sovereignty in Polish Prussia, and the Russians formally confirmed Sweden's possession of the Baltic provinces. For the first time in the seventeenth century the Baltic was at peace.

SWEDEN AND BRANDENBURG, 1660–1700

The Regency and the Reign of Charles XI, 1660–97

The death of Charles X, though it gave Sweden a respite from war, resulted in other ills so serious that the fruits of peace could not be enjoyed. Since Charles XI was a minor the *rad* seized power in his name, and the government fell into the hands of his uncle, Magnus de la Gardie. Of French ancestry, both rich and handsome, he was a glittering figure at Court and a great patron of the arts, but he had no understanding of government finance nor of foreign affairs. He was not the man to withstand the nobles who, indifferent to any interests but their own, renewed their spoliation of the crown, the victims of the 1654 *reduktion* jostling with the families who had failed to gain advantage from the earlier alienations. Under la Gardie's lax direction the worst excesses of Christina's reign were repeated. For this there was no excuse since the price to be paid in terms of administrative collapse and social unrest was already known to all.

The government soon became bankrupt, a predicament for which la Gardie proposed an unconventional solution: 'Cease paying off debts, and borrow, anticipate, take foreign subsidies ... and not a doit of deficit will remain.' His foreign policy was therefore designed less to safeguard the Baltic empire than to find a wealthy backer, whatever the consequences. Indeed many of la Gardie's colleagues were determined that there need be no consequences at all. 'Let us act like merchants', said one of them, 'so as to get money enough, and do naught else for it than sit still.' After a brief association with the Dutch in the Triple Alliance of 1668, the Swedes sold out to France for an annual subsidy of 400,000 *livres*. When Louis XIV invaded the United Provinces in 1672 la Gardie deceived himself that Sweden would have nothing more onerous to do than to close the Sound to Dutch shipping, a task made even more easy by the fact that Denmark too was in the French camp. Unfortunately, when the Dutch found an ally in the Elector of Brandenburg (1674), a Swedish army had to be sent to Pomerania in order to neutralise the Elector's forces in north Germany. La Gardie had no intention of provoking a fight with Brandenburg — his sole concern being to satisfy Louis XIV that his subsidies were being put to good use — but so badly were his men supplied that within a few weeks they were compelled to cross the border into Brandenburg in search of food. There they were defeated at Fehrbellin in February 1675.

The battle itself was little more than a minor engagement, but so consistently had Sweden triumphed in the past that the news of her defeat by a north German princeling had important repercussions. The immediate result was to advertise her impotence before all her enemies, who were quick to take advantage of it. The Elector's troops overran Pomerania, the Bishop of Münster occupied Bremen and Verden, and Christian V of Denmark set about the recovery of the provinces lost in 1660. The Danish fleet won command of the Sound, and an invading army swarmed across Scania, to the great delight of the peasants who ransacked the houses of the nobility and hailed the Danes as liberators.

The crisis served one good purpose in that it galvanised Charles XI into action. So backward and shy had he been as a boy that many had believed him illiterate, and it had been an easy matter for la Gardie to win complete ascendancy over him. Even when Charles came of age in 1672 he passively accepted his uncle's leadership, until he discovered in 1674 that his army, the one thing to interest him, had virtually ceased to exist. This prompted him to demand, and to secure, the *reduktion* of several hundred home-steads whose income had traditionally maintained the army. When, in the succeeding year, he saw his empire on the brink of dissolu-tion, he abandoned la Gardie altogether and put himself at the head of his people. It was almost too late. With 15,000 men he fought a harsh campaign in 1676 against the Danes in Scania, a campaign made all the more bitter by the peasantry who formed guerrilla bands to harass the royal army. Charles's strategy was simple, almost simple-minded. With sword in hand he sought to meet the enemy face to face, to challenge him for the mastery of the kingdom in one great pitched battle. But the Danes were too cautious, the guerrillas too wise, to play into his hands, and during the winter of 1676-7 his numbers were reduced to 8,000 by hunger and disease. Finally, at Lund, he forced the Danes to stand against him, and after a bloody encounter in which a total of 8,000 lost their lives, Charles emerged victorious. If the battle proved to be less decisive than he had hoped it at least made possible the recovery of Scania.

By 1678 the mainland had been secured, but it seemed that the north German territories were lost for ever. Ironically, however, what had been lost on account of the French alliance was recovered immediately by the same means. Louis XIV could not afford to earn a reputation for deserting allies; consequently, when a peace settlement was being negotiated at Nijmegen, he made separate treaties with Denmark at Fontainebleau, and with Brandenburg at Saint-Germain, compelling them to evacuate their troops from Wismar, Holstein-Gottorp and Pomerania.[1] It was in its way a gesture typical of Louis's arrogance since Charles was not consulted by the French, and so angry were both he and Christian that they salved their pride by embodying the terms of Fontainebleau in a special treaty between themselves. Thereafter Charles XI never forgave Louis for embroiling Sweden in so disastrous a war, nor for rescuing her so contemptuously from its consequences.

The war transformed Charles XI into a ruthless autocrat, bent on punishing those who had imperilled the kingdom during his youth. Like his father he was a soldier at heart, and it was only on the parade ground that he lost the inhibitions which at other times made him appear solitary and reserved; but he also possessed a political skill which smacked more of Christina than of Charles X. As Christina had achieved her abdication on her own terms by exploiting the rivalry of *rad* and *riksdag*, so Charles XI used this same conflict to make the monarchy absolute. His first step was to destroy the power of the nobles but this he did as though to please the other estates. In 1675 he acceded to a petition from the *riksdag* for the appointment of a commission of enquiry into the conduct of the regency. The commission's brief was too general,

[1] See Chapter VII, page 297. As French troops were in temporary occupation of Oldenburg and Cleves, neither Christian nor the Great Elector dared to resist.

however, and in 1680, at the *riksdag*'s request, it was superseded by two new commissions, each with greater powers than their predecessor, each with a more specific task. One was to investigate 118 families which had been involved in the regency administration, and to punish them for the consequences of their misrule; the other was to recover all crown lands alienated since 1638. At this the nobles threatened civil war, but, as Charles had foreseen, they were impotent against the combined strength of king, clergy, townsmen and peasantry. Isolation was the penalty they paid for governing in the exclusive interests of their class. The commissions worked zealously, the one collecting no less than four million *thalers* in fines, the other transferring to the crown the landed wealth of the nobility. As a result of this drastic *reduktion* the crown was assured of an additional income of 2,500,000 *thalers* a year.

The *riksdag*, believing that the king was indeed the only true guardian of its interests, and determined to remove all trace of noble oligarchy, willingly created a royal despotism by abolishing the powers of the *rad*. Thus ended the tradition begun in 1611 by Gustavus II Adolphus. Humiliated by the *riksdag*'s commissioners and deprived of much of their land, the nobles withdrew from public life, to be replaced in the administration by a new class of professional civil servant.

The collegiate system remained as before, but the nature of local government was developed to a degree of excellence unparalleled in Europe. The smallest unit, the *socken*, was made up of a small group of peasant farmers under their headman, who joined with the pastor and the elected magistrates to assess each taxpayer's contribution. The system demanded a peasantry wealthy enough to sustain the burden of taxation, in which Sweden was fortunate, but even more striking was its fairness and efficiency, demonstrated by the general readiness of the peasantry to pay their due amount. Above the *socken* came the district of one thousand hearths with its staff of magistrates and permanent officials: seven or eight districts comprised the province whose affairs were directed by a governor and four other officers: their work in turn was integrated with the five colleges of the central administration. The result was a highly organised system, methodical and meticulous, and particularly successful in the assessment and collection of taxes. Even during the disastrous years which followed Charles

XI's death, when Sweden was burdened with the continuous and extensive campaigns of his successor, this local administration, based on honesty, justice and efficiency never collapsed.

As revenue began to exceed expenditure Charles XI could afford to establish permanent garrisons, numbering about 25,000 troops in all, throughout his overseas possessions. In addition, the recovery of crown lands made it possible to maintain an army of 38,000 men on the land, ready for active service. A similar territorial system maintained 11,000 men for the Swedish navy which was re-equipped with thirty-eight new ships of the line. Though he was at heart a soldier, Charles resisted the impulse to use his military force since he realised that Sweden could benefit more by peace in the Baltic than from war. He gave nominal support to the European coalitions against France but avoided continental entanglements. He died in 1697, leaving the Swedish empire more powerful than it had ever been.

Brandenburg to 1660

Sweden's defeat by Brandenburg at Fehrbellin took Europe by surprise and marked the emergence of the Elector Frederick William as a major figure in Baltic politics. Thirty-five years earlier, at the time of his accession in 1640, the position had been very different. One of the largest principalities in Germany, Brandenburg had no assets: it was cut off from the sea, its towns had ceased to be centres of trade, it lacked natural resources, and because of its poor soil it was known as the sandbox of the Holy Roman Empire.

The depopulation of the countryside and the impoverishment of the towns, evident before 1618, were accelerated by the Thirty Years War, especially as Brandenburg was in the unhappy position of a buffer state between Sweden and Austria. Her ruler, however, as one of the seven imperial electors, had an important title, and as a Hohenzollern he was the heir to many carefully planned marriage alliances which had extended his territories. The duchy of Cleves, with the counties of Mark and Ravensberg, had been salvaged in 1614 from the Jülich–Cleves crisis;[1] the duchy of East Prussia had been acquired in 1618 as a Polish fief; in 1637 the last duke of Pomerania had bequeathed his duchy to the Hohenzollerns. These separate duchies were each of strategic and political importance, which, in the circumstances, was their chief disadvantage since

[1] See Chapter II, page 112.

this made them highly desirable to other powers. Cleves had close links with the United Provinces, and in 1640 was actually under Dutch occupation in order to protect it from Spain: Prussia was coveted by Poland, with whose king the Prussian nobility had more in common than with the Elector of Brandenburg: Pomerania with its valuable ports on the Baltic was under Swedish occupation.

Scattered though his territories were across Europe, and sharing no common institutions, bound together by no ties and virtually controlled by the armies of other powers, the new Elector was none the less inspired by a vision of a Hohenzollern state which should be both independent and united. His character was well suited to his self-appointed task. Like his father, George William,[1] he was a tall big man, but it was only the son whose spirit could match the frame: where his father had been hesitant, timid and unimaginative, Frederick William was a man of enterprise with a talent for bold decision. Above all, he had the courage to accept his predicament in 1640 as a challenge. With only 4,600 mercenaries, and with no money to pay them, his determination might well have appeared rash, since he had only his wits to rely upon. These, however, were unusually sharp. In subsequent years he was to acquire a reputation for unscrupulous diplomacy, 'le plus fin renard de l'Europe', as the French called him, and since it is only the strong who can win their way by force he had no other weapon but duplicity. Even so the legend was exaggerated. Skill and intelligence, resolution and ruthlessness, were qualities which all rulers required and which only successful ones shared. There were no more broken compacts in the history of Brandenburg than in that of other states.

Although his father had allied himself with the emperor after the Peace of Prague (1635), Frederick William spent his youth in the courts and camps of Austria's enemies. At the age of ten he was presented to Gustavus II Adolphus on his landing in Pomerania, he accompanied Frederick Henry of Orange at the siege of Breda, and so marked did his hostility to Austria become that his father summoned him home in 1638. Two years later he was free to pursue his own policy. The Austrian alliance was clearly played out. The emperor was no longer a power in north Europe after 1640; his friendship gained Brandenburg nothing but the hostility

---

[1] See Chapter II for George William, and for all subsequent references to events in the Thirty Years War.

Map 19   The territories of Brandenburg, 1660

of Sweden, France and Holland, and with rare percipience Frederick William realised that these were the very states who would emerge victorious from the war. By a supreme confidence trick he succeeded in convincing them that Brandenburg's friendship or neutrality were of value. He took a wife from the Orange family in order to ease his way back to Cleves, he attracted Mazarin's friendly interest without committing himself to any precise agreement, and, though it did nothing to secure the evacuation of Swedish troops from Pomerania, he secured from Sweden recognition as a neutral in the Treaty of Stockholm (1641). More than this he dared not do lest Austrian troops be directed to his defenceless frontier, but, as the negotiations at Westphalia demonstrated, his policy paid.

Mazarin was eager to restrain the emperor by creating a more powerful Protestant state in north Germany, and Sweden, once assured of western Pomerania, was prepared to assist the Elector to gain compensation elsewhere. In the event, Brandenburg gained territory out of all proportion to her importance in the war.

(i) The emperor confirmed the Treaty of Xanten (1614), which had assigned Cleves, Mark and Ravensberg to the Hohenzollern claimant;

(ii) Ravensberg was strengthened by the acquisition of its neighbour, the secularised bishopric of Minden;

(iii) The Elector also acquired the secularised bishoprics of Cammin and Halberstadt on Brandenburg's frontier, together with the reversion of the secularised archbishopric of Magdeburg after the death of its existing ruler. This prince did not die until 1680, but as early as 1650 Frederick William ensured that an electoral garrison was posted there;

(iv) Sweden took possession of Western Pomerania, with Stettin and the mouth of the Oder, but the eastern half of the duchy, barren of ports, was restored to the Elector.

Once the war was over the Elector was able to turn his mind to something more ambitious than mere survival. His object was to bring together his scattered territories in an administrative union, to make them *membra unius capitis*. The problem was to convince the states that this was desirable. In Brandenburg the dominant group was the *junker* squirearchy. Though not so wealthy as the nobles of Poland, the *junkers* too ran their estates on serf labour, making their profit from the sale of corn and beer. Their political creed was simple: they refused to pay taxes, they disliked warfare, which only brought foreign troops to ravage their fields, and they rejected out of hand the Elector's notion of a government common to all his territories. All these beliefs were evinced in 1650 when the Elector appealed to them for money, in order to raise troops to settle a frontier dispute with Sweden in Pomerania. The *junkers* refused the money, advised against any action threatening war, and pointed out that the Pomeranian nobles would never vote money for the defence of Brandenburg. The Elector was hamstrung since there was no one else to appeal to: the clergy no longer sat in the Diet, the poverty of the towns was reflected in the impotence of their representatives, and the peasantry had been reduced to serfdom. Nor could the Elector dispense with the Diet since it controlled not only the granting of revenue but also its assessment and collection.

When it became obvious that the *junkers* would never assent to his plans, Frederick William summoned a full session of the Diet in 1652. This in itself was an innovation since representative committees usually met on behalf of the Estates, but the surprise of the members at being summoned was nothing to their indignant alarm on learning the Elector's proposals. Instead of the excise on beer and the customary contributions levied separately on the towns and the countryside, he demanded a general excise on the Dutch model, the *modi generales*, a series of indirect taxes to which all subjects were to contribute. In the angry debate which followed, the Diet counter-attacked with every possible grievance it could bring against the elector. Finally it came to terms with him in the Recess of 1653 which concluded the Diet.

   (i) The serfs were to be abandoned more completely than ever before into the hands of the *junkers*;

  (ii) The practice of the Elector, a tolerant Calvinist, of employing Catholics in his service was to stop;

 (iii) All treaties contracted by the Elector were to be ratified by the Diet;

 (iv) The *modi generales* were not to be adopted;

  (v) The sum of 500,000 *thalers*, to be collected over a period of six years, was to be granted to the Elector.

The Recess was apparently a victory for the *junkers*, who sought absolute control over their serfs, who hated Catholicism, who distrusted their ruler's diplomacy, and who refused to pay taxes. Their one concession cost them nothing, the burden of the contribution falling upon the towns since they themselves were exempt. But Frederick William as the greatest landowner in Brandenburg was also a *junker*, sharing the prejudices and emotions of his class. The social terms of the Recess were not concessions wrung unwillingly from his hands. Moreover he secured what had formerly been denied him, a grant of money sufficient to raise 1,800 troops. It was only a beginning, but if the vision of a Hohenzollern state was to be given reality then, as Frederick William realised, force was the only means of achieving it.

The Swedish invasion of Poland,[1] culminating for Frederick William in the Treaty of Königsberg (1656) almost destroyed his plans. He surrendered not only half the revenue of his Prussian ports but also the use of his hard-won troops. Worst of all he had to recognise Charles as king of Poland and do homage to him for his fief of East Prussia, an act for which he might forfeit it for ever should John Casimir return victorious, and with the emperor sending aid from Austria, and with Swedish troops unwittingly seconding his efforts by their sacrilege and depredation, his return was not improbable. By good fortune, and the skill to recognise it when it appeared, Frederick William survived. When Charles X became hard pressed the Elector demanded full independence for Prussia as the price of his aid. When Charles turned to deal with Denmark, abandoning Poland to John Casimir, Frederick William survived the crisis, and preserved his independence in Prussia, by assisting Casimir against the Cossack and Russian armies which still plundered Poland.[2]

The Polish war proved to be the turning point of Frederick William's reign. Not only did he win general recognition of his sovereignty in Prussia, but he turned the war to such good account in Brandenburg that he was never again compelled to petition the Diet for money. He exploited the crisis to levy taxes on his own authority, and where protests arose that the taxes were illegal the troops who depended upon them were employed in their collection. in 1655–6, 700,000 *thalers* were collected by the army, whose numbers quickly grew to 22,000, and supplies of food and fodder were also appropriated. By 1659, 110,000 *thalers* were being

[1] See above, page 395.   [2] See Chapter IX, page 365.

collected monthly in Brandenburg alone, and even in the Rhineland duchies 1,500,000 *thalers* were seized before 1660. The Recess
which had given Frederick William the first sum to raise troops had
thus indirectly provided the means to raise all future contributions.

The Creation of the Hohenzollern State, 1660–1700

Burdensome though it was to the economy, the Elector retained
as many as 12,000 troops in service after peace had been made at
Oliva in 1660. If they had yet to prove their value on the battlefield,
they had already begun to play so vital a part in the collection of
taxes as to be indispensable. The *Generalkriegskommissariat*,
appointed originally as a general supply organisation for the army,
was made responsible for collecting the taxes by which the army
was maintained, and thus became a central department of the
administration. Its officers, though trained as soldiers, were
transformed into the servants of a centralised bureaucracy, as
efficient as their civilian counterparts in the Austrian *hofkanzlei*.[1]

There was no pretence of winning popular support. The Diet
complained repeatedly, but ineffectually, of the army's fiscal
activities and it failed to prevent the elector replacing in some areas
the traditional contribution by the excise, or *modi generales*. The
towns were fatally handicapped by social divisions. Many burghers
resented the close oligarchy of the older families, and advocated
the excise in order to win the Elector's favour in their local conflict.
Others preferred the excise since it was at least paid by everyone
whereas the older families had in the past exempted themselves
from payment of the contribution. For these reasons several towns
voluntarily submitted to the excise; after that it was not difficult to
impose it upon the remainder.

In any case the towns were politically unimportant no matter
how much they might contribute in taxation. Power lay with the
junkers; and their acquiescence in the virtual eclipse of the Diet, in
which they had always played the dominant part, was one of the
most striking developments of the reign. Curiously enough there
was little conflict. The Recess of 1653 had assured the social
privileges of the *junkers*, and they paid none of the *modi generales*
which the army collected from the rest of the community. Moreover they had everything to gain by approving the Elector's plans.
The *junkers* were only gentry, substantial landowners in their way

[1] See Chapter IX, page 357.

but not a wealthy leisured class. Instead of living on the rents of their estates they had to work them themselves, and no matter how energetically they did so, no matter how cheap serf labour, they could rarely provide a good living for all their family. Since the Reformation there were no longer benefices for their younger sons; the convention of their class forbade trade; employment in government service was therefore necessary to augment their incomes, and the army was the most favourably regarded as a suitable career. Any extension of the army's function, along with an increase in both its numbers and its importance, was bound to meet with the *junkers'* approval. Consequently, the eclipse of the Diet was of no interest to the class which enjoyed new and greater opportunities for employment in the Elector's service; especially since Frederick William so nicely reflected their own prejudices and interests.

In pursuit of his goal of a unified Hohenzollern state, the Elector had to extend his administration to his other territories, but the Rhineland duchies were in no mood to welcome interference from Berlin. Their towns were wealthy, and in the Estates the burghers joined with the nobles to oppose the Elector's plans. In two sessions of particular importance, in 1649 and 1653, they won substantial concessions, among them the right to meet on their own initiative, to negotiate independently with foreign powers, and to prevent the appointment of any official not locally born: in addition, the Elector could not raise taxes nor introduce his troops into the duchies without their consent. All these liberties were violated during the Swedish war of 1655–60, when, in spite of the threat of a general rising, over a million *thalers* were collected by the army. In 1660 the Elector challenged the opposition to show its hand by sending an ultimatum: unless their liberties were curtailed he would march upon the duchies. The fact that after the Peace of Oliva the Dutch were on good terms with Frederick William meant that the towns could not rely upon them for assistance as in the past; there were also many nobles who were eager to follow the example of the *junkers* by selling out to the Elector in return for privileges and employment. The final outcome was a compromise since Frederick William was scarcely able to fulfil his threat. The Estates abandoned their claims to negotiate independently and to refuse admission to the Elector's troops: their other privileges remained intact. Though on occasion the army subsequently collected forced taxes, the process of integrating the Rhineland duchies with Brandenburg

went no further, and they remained an exception to the general
pattern of Hohenzollern despotism.

At first sight the problem of Prussia seemed greater than that of
Cleves. The administration was headed by four locally appointed
oberrathe, whose collective powers were those of a viceroy, save
that they answered to no king. Frederick William found their
arrogance intolerable: 'These Prussians make the inhabitants of
Cleves seem like little saints.' The Prussians had only to look
across into Poland to see the type of anarchy which most appealed
to them. Consequently they would rather have been integrated
with Warsaw than with Berlin, and when Frederick William
removed all hope of this by winning Prussia's independence in
1660 he was faced with revolt. The city of Königsberg, spurred on
by Hieronymus Roth, a popular demagogue, led the way in
appealing to John Casimir to recover his rights in Prussia. Frederick
William, faced with the loss of the sovereignty he had so recently
acquired, reacted swiftly by marching on Königsberg in 1662 with
2,000 troops and by arresting Roth. Confronted with this show of
force, the Prussian Diet was taken unawares: it recognised the
Elector's sovereignty and even voted him a tax, but it retained
enough innate obstinacy to reject instinctively his proposals to
enforce the *modi generales*.

The compromise between independence and integration did not
last long. A powerful group of nobles was soon deep in conspiracy, and when Kalckstein, its leader, suspected that the Elector
was informed of the plot he simply crossed the frontier into Poland
in 1669. Such immunity, creating a dangerous precedent for other
traitors, could not be tolerated. Kalckstein was kidnapped by the
Elector's Resident in Warsaw and smuggled across the frontier to
Königsberg. There, after torture, he was executed in 1672. Two
years later, when Königsberg refused to allow the Elector's troops
to collect taxes, the citizens found themselves the unwilling hosts
of the army, which remained billeted upon them until the taxes
had been fully paid. Strong measures such as these employed
against a factious people won the day. After 1674 there was no
further conspiracy, the administration was geared to that of
Brandenburg, and the independent power of the *oberrathe* was
destroyed: 'They are councillors and servants who derive their
power only from their lord', wrote Frederick William, 'without his
will and approval they have no power to do or decide anything in

his affairs, except in conformity with their instructions and commission. It belongs to His Electoral Serenity to make the decisions which he thinks best and most useful.'

Of all the diverse and scattered elements of his inheritance the Elector could scarcely make one nation. His achievement was to make one state, and though it was two hundred years before Berlin became the capital of a territorially united Hohenzollern empire, by 1688 it had been established as the administrative centre of the Elector's territories, directing and controlling all the important features of their political life. The secret of Frederick William's success had been the army, and in the *Generalkriegskommissariat* he had created an organisation whose ruthless efficiency made possible the imposition of administrative unity. From its original function of military supply it had advanced to military finance, to national finance and finally to all economic matters. This was a rational progression since the maintenance of a standing army imposed tremendous strains upon the state's resources: by 1688 a population of 1,000,000 supported a standing army of 30,000, in contrast to France at that date where 18,000,000 maintained no more than 300,000. About one-tenth of the cost was met by foreign subsidies, but the remainder had to be found from taxation, which could not be done unless the national wealth was increased. Hence the *Generalkriegskommissariat* was assigned to the task of supplementing with state aid the scanty resources of private initiative.

The Elector's propagandists did their utmost to blacken the picture of Brandenburg's plight in 1640 in order to enhance the achievements of his reign, but there was little need for exaggeration. The economy which had been gravely weakened by the decline of the Hanseatic League and the by-passing of transcontinental trade routes, was well-nigh destroyed by the perpetual passage of armies during the course of the Thirty Years War. The process of recovery was both slow and spasmodic. Wisely the Elector turned for advice to Holland, and faithfully reflected it in a subsequent edict claiming that 'commerce and shipping are the main pillars of a state'. Little was achieved, however, since his mentor had no wish to create a rival. Nevertheless a Dutch merchant, Raule, whose audacity and enterprise were such that it became necessary for him to leave the United Provinces, found a welcome at the Elector's court, and became Director-General of the navy in 1672. Four years later, appointed to direct the Electoral

O2   M.E.S.C.

Board of Trade and Admiralty, he sent out privateers to win silver from the Spanish treasure fleets, and in 1682 he established the Brandenburg African Trading Company. It was a waste of time. The Dutch discouraged competition, and Brandenburg was scarcely in a position to offer any. Though his commercial ventures failed, Raule did equip a fleet of Ruritanian proportions, boasting a frigate and two small craft at Königsberg, and a North Sea squadron of seven other vessels at Emden.

At home much effort was made to improve communications, the most striking work being the construction of a canal from the Oder, above Frankfurt, to the Spree, whence barges could travel to Berlin, down the Havel and into the Elbe. This cut out the Baltic ports where Swedish commissioners waited to tax the transports which in the past had had to descend the Oder and sail round to the Elbe. It also attracted trade from the overland route running from Silesia and Saxony to the valleys of the Elbe and the Weser. In addition to improving communications, Frederick William did much to encourage immigration. Settlers not only brought new skills and industries to a population which had been traditionally agricultural, they also bred more consumers to stimulate industry and more taxpayers to support the army. The Dutch were especially welcome since their skill in land reclamation was invaluable in transforming the sandy wastes and marshy swamps of Brandenburg into fertile farmland, and the Elector offered them leases free of rent for ten years. He was quick to respond to the revocation of the Edict of Nantes, and 20,000 Huguenots found a home in Brandenburg. Though they did much to establish horticulture around Berlin, it was in the manufacture of textiles that they made their greatest contribution. The Elector's army was soon equipped with uniforms of their making, and was swollen by the addition of five infantry regiments of French refugees.

After 1660 the Elector was content to avoid dangerous commitments in foreign affairs, and to join his fellow Germans in accepting French subsidies. When the Dutch war broke out in 1672 he intervened,[1] after two false starts, on the Dutch side, and defeated Louis XIV's ally, Sweden, at Fehrbellin (1675). Though he overran Pomerania his conquest was short-lived. Louis XIV in 1679 was too powerful, and Cleves too vulnerable, for the Elector to retain it. After this, Frederick William returned to the receipt of

[1] See Chapter VII, pages 294-7.

French subsidies, playing an acquiescent, unheroic part in the *réunion* controversy. In 1688, the year of his death, he was stung to action by the French invasion of the Palatinate, at which he immediately offered his alliance to the emperor, and sent aid to William of Orange on his voyage to England. It was left to his son Frederick to join in the War of the League of Augsburg, and in return for his promise of aid in the War of Spanish Succession the emperor granted him the title of King in Prussia. In 1640 the Prussians had been the most recalcitrant of Frederick William's subjects, and Prussia itself a fief of the Polish crown: in 1700, tamed and transformed, it was deliberately chosen to give its name to the Hohenzollern monarchy since, lying beyond the frontiers of the Holy Roman Empire, it symbolised the emergence of a new and independent power in Europe.

THE GREAT NORTHERN WAR, 1700–21

Charles XII: from Narva to Poltava

When Charles XI died in 1697 he left his fifteen-year-old son in the care of a council of regency. As Sweden had suffered too often from the misrule of nobles in the past, Charles had appointed the regents with care, selecting men who were wholly committed to his policy of *reduktion*. So loyally did they carry out his intentions that the nobles, who had looked for a respite from the persecution of their class, began to cast about for some means to get rid of them. In the *riksdag* they appealed to Charles XII to free himself from the council's control. The other three estates supported them, partly because of their innate suspicion of all regency government, partly because once the proposal had been made no one wished to be seen in opposition to it. Even the regents themselves did not oppose the measure for long, and within six months of Charles XI's death they had surrendered their powers to his son.

At the age of four Charles had been removed from the care of women in order that no trace of effeminacy might mar his character as a warrior prince. Brought up by his father in a wholly masculine society, his regime was one of austere simplicity, in which exercise, drill and hunting — he killed his first wolf when only ten — alternated with the study of languages and military history. It was a cold, harsh upbringing which made him insensitive to physical discomfort and imperceptive to beauty. His isolated childhood left

MAP 20   The Great Northern War

him friendless and solitary, whilst his rare revels were the gloomy
excesses of one to whom revelling is unnatural; to observers he
appeared 'shy as a nun', 'a peasant lad new 'listed who kept his
eyes downcast with rustic shyness'. Scorning all arts save those of
war he seemed a leader in the tradition of Norse Saga, a reincarna-
tion of the untamed spirit of the Viking hero, choosing to fight
because for him the sword was the best and the only argument. His
powers of leadership, his disdain of personal suffering and his
burning delight in war, won him the utter devotion of his men,
who fashioned a legend around his exploits and blindly followed
him to the portals of Valhalla.

Charles was only fifteen when sovereignty was thrust upon him.
He needed time to gain experience without the urgency of crisis to
force his hand, especially since the Swedish crown had become so
autocratic that his people's destiny depended upon his judgement
alone. But his judgement was never given the chance to mature. No
sooner was he established on the throne than a coalition of
European powers threatened the entire Swedish empire.

The problems of Gustavus II Adolphus in establishing the Swedish empire in the Baltic were as nothing to those facing his successors, who sought to preserve it. The separate provinces were bound together by no emotional or racial ties, and as an empire were strategically indefensible. Scattered around the Baltic shores, they were open to attack from all quarters, nor was it possible to penetrate into the interior in search of natural boundaries: there were none to be found east of the Urals or north of the Alps. Instead, they perpetually excited the hostility and greed of the inland powers. Local victories over local rulers had assured Sweden of local supremacy for limited periods, but it was only a matter of time before those rulers who had most to gain from the 'disruption of the Swedish empire should combine to attack its vulnerable frontiers simultaneously.

The catalytic agent in this volatile situation was the desire for vengeance of an exiled Livonian noble, Johann Patkul. When the *reduktion* had been enforced in Livonia, the commissioners had restored to the crown many estates which had been alienated in good faith at an earlier date. Patkul led a deputation to Stockholm in 1692 to secure redress, but he was ill suited to so delicate a mission. Violent and intemperate, his outspoken words only angered Charles XI: Patkul was arrested and, after his escape into exile, condemned for treason. On Charles XII's accession he appealed for a pardon, but, in company with the Swedish nobles who too had looked for favours from the new king's hand, was brusquely repulsed. From that moment Patkul determined on nothing less than the destruction of the Swedish empire, and his pursuit of vengeance led him from one northern capital to another, fomenting jealousy of Sweden's power and inciting greed for her possessions. His principal patron was Augustus the Strong, the Elector of Saxony, who had abandoned Lutheranism to win the crown of Poland: he was not a great soldier,[1] his title of Strong derived from his reputed prowess in raising illegitimate children, but he was ambitious to extend his influence in the Baltic, and with both Saxony and Poland in his hand he was well placed to do so.

The Elector of Brandenburg seemed to be an obvious ally since Western Pomerania still remained under Swedish occupation, but Frederick was preoccupied with his coming coronation as king in

[1] See Chapter IX, page 376.

Prussia, and in any case was far too cautious to be first in the field. Not so his namesake, Frederick IV of Denmark, who inherited all the frustrated ambitions of his predecessors to recover former Danish territory across the Sound. Nearer home, too, he urgently desired to expel the Swedish garrisons from Gottorp, where they stood poised behind his back. Welcoming Augustus's overtures he concluded negotiations in 1699 with both Saxony and Russia[1] to launch simultaneous attacks at all points in the widely scattered Swedish empire. Denmark was to gain whatever she might recover, Saxony was to have Livonia, and Russia the other Baltic Provinces.

Dangerous though the situation was, it was precisely the one for which Charles XII had been trained to meet, and he responded brilliantly to the challenge. While Danish forces invaded Gottorp, secure in the belief that their navy held the Sound, an Anglo-Dutch fleet entered the Baltic in order to prevent this local conflict from becoming a serious distraction from the more pressing problem of containing the ambitions of Louis XIV. The Danish navy, led by an unusually timid and irresolute commander, allowed itself to be immobilised, but Charles XII, by a swift and daring stroke, forced a passage through the eastern end of the Sound, the *Flinterend*, which all naval authorities, including Charles's own captains, believed to be unnavigable; this the Anglo-Dutch fleet had therefore left open, and Charles XII landed wholly unexpected on Zealand with 11,000 men. To avert an attack on Copenhagen Frederick at once capitulated and signed the Treaty of Travendal. All that Charles demanded was an assurance of Danish neutrality; this secured, he wasted no time in turning his attention to the eastern shores of the Baltic.

In Livonia his enemies had already suffered a set-back. Patkul, like many exiled leaders, had overestimated the warmth of feeling for him in his own country, and his arrival with the Saxon forces aroused none of the support he had anticipated. The Livonian gentry failed to join him, and the Swedish garrisons, having no local rising to contend with, swiftly expelled the invaders. At this unlooked-for defeat of his allies, Peter the Great hastily intervened. A vast Russian horde poured into Ingria, the most northerly of the Baltic Provinces, where, on the frontier with Estonia, it laid siege to Narva. Since Charles was presumed to be fully occupied in the west the outcome of the siege seemed assured, until it was learned

[1] See below, page 425, for Peter the Great's ambitions and foreign policy.

that Charles had arrived on the Estonian coast with 7,000 men. Peter had no illusions about his army's fate. Though the Russians outnumbered the Swedes by five to one, they were dispersed in siegeworks around the city and lacked experience of war; in fact they would never have been risked in a campaign at all had Peter anticipated that they would encounter Charles XII. With ruthless logic he promptly deserted them, taking with him those officers who might be useful in raising a new army. On November 20th, Charles stormed the Russian lines under cover of a snowstorm, and within a few hours all resistance was ended.

Elated by his victories Charles determined to exploit them even though Sweden was no longer in danger. It was the natural response of a man for whom peace had no meaning; it was also a deliberate decision to teach aggressors a lesson which their successors at least might value, for there seemed to be no other way to preserve the empire except by successive campaigns of intimidation. His advisers urged him to chase after Peter and compel his acceptance to a treaty which might render Russia harmless for a decade or more, but Charles was rendered scornful of the Russians by his easy victory at Narva: 'There is nothing in winning victories over the Muscovites; they can be beaten at any time.' Instead he turned on Augustus, whose army had begun to counter-attack at Riga. It was probably the right decision, since to have invaded Russia with an enemy in the south, able to disrupt his supply lines and to attack his flank, would have been to court disaster. What was mistaken was Charles's contempt for Russia's recuperative powers, since he left only 15,000 men to guard a frontier over 600 miles long, and stripped the garrisons of their best men to strengthen his campaign to the south. Throughout 1701 he drove the Saxons before him from the Baltic Provinces and burst through into Courland. The Poles, loudly protesting, awaited his invasion with alarm since Poland herself was at peace with Sweden whatever her king might be doing as Elector of Saxony. Charles was more than tactless: declining to negotiate, he bluntly demanded the deposition of Augustus, and drove the reluctant Poles into line behind their king. The invasion of Poland took place in January 1702, and after four months of fighting Charles occupied the two capitals of Warsaw and Cracow. At Klissow, midway between them, he then destroyed a combined force of Poles and Saxons.

Klissow gave Charles an excellent occasion to end the war, since

Augustus was willing to concede defeat and to guarantee Sweden's imperial frontiers. It was to achieve this that Sweden had fought, and the menace came now from Russia rather than Saxony. Taking advantage of Charles's campaign in Poland, Peter the Great had overrun Livonia, which, as it was assigned to Augustus and not to himself, he devastated with methodical barbarity on the plea that he was denying vital supplies to the Swedes. To the north, in the provinces earmarked for himself, his troops were more careful. Ingria was occupied, and at the mouth of the river Neva work was begun on the construction of St. Petersburg,[1] an act of faith that the territory was to be permanently held by Russia. But Charles was for the moment indifferent to the Russian advance. In Augustus he faced an enemy whom he hated above all others, an enemy who had concealed his hostile intentions up to the very outbreak of war. Such duplicity Charles found intolerable: the stark simplicity of his Viking code taught him that vengeance must be exacted, a concept whose rigidity and narrowness made it as anachronistic as the longship and the Viking helmet. So personal a view of international affairs, so remorseless a quest for personal satisfaction were the characteristics not of courageous patriotism but of insane egoism, and Charles's advisers sought in vain to moderate its excesses. In Europe the War of Spanish Succession had begun, and Charles was being urged to join the Grand Alliance. Its chief members had not only been allied to his father, but were willing to guarantee security to Sweden in the Baltic, which was something that Charles's own campaigns could not do, if he would but take part against France. There was in fact an opportunity for so redoubtable a soldier to do more than join an alliance: Charles, in the words of his counsellor, Bengt Oxenstierna, could become 'the arbiter of Europe'. But the first step along such a course was of necessity the making of peace with Augustus, to which Charles obstinately refused assent. 'It would put our glory to shame if we lent ourselves to the slightest treaty accommodation with one who has so vilely prostituted his honour.'

Charles's first objective was to depose Augustus from the Polish throne. His victories in 1703 compelled a confederacy of Polish nobles to elect his own nominee, Stanislas Leszczinski, but Augustus counter-attacked with sufficient force to recover Warsaw itself for a week in August 1704. It was not until a year later

[1] See below, page 426.

that the Saxons were finally driven out, and Stanislas received the crown. Even then, though the Russians had massacred the population of Narva and had established effective control of the Baltic Provinces, Charles pursued his vendetta against Augustus into the very heart of Saxony. Bemused at his persistence, Augustus had no other course but abject submission. In the Treaty of Fraustadt, 1706, he recognised Stanislas as king of Poland, and handed over Patkul for summary execution. Charles was at last prepared to turn against Russia, but not before provoking a conflict with the Emperor Joseph over the persecution of Lutherans in Silesia. For the best part of a year the Swedish army encamped at Leipzig until the emperor became so incensed that it needed Marlborough's intervention to prevent open warfare between them. In order to concentrate on the struggle with France, Joseph reluctantly agreed to humour the mad Swede, and at Altranstädt, 1707, he granted the necessary concessions to the Silesian Lutherans.

In September 1707 Charles at last left Silesia for Russia. Peter the Great had used every device to stave off an attack, even to the extent of offering Marlborough either Kiev or Smolensk, in addition to a pension of 50,000 *thalers*, if he would mediate between Sweden and Russia. Charles refused all offers. Peter had deceived him by renewing the Treaty of Kardis[1] just before the war began; Peter had challenged him to combat. Neither the treachery nor the challenge could be forgiven. The punitive expedition moved fast. Crossing the Vistula on Christmas Day, it reached Grodno on the Niemen in January 1708, only two hours after Peter had left the town in haste. Blindly ignoring the presence of a Russian army in the Baltic Provinces, Charles continued the chase eastwards into Russia. His plan was to reach the Dnieper by midsummer, and to be joined there by a second Swedish force of 11,000 despatched from Riga under Count Levenhaupt. The two armies would then move south down river to winter in the Ukraine, where there was not only corn but the promise of 30,000 Cossacks led by their hetman, Mazeppa.

The alliance of Viking and Cossack was a theme to excite the imagination, but Mazeppa was anything but romantic. The landowner of more than 19,000 farmsteads, he exploited his vast estates with the prosaic business acumen of a Dutch burgher and monopolised the mining of saltpetre in the Ukraine. As leader of

[1] First made in 1660. See page 398.

the Dnieper Cossacks he was also a soldier, but he regarded wars as investments and selected his allies with the same shrewd care with which he chose his bailiffs. He had gone to Peter's aid at Azov,[1] and had fought against Charles XII in Poland, but in 1700 Peter ordered him to the Baltic front, appointing Menshikov, his own general, to defend the Ukraine. This was not merely insulting; Mazeppa suspected an underhand scheme to integrate the Ukraine with Russia, and, as it became increasingly evident to him that Charles would be victorious yet again, he decided to change sides. His only problem was to play for time while Peter demanded his presence in the north to meet the advancing Swedish army.

Charles left Grodno and successfully fought his way eastwards, winning what was to be his last great victory at Holowczyn on the river Drucz, where the Russians' position appeared impregnable until the Swedes overran it. He then advanced a further twenty-five miles to a point on the Dnieper, a little to the south-west of Smolensk. There he waited until October when he suddenly marched south even though Levenhaupt had not yet arrived from Riga. Peter's ruthless destruction of all farms and fields in the path of the Swedish army was partly the cause of this unexpected move, but Charles was also racing against time since Peter had called the Cossacks' bluff. Though Mazeppa protested that he had to take to his bed, 'being on the point of death', Peter's final despatches left no doubt that he had uncovered the treachery, and Charles, to save himself as well as Mazeppa, left the Dnieper and struck across Severia to the Ukraine. According to a British officer in Swedish service, the army was in high spirit: 'We find ourselves at present with the hopes of coming into a country flowing with milk and honey, that Count Levenhaupt will soon reinforce our army with the addition of eleven or twelve thousand men and that General Mazeppa will declare for us.'

The vision of a promised land was soon dispelled when the army ran into Mazeppa, fleeing north with only 1,300 men. The Cossack had been taken unawares by Menshikov's arrival, and his capital, Bakurin, was under siege. Swiftly though Charles advanced, he was yet too late, and in November his army passed the smouldering ruins of the city. Moreover, Levenhaupt's levies had been so badly mauled in their chase after Charles that on arrival only 8,000 had survived: worse still, they had lost their cannon and 2,000

[1] See below, page 423.

wagons of provisions. With his army augmented but without the ability to feed it, Charles continued the march southward in a desperate search for supplies. He marched into the teeth of the worst winter of the century, when birds fell dead in flight from the cold. On the endless steppes of the Ukraine, where there was neither shelter nor food, the attacks of Russian troops were the least of all the perils. Exposure and starvation reduced the army from 44,000 to 20,000. Charles suffered the same privations as his men, and it was only his example and determination which held together the remnants of the army. But the terrible ordeal drove him yet further into insanity. The single-minded pursuit of vengeance which had characterised his campaigns, first against Augustus and then against Peter, became wholly obsessive. With the spring of 1709 his spirits lifted, and all his talk was of reserves to be raised in Poland and Sweden and of victory to be won against Peter. But the real problem was still that of survival, and the army still continued its march southward for supplies. In June it reached the town of Poltava on the river Vorstkla, fifty miles above its junction with the lower Dnieper.

As the 20,000 weary men of Charles's army began the siege upon which their fate depended, Peter, remembering Narva, closed in cautiously. As before, the Russians outnumbered the Swedes by four to one, but on this occasion it was the Swedes who were dispersed in siegeworks. Nevertheless, Peter refrained from attack until he learned that the Swedish sappers were about to open a breach in Poltava's walls and that Charles himself had been wounded in the foot from a chance encounter with a patrol. The Russian attack was accompanied by a devastating artillery barrage which took tremendous toll of the Swedish infantry. The Swedes had no guns with which to retaliate; and, though Charles was carried hither and thither in a palanquin to survey the battlefield, there was no room in which to manœuvre as the Russians, arrayed in a vast arc, closed in upon the town. The Swedish army was destroyed, Charles and Mazeppa fled to the south with less than 2,000 survivors, to take refuge on Turkish soil.

Peter the Great and Europe

Peter the Great's ambition was to transform an Asiatic community into a European state: its corollary was to effect a fundamental change in foreign policy, to acquire for Russia not merely a window on the west but a place in the European concert of nations. Poltava, 'the Russian resurrection', as Peter described it to his wife, was therefore a victory of enormous consequence for Europe since it enabled Peter to break through, once and for all, the barrier insulating Muscovy from the West.

MAP 21   Russia in the Reign of Peter the Great

The Europe civilisation of Kiev and Smolensk had been destroyed in the thirteenth century by Genghis Khan and the Tatars of the Gobi Desert, and for four hundred years Muscovy was isolated from the original sources of her culture. The refugees from Kiev made their way up the river Desna to the present site of Moscow, and there they attempted to preserve some continuity with the past by preserving the Orthodox religion they had received at the hands of Byzantium. Moscow, too, was overrun and Muscovy became a province of the Tatar empire, but her grand dukes were granted particular privileges as the tax-collectors of the Khans. As the centuries passed, the dukes began to extend their authority, and finally to strike at the heart of the Tatar empire. Ivan the Great (1462–1505) and Ivan the Dread (1533–84), no longer dukes but self-styled tsars, plunged further into Asia. Their colonists trekked across Siberia, reaching the Pacific about 1640, and Dezhnov's expedition proved the existence of the Bering Strait in 1648, but the tsars were more interested in expansion to the south-east, through Kazan and Astrakhan, until it was only the power of Abbas the Great of Persia which checked their advance beyond the Caucasus.

Peter was not the first tsar to look towards the west: Michael Romanoff would have secured a foothold on the Baltic coast had it not been for Gustavus II Adolphus; his successor, Alexis, had changed the point of attack by recovering Kiev and Smolensk from Poland.[1] What was new was the unparalleled fascination that Europe exercised over Peter, a Europe first created in his imagination by conversation with the hundreds of European doctors, traders, soldiers and engineers who lived in Moscow. It was a Dutchman, Timmermann, who first showed him how a boat could sail not only with the wind but against it, and prompted him in 1680 to travel to Archangel to see for himself the merchantmen arriving from Holland and England. The excitement this engendered in Peter caused him, once he was tsar, to determine on a great campaign in 1695 to seize possession of the Ottoman-held port of Azov, from where he could build a fleet to challenge the Turks in the Black Sea. If the campaign was a failure, the manner of it confirmed his view of sea power since it was from the sea that the Turks sustained the siege of Azov. Immediately Peter ordered the construction of his own fleet during the winter of 1695–6 at Voronezh on the Don. It was a good centre for shipbuilding, standing in the heart of pine forests and with access to the Black Sea, but the first ships to be launched there were in fact made four hundred miles away outside Moscow. There Peter had secured a Dutch galley to serve as a model; twenty-five copies were then shipped overland to Voronezh, and commissioned for action in the Sea of

[1] See Chapter IX, page 365.

Azov. The first victory of the Russian navy was thus the successful blockade of Azov, which fell to Peter in July 1696.

Peter could no longer contain himself: the west had so much to offer that he took the unheard-of step of going there in person in 1697. But it was not to see the stately splendours of the Escurial and Versailles, but to tour the dockyards of Holland and England. He worked for some time in Amsterdam, in the yards of the East India Company, but finding the Dutch too empirical for his taste he crossed the North Sea to study the theory of shipbuilding in London. Apart from the great concourse of merchantmen which excited his admiration and envy, he was equally struck by the industry and invention of the craftsmen whose skills alone made commerce possible. It became vital to his plans to return not merely with European shipbuilders but with technicians of every kind. Among the many hundreds who accompanied him home were several Englishmen, among them John Parry, an expert in hydraulics, to construct a canal between the Volga and the Don, and Henry Farquharson of Aberdeen University, who established a school of mathematics and navigation at Moscow. Peter intended to visit Venice, too, for he had heard of its famous arsenal and of the commercial prosperity of the lagoons, but his plans were suddenly changed by news of a revolt at home by the *Streltsi*.

The *Streltsi* were the élite of the army, the officers of the palace guard, who throughout the century had engineered a succession of palace revolutions, each marked by barbaric cruelty. They represented the most conservative, the most traditionalist, force in Russia, and though they had supported Peter's accession against his half-sister Sophia, they were outraged by his novelties, above all by his visit to Europe. Fortunately for Peter, he had left command in the hands of a Scot, Patrick Gordon, who, by his quick action in summoning the aid of loyal troops led by other foreign officers, suppressed the revolt. Peter returned to make a terrible example of the rebels. More than a thousand suffered torture and death, some at Peter's own hands as, in order to garnish a night of drunken revelry, he summoned them from their cells to be despatched with savage brutality among the trestles and the drinking-cups. The bloody orgies revealed the pathological blemish in his character; violent and unstable, he was as intolerably energetic in his barbarism as in his moments of construction. There was, however, some political intent behind the slaughter.

At one blow Peter destroyed the *Streltsi* and made it possible to create a new army. Gordon and another Scot, Bruce, became his chief advisers, and through them he recruited more foreigners to lead and to command his army. This was essential; if Russia were to become a political force in Europe, her troops would have to defeat the armies of countries far more advanced than herself.

Equally essential, if Russia were to fulfil the ambitions which Peter entertained, was the creation of the navy. Before he left for Europe Peter had drawn up plans which despite their ruthless innovation were remarkably fulfilled in his absence. Twenty thousand men from the Ukraine were drafted to build a town and a harbour on the shores of the Sea of Azov at Taganrog, while the fleet which was to ride at anchor there was swiftly constructed at Voronezh. Every landowner was required to provide one ship for every 10,000 serf households attached to his estates, the Church a ship for every 8,000 households, and the lesser landlords were taxed in proportion. Peter's government supplied the timber at Voronezh, but everything else had to be provided by the reluctant patrons down to the last item of rigging. Skilled labour was secured by importing fifty shipbuilders from Europe in the first half of 1697, and, a radical innovation of great importance, by sending Russians to Europe for training. But the Voronezh fleet never sailed upon the Black Sea. Azov had been an easy capture, but to destroy the Ottoman hold along the Black Sea coast would require the help of European allies: Peter sought this throughout his journeyings, but he soon realised that the issues of the Spanish Succession were paramount in the minds of Europeans. His volatile temperament could not be discouraged. The fleet should sail on the Baltic instead, and a timely meeting with Augustus of Saxony led Peter to join the coalition of Sweden's enemies.

No sooner had Peter decided upon this change of front than he recalled his troops from the Crimea, made peace with the Turk, and invaded Livonia.[1] This campaign, even though it was disastrous, did more than any other single incident to project Russia into the sphere of European diplomacy and warfare. In later years it was perhaps characteristic of Peter to declare that an early victory would not have been in the best interests of Russia and that the lessons learned in 1700 paved the way for his ultimate success. None the less, the defeat at Narva left Russia humiliated and

[1] See above, page 416.

defenceless, and there would have been no opportunity to learn any lessons at all had not Charles XII preoccupied himself with Poland and Saxony for the next five years.

During these years Peter knew exactly what to do. First he recreated his army. One hundred thousand men were raised for immediate service, while local conscription maintained a steady supply of recruits from the provinces. From this date the vast reserves of Russia's manpower were tapped to make the army indestructible: as one battalion was annihilated, another was conscripted in its place. At Narva Peter had lost his artillery, and new supplies were ordered from Europe. At Narva, too, Peter lost some of his confidence in his foreign officers. Many were retained in service since he could not do without them, but a Russian, Sheremetieff, was appointed to command, and the proportions of Russians to European officers was increased. It was typical of this trend that as European weapons were imported, factories were set up to imitate them, and finally the army was munitioned mainly from Russian resources.

Peter's second decision was to hammer at the Baltic coastline in pursuit of his dream of making Russia a great naval power. While Charles XII fought Augustus, Peter overran the Baltic Provinces and seized upon the delta of the Neva to be his naval base. Here he would build a fortress to safeguard the delta from Swedish counter-attacks: here, in a harbour less remote and less ice-bound than Archangel, Russia might compete in the commercial enterprises which underlay the power of European civilisation: here could be the window on the west from which to intervene in Europe, and through which European ideas might illuminate Muscovy. It was an enthralling prospect, but in 1703 it seemed scarcely attainable. The delta was a waste of swamps and islands, frequently flooded, with no local stone and no local labour. Thousands of serfs were conscripted from elsewhere, and, though they perished in their thousands from exhaustion, exposure and disease, though Swedish raiding parties hampered the work of construction, though Russia had to be ransacked for stone and Europe for technicians and craftsmen, the city began to rise. In 1703 the Peter and Paul fortress was completed on the island dominating the delta. In 1704 the foundations of the Admiralty were laid, and then of the docks and the warehouses. All would have been in vain had Charles turned north from Grodno in

January 1708, but his long march into Russia, ending at Poltava, saved the city: 'Now', said Peter, 'the final stone has been laid of the foundations of St. Petersburg.'

After this date the city could be embellished. A decree of 1712 forbade any construction in stone elsewhere in Russia so that St. Petersburg should not run short of its raw material, and a second tour of Europe in 1717 raised a new army of architects and engineers, since it was only fitting that the window on the west should be constructed in western style. A French architect, Le Blond, prepared a master plan for the whole capital, with terraces, palaces and gardens on a scale to dwarf Versailles, but the project was not to Peter's taste. He was not aping Louis XIV nor did he think that France provided the best models. 'I have been in France myself', he wrote to a group of Russian architects visiting Europe, 'where they have no decoration in architecture and do not want it. They build smooth, straight and very heavily, and only in stone not brick. I have heard quite enough about Italy and already have three architects who have studied there. But the conditions of building here are similar to those in Holland. Therefore you must stay in Holland and learn about the Dutch manner of building, especially of laying foundations which are so essential here.' The buildings which have remained from Peter's reign indicate his preference for the simple burgher's houses with curly gables and plaster decoration which he had seen in Amsterdam. Though the city was not completed before his death in 1725, its purpose was fulfilled. From St. Petersburg Russia became a naval power in the Baltic,[1] through it passed the commerce and the techniques to speed the internal development of Russia, in it was established the new capital of the new Russia looking firmly to the west.

The Northern War concluded, 1709-21

The Swedish empire was the artificial creation of the sword: when that sword was splintered at Poltava her empire collapsed. Swiftly Sweden's enemies began the work of partition. Augustus regained possession of Poland, Peter seized Riga and Reval, Frederick of Denmark attacked both Scania and Holstein, and even the cautious Frederick I of Prussia judged the moment opportune to invade Pomerania. Though Stanislas Leszczinski thankfully abandoned his Polish throne, elsewhere the brilliance of

[1] See below, page 429.

local commanders and the loyalty of the troops to their absent monarch sufficed to delay the advance of the invaders. In one grim rearguard action after another, the Swedes clung desperately to their territories until such time as their king could return to save them. But their king was an uncommon long time coming. The refugee on Turkish soil would neither negotiate with his enemies nor return to fight them. Refusing to accept that his campaign to bring retribution upon Peter had ended at Poltava, he first caballed at the Ottoman court to remove a grand vizier who advocated peace with Russia, and then persuaded the sultan to attack. At the crossing of the Pruth the Russians were defeated in 1711, but when the sultan regained possession of Azov he decided not to push his luck too far and concluded a treaty of peace.

Far from accepting this as the moment to abandon his vendetta against Peter, Charles settled down at his headquarters in Bender on the river Dniester to plan yet another campaign. His subjects begged him to return; his hosts urged him to depart; even his enemies wanted him back in order to negotiate a settlement in the Baltic, and Peter the Great offered him safe conduct across Russia. But the shutters of Charles's mind were tragically closed to any but immediate issues. He sought to avenge Poltava and would therefore stay in Turkey until the sultan joined him in the venture, and if the sultan chose to expel him then he would fight him too. This is what it finally came to. On February 1st, 1713, while his subjects at home were at their wits' end to defend themselves, Charles, with forty men, challenged an army of 12,000 Turks to remove him from his headquarters. 'The affray of Bender' became one more incident to add to the saga, the last stand of the Viking. It took eight hours to dislodge Charles and cost the lives of 200 Turks. Though Charles was still treated with courteous respect, the sultan, with the firm indulgence afforded to the insane, insisted upon his departure. After many delays and false starts Charles left for home in September 1714, over five years since his escape from Poltava.

After a secret journey across Europe Charles arrived in November at Stralsund, the last surviving remnant of the Swedish empire. Sweden was near collapse: her finances were strained to the full, her trade was in ruins and, since the outbreak of the war, 146,000 casualties had been sustained by a population of scarcely one million. She could no longer sacrifice men to Charles's insane career. It was a time for negotiation, an opportunity to reap advantage from discords among her enemies. Charles heeded no one. By the end of 1715, though every country at war with him sought to make peace, he had provoked a new alliance against him of Russia, Prussia, Saxony, Denmark and Great Britain, through George I's connection with Hanover. In addition he lost Stralsund.

The rival allies were left in a quandary. Charles was clearly determined to drag on the war indefinitely and nothing less than the conquest of Sweden would silence him, but over this the allies were hopelessly divided. Denmark excited the jealousy of Hanover and Saxony, who disliked the notion of her recovering control of Scandinavia but who refused to attempt the invasion themselves: all were united in their suspicion of Russia, especially as Peter seemed to be the only commander capable of launching a successful invasion. Russia was at last a naval power, thanks to Peter's determination and the efforts of Patrick Gordon's kinsman Thomas, a Jacobite and a former naval officer. In 1713 Gordon defeated a Swedish fleet and landed 11,000 troops to overrun southern Finland. In the following year, off Cape Hangö, a vast fleet of 20 ships of the line accompanied by nearly 200 galleys defeated 21 Swedish ships after three hours of heavy fighting in which the Russian galleys rammed and grappled as though born to the Mediterranean tradition. Galleys in fact were particularly useful in the Baltic since they could get under way and manoeuvre easily among the clustered shoals and islands, where lofty cliffs stole the wind from the sails of other ships. The victory at Hango established Peter's dream of naval power, and he rightly celebrated it as great a triumph as Poltava. Britain was aghast: in 1698 one of her poets had apostrophised the achievements of Peter on land against the sultan,

> 'May Roman conquests be outdone by thee
> And Czar to more than Caesar then extended be,'

but when Peter won conquests on the waves as well a despatch was sent to the British commander in the Baltic to watch with wary eye, 'that fleet which will disturb the world whilst it is steered by ambition and revenge.'

With public opinion throughout north Europe more hostile to Peter than to Charles, the opportunity for sowing dissension among the allies could not be missed, especially as the Baltic Provinces were not only the very territories which Sweden most wished to recover but also the ones which Britain, Saxony, Prussia and Denmark wished to see denied to Russia. But though Charles permitted his diplomats to negotiate if they wished, he himself remained adamant: no territory was to be ceded, no concessions made, and, to teach Britain a lesson for daring to intervene in Baltic politics, he promptly gave support to a Jacobite conspiracy. Having struck both his advisers and his enemies speechless with dismay he then began an invasion of Norway. His death in the trenches outside Frederickshald on December 12th, 1718, came·as a relief to both sides.

Charles's sister succeeded him and speedily made peace. The Treaties of Stockholm (1719 and 1720) ceded Bremen and Verden to Hanover, and Stettin with most of Pomerania to Prussia: the Treaty of Fredericksburg (1720) restored to Denmark her control of the Sound and her right to tax Swedish shipping, and also gave her the duchies of Holstein and Gottorp. Russia alone remained at war, since Sweden could not be reconciled to the loss of the Baltic Provinces until a series of damaging raids on her mainland accelerated her decision to give way. At Nystad (1721) Peter was granted formal recognition of his title to Estonia, Livonia, Ingria, Kexholm, Viborg and part of Finland. It was the culmination of twenty-one years of endeavour: 'Most apprentices generally serve for seven years; but in our school the term of apprenticeship has been thrice as long. Yet God be praised, things could not have turned out better for us than they have done.'

In Sweden the spell of the saga was too powerful to be dispelled: the madman fighting his fruitless wars became a hero king to be enshrined in the national pantheon, but his country was reduced to the rank of a third rate power. Fortunately, if imperial glory was denied her in the eighteenth century, Sweden found solace in happier activities. Her forests produced the timber for which the maritime powers competed, her iron mines were systematically exploited, and her overseas trade began to flourish. With the wealth thus gained, universities were founded at Lund, Uppsala and Stockholm, a great achievement for so small a country. The free peasantry survived the holocaust which had decimated their ranks, and the ideals of local liberty, good order, honesty and justice in the internal administration of Sweden were of permanent value, even though the pretensions to a *dominium maris balticae* had been irrevocably shattered.

Peter the Great and Russia, 1694–1725

Peter succeeded in bringing Russia into Europe: it was more difficult to bring Europe into Russia. He ruled a country which was not only alien to the European community but which preferred to remain self-contained and self-regarding. Yet from 1700 to 1721 Russia was involved in a European war, and unless she herself became something of a European state herself she could not hope to survive against her more advanced opponents. To further the war effort Peter had to grasp whatever the west could offer, and as he copied European weapons of war so he proposed to adopt European techniques of industry and administration. Though the speed at which he moved was unparalleled, the direction he took was not altogether novel since western ideas were already entering the country and there were precedents for much of what he did. Nor was Peter's programme wholly revolutionary since he sought no alteration in the basic structure of Russian society. What he did attempt with tremendous vigour and violence was to graft European institutions and attitudes upon the semi-Asiatic, Muscovite state of his predecessors.

One unprecedented action was to send groups of Russians abroad to complete their education, but only in a special sense: Peter regarded Europe not as a finishing school but as a technical college, where practical skills could be acquired in navigation and gunnery to benefit the armed forces, in metallurgy, economics and foreign languages for industry and trade. Technical schools were set up at home, and even the proposed academy of Fine Arts at St. Petersburg was to teach carpentry, turnery, hydrostatics and instrument making, and by means of such education Peter hoped to establish in Russia the bases of the prosperity he had witnessed in England and Holland. But Russia lacked the principal driving force of the English and Dutch economics, an ambitious middle class equipped with capital, skill and enterprise. For this the social structure of Russia was to blame. There was no free labour market, no free migration from country to town, since the entire labour force was bound in serfdom to the soil. So jealous were the *boyars*, the nobles, of their privileges that none but themselves might own land or purchase serfs, and it was only with great difficulty that aspiring industrialists could assemble a labour force. What aggravated the problem was that most of the middle classes were resigned to their difficulties. Even when trade was opened up with Europe during the seventeenth century they let it fall into European hands. This was not due, as many have claimed, to the lack of a Protestant ethic, but to lack of numbers: they constituted barely 3 per cent of the population, they enjoyed no social prestige, and were utterly lacking in self-confidence. They had no idea at all of the wealth and position enjoyed by their class in other countries and, in their isolation, they too easily gave way to the forces and conventions which inhibited their expansion.

It was scarcely surprising that the burden of promoting industrial expansion fell principally upon Peter. Three-quarters of all industry established between 1695 and 1709 was owned by the state, and all of it was promoted by the state in order to supply the armed forces. Most of Russia's industrial expansion was therefore in the field of metallurgy and in mining the great deposits of ore in the Ural Mountains. This was not novel: the Demidovs, a famous family of ironmasters, had built up a tradition over several generations, and since they had been ennobled they were no longer denied the right to employ their own serfs to work the furnaces and mines, but private enterprise generally had to be supplemented by the state. Five thousand tons of pig-iron were produced in 1700, 20,000 tons in 1725. The initiative and capital were provided by the state: technicians were recruited abroad in vast numbers, Great Britain, for example, had to pass special legislation to prevent the loss of English craftsmen, while unskilled labour was conscripted from the serfs. So necessary was this for the success of all industrial enterprise that Peter took the revolutionary step in 1721 of authorising industrialists to purchase serfs, a step which was revoked by the *boyars* after his death.

To collect taxes and to conscript labour for his public works and his armies, Peter required a more efficient administration than that evolved by his predecessors. No one questioned the absolute authority vested in the tsar, but, arbitrary and despotic though he might be, it was often impossible to secure compliance with his orders. For one thing the very vastness of Russia was bewildering: stretching 1,500 miles from Archangel to Azov, 1,200 miles from the Dnieper to the Urals, with another 3,000 miles across Siberia to the Pacific, Russia presented an administrative problem which would remain insoluble until the age of the telegraph and the railway. Inspector-generals and Guards officers assigned to investigate particular problems were given powers as arbitrary as those of their sovereign, and their irruptions into provincial life invariably resulted in the wholesale dismissal, and frequently the execution, of incompetent and dishonest officials. Local government was thus temporarily galvanised into unusual activity, but visitations of this sort were spasmodic, short and all too few.

Since the government departments in Moscow were failing in the perennial task of supplying him with money and recruits, Peter in 1708 tried to ease the problem by decentralisation. Eight provincial governments were created, each primarily responsible for taxation and conscription; but the areas under their control were still too vast, and decentralisation without effective direction from the centre merely caused confusion by abdicating responsibility from one department to eight separate ones. This was soon evident, and Peter, who was learning more of western techniques of government, restored the emphasis on central control. In 1711 he created a new institution, the senate, whose functions were to determine policy and to supervise its execution: this was too much for one body to handle in detail, and after long correspondence with the German philosopher Leibniz, Peter adopted his recommendations to allocate responsibility for specific tasks to colleges on the Swedish model.[1] 'There cannot be good administration except with colleges,' wrote Leibniz, 'their mechanism is like watches whose wheels mutually keep each other in movement', a striking parallel with his theory of the operation of monads in the universe.[2]

Nine colleges were set up, each run by its own board with a president, working under the general supervision of the senate. It was equally sensible to borrow administrative devices from abroad as to imitate industrial techniques, but since these devices had sprung from a peculiar social structure, their transference to an alien environment created difficulties. Despite Leibniz's assurances, there was nothing magical about the collegiate system, and Peter discovered that in practice it often resulted in the employment of five men to do the work of one. Bureaucracy of this sort was an innovation of which few Russians had had any experience. Consequently the colleges had to be staffed in the first place by foreigners, Swedish prisoners of war were especially useful, but when, by 1722, Peter began to weed them out in order to establish

[1] See above, page 382.   [2] See Chapter I, page 66.

Russian control of the administration, the collegiate boards became merely nominal organisations with real power in the hands of the presidents. Nevertheless the colleges relieved the senate of much detailed work, leaving it freer to co-ordinate and to direct the administration as a whole. In the senate the appointment of a Procurator-General in 1722 strengthened the work of centralisation. The Procurator-General had his own procurators in each of the separate colleges, presided over the senate in Peter's absence, and had charge of the revenue officials in the provinces. He thus became the central figure in the administration, combining knowledge of Peter's intentions with detailed information not only of the colleges but also of the provincial government.

Yet for all the innovations and reforms the Russian administration was not a success. Some of Peter's work was invalidated by passive resistance, concealed behind a front of incompetence and assisted by the difficulty of communication. More deep-rooted than this was the general tradition of peculation. What was commonplace throughout Europe had grown out of hand in Russia, where never more than a third of estimated revenues reached the treasury. Peter took violent action against known offenders, and introduced special agents, the *fiscals*, to check on dishonesty; but it was an *ober-fiscal* who had to be executed in 1717, and as one official reported to Peter, 'In the end you will have no subjects at all for we are all thieving.' What finally compromised Peter's achievement was the fact that even his most loyal officials were wholly disinclined to assume responsibility for anything. Departmental decisions were referred to higher authorities; 'the official was kept like a child,' said Peter, 'swaddled in long, meticulous edicts, and on each new unforeseen occasion the grown child asked for instruction'. Unfortunately the root cause was irremediable. Peter was held in such terror by his subordinates that there were few who dared to assume responsibility, especially as the pace of Peter's innovations and reforms obliterated the conventional landmarks of their experience.

Many of Peter's reforms were concerned with the superficial imitation of western habits. Peter was not so foolish as to believe that clothes could transform a Russian into a European, but he persisted with his insistence on apparently trivial points because he realised that the customs he sought to change had acquired an aura of traditional, even of religious, associations which retarded the acceptance of western ideas in general. For this reason he abolished the Russian calendar, brought the New Year from September to January, and abandoned the tradition of dating events from the Creation which had resulted in a discrepancy of eight years between Russian and European calendars. Above all he struck at the beard, forcibly shearing his own courtiers should they be obdurate, and supplying all customs posts along the roads with pairs of scissors to deal with travellers. Ivan the Dread had expressed the Muscovite veneration of the beard: 'To shave the beard is a sin that the blood of all the martyrs cannot cleanse. Is it not to deface the image of God created by men?' Peter's attack on beards and the calendar was a stroke at the heart of Russian tradition, and caused trouble with the clergy, the most reactionary body in Russia.

This might have been a serious matter since the Orthodox Church has always possessed a very great influence in political affairs but, luckily for Peter, the Church itself was then divided by a prolonged dispute over the revision of the Scriptures. The battle between the innovators who wanted to amend the Russian version in the light of their Greek scholarship, and the so-called Old Believers who stood four-square against all change, and who were eventually to triumph, distracted the Church from the more fundamental innovations going on around it. Nevertheless there was always the danger that the Patriarch, whose authority and prestige made him second only to the tsar, might precipitate a quarrel between Church and State. Peter scotched this by letting the patriarchate lapse in 1700 and, after twenty-one years, by putting it into commission under a layman, the Procurator of the Holy Synod. In a way Peter's policy resembled that of Henry VIII of England: his concern was political not doctrinal, and having won control over the church he could not resist encroaching upon its wealth by secularising its land, a process completed in 1764. Not surprisingly the lesser clergy took secret delight in reviling him as Anti-Christ, not least for his abandoning of Holy Moscow, centre of 'the old and ancient faith, of holy orthodox Rus', for St. Petersburg.

More difficult than the priests were the landlords, the *boyars*, who had frequently led Russia into civil war. Peter had tried to dispense with them by creating a new administration in which a new class of officials could attain nobility by loyal service: he drew up a table of military, civil and legal offices containing fourteen

P

grades, of which the eight senior grades ranked as noble and were exempted from taxation. This seemed to presage the French Revolution and the career open to talent, an impression strengthened by the rise of Alexander Menshikov from pastry cook's son to Peter's greatest soldier and close friend; but nothing so radical transpired in practice. The *boyars* were still employed since there were not enough middle class officials to supplant them, and Peter had even to compel them, at the price of their privileges, to serve the state either in the army or in the administration. Indeed Peter's policies tended to emphasise the gulf between the *boyars* and the rest of the community. Though his edicts often proved abortive, in particular that no *boyar* was to marry until he had passed written examinations in arithmetic, geometry and navigation, there is no doubt that the Russian noble became sufficiently westernised to play his part in Peter's administration, and thus grew further away from his fellow Russians. Moreover, the *boyars* remained the landlord class, and the essential divisions of Muscovite society into tsar, *boyar*, and serf, were confirmed and indeed strengthened. The lowest unit of administration for the purposes of taxation and conscription was the landed estate; the *boyar* was thus made more powerful than ever since his serfs had to obey him not only as landlord but also as the agent of Peter's government.

Frederick the Great considered that Peter worked upon Russia like nitric acid upon iron, merely scarring the surface. It is true that the social structure remained unchanged; it is also true that many of the changes brought about were already in train, merely accelerated by Peter's overriding enthusiasm, his stubborn determination and his brutal treatment of opposition; but the creation of the navy, the choice of St. Petersburg as capital, the education of Russians abroad and the abolition of the patriarchate were innovations which were wholly unprecedented and of fundamental importance in the history of Russia. Peter acted as a turbulent force whose impact could neither be forgotten nor reversed: for good or for ill Russia could never revert to her Muscovite seclusion. Equally, and with far greater significance for the history of the world, Peter's success in the Great Northern War ensured that Russia, whether Europe liked it or not, was henceforward to be a European power.

Bibliography

The arrangement of titles under each of the main headings of this bibliography follows that of the text, except for works of a more general nature which are always mentioned first.

GENERAL HISTORIES

1. H. A. L. FISHER, *History of Europe* (Arnold, 1936).
2. LORD ACTON, *Lectures on Modern History* (Macmillan, 1906).
3. J. M. THOMPSON, *Lectures on Modern History* (Blackwell, rev. ed., 1956).
4. G. N. CLARK, *The Seventeenth Century* (O.U.P., 2nd ed., 1947).
5. E. BARKER, G. N. CLARK, and A. VAUCHER (eds.), *The European Inheritance*, vol. ii (O.U.P., 1954).
6. E. L. CARSTEN (ed.), *The New Cambridge Modern History*, vol. v, *The Ascendancy of France, 1648–88* (C.U.P., 1961).
7. R. MOUSNIER, *Les Progrès de la Civilisation Européene et le Déclin de l'Orient* (Presses Universitaires, Paris, 1951).
8. H. HAUSER, *La Prépondérance Espagnole, 1559–1660* (Presses Universitaires, Paris, rev. ed., 1948).
9. P. SAGNAC and A. DE ST. LÉGER, *La Prépondérance Française, 1661–1715* (Presses Universitaires, Paris, rev. ed., 1949).
10. C. J. FRIEDRICH, *The Age of the Baroque, 1610–1660* (Harper, New York, 1952).
11. F. L. NUSSBAUM, *The Triumph of Science and Reason, 1660–1685* (Harper, New York, 1953).
12. J. B. WOLF, *The Emergence of the Great Powers, 1685–1715* (Harper, New York, 1951).
13. V. H. H. GREEN, *Renaissance and Reformation* (Arnold, 1952).
14. D. OGG, *Europe in the Seventeenth Century* (Black, 8th ed., 1960).
15. L. W. COWIE, *Seventeenth Century Europe* (Bell, 1960).
16. M. BELOFF, *The Age of Absolutism, 1660–1815* (Hutchinson, 1954).

No. 14 is probably the best one-volume textbook available in English; it is dated of course and some of its most illuminating chapters, e.g. 'Jesuit and Jansenist', may perplex the less gifted reader. For him 15 is uninspiring but straightforward. No. 13 is an excellent textbook, but unfortunately ends at 1648; 16, which begins at 1660, will be enjoyed by those with some previous knowledge of the period who can benefit from the broad survey of seventeenth- and eighteenth-century states and governments. Nos. 8 and 9 are authoritative and comprehensive histories for those who read French — and even those who find the language difficult ought to sample sections of 7, if only to admire the author's idiosyncratic but apparently total grasp of the period. Nos. 10 and 11 are essentially for the intelligent reader who can withstand the authors' determination to cram the diversified history of their periods into oversimplified patterns; a good student will enjoy annotating, for example, Friedrich's extension of the term 'Baroque' from art to economics, politics and even warfare. None the less the material is good and easily abstracted, the bibliographies are excellent, and 12, in the same series, is more straightforward in its thesis. No. 6 must be used whenever possible; it is laid out clearly and is far more readable than the old Cambridge Modern Histories. Everyone should at least browse in 4 and 5 to savour some of the rich variety of the century's life and thought, and, taking care to check occasionally with more modern books, enjoy the stimulating observations to be found in 1, 2, and 3: these are the works of masters; they make history intelligible, illuminating, and full of interest.

* * *

NATIONAL HISTORIES, MONOGRAPHS, AND
BIOGRAPHIES

France

1. J. LOUGH, *Introduction to Seventeenth Century France* (Longmans, 1954).
2. L. ROMIER (trans. A. L. ROWSE), *A History of France* (Macmillan, 1953).
3. E. LAVISSE, *Histoire de France depuis les origines jusqu'à la Révolution*, vols. vi, pt. ii, vii, pt. iii, and viii, pt. i (Hachette, Paris, 1900–11).
4. G. PAGÈS, *La Monarchie d'Ancien Régime* (Colin, 5th ed., 1952).
5. P. SAGNAC, *La Formation de la Société Française Moderne, 1660–1715*, vol. i (Presses Universitaires, Paris, 1945).
6. C. V. WEDGWOOD, *Richelieu and the French Monarchy* (E.U.P., 1949).
7. H. HAUSER, *La Pensée et l'Action Économique du Cardinal de Richelieu* (Presses Universitaires, Paris, 1944).
8. P. R. DOOLIN, *The Fronde* (Harvard U.P., 1939).
9. C. W. COLE, *Colbert and a century of French Mercantilism* (Columbia U.P., 1939).
10. M. ASHLEY, *Louis XIV and the Greatness of France* (E.U.P., 1946).
11. W. H. LEWIS, *The Splendid Century* (Eyre & Spottiswood, 1953).
12. W. F. CHURCH (ed.), *The Greatness of Louis XIV, Myth or Reality* (Heath/Harrap, 1959).

United Provinces

13. G. J. RENIER, *The Dutch Nation* (Allen, 1944).
14. P. J. BLOK, *History of the People of the Netherlands* (trans., Putnam's, 1912).
15. G. EDMUNDSON, *History of Holland* (C.U.P., 1922).
16. P. GEYL, *The Netherlands Divided, 1609–1648* (Williams & Norgate, 1936).
17. M. C. TREVELYAN, *William III and the Defence of Holland, 1672–74* (Longmans, 1930).
18. C. R. BOXER, *The Dutch in Brazil* (O.U.P., 1957).

19. A. HYMA, *The Dutch in the Far East* (Wahr, 1942).
20. V. BARBOUR, *Capitalism in Amsterdam* (Johns Hopkins, 1950).

Spain and Portugal

21. R. ALTAMIRA, *History of Spain* (Macmillan, 1948).
22. J. B. TREND, *The Civilisation of Spain* (O.U.P., 1944).
23. J. H. ELLIOTT, *Imperial Spain 1469–1716* (Arnold, 1963).
24. R. TREVOR-DAVIES, *The Golden Century of Spain, 1501–1621* (Macmillan, 1937).
25. *Idem, Spain in Decline, 1621–1700* (Macmillan, 1957).
26. P. VILAR, *Histoire d'Espagne* (Paris, 1956).
27. E. J. HAMILTON, *American Treasure and the Price Revolution in Spain* (Harvard U.P., 1934).
28. J. KLEIN, *The Mesta* (Harvard U.P., 1920).
29. C. H. HARING, *Trade and Navigation between Spain and the Indies* (Harvard U.P., 1918).
30. J. NADA, *Carlos the Bewitched* (Cape, 1962).
31. H. V. LIVERMORE, *History of Portugal* (C.U.P., 1947).

Germany, Austria, and Eastern Europe

32. G. BARRACLOUGH, *The Origins of Modern Germany* (O.U.P., 1929).
33. C. V. WEDGWOOD, *The Thirty Years War* (Cape, 1938).
34. G. PAGÈS, *La Guerre de Trente Ans* (Payot, Paris, 1949).
35. F. L. CARSTEN, *Princes and Parliaments in Germany* (O.U.P., 1959).
36. *Idem, The Origins of Prussia* (O.U.P., 1954).
37. F. SCHEVILL, *The Great Elector* (Chicago U.P., 1947).,
38. P. FRISCHAUER, *The Imperial Crown: The Story of the Rise and Fall of the Holy Roman and Austrian Empires* (trans., Cassell, 1939).
39. H. F. SCHWARZ, *The Imperial Privy Council in the Seventeenth Century* (Harvard U.P., 1943).
40. H. MARCZALI, *Hungary in the Eighteenth Century* (C.U.P., 1910).
41. O. LASKOWSKI, *Jan III Sobieski, King of Poland 1629–1696* (1941).
42. W. F. REDDAWAY (ed.), *The Cambridge History of Poland*, vols. i and ii (C.U.P., 1941 and 1950).
43. D. M. VAUGHAN, *Europe and the Turks, 1350–1700* (Liverpool U.P., 1954).
44. A. H. LYBYER, *The Government of the Ottoman Empire in the time of Suliman the Magnificent* (Harvard U.P., 1913).

The Baltic States and Russia

45. L. KRABBE, *Histoire de Danemark, des origines jusqu'à 1945* (Copenhagen, 1950).
46. E. F. HECKSCHER, *An Economic History of Sweden* (trans., Harvard U.P. 1954).
47. M. ROBERTS, *Gustavus Adolphus, A History of Sweden*, vols. i and ii (Longmans, 1953 and 1958).
48. F. BENGTSSON, *The Life of Charles XII* (Macmillan, 1960).
49. B. PARES, *History of Russia* (Cape, rev. ed., 1955).
50. B. H. SUMNER, *Peter the Great and the Emergence of Russia* (E.U.P., 1950).

51. *Idem, Peter the Great and the Ottoman Empire* (Blackwell, 1950).
52. I. GREY, *Peter the Great, Emperor of all Russia* (Hodder & Stoughton, 1962).

Textbooks generally attach so much importance to French history (and their authors are generally more knowledgeable in this field) that often the reader feels no need to look further afield. He should, however, browse through 1, an invaluable supplement to textbook reading, whose extracts will provide many useful quotations for history essays. For those who are still hesitant to leave the textbooks, 6 and 10 are particularly helpful, being short, clear, accurate, and interesting. No. 12, a symposium of contrasting views on Louis XIV, is also valuable for revealing that, where the textbooks may pontificate, other historians may hold a variety of opinions.

No. 16 should not be missed even if the period is so rarely examined directly, since it reveals the latent tensions in Dutch society as it emerged from rebellion to independence. Equally valuable, and a book frequently to return to, is 13, which not only describes how these tensions were worked out subsequently, but also makes wholly intelligible the political and constitutional fabric of the United Provinces. There is no such book in English on Spanish history. No. 23 is a sound new book with helpful chapters on the seventeenth century; 24, though excellent, ends at 1621, and 25 is a weak, even misleading, successor. No. 30 may be too sensational and too condescending to the Spaniards, but it will none the less fascinate many readers.

C. V. Wedgwood writes brilliantly for students, who should not miss No. 33. Though the scale of the detail may alarm, the firmly held theme and the careful characterization of the individual actors in the story make this an excellent book. Though they are not so directly suited to the needs of the student, 35 and 36 represent the fruit of much research and are wholly authoritative. It is a great pity there is nothing so good on the Austrian Empire. Another recent book which has superseded all others is 47 — very detailed but invaluable, especially if it is used to illuminate topics as they arise rather than being read straight through. No. 50 however can be swallowed whole, though the reader will return frequently to make notes; on the same subject, 52 is a recent scholarly and sympathetic study.

* * *

THE SEVENTEENTH-CENTURY BACKGROUND

1. G. N. CLARK, *The Seventeenth Century* (O.U.P., 2nd ed., 1947).
2. E. BARKER, G. N. CLARK, and A. VAUCHER (eds.), *The European Inheritance*, vol. ii (O.U.P., 1954).

Economic and political studies

3. C. W. COLE and S. B. CLOUGH, *Economic History of Europe* (Heath, Boston, 3rd ed., 1952).

4. H. HEATON, *Economic History of Europe* (Harper, New York, 2nd ed., 1948).
5. H. SÉE, *Les origines du capitalisme moderne* (Colin, Paris, 1926).
6. E. F. HECKSCHER, *Mercantilism* (trans., Allen & Unwin, 2nd ed., 1955).
7. R. W. GREEN (ed.), *Protestantism and Capitalism* (Heath/Harrap, 1959).
8. R. S. MERRIMAN, *Six Contemporaneous Revolutions* (O.U.P., 1938).
9. M. ROBERTS, *The Military Revolution, 1560-1660*, Inaugural lecture, Belfast (Boyd, 1956).
10. G. N. CLARK, *War and Society in the Seventeenth Century* (C.U.P., 1958).
11. G. MATTINGLEY, *Renaissance Diplomacy* (Cape, 1955).
12. G. H. SABINE, *A History of Political Theory* (Holt, New York, rev. ed., 1950).
13. H. SÉE, *Idées Politiques en France au XVIIme Siècle* (Hachette, Paris, 1920).
14. J. B. BURY, *The Idea of Progress* (Macmillan, 1920).

Science, Philosophy and Religion

15. C. SINGER, *A Short History of Science to 1900* (O.U.P., 1959).
16. W. C. DAMPIER, *A History of Science* (C.U.P., 4th ed., 1948).
17. R. J. FORBES and M. J. DIJKSTERHUIS, *History of Science and Technology*, vols. i and ii (Penguin, 1963).
18. S. TOULMIN and J. GOODFIELD, *The Fabric of the Heavens* (Hutchinson, 1961).
19. H. BUTTERFIELD, *The Origins of Modern Science* (Bell, 1949).
20. A. R. HALL, *The Scientific Revolution, 1500-1800* (Longmans, 1954).
21. A. WOLF, *A History of Science, Technology and Philosophy in the Sixteenth and Seventeenth Centuries* (Allen & Unwin, 1950).
22. G. N. CLARK, *Science and Social Welfare in the Age of Newton* (O.U.P., 2nd ed., 1949).
23. A. KOESTLER, *The Sleepwalkers* (Hutchinson, 1959).
24. G. DE SANTILLANA, *The Crime of Galileo* (Heinmann, 1958).
25. B. WILLEY, *The Seventeenth Century Background* (Chatto & Windus, 1934).
26. B. RUSSELL, *History of Western Philosophy* (Allen & Unwin, 1946).
27. R. PETERS, *Hobbes* (Penguin, 1956).
28. D. J. O'CONNOR, *Locke* (Penguin, 1952).
29. S. HAMPSHIRE, *Spinoza* (Penguin, 1951).
30. R. L. SHAW, *Leibniz* (Penguin, 1954).
31. S. HAMPSHIRE (ed.), *The Age of Reason* (Muller, 1956).
32. J. R. RANDALL, *The Making of the Modern Mind* (rev. ed., New York, 1940).
33. P. HAZARD, *The European Mind 1680-1715* (trans., Penguin, 1964).
34. G. R. CRAGG, *The Church and the Age of Reason* (Penguin, 1960).
35. F. L. CROSS (ed.), *The Oxford Dictionary of the Christian Church* (O.U.P., 1957).

36. L. VON RANKE, *History of the Popes* (trans., Bohn ed., 3 vols., Bell, 1907).
37. M. DE LA BEDOYÈRE, *The Archbishop and the Lady* (Collins, 1956).
38. R. A. KNOX, *Enthusiasm* (O.U.P., 1950).

Art and Architecture

39. E. H. GOMBRICH, *The Story of Art* (Phaidon Press, 1956).
40. N. PEVSNER, *An Outline of European Architecture* (Penguin, rev. ed., 1963).
41. E. NEWTON, *European Painting and Sculpture* (Penguin, rev. ed., 1963).
42. G. HIGHET, *The Classical Tradition* (O.U.P., 1949).
43. V. L. TAPIÉ, *The Age of Grandeur: Baroque and Classicism in Europe* (trans., Weidenfeld & Nicolson, 1960).
44. H. WÖLFFLIN, *Principles of Art History* (Bell, 1932).
45. Idem, *Renaissance and Baroque* (trans., Collins, 1964).
46. T. GERSON and TER KUILE, *Art and Architecture in Belgium, 1600–1800* (Penguin, 1960).
47. R. H. WILENSKI, *An Introduction to Dutch Art* (Faber & Faber, 1955).
48. J. ROSENBERG, *Rembrandt* (Harvard/Oxford, 1948).
49. G. KUBLER and M. SORIA, *Art and Architecture in Spain, Portugal and their American Dominions 1500–1800* (Penguin, 1959).
50. W. WEISBACH, *Spanish Baroque Art* (C.U.P., 1941).
51. A. BLUNT, *Art and Architecture in France, 1500–1700* (Penguin, 1953).
52. R. SCHNEIDER, *L'Art Française au dix-septième siècle* (Paris, 1925).
53. L. HAUTECOUR, *Histoire de l'architecture classique en France, vol. ii, Le Règne de Louis XIV* (Paris, 1948).
54. R. WITTKOWER, *Art and Architecture in Italy, 1600–1750* (Penguin, 1958).
55. A. MCCOMB, *The Baroque Painters of Italy* (Harvard U.P., 1934).
56. J. BOURKE, *Baroque Churches of Central Europe* (Faber & Faber, 1958).
57. H. A. MILLON, *Baroque and Rococo Architecture* (London, 1963).
58. E. HEMPEL, *Baroque Art and Architecture in Central Europe* (trans., Penguin, 1965).

For any study of the background to the seventeenth century the relevant pages in 1 and 2 will provide in most cases the best introduction to more detailed study.

Nos. 3 and 4 are dull but very useful; 5 and 6 are books to provoke thought; 7 provides an interesting symposium of views on the much debated connection between capitalism and religion. On economic history especially it is advisable to follow the recent discussions of particular points in the journals. No. 9 is an interesting comparative study of the mid-century revolutions, a subject which is also currently attracting much attention in the journals (*see* p. 443). No. 10 is a book to stimulate interest and thought, and 11, though mainly concerned with the sixteenth century, throws much light on seventeenth-century diplomacy.

This century is of such importance in the history of science that it has recently attracted many first-rate historians. Nos. 18 and 19 are probably the most helpful and illuminating for those who have previously studied only political and military history. No. 23 is a brilliant book, but not all its conclusions are accepted by all historians. The impact of science on contemporary thought is treated well, and variously, by 21, 22, and 25. No. 26 is excellent for this period and, in conjunction with 31, may well help the novice to approach the philosophers of the century. No. 33 is a famous detailed study, now available in English, of the crucial relation of science and religion at the end of the century, and is probably the most stimulating book of its kind for the more gifted student to dip into. Nos. 34 and 35 are excellent works of reference for religious history; 37 throws a fascinating light on Fénélon and Quietism at the court of Louis XIV; and 38 relates both to Quietists and Jansenists.

The history of the arts is attracting so much expert attention, apart from a lack of good biographical studies, that it is difficult to select a few from the many. For the novice 39 will provide an excellent introduction; 40 and 41 will together take him a little further — to make him bold enough to read 42 which provides the best description in English of the nature of the Baroque, a task undertaken also by 43 and 45.

*　　*　　*

RECENT ARTICLES

Articles in historical journals are very helpful in two ways. Frequently they inform the public of recent trends in research long before these have percolated through to the textbooks; they can also give much more detailed treatment to the description of a man or an incident than is usually possible in a textbook. Not all the historical journals are of equal value for the student; some are essentially for the postgraduate, others may be too expensive, but, by and large, many schools are able to shelve *History, Past and Present,* and *History Today.* The following articles are therefore selected from these publications. (*H — History*; *P — Past and Present; HT — History Today*).

P, nos. 5, 6, 16, and 18 contain a fascinating series of articles on the 'Crisis of the Seventeenth Century', the mid-century coincidence of rebellion and revolutionary situations in most European states. The student should not, however, expect to find a cut and dried answer to the problem, and may well come to believe that many of the authorities tend to cancel each other out. Mercantilism, another issue which has raised much controversy, is covered in *H,* xxix. 24, and the current views are most helpfully summarized in the Historical Association's pamphlet G 37, *Mercantilism.*

French history has attracted many recent articles. There are well-illustrated essays on 'Marie de Medici' (*HT,* May 1963), 'Richelieu' (*HT,* Oct. 1959), 'Mazarin' (*HT,* July 1957), and 'Louis XIV' (*HT,* Mar. 1954), which will help and interest all students. 'An Incident of the Fronde' (*HT,* Apr. 1960) and 'English Visitors at Louis XIV's Court' (*HT,* June 1959) are interesting fringe articles. For the more confident reader there is much to be gained from 'Alsace and Louis XIV' (*H*, xiii. 50), 'Church and State under Louis XIV' (*H*, xlv. 155), and 'The French Peasantry in the Seventeenth Century' (*P*, 10). This last article is important for revealing the true plight of the peasantry in its perennial fight against starvation.

'The Thirty Years War, A new interpretation' (*H*, xxxii. 116) and 'The Thirty Years War' (*P*, 6) will do much to help in the study of this topic. There is also an interesting account of the short-lived reign of Frederick, Elector Palatine in Bohemia, 'The Bohemian Revolution and The Reign of the Winter King' (*HT*, June 1955). 'John Sobieski' is given full treatment in a double article (*HT*, Mar. and April 1962) which will do something to compensate for the lack of textbooks on Eastern European history, as will 'Francis Rackoczi and the Hungarian Rising of 1703–11' (*HT*, Aug. 1959).

The remaining articles fall into two very marked regional categories, Holland and the Baltic Powers. Of the first, there is an excellent study of 'Johan de Witt' (*H*, xx. 80) and of 'The Golden Age of Amsterdam' (*HT*, Dec. 1957); but it is the Dutch overseas who have attracted most attention, principally from C. R. Boxer, in 'The Time of the Flemings; the Dutch in Brazil' (*HT*, Mar. 1954), 'Peter Stuyvesant, Director-General of the New Netherlands' (*HT*, May 1960), 'Piet Heyn and the Silver Fleet' (*HT*, June 1963), 'Cornelis Speelman and the Expansion of Dutch Power in Indonesia' (*HT*, Mar. 1954), and 'The Coast of Lost Treasure' (*HT*, Feb. 1961), an account of Dutch voyagers to the East Indies who lost their way and touched Australia. Finally, 'The Tromps and the Anglo-Dutch Wars, 1652–1674' (*HT*, Dec. 1953) will be of interest both for Dutch and for English history.

The achievements of 'The Great Elector' are well summarized (*HT*, Feb. 1960), and M. Roberts continues his masterly studies of Swedish history with 'The Abdication of Christina' (*HT*, Dec. 1954) and 'Christina and the General Crisis of the Seventeenth Century' (*P*, 22). One of the major battles of the period is analysed in 'Pultava, 1709' (*HT*, Feb. 1963); the vanquished is treated of in 'The Death of Charles XII of Sweden' (*HT*, Dec. 1963) while the victor is handsomely dealt with in 'Peter the Great, (*H*, xxxii. 115), 'Peter the Great and the Creation of the Russian Navy' (*HT*, Sep. 1961), 'Church and State in Russia' (*HT*, Aug. 1963), and a romantic footnote is provided by 'Mazeppa' (*HT*, Sep. 1957). Though there is little meat to it, many will enjoy 'Peter the Great in England' (*HT*, April 1956), an account of his short visit of 1698.

There are only two articles on Spanish history, but both are worth reading: 'The Decline of Spain' (*P*, 20) and 'Olivares' (*HT*, June 1963).

Index

I HAVE not thought it necessary to distinguish between Venice and Venetian, and so on, and have placed all such references under the proper noun rather than the adjective. Throughout the book I have frequently referred to a country when, more precisely, I meant the ruler of that country: for example, 'Louis XIV won over Brandenburg' for 'Louis XIV won over Frederick William of Brandenburg'. In compiling the index I have taken all such references as though they relate to the ruler.

The important references are given in bold type; those in italics refer to maps.